# THE LAST INDIAN WAR

ALSO BY ELLIOTT WEST

*The Contested Plains: Indians, Goldseekers, and the Rush to Colorado*

*Growing Up in Twentieth-Century America: A History and Resource Guide*

*The Way to the West: Essays on the Central Plains*

*Growing Up with the Country: Childhood on the Far Western Frontier*

*The Saloon on the Rocky Mountain Mining Frontier*

PIVOTAL MOMENTS IN AMERICAN HISTORY

*Series Editors*
David Hackett Fischer
James M. McPherson
David Greenberg

James T. Patterson
*Brown v. Board of Education:*
*A Civil Rights Milestone*
*and Its Troubled Legacy*

Maury Klein
*Rainbow's End:*
*The Crash of 1929*

James McPherson
*Crossroads of Freedom:*
*The Battle of Antietam*

Glenn C. Altschuler
*All Shook Up:*
*How Rock 'n' Roll Changed America*

David Hackett Fischer
*Washington's Crossing*

John Ferling
*Adams vs. Jefferson:*
*The Tumultuous Election of 1800*

Joel H. Silbey
*Storm over Texas:*
*The Annexation Controversy*
*and the Road to Civil War*

Raymond Arsenault
*Freedom Riders: 1961 and*
*the Struggle for Racial Justice*

Colin G. Calloway
*The Scratch of a Pen: 1763*
*and the Transformation*
*of North America*

Richard Labunski
*James Madison and the*
*Struggle for the Bill of Rights*

Sally McMillen
*Seneca Falls and the Origins*
*of the Women's Rights Movement*

Howard Jones
*The Bay of Pigs*

Lynn Hudson Parsons
*The Birth of Modern Politics:*
*Andrew Jackson, John Quincy*
*Adams, and the Election of 1828*

Glenn C. Altschuler and Stuart M. Blumin
*The GI Bill: A New Deal for Veterans*

Richard Archer
*As If an Enemy's Country:*
*The British Occupation of Boston*
*and the Origins of Revolution*

Thomas Kessner
*The Flight of the Century: Charles Lindbergh*
*and the Rise of American Aviation*

# THE
# LAST
# INDIAN WAR
## THE NEZ PERCE STORY

ELLIOTT WEST

OXFORD
UNIVERSITY PRESS

# OXFORD
### UNIVERSITY PRESS

Oxford University Press, Inc., publishes works that further
Oxford University's objective of excellence
in research, scholarship, and education.

Oxford  New York

Auckland   Cape Town   Dar es Salaam   Hong Kong   Karachi
Kuala Lumpur   Madrid   Melbourne   Mexico City   Nairobi
New Delhi   Shanghai   Taipei   Toronto

With offices in

Argentina   Austria   Brazil   Chile   Czech Republic   France   Greece
Guatemala   Hungary   Italy   Japan   Poland   Portugal   Singapore
South Korea   Switzerland   Thailand   Turkey   Ukraine   Vietnam

Published by Oxford University Press, Inc.
198 Madison Avenue, New York, New York 10016
www.oup.com

First issued as an Oxford University Press paperback, 2011

Library of Congress Cataloging-in-publication Data
West, Elliot, 1945–
The last Indian war : the Nez Perce story / Elliott West.
    p.   cm.— (Pivotal moments in American history)
Includes bibliographical references and index.
ISBN  978-0-19-513675-3; 978-0-19-976918-6 (paperback)
1. Nez Percé Indians—Wars, 1877.   2. Nez Percé Indians—History—19th century.
3. Joseph, Nez Percé Chief, 1840–1904.   4. Big Hole, Battle of the, Mont., 1877.
I. Title.
E83.877.W47 2009
973.8'3—dc22       2008051382

Printed in Canada
on acid-free paper

*For my students*

# CONTENTS

List of Illustrations and Maps                                    xi
Editor's Note                                                     xv
Preface                                                          xvii
Timeline                                                        xxvii

PART I

Chapter 1    Real People                                           3
Chapter 2    Marks of Friendship                                  20
Chapter 3    The Place of the Butterflies                         35
Chapter 4    "God Named This Land to Us"                          52
Chapter 5    Gold, Prophecy, and the Steal Treaty                 75
Chapter 6    "Conquering by Kindness"                             98

PART II

Chapter 7    "It Will Have to Be War!"                           123
Chapter 8    Maneuvering and Scrapping                           137
Chapter 9    Ways of Life, Ways of War                           152
Chapter 10   Leaving Home                                        169
Chapter 11   Big Hole                                            186
Chapter 12   Toward Buffalo Country                              201
Chapter 13   War in Wonderland                                   214
Chapter 14   "The Best Skirmishers in the World"                 230
Chapter 15   Toward the Medicine Line                            243

PART III

Chapter 16   Under the Bear's Paw                    267
Chapter 17   Going to Hell                           283
Chapter 18   Eeikish Pah and Return                  301


Epilogue                                             315
Acknowledgments                                      322
A Note on Sources                                    325
Notes                                                329
Index                                                381

# LIST OF ILLUSTRATIONS AND MAPS

## Illustrations

Figure 1.1  The Heart of the Monster, birthplace of the Nez Perces   5

Figure 1.2  Wallowa Lake and valley, shielded
by mountains to the west   14

Figure 2.1  Weippe Prairie, with camas in bloom,
where Lewis and Clark met the Nez Perces   22

Figure 2.2  Elijah White tried to impose both laws
and a social order on the Nez Perces   30

Figure 3.1  Henry H. Spalding, missionary to the Nez Perces   40

Figure 3.2  Spalding's published version of Elijah
White's imposed arrangement   42

Figure 4.1  The Nez Perces' dramatic arrival at the
Mill Creek council   63

Figure 4.2  Looking Glass, whose sudden arrival
threatened to upset Isaac Stevens's treaty   66

Figure 4.3  Tuekakas, or Old Joseph, chief of the Wallowa band   73

Figure 5.1  Lewiston early in the 1860 gold rush   77

Figure 5.2  Early Dreamers, whose religion opposed
changes brought by the white frontier   83

Figure 5.3  Lawyer, the Christian Nez Perce who was the
leading advocate for the treaty in 1863   91

Figure 6.1  Heinmot Tooyalakekt, Chief Joseph, in 1877   113

Figure 7.1  Nez Perce drawing of a tel-lik-keen like that
at Tepahlewam   125

Figure 8.1  Oliver Otis Howard early in the Civil War   138

Figure 8.2  Fort Larned in Kansas, a typically bleak
western army post   147

Figure 9.1   Fanciful drawing of Chief Joseph as stern
             commander of the Nez Perces                         161
Figure 9.2   Red Heart, imprisoned with his band in 1877,
             at a happier time in later life                     167
Figure 10.1  Civil War soldiers string out the wire
             that would help unify the continent                 178
Figure 11.1  At the Battle of the Big Hole, John Gibbon
             barely avoided George Custer's fate                 192
Figure 11.2  A Nez Perce drawing of the animal that
             revolutionized Native American life                 198
Figure 12.1  An English view of O. O. Howard's "pursuit"         207
Figure 13.1  Members of the Cowan party of Yellowstone
             tourists after their ordeal                         222
Figure 14.1  Samuel Sturgis, outmaneuvered by the
             Nez Perces outside Yellowstone Park                 233
Figure 14.2  As with these Crow warriors, soldiers and
             Indians often met on close but peaceful terms       239
Figure 15.1  The reading public kept up with the war and
             battles like that at Canyon Creek                   246
Figure 15.2  Nelson Miles, "Bear Coat," led the final
             pursuit of the Nez Perces                           252
Figure 15.3  The "Great Hunt" devoured the plains
             bison with a factorylike efficiency                 261
Figure 16.1  Site of the final battle, looking south
             from Snake Creek to the Bear's Paw mountains        268
Figure 16.2  Miles's initial attack at Snake Creek               277
Figure 17.1  Charles Erskine Scott Wood soon after
             graduation from West Point                          286
Figure 17.2  William Sherman pressed to send the
             Nez Perces into a punishing exile                   294
Figure 18.1  John Monteith stands above Archie Lawyer,
             James Reuben, and Mark Williams who
             joined the exiles                                   303
Figure 18.2  An older Chief Joseph learned to read
             shrewdly the public and its needs at the
             end of the Indian wars                              312
Figure E.1   Yellow Wolf two years after he began his friendship
             with Lucullus McWhorter                            320

## Maps

Nez Perce War                                    XXIV–XXV
Nez Perce Territory                                     6
Nez Perce War Outbreak                                132
Battle of Big Hole                                    188
Battle of Bear's Paw                                  270

# EDITOR'S NOTE

Many scholars agree that the years 1876–77 were defining ones in American history, but they do so for different reasons. Some remember this period as a turning point for Reconstruction in the American South. Others view it as a critical era in the history of capital and labor throughout the northeastern states—with massive strikes, bloody violence, and bitter conflict between rival ideas of human rights. Elliott West believes that they were a pivotal moment in western history, when native American nations met the expansive power of the United States in the last great Indian wars. This pathbreaking work connects them all.

West brings two great strengths to this project. He has a depth of special expertise in western history (for which his peers have elected him president of the Western History Association). He is also a "generalist," interested in putting large problems in a broad context. This book combines both approaches.

Its particular subject is the Nez Perce War of 1877. West begins by introducing us to the great Indian nation who called themselves the *Nimiipuu* ("the real people"), and were nicknamed the Nez Percé—"pierced nose people"—by French *coureurs de bois* who traded with them. He takes us to their magnificent homeland in what is now Idaho and its neighboring states protected by the barriers of Blue Mountains to the southwest and by the Bitterroot range to the east, and riven by huge canyons—one of them half again deeper than the Grand Canyon, which made them among the "most geographically blessed people" in America. High above the rushing streams of this region (the Snake, Salmon, and Clearwater rivers) were great expanses of forest-fringed grasslands, which were perfect country for horses. The Nez Perce became legendary horsemen. An expert rider observed them galloping their animals "as though grown to their backs," with the aid of a barely visible buffalo string, and was put in mind of a nation of centaurs by that sight. They were also famed for their skill in breeding some of the finest bloodstock in America and won the reputation of being able to "beat a Yankee on a trade." The Nez Perce were able to control their homeland until the 1860s, when gold was found in the northern Rocky Mountains. Treaties were solemnly made and swiftly broken. Fear and rage grew on every side, and it was followed by violence and war. Leaders such as William Tecumseh Sherman ordered that the Nez Perce should be "treated with extreme severity."

On one side were the great Nez Perce warriors Ollokut, Toohoolhoolzote, Five Wounds, Rainbow, Looking Glass, and the brilliant political leader Young Joseph. Fighting against them were regular soldiers of the United States Army, some of whom greatly respected the Nez Perce and sympathized with their cause. General John Gibbon, who nearly suffered Custer's fate, described the Nez Perce War in his own words as "an unjustifiable outrage upon the red men, due to our aggressive and untruthful behavior." General Nelson Miles reflected on his long experience and wrote that the military skill of the Nez Perce was "unequalled in the history of Indian warfare."

As this book shows us with vivid and memorable clarity, the Nez Perce outfought their enemies many times and were never defeated in battle. They tried to reach Canada, in a long march through the Yellowstone country where war parties met groups of tourists in a surreal collision of two eras. At one point they nearly captured General Sherman himself. Finally, after trekking 1,500 miles, and only miles short of their goal, the Nez Perce were overwhelmed by the strength of the forces arrayed against them. Their leaders surrendered to save their people, and Joseph spoke the words for which he is known: "From where the sun now stands I will fight no more."

The Nez Perce were exiled to distant reservations, but they continued the struggle by other means. Speaking with an eloquence that moved even his enemies, Chief Joseph went East and demanded justice from the great republic, which, as West shows, was attempting to "reconstruct" native Americans into the broader polity, but on its own limited terms. Partly on the strength of his appeals, some of the Nez Perce returned to their homeland. The great issues of 1877 remained unresolved. The United States demanded the full allegiance of African Americans in the South, Indians in the West, and impoverished workers in the Northeast. But were they full citizens of the great republic? It is still an open question.

# PREFACE

In late July 1877, about eight hundred Nez Perce Indians made their way in a long column up a steep and twisty trail into the Bitterroot Range of the northern Rocky Mountains. The column included what had been several villages—warriors, women, children, and elderly—as well as more than two thousand horses, dozens of dogs, and all that they would need to start their lives over. Just where that might be, or how long they might be there, they didn't know.

They were leaving home, eastward out of central Idaho toward Montana. Already they had fought two battles and several skirmishes with the U.S. army, and several more times over the next two months they would confront hundreds of troops pulled together from much of the northwestern quadrant of the nation. Their running would take the Nez Perces three times over the continental divide, through arid valleys and beds of lava, past geyser basins, along great rivers, and across the rolling, grassy expanse of the northern Great Plains. Their final goal was asylum beyond what they called the "medicine line," the international boundary with Canada. Some would make it. Most would be caught barely forty miles shy of the border.

All told, they would travel roughly fifteen hundred miles. For an equivalent, imagine that after the Civil War the residents of a small town in Culpeper County, Virginia, feeling alienated and threatened, decided to pick up and head west. Imagine them led by Confederate veterans, chased by Union troops, crossing the Appalachians and pushing on beyond the Mississippi, driving large herds of livestock and pulling wagonloads of wherewithal. To cover the same distance the Nez Perces did, the Virginians will have to go as far as Denver.

That remarkable odyssey alone makes the Nez Perce War one of the most compelling stories of nineteenth-century western history. It was also an event well suited to be part of this series—a pivotal moment in American history. It has a claim to being the nation's last Indian war. Looking back, tracing the long-running developments that led to it, we can learn plenty about how the young nation extended its control over Indian peoples, worked to undermine their material and spiritual ways of life, and sought to incorporate them into the growing republic. Looking ahead, we can see something of the fate of Indians after their final resistance.

The Nez Perce War was pivotal in another sense. It was a culminating moment in the transformation of the nation, an era of wrenching changes that transformed America physically, economically, politically, and culturally. Looking back on that transformation from the historical pivot of the Nez Perce War is a useful view. It challenges some common assumptions and perspectives. For me, in fact, it is a chance to rethink how America was remade in the middle of the nineteenth century. It pushes me to question how we have pictured those years and arranged them in our heads.

Historians segment time. Usually, we name a segment for a dominating event we say turned the course of history in a new direction and then kept shaping what was happening until something else came along big enough to shift history onto a new course. American segments include the revolutionary and Jacksonian eras, the progressive period, and the New Deal.

Segmenting time, or periodization, is something we have to do if we want to organize the past and give it meaning. But it's dangerous. By choosing some dominating event and saying that its period starts here and ends there, we run the risk of neglecting other events that don't fit well into the scheme we've created, and that in turn risks distorting our view of how events have worked and built on each other to make the America we have come to know. Periodization matters. History is not the same, no matter how you slice it.

The crisis of the Nez Perces and the war that came from it fell within the period usually called the "Civil War era" and dated between 1861 and 1877. This label presumes that the preeminent force of its time was the war to save the union. The war, the developments that caused it, and its historical aftershocks dominate not only the story but also the terms of significance. How valuable an event is to understanding mid-nineteenth-century American history depends on whether and how much it had to do with the Civil War, its causes, and its aftermath.

The problem with this big picture is that many developments with great long-term consequences have little or no place in it. Consider those shown in the Nez Perce story. Through it, we see the extension of national presence to the Pacific coast—the flood of white settlement, the implanting of lifeways and economies, and the establishing of an increasingly muscular federal presence. We watch the tapping of resources that would go far toward making the nation the richest and most powerful in history. We see the West's mythic meaning take shape and become an essential part of the nation's understanding of itself. And in the ordeal and survival of the Nez Perces themselves, we can follow the opportunities and threats to indigenous peoples that began with the first touch of white newcomers in the far West and proceeded through the intricate exchanges that followed. We see the challenges to Native America's physical and cultural independence, their conquest and dispossession, and their tenacious efforts to preserve their identities.

These events and issues and conflicts are vital to understanding the full American story of the mid–nineteenth century. Yet when we hold them in our minds, and then put beside them the usual narrative of the Civil War era, there seems little or no connection between the two. What do the overland migration to Oregon, Protestant missions to the Pacific Northwest, and Indians' prophetic religions have to do with the crusade against slavery and the secession crisis? Where is a common thread to emancipation, the Freedmen's Bureau, and federal occupation of the South on the one hand and western railroad surveys, reservations, Indian wars, and Yellowstone National Park on the other? It's as if there are two independent historical narratives, and because the one that is set in the East and centered on the Civil War has been tapped as the defining story of its time, the one that is set out West seems peripheral, even largely irrelevant, to explaining America during a critical turn of its history.

The trick would seem to be to find a way to rethink these crucial years so that its historical segment and its great defining events both accommodate what happens in the big story as it is now told while also admitting what has been kept at the margins. This book suggests an option, offering the Nez Perce War, with its origins and its aftermath, as a pivotal moment that especially illuminates one of the most consequential periods of our history.

This approach has three simple premises. First, the period itself, the historical segment, covers the thirty-two years 1845–77. Second, this period was defined by two events that together set American history in a new direction. One was the Civil War; the other was the acquisition of the far West that came in three episodes over three years—the annexation of Texas (1845), the Mexican War (1846–48), and the acquisition of the Pacific Northwest, including Nez Perce country (1846). Third, far western expansion and the Civil War raised similar questions and led to twinned crises. Grappling with those questions and resolving those crises essentially remade the nation, a transformation that was genuinely continental in scope and with implications, including nagging questions, that have rippled ahead to the present day.

I have called this period the Greater Reconstruction. This risks confusing readers, I know, because in standard histories the familiar term "Reconstruction" applies only to the years 1865–77 and focuses almost wholly on reintegrating the South into the union. Nevertheless, I use the term, first, because, if taken literally, it stresses that transforming the nation began with a physical rebuilding, a reconstructive burst of territorial growth that increased the size of the nation by roughly 70 percent. Second, the term helps make another basic point: far western expansion and the Civil War, as just noted, raised similar issues. We associate all those issues to some degree with events during Reconstruction as usually defined, the dozen years following the Civil War. Think of those events— for instance, the fights over readmission of southern states; efforts to assist freedmen and to secure their political participation; investment in the southern economy and extending railroads to the South's cottonlands and ports. Now ask what fundamental questions were behind them. Those questions were being asked as much about the West as about the South, and they were pushed to the front of national concern as much by territorial expansion as by the Civil War. By adding the modifier "Greater" to "Reconstruction," I'm suggesting that we should keep our focus on the usual issues associated with Reconstruction but extend our thinking through both space and time.

The issues were threefold. One was about size. Could a large and diverse nation, especially a republic, hang together? In the East, the tension pulling apart North and South arose not just from questions of slavery but also from regional diversity, from the diverging economic trajectories of two large, quite different parts of the nation, and from the weakening bonds between the two as the skein of railroads developed faster and more fully in the North than in the South. Western expansion aggravated the size question even more obviously. Could we really add one and a quarter million square miles to the nation, deserts and cordilleras and plateaus radically unlike anything to the East, while keeping the nation as one thing? By 1877, the responses, East and West, were efforts at a vigorous integration of regions into a national whole—militarily, economically, and through expanded and consolidated systems of roads and rails, including the first transcontinentals.

A second issue was political—the central government's relation to the nation's parts. The immediate question in the East, the one dominating the story told in textbooks, concerned where national and state authority stopped and started and what recourse was available when a boundary was breached. But the West had its own questions. How would federal authority be structured and exercised in a region larger than western Europe? An area with scores of other centers of power, each with people who had never contemplated being part of the nation and who had vastly different notions of power itself? The Union victory back East, including the reshaping of southern state governments, confirmed federal sovereignty throughout the nation. Out West, a centralized authority was extended and given form—states and territories, reservations and a bureaucracy to control native peoples—over an area half again the size of the Confederacy.

A third, especially nettlesome issue concerned citizenship, its nature, prerogatives, and demands. The question back East at first was whether southern whites would be allowed to end their citizenship collectively through secession. The answer to that question (no) spun off another—whether and how citizenship might expanded to another southern group, freed slaves. Out West, the question involved dozens of Indian peoples who were, at least on paper, suddenly inside the nation yet far outside its cultural mainstream. Could such peoples ever really fit inside even the loosest conception of membership in the republic? Answering this question (yes) raised another. If Indians were told they were to become citizens, what if they said no? It was one thing to force southern whites, a group with deep historical roots in the union, to stay inside the national household. It was quite another to force independent, culturally alien peoples to *come* in. Washington's answers for East and West were much the same. Freedpeople and Indians would ultimately be citizens. They would be ushered in, assimilated, via strikingly similar programs of Christian mission, common school education, and integration into the economy of agriculture and the manual arts. If the approach was the same, however, responses were not. Freedpeople embraced these programs and the vision behind them. So did some Indians. But some didn't, and for them the government's answer was what it had been for southern whites who had earlier tried to opt out of citizenship—military conquest.

These three essential issues of the Greater Reconstruction had always been there, but after 1845 they took on a new urgency. Expansion and the tensions between North and South made those questions both much harder to resolve and impossible to avoid. During the Civil War, fundamental answers emerged, and Washington's power to implement them expanded. During the dozen years after Appomattox, Washington used that power to subdue the last resistance to its answers and to consolidate the new order that resulted.

Two great events reconstructed America. Each influenced the other, yet each had its own strings of consequences, equally transforming, and so each requires equal billing if we are to reimagine a full, balanced picture of the nation's remaking. This book's perspective considers the Greater Reconstruction from out of the West. This view stresses that the forces transforming America were at work in Idaho and Oregon as much as in South Carolina and Massachusetts and emphasizes that the consequences were decidedly different in different regions and for different Americans. Those broad points are best shown by giving them body through particular human experiences. Nothing shows that better than the story of the Nez Perces.

When Chief Joseph surrendered on a snowy battlefield just below the Canadian border, the *Chicago Tribune* declared that after more than two and a half centuries, "the end of Indian wars seems to be at hand."[1] While not absolutely accurate, the claim was close enough. The next year, there was a brief outbreak among the Bannocks, neighbors to the Nez Perces. In the Southwest, the Apaches would put up resistance for nearly another decade, with fighting that was nasty, brutish, and long but less a war than sporadic raid-and-response, much like today's police fighting urban gangs. The sad events around Wounded Knee in 1890 were a brief slapping-down of spiritual independence. Native opposition had begun soon after the first intrusions into the Southwest and on the Atlantic coast. On October 5, 1877, it essentially ended.

The United States fought its last war against an Indian people who could claim the longest friendship and firmest alliance with the nation. The Nez Perces' first contact, in 1805, was with the republic's most famous western explorers, the Corps of Discovery of Meriwether Lewis and William Clark. The bond of peace made then lasted seventy-two years. That span, starting with the first touch of national power and ending as the nation was completing its conquest and consolidation, lets us follow with rare detail how Indians were subsumed within a new political and social order as America remade itself. The fact that this last war was with such a consistent ally also raises the troubling question of whether those doing the reconstructing could have found a way for native peoples to live more fully and freely with what they valued most—cultural integrity as their own distinct people.

The first part of this book covers the Greater Reconstruction as experienced by the Nez Perces—ultimately a conquest in many forms, as much as anything an assault on their understanding of who they were. This part ends with the United States and Nez Perces on the lip of war. The second part follows the war itself, an episode worthy of our attention in its own right and one that further illuminates how America's remaking played out in the West. This part ends on the eve of the battle that would end the Nez Perces' extraordinary effort to stay free. They were learning painfully what it meant to live inside a modern state—the thread of the book's third part, which covers their capture, their exile, and finally their return. As they responded to Washington's continent-wide effort to consolidate the nation, including programs parallel to those bringing newly freed slaves toward citizenship, they also shrewdly crafted how they were seen, playing to role, and winning their way home.

Every so often in the narrative, I pull back to consider how the story says something crucial to understanding the western side of the Greater Reconstruction. I think of these as "step-asides." Their topics range from epidemics and empire, religious prophecy, mountain men, and Yellowstone National Park to the telegraph, Native American diplomacy, and army life in the West.

The Nez Perce story has much to say about its time and about how that time helped make the America we know. This book also respects this story simply for what it is. Its cast includes cavalrymen and officers and their wives, bureaucrats and politicians, trappers, prospectors, missionaries, and ranchers, but the key actors were the Nez Perces. They were themselves a very mixed group, but they had one thing in common—a homeland.

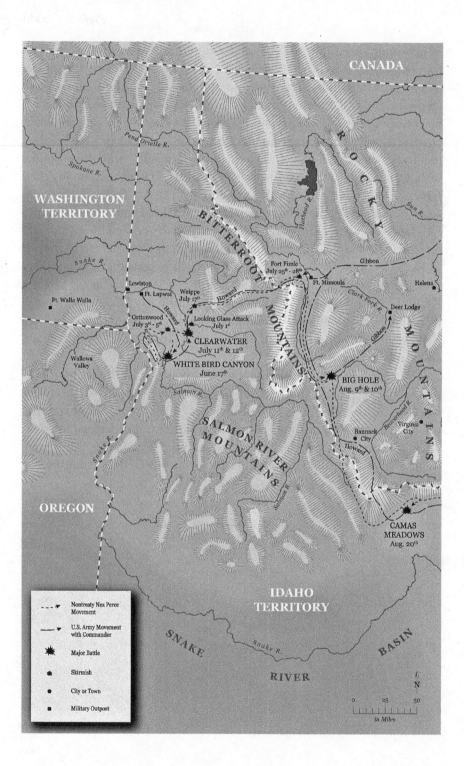

CANADA

WASHINGTON
TERRITORY

*Pend Orielle R.*

*Spokane R.*

ROCKY

*Flathead R.*

*Sun R.*

*Snake R.*

BITTERROOT

Gibbon

Helena

Lewiston

Weippe
July 17th

Howard

Ft. Missoula

*Clark Fork R.*

Fort Fizzle
July 25th - 28th

MOUNTAINS

Deer Lodge

Ft. Walla Walla

Ft. Lapwai

Howard

Looking Glass Attack
July 1st

Cottonwood
July 3rd - 5th

CLEARWATER
July 11th & 12th

Gibbon

MOUNTAINS

Wallowa
Valley

WHITE BIRD CANYON
June 17th

BIG HOLE
Aug. 9th & 10th

*Salmon R.*

SALMON RIVER

*Beaverhead R.*

*Snake R.*

MOUNTAINS

Bannack
City

Virginia
City

Howard

*Salmon R.*

CAMAS
MEADOWS
Aug. 20th

OREGON

IDAHO
TERRITORY

SNAKE

*Snake R.*

BASIN

RIVER

N

Nontreaty Nez Perce
Movement

U.S. Army Movement
with Commander

Major Battle

Skirmish

City or Town

Military Outpost

0        25        50

in Miles

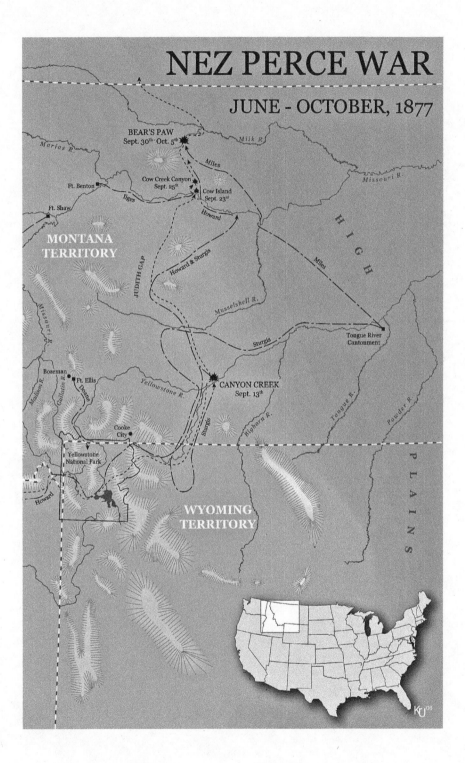

# NEZ PERCE WAR

## JUNE - OCTOBER, 1877

BEAR'S PAW
Sept. 30th - Oct. 5th

*Milk R.*

*Marias R.*

*Missouri R.*

Ft. Benton

Cow Creek Canyon
Sept. 25th

Cow Island
Sept. 23rd

*Miles*

Ft. Shaw

*Ilges*

Howard

HIGH

MONTANA
TERRITORY

JUDITH GAP

Howard & Sturgis

*Miles*

*Musselshell R.*

Sturgis

Tongue River
Cantonment

Bozeman

Ft. Ellis

*Doana*

*Yellowstone R.*

CANYON CREEK
Sept. 13th

*Madison R.*

*Gallatin R.*

*Missouri R.*

Cooke
City

Sturgis

*Bighorn R.*

*Tongue R.*

*Powder R.*

Yellowstone
National Park

PLAINS

Howard

WYOMING
TERRITORY

KU '06

# TIMELINE

## European Contact to War: 1730s–1877

| | |
|---|---|
| 1730s | Nez Perces acquire horses |
| 1780–81, 1800 | Smallpox epidemics sweep through Pacific Northwest; prophet dance and other prophetic religious movements |
| Sept. 20, 1805 | Lewis and Clark meet Nez Perces at Weippe Prairie; pledge of friendship on return trip in May 1806 |
| 1829–32 | Spokan Garry returns from Anglican school, leads revival; four emissaries from Nez Perces and Flatheads visit St. Louis |
| Summer 1836 | Whitmans and Spaldings arrive as missionaries at Waiilatpu and Lapwai |
| 1840 | Young Joseph (Heinmot Tooyalakekt) born |
| 1842 | Elijah White appointed Indian agent, meets with Nez Perces to establish basic laws and name first head chief |
| June 1846 | United States acquires Pacific Northwest through Oregon Treaty with Great Britain; Oregon Territory organized August 1848 |
| Nov. 1847 | Whitmans killed at Waiilatpu and Spaldings driven from Lapwai mission |
| 1855 | Isaac Stevens negotiates series of treaties, including one with the Nez Perces and two others with tribes of the Plateau |

| 1855–58 | War on Plateau breaks power of Yakimas, Wallawallas, Coeur d'Alenes, and other neighbors of Nez Perces; stresses over the war, the treaty of 1855, and pressure to assimilate divide Nez Perces between "treaties" and "nontreaties" |
|---|---|
| 1850s | Rise of Dreamers, prophetic movement opposing farming, selling land |
| Oct. 1860 | Gold discovery on northern fringe of Nez Perce reservation triggers flood of white immigration |
| June 1863 | Government claims new treaty negotiated, although several bands reject it and formally break with those supporting it |
| 1869–71 | President Grant initiates Peace Policy; Presbyterian minister John Monteith appointed agent to Nez Perces; Henry Spalding returns to reservation |
| Aug. 1871 | Old Joseph (Tuekakas) dies, succeeded by Young Joseph/Chief Joseph |
| June 1876 | Killing of Wilhautyah in Wallowa valley precipitates crisis between Nez Perces and white settlers |
| Nov. 1876 | In meeting with Joseph, government commission demands that resistant Nez Perce bands move to reservation, recommends suppression of resistant Dreamers |
| May 3–14, 1877 | In showdown at Lapwai, Howard and Monteith demand compliance with 1863 treaty; after arrest of Toohoolhoolzote, the other leaders agree; dead line for moving onto the reservation is set for June 15 |

## The War: June–October, 1877

| June 14–17, 1877 | Nez Perce attacks on settlers; battle of White Bird Canyon |
|---|---|
| July 1: | Whipple attacks village of Looking Glass band |
| July 3–5 | Skirmishing around Cottonwood Creek; Rains party killed; attack on the Brave Seventeen |
| July 11–12 | Battle of the Clearwater |
| July 15 | Nez Perces decide to leave home; Looking Glass assumes leadership for journey to Crow country |
| July 16–28 | Nez Perces cross Lolo Pass, confront Rawn, and bypass "Fort Fizzle" |

| | |
|---|---|
| July 28–Aug. 8 | Gibbon joins the pursuit |
| Aug. 9–10 | Battle of the Big Hole; Poker Joe (Lean Elk) assumes leadership of Nez Perces |
| Aug. 20 | Nez Perces attack Howard at Camas Meadows; fight with Norwood |
| Aug. 26–Sept. 5 | Nez Perces, Howard, and Doane maneuver in Yellowstone National Park |
| Sept. 5–11 | Nez Perces leave Yellowstone, elude Sturgis, reach Yellowstone River |
| Sept. 13–14: | Battle of Canyon Creek and Crow pursuit of Nez Perces |
| Sept. 14–22 | Nez Perces break for Canada; September 17, Miles begins pursuit from Tongue River Cantonment |
| Sept. 23–25 | Nez Perces cross Missouri River; skirmishing at Cow Island; Looking Glass reassumes leadership |
| Sept. 30–Oct. 5 | Battle and siege of Bear's Paw Mountains (Snake Creek) |
| Oct. 5 | Joseph surrenders; White Bird and more than two hundred Nez Perces escape toward Canada |

## The Aftermath: 1877–1904

| | |
|---|---|
| Nov. 1877 | Nez Perce captives sent to Fort Leavenworth, Kansas |
| July 1878 | Exiles moved to eastern Indian Territory |
| Jan. 1879 | Joseph and Yellow Bull visit Washington, D.C. |
| Apr. 1879 | Joseph's dictated story appears in *North American Review* |
| June 1879 | Exiles moved to Ponca agency |
| 1878–81 | Most Canadian exiles return to Idaho |
| 1883 | Twenty-nine exiles allowed to return to Idaho |
| 1885 | Congress authorizes return of remaining exiles; in May, 118 move to Lapwai; 150, including Joseph, to Nespelem on reservation in Colville, Washington |
| 1897 | Joseph visits New York City, rides in parade for dedication of Grant's Tomb; pleads for return to Wallowa |
| 1900 | Final refusal of return to homeland |
| Sept. 21, 1904 | Joseph dies at Nespelem |

# PART I

## CHAPTER 1

# Real People

The attack came during breakfast. On a high bluff, a scout wheeled his horse in a tight circle while waving a blanket, the signal that an enemy was right on the Nez Perces. Almost immediately, the first cavalrymen were there. They came at a full gallop out of the south, the Bear's Paw mountains behind them. In the "wild stir" that followed, Yellow Wolf (Hemene Moxmox) and several other warriors sprinted for the horse herd pastured on the far side of the camp from the attack, but soldiers and their Cheyenne scouts were soon there. Women and children, including Yellow Wolf's mother, were with the horses when the cavalry charged, and he helped send them off to escape to the north, toward Canada—forty miles away. Back in the camp, other warriors stopped the cavalry's charge, drove back a second attack, and dug in for a defense. It began to snow. After midnight, Yellow Wolf slipped between sentries and joined the besieged camp.

He heard keening, the moans of the wounded, and the crying of cold, frightened children. Many warriors had died, "swept as leaves before the storm." With dawn, the fighting began again, with furious fire from both sides, "bullets from everywhere." Rifles flashed in the blue battle smoke. The day was "wild and stormy, the cold wind was thick with snow," and the Nez Perces fought as bravely and as well as they had at any of several battles since the first one in early summer.

This time there was no way out. After traveling farther than most could have imagined, after all the fighting, and with more than a hundred dead, Yellow Wolf knew it was over. "I felt the coming end," he remembered: "All for which we had suffered lost!" And then: "Thoughts came of... where I grew up. Of my own country when only Indians were there. Of tepees along the bending river. Of the blue, clear lake, wide meadows and horse and cattle herds. From the mountain forests, voices seemed calling. I felt as dreaming. Not my living self."[1]

Out of despair, the call of home.

The Nez Perces have been some of the most geographically blessed people on this continent. They have Coyote to thank. Long time ago, a gigantic and voracious monster entered the valley later called Kamiah and proceeded to eat all the people. (This was before humans, so these were nonhuman people that others would call animals.) Coyote decided this was no good, and, clever as always, he got himself inhaled by the monster, taking with him pitch, a fire-making kit, and five sharp flint knives. He explored inside the monster until he found the heart, along the way kicking Bear and Rattlesnake, flattening their respective nose and head. Coyote lit a fire, and as smoke poured from the monster's mouth, nose, eyes and anus, he began to cut the heart loose from its moorings. He broke all five knives, but by hanging on the heart he pulled free the last bit of flesh that held it in place. With that the monster died, and the surviving people all fled back into the world, carrying the bones of their own dead. These Coyote revived with the monster's blood. Then he began cutting up the monster and flinging its parts far away in all directions. As each piece landed, a group of humans sprang up: Coeur d'Alenes, Blackfeet, Cayuses, Pend Oreilles, even the Crows and Sioux. When he had finished, the monster's body was all gone.

Then Fox asked Coyote: Who will live *here?* Coyote washed his gory hands and began sprinkling the blood-water right around him. Where the drops landed, another group of human people sprang up. They were a little smaller, born not from flesh but from water. Nonetheless, Coyote assured them, while you may be little people, you will be powerful, and very manly.[2]

Thus were born the Nimiipuu (the Real People).

The heart of the monster remains today, described by geologists as a basaltic mound along U.S. Highway 12 near the town of Kamiah, Idaho. In time, the Nimiipuu would become most widely known as the Nez Perces, derived from the French for "pierced nose" and pronounced "Nezz Purse." They may have gotten the name from wearing ornaments in their noses, something they did occasionally but not commonly. More likely, the name came from the sign they used to identify themselves to outsiders. Periodically, they crossed the Bitterroot Mountains eastward to hunt bison on the Great Plains. Their sign reflected that journey. With the right hand, the index finger extended, they made an up-and-over movement to the right of the head, as if crossing a divide, then swept down to the left under the nose. To the uninitiated, it looks like an extravagant nose-piercing.[3]

**Figure 1.1** The Heart of the Monster, birthplace of the Nez Perces

The people Coyote flicked to life out of bloody water called home a land covering more than twenty five thousand square miles of the inland Pacific Northwest in what is today southeastern Washington, northeastern Oregon, and north central Idaho.[4] Their country was strikingly diverse. It overlapped three geological provinces. Its northwestern part was in the Columbia Plateau, a vast lava sheet stretching to the north and west. Its southwestern portion, at the base of the Kill Devil and Wallowa Mountains, was part of the Blue Mountains province, which ran north and south across modern northeastern Oregon. To the east, their country abutted the northern Rocky Mountain province, specifically the Bitterroot Mountains, which rose to the continental divide. The center of Nez Perce country, where much of the following story took place, shared some traits of all three provinces.

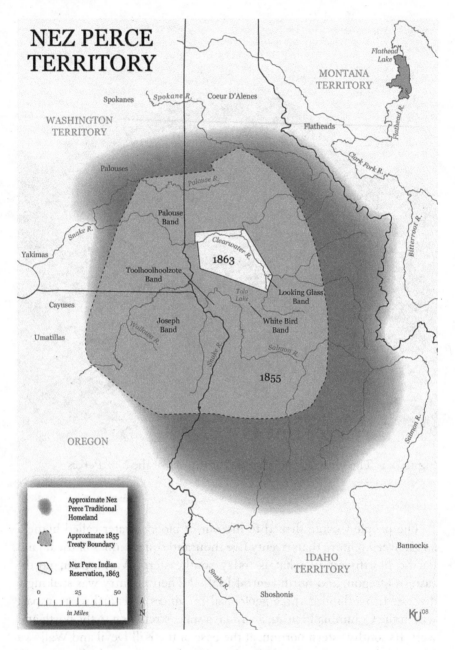

# NEZ PERCE TERRITORY

WASHINGTON TERRITORY

Spokanes    *Spokane R.*    Coeur D'Alenes

MONTANA TERRITORY

*Flathead Lake*

Flatheads

*Clark Fork R.*

Palouses

*Palouse R.*

Palouse Band

*Clearwater R.*

1863

*Snake R.*

Yakimas

Toolhoolhoolzote Band

*Tolo Lake*

Looking Glass Band

*Bitterroot R.*

Cayuses

Joseph Band

White Bird Band

*Wallowa R.*

Umatillas

*Salmon R.*

*Snake R.*

1855

OREGON

*Salmon R.*

Approximate Nez Perce Traditional Homeland

Approximate 1855 Treaty Boundary

Nez Perce Indian Reservation, 1863

0    25    50

*in Miles*    N

Bannocks

IDAHO TERRITORY

*Snake R.*

Shoshonis

KU '08

Several magnificent rivers nourished the Nez Perce homeland. Largest was the northward-flowing Snake River. Draining into the Snake from the west were the Imnaha and Grande Ronde rivers, and from the east the Salmon and the Clearwater. After gathering these waters, the Snake bent westward and left Nez Perce country before joining the Columbia. Fed by snows in the high country, all these streams had healthy flows from midspring until midautumn. All hosted native fish and were spawning grounds for migrating salmon.

Like all of the inland region, Nez Perce country lay in the "rain shadow" of the Cascade Range to the west. Saturated air roiling inland from the coast dumped most of its moisture in the lofty Cascades, so as these fronts passed inland, they were like sponges wrung almost dry. Much of the land below was semiarid, receiving on average from thirteen to twenty inches of precipitation a year. The Cascades, the Blue Mountains, and the Rockies also sheltered this country from the worst buffeting from the outside, in particular the powerful storms that struck the northern Pacific coast.

The Nimiipuu homeland was a country of extremes—of temperature and precipitation, and therefore of threat and opportunity. The great range of landforms, especially in altitude, were the reason. The Bitterroots and Wallowas rose high up to the east and west. Over the millennia, the high country's snowmelt, churning downward, had gouged deep canyons into the basalt below. On the southern edge of Nez Perce country is the lower end of the deepest gorge in North America, Hell's Canyon, nearly half again as deep as Arizona's Grand Canyon. At their highest, the Wallowas and Bitterroots were around ten thousand feet above sea level; the lowest point in Nez Perce country, around present Lewiston, Idaho, was less than a thousand feet. The equivalent east of the Mississippi would be starting from its highest point, the top of North Carolina's Mount Mitchell, and dropping down to New Orleans—then burrowing three thousand feet more into the earth. The long reach from mountaintops to canyon floors allowed a remarkable environmental range. Of the six life zones from low desert to alpine tundra, four can be found in Nez Perce country.

Any traveler knows that moving upward in elevation generally means finding lower temperatures and higher precipitation, while heading the other way brings warmer, drier conditions. The range of moisture and heat in Nez Perce country is exaggerated still more by the country's exposed highlands and its confined, heat-trapping canyons. Today Lewiston, at the junction of the Clearwater and Snake rivers, receives an average of about twelve and a half inches of rain a year, well less than Salt Lake City, while Grangeville, Idaho, forty miles to the southeast, on a plateau that drew lots of attention from white cattlemen, gets about twice that. Elk City, less than fifty miles farther on, gets about thirty inches. While precipitation is modest overall, because most of it comes in the winter, little is lost to evaporation, so much of the open plateaus at midelevations still green up nicely with only modest rains. Besides that, how the land lies and drains helps determine rainfall's practical effects, leaving some places desiccated, others marshy and lush.

Temperatures vary, too. The Wallowa valley sits high and exposed west of the Snake River. In the deep winter, it could be nearly unliveable, while temperatures on the floor of the Imnaha River canyon, scarcely twenty miles away, were quite moderate. In high summer, the Wallowa is cool and pleasant, while the Lewiston area bakes, as do canyon towns in even higher country. Orofino, up the Lochsa River, a tributary of the Clearwater, reported Idaho's highest recorded temperature on July 28, 1934—118 degrees F.

A visitor touring Nez Perce country would have passed through vegetation ranging from sagebrush and rabbitbrush in the desert-like canyons to bunchgrass, fescue, snowberry and chokecherry at midelevations, plus a variety of shrubs and forbs and limited trees, notably hackberries, along watercourses. Moving into the mountains, he would have found forests ranging from ponderosa pine to Douglas fir, western hemlock, and subalpine fir, with several varieties of berries flourishing in higher areas. Springs and seeping hillsides, poorly drained marshlands, and small protected mountain valleys, or "holes," formed atypical niches with still other vegetation.

It was quite a show, and while the extremes of terrain, temperature, and precipitation posed obvious challenges, they were also blessings. They allowed a variety of life that the Nez Perces could use to support their own.[5] The Nez Perces relied on three broad categories of food. Fish were most important. They took resident species like cutthroat trout and whitefish, but most vital were salmon, taken as they swam upstream to spawn. Three species, silver, bluebacks, and the large chinook, migrated at different times, so the people were pulling them from streams from early spring into the autumn. The salmon harvest at the time of white contact was astonishing—between two and three million pounds per year, or between three and five hundred pounds per person. Gutted, cleaned, and dried, salmon were eaten from spring until nearly the end of the winter. They provided about half the people's annual calories. The knowledge that was essential for fishing was how the patterns of migration and spawn overlapped with the spots where salmon were most vulnerable—when and where people needed to be to take best advantage of the harvest.

Another 10–25 percent of their food came from wild game (unlike some other Indian peoples, they did not eat their dogs). They hunted with splendid bows that were highly prized regionally as trade goods. Their favored game were whitetail and mule deer and elk, although they occasionally took mountain goats, mountain sheep, and, less often, bears as well as rabbits and other smaller animals. Nez Perces living in the northern homeland, in the Clearwater River area, crossed the Bitterroot Mountains to the Great Plains to hunt bison and antelopes, a practice that became more common and important once they had horses. Different game animals moved around the country in different patterns in response to changes in weather and forage. The knowledge that was essential for hunting, then, was how best to break into those various patterns—how and when to move among places scattered across large areas.

Wild plant gathering, women's work carried on in all seasons but winter, provided the other 25–40 percent of the Nez Perces' food. One authority has identified thirty-four food plants. Some, like serviceberry, elderberry, chokecherry, and sunflowers, were familiar in many parts of the West. Others were more localized. Some, like the sego lily, frasera, and elk thistle, were seasonal supplements eaten when picked; others were processed to be stored for the winter. Two of these were far and away the most important. Cous (*Lomatium cous,* common name biscuitroot) flourished in canyons and on plateaus. Its roots were gathered after its seeds had matured in May and early June. A vigorous digger could unearth fifty to seventy-five pounds a day. Cous roots could be eaten raw, tasting something like parsnips, or cooked and peeled, or dried and ground into flour. Most valuable of all were the roots of the camas lily (*Camassia quamash*), which grew so thickly in marshlands that from a distance their waving blue blossoms could be mistaken for a shimmering lake. As with cous, gatherers waited until the seeds had matured, which made the roots tastier, and because maturation varied with altitude, the Nez Perces dug camas from mid-June into September. The harvest was great—forty, fifty, or even more pounds a day per woman—and like cous the processed camas root was a major staple during winter. It was remarkably rich in energy, providing about seventeen hundred calories per pound.[6] To put it in modern terms, a pound of camas root had the caloric clout of nearly half a large pizza, with three times as much protein. Berries offered a lot, too. Serviceberries had more than twice the calories of braised beef liver; a pound had nearly four times the calories of a six-ounce fried chicken breast.

Each plant had its favored conditions. Cous was found in well-drained soils in canyons and on plateaus, camas in poorly drained, soggy meadows. Other plants were more widely distributed. Chokecherries were found in canyons and on plateaus, gooseberries on plateaus and foothills, yampa (wild carrot) on prairies and near pine stands, serviceberry and fireberry in the high country. The knowledge that was essential for gathering, then, combined those for fishing and hunting: knowing when some plants would be ready to take from the same spots, as with cous and camas, and when others were likely to appear in which scattered locations.

The country's obvious upside—the abundance, variety, and geographical spread of its resources—had its downside. With so many different plants and animals living in so many habitats, some were likely to falter or fail in any given year. And because virtually all harvesting and hunting was between midspring and midautumn, with the months from June through August by far the busiest, people had to choose to exploit one place and one kind of food over others. This had two practical effects. First, the Nez Perces had to spread themselves out in relatively small groups to take advantage of all their country's possibilities. Second, since none of these groups could provide all of its own needs, they all had to rely on each other to make up the difference.

The tug between these two demands helps explain how the Nez Perces had set themselves up as a society.[7] That society was so alien to white newcomers that few grasped more than its crudest outlines. Nor, of course, did most Nez Perces have the slightest inkling of the whites' social arrangements. The mutual misperceptions fouled communication and frustrated honest efforts to harmonize relations between the peoples, which made the Nez Perce social arrangement, as it was in fact and how it was misunderstood, vitally important in the story that follows.

The most stable point in the Nez Perce society was the village. It was a firm reference point in two senses. It was a political unit—an important focus of an individual's identity—and it was anchored in place.

The Nez Perces lived in villages during the winter, when weather was most dangerous and resources the scarcest, so they chose spots where they could best hedge their bets: the river canyons, those low, claustral places that shielded them from storms and provided the mildest temperatures.[8] Winter, not as a time on the calendar but a condition, was shortest in the canyons. In effect, spring began there and moved gradually into the upcountry. In these bottoms, the people could find the earliest spring offerings just as their stored winter food was running out. The best locations were along feeder streams close to where they entered larger rivers. Resident fish spawned there before the first salmon runs. There was driftwood for fires and, after the Nez Perces acquired horses, grass for grazing. Here, in the lean late winter, appeared the season's earliest edible plants, "starvation foods" like *Lomatium canbyi*—nourishing, though it tasted, some said later, like kerosene.[9]

There were about 130 villages in Nez Perce country, ranging from a single family of about ten or so to seventy-five members of several extended families.[10] Structures and facilities changed dramatically with European influence, but before that families in a typical village lived together in a long lodge that was bermed two or three feet into the earth, framed with driftwood logs, and roofed by large mats sewn from cattail stalks. Nearby were two sweat lodges, one for men that doubled as a sleeping place for unmarried males and another for women's general use and for living quarters during childbirth and menstruation. Many villages also had a ritual dancing area, well removed because of its spiritual power, where a mat lodge was built and taken down before and after annual ritual dances.

Villages were also economic units. Villagers embarked on an annual round as the weather warmed and as plant sequences and salmon migrations began. Each village typically controlled a salmon fishing station, a vital site given how much of a year's food was gathered there. Each station had equipment—traps, weirs, and platforms from which men pulled out the flashing fish with nets and spears—that required considerable maintenance. Here others came to fish and work at repairs; these shared labors helped bind villages together. From midspring to early fall, villagers also traveled and camped together to gather camas and other plants as each matured in its particular time and niche—first yellowbell and balsamroot sunflower, then serviceberry and wild hyacinth and cous, then gooseberry and chokecherry and yampa, and finally mountain serviceberry, fireberry, and huckleberry. As the women gathered, the men hunted game that moved with their own seasonal patterns. Movement was generally upward into higher country as the weather warmed and the summer progressed, then back down into the canyons with the year's harvest of fish, plants, and game.

Villages were part of larger social groupings, called combines, made up of villages clustered on the same sidestream flowing into the Snake, Salmon, and Clearwater rivers. Members of a combine easily switched residence among member villages, intermarried, met together for religious ceremonies, and cooperated in common work. A combine of two or more villages with especially strong ties went by another name—a band. Beyond the village, the band was the highest level of political integration and an individual's firm identity. A man or woman would certainly recognize wider social connections, but his or her sense of belonging and allegiance came most sharply into focus in these local groupings.

Each village had a headman, usually the most respected older male, who was expected to speak for the village and to promote harmony and resolve disputes within it.[11] He earned his respect partly by living up to Nez Perce ideals. He should be like "foxes," according to a modern informant—modest, generous, capable, fair, and a "man with kind words." He should cultivate ties beyond the village for help in an economic crunch.[12] A village council of older men advised the headman. The band or village combine also had its central figure, sometimes called a "headman," sometimes a "chief," also a highly respected older man who was often from the group's largest village. He would speak for the band, and like the village headman he was advised by a council of elders and was measured by standards of high morality, poise, outside influence, and political skill. There were others with particular duties. The village "fish headman" distributed the catch at a fishing station. The "whipman," a kind of anticheerleader, verbally chastised misbehavior. The "herald," like a medieval town crier, announced decisions by the headman and other significant news. Another figure, the *tewat* (shaman), was recognized for special gifts of healing, cursing, prophecy, and in general having an unusually immediate access to spiritual powers and the unseen. Because Nez Perces believed that unseen power was at work in every aspect of life, a *tewat*'s influence was potentially as great or greater than that of any headman or chief, and in fact he might be recognized as a leader in such other areas as war and diplomacy.

Sketched in this way, there appears to be a structure of authority, with chiefs and headmen and their councils on top, that a white outsider then and a reader today might presume enforced the rules and standards found in every human community. Presuming that, however, would be a mistake. By the terms of white society, nobody was in charge. No one could legitimately require anyone else to do anything. A headman might make a decision for his village, but he could not force a single person to follow it, and he would likely be rebuked if he tried. The same applied to a band chief. There were certainly standards and rules of behavior, but they were maintained not by the power to punish but by two other influences. One was a sense of responsibility instilled from earliest youth, buttressed by what everyone knew by living day to day—that survival was possible only if each individual respected the needs and security of the group. If someone did act improperly, the second influence could come into play. In these small, tightly knit communities, shaming and humiliation were powerful tools. The violator might endure public chastisement, led by the village "whipman."

For special occasions, leaders emerged above the band and village level. One such time was large-scale hunting. Bands among the upper Nez Perces on the Clearwater River traveled periodically across the Bitterroots to join with Flathead allies to hunt bison, which often meant fighting plains tribes like the Blackfeet. At these times, bands followed the lead of the men who were especially adept at following trails to the buffalo country, organizing and executing the hunt, and battling rivals.[13] Diplomacy was another such occasion. In dealings with other peoples, the person conceded to be the best negotiator—the most articulate, the coolest under pressure, the shrewdest and subtlest in gauging and defending his people's interests—took the lead, with the full support of several otherwise independent bands. These roles, however, were temporary, pegged to the needs of the moment, and once the hunting, fighting, or bargaining was done, so was the man's authority. Leadership reverted to headmen and chiefs.

Collective hunting and war parties were reminders that villages and bands were never self-contained. They relied on each other, which called for devices of connectedness. Marriage among different villages created bonds of kinship, which in turn brought an exchange of resources. Villages joined in annual ceremonies, notably the guardian spirit dance and the first fruits ceremony. On those occasions, social ties were formed and strengthened and information exchanged about conditions across the region. Villages used one another's fishing stations and hunting camps, and persons from different communities, usually women with women and men with men, joined in the common efforts of hunting or gathering. Finally there were simply bonds of friendship across villages and bands. Being well regarded and liked among several communities was a real asset that played into a man's rising to headman or chief.[14]

It went farther. The Nez Perces were tied by blood, trade, and friendship to several other peoples across the Columbia Plateau and beyond, some those born when Coyote tossed around the bloody pieces of the monster. To the west and north were the Cayuses, Palouses, Wallawallas, Umatillas, Yakimas, Coeur d'Alenes, Spokans, and others. To the east, across the Bitterroots, were the Flatheads. Each people spoke their own language, which in turn fit into two linguistic families, the Sahaptin (Nez Perces, Cayuses, Wallawallas, Yakimas, Umatillas, Palouses) and the Salish (Flatheads and Spokans). Nez Perce bands in the west intermarried frequently with the neighboring Palouse, Cayuse, Wallawallas, and Umatillas, while those to the east on the upper Clearwater River intermarried with the Flatheads and lived with them, sometimes for years at a time, while hunting plains bison. The Nez Perces and all groups were necessarily multilingual and conversant in various traditions.

From one perspective, then, the Nez Perces were a collection of smallish villages and bands clustered along streams.[15] From another, they were a series of functional relationships among peoples of different bands bound by cooperation, blood, and amity.[16] From still another, they were part of a far wider nexus of peoples who went by many names and spoke many languages yet felt connected by bonds both practically and emotionally weighted.

Small wonder that arriving whites found it hard (if they tried at all) to comprehend how the Nez Perces were organized and operated. Leadership would seem maddeningly difficult to pin down, something there but not there. All authority was situational and informal, all rules essentially self-enforced. Society seemed at best odd and at worst no society at all.[17]

Whites responded by projecting onto the Nez Perces and others what they expected to be there—or in some cruder cases, what suited their needs at the time. Generally they assumed they were dealing with a rough equivalent of a state or nation, with parts knit into a whole that was firmly bounded and governed by a descending order of power. The gap between the society white authorities expected or needed to find and the subtle, multilayered society that was actually there relentlessly plagued the relations between whites and Nez Perces.

Geography shaped the Nez Perces' history in one more way. The mountains that ringed their homeland were barriers against enemies. The Blue Mountains to the southwest and the Bitterroots to the east stood as bulwarks against the Shoshonis, Bannocks, and Blackfeet. For a while they stood also against the pressures brought from the white frontier.

Figure **1.2** Wallowa Lake and valley, shielded by mountains to the west

Nez Perce country was no Shangri-la, however—no timeless land untouched by the world outside. Long before Europeans appeared, in fact, all of North and Central America was an intricate mesh of trade and diplomatic allegiances. In uncountable contacts and through annual trade fairs, one of the largest of which took place among the Nez Perces' Shoshoni neighbors, the goods circulated—conch and mussel shells from both coasts, mica from the Appalachians, flint from Texas, grizzly claws and obsidian from the Rockies, bison hides and skulls from the Great Plains, turquoise from the Southwest, parrot feathers from Mexico, and much more. Along with them came habits, customs, cosmologies, dress, stories, cultural wrinkles. Potentially every native group in the Americas might feel some effect, good or ill, from every other.

Most Indian peoples, including the Nez Perces, first encountered Europeans through that network—not directly, in the flesh, but through what the newcomers brought with them. First, the detritus tossed off or taken from the invaders—bits of metal, caps and cloth scraps, leather saddle cinches—was sucked into and along trade routes to travel hundreds or thousands of miles into the American interior. Next, with face-to-face contact, all parties quickly began seeking from the others what they wanted most. Increasingly, Europeans sought the pelts of fur-bearing animals: fox, bears, martins, wolves, ermines, and especially beavers. Indians acquired knives, hide-scrapers, blankets, awls, amulets, copper bells, beads, metal fire-sparkers, and more. Inventories of British traders included deworming pills, peppermint candy, and corduroy pants. By the time the United States acquired the far West in the 1840s, this exchange was well advanced. Indians lined their tipis with bed ticking from eastern textile mills. They used steel knives to cut off twists of Virginia tobacco that they smoked in pipes made in Massachusetts. After grinding African coffee in New England handmills, they drank it sweetened with West Indian sugar and New Orleans molasses.

The two most coveted imports were guns and horses. Firearms, especially more sophisticated versions that became available in the later eighteenth century, offered the obvious advantage of killing game and enemies from longer distances, especially in the more open landscapes of the Great Plains and unforested areas like the Columbia Plateau (which I will refer to from now on as the Plateau). There was the disadvantage of relying on whites for gunpowder and parts for repair, but the appeal still was nearly irresistible. Because the gun trade flowed almost wholly out of the East from the French and British, however, the spread of firearms across the West was uneven. In 1800, the Nez Perces were still without them.

They did, however, have lots of horses. Horses were at least as alluring as guns. They vastly expanded a people's range in trading and fighting and in some settings increased hugely a person's ability to hunt, most notably among the plains bison. Horses became measures of prestige, adding a cultural appeal, and unlike guns they could replace themselves. One testimony to the allure of horses is how rapidly they spread across the West. Although horses first appeared in the West in the 1540s (or rather reappeared—see chapter 11), Indians got them in large numbers only after the Pueblos drove the Spanish out of northern New Mexico for a dozen years in 1680. From there, horses spread northward through the Rocky Mountains, into the Pacific Northwest, and then into the Great Plains. The process was completed by about 1780, a mere century after it started.

The Nez Perces got their first horses sometime during the first thirty years of the eighteenth century, probably from Shoshonis to the south. Tribal tradition says that a pregnant white mare became the seed of what in time became enormous herds.[18] The Nez Perces' situation was unusual, if not unique. Horses could not give any great boost to their economic basics of salmon fishing, gathering camas and berries, or hunting elk and deer. But geography had blessed them in yet another way: their homeland was as close to perfect horse country as anywhere on the continent. High stream valleys like those of the Wallowa and Grande Ronde had magnificent pastures during the warm months, and during the winters the canyons provided sanctuary from the weather and bunchgrass for feed. The Plateau had few natural predators, and the mountain barriers discouraged raids from other horse-hungry groups.

The Nez Perces not only took to horses, they became one of the continent's greatest horse cultures. By the time this was accomplished, one of their earlier names, "The Walking People" (Tssop-nit-palu) would have seemed odd indeed.[19] Their herds rivaled or surpassed in size any others. Meriwether Lewis and William Clark told of one prominent chief possessing "more horses than he can Count," and in 1814 a British trader visited a camp of Nez Perces and some neighbors that had a pony herd he estimated at nine thousand.[20] The Nez Perces were also among the few western tribes to practice selective breeding, gelding some stallions and mating others with selected mares to encourage certain traits and suppress others. The result was what a visitor in 1861 described as "elegant chargers, fit to mount a prince," tall and long-limbed, "sinewy and sure-footed."[21] (Contrary to popular belief, they did not produce the colorful, spotted Appaloosa, though they had such horses and favored them.)

All this the Nez Perces did while still living by a traditional means of fishing, hunting, and gathering that horses did little to help. It is hard to avoid the impression that behind the equestrian flourish were feelings of mastery and sheer pleasure.

Horses did enhance two parts of the Nez Perces' economy. They could trade farther and more vigorously, and across the Bitterroots they could hunt bison more effectively. To the west, they expanded their exchanges with Plateau groups at annual gatherings at The Dalles and elsewhere. To the east, their trips to the Great Plains increased in tempo and scope. Not relatively small all-male parties but large groups of families now made the journey. They moved over a much longer radius and sometimes were gone for two or three years. They met and mingled with new groups, other horse-powered peoples hunting more widely and vigorously— Sioux, Cheyennes, Arapahoes, Crows, Hidatsas, Comanches, Kiowas, and Utes. There were some clashes, but the encounters apparently were relatively peaceful at first.

Peaceful—and rich in material and cultural exchange. The Nez Perces left home loaded with their superb bows (so valuable that a single bow might trade for a good horse), salmon oil, and dried salmon packed in salmon skins, shells traded from The Dalles, bowls and spoons carved from mountain sheep horns, baskets of cedar root, flat embroidered wallets woven of hemp, camas cakes, and dried mountain berries. They came home with bison horns and ornamented bison robes, rawhide parfleches, tipi coverings, and pemmican. Dried bison meat became increasingly a staple of their diet. Within a few generations, tipis had all but replaced traditional mat-covered lodges, and men took to wearing the flowing eagle war bonnets of the western Sioux.

The Great Plains connection encouraged a deep-rooted distinction among the Nez Perces, one essential to understanding the story to come. That division was between the bands on the Clearwater River, at the western base of the Bitterroot Mountains and closest to the plains, and the bands living farther south and west, along the watersheds of the Salmon and Snake rivers. The former group would be called the upper Nez Perces, the latter the lower. The upper Nez Perce bands crossed the Bitterroots more often to hunt the plains bison. They cultivated an image of dash and flair, of bold, adventuresome roamers known for horse-stealing, fighting, and scalp-gathering. They sometimes were called *k'usaynu ti-to-gan,* "sophisticates."[22] The lower bands were less likely to join the journeys. They took on something of a stay-at-home reputation, that of borderline rubes who stuck with the old ways, preferring huckleberries and salmon fat to bison steaks. Sometimes they were called *eneynu ti-to-qam,* "provincials." In the crisis leading to war, the division between upper and lower bands played out in complicated ways. Once the war began, the reputation of some among the upper bands, that of savvy navigators of the country to the east, made for a crucial turning point in the story.

While the horse greatly expanded the Nez Perce world, its greater reach could deliver more than was bargained for. It was not entirely a coincidence that the West's first smallpox pandemic—the first epidemic to expand beyond its point of initial infection—occurred in 1780, generally noted as the year the horse culture was fully in place across the West. The contagion moved via trade routes used for centuries, but before horses, movement had been so slow that diseases like smallpox burned themselves out before reaching a fresh population. Travel by hooves got the infection into virgin soil in time to set its horrors loose. How many died in 1780–81 we can't know, but it may have been as many as twenty-five thousand in the Pacific Northwest, including great numbers of Nez Perces.[23] Had they understood what was happening, victims might have resonated with an image from the Christian Book of Revelation: death riding a horse.

Horses and guns had another disruptive effect: they unsettled relations among native peoples. Newly horsed peoples moved permanently onto the Great Plains, one of the planet's great pastures—Comanches from the Great Basin, Sioux and Cheyennes from the eastern woodlands, Kiowas from the northern Rockies, and others—while periodic hunters like the Nez Perces came in greater numbers and stayed longer. The mingling grew more tense with competition and as some gained an edge over others. Here, the uneven spread of guns—traded freely in the East, rare or absent in the West—was critical. Groups to the east had both of the new keys to power, guns and horses, while those to the west had only horses. By the late eighteenth century, the Blackfeet had acquired enough firepower to expand aggressively westward, challenging the Nez Perces, Shoshonis, Flatheads, and others for use of the buffalo plains on the eastern slope of the Northern Rockies.

So by the opening of the nineteenth century, although no whites had come into Nez Perce country, they had altered it profoundly. They had brought the Nez Perces great opportunity and given them expanded power. Along with that had come epidemics and mass death. The same indirect influences had shaken the people's security. Coyote's gift to the Nimiipuu, their ancient protective isolation, was beginning to erode.

In an audacious move in the spring of 1805, the Nez Perces sent three young men hundreds of miles to the east through hostile territory to the

Hidatsas living with the Mandans along the Missouri River. Their villages, longtime trading pivots, had firearms. Remarkably, the three men made it there and back with the first six guns acquired by the Nez Perces. It was a promising break. Along with the guns, the three brought home a rare firsthand view of a faraway world.[24]

Tucked into their stories was an intriguing bit of news. The previous winter, a clutch of white men had stopped in the same trading villages. They sounded interesting. They said they were pausing on a long journey of peace in hopes of establishing trade (guns?) with western peoples. The young emissaries had not seen these newcomers, however. Just as the three had set off for the Hidatsas, the whites had continued up the Missouri, toward Blackfoot country. Their advance was toward the snowy wall of the Bitterroots, maybe beyond.

# CHAPTER 2

# Marks of Friendship

Meriwether Lewis, William Clark, and their men were the first whites the Nez Perces saw in their homeland.[1] On September 20, 1805, Clark and an advance party of the Corps of Discovery came on three boys, who hurried to alert the villagers who had camped nearby at Weippe Prairie for one the season's last camas harvests. The boys carried the nation's first gifts to the Nez Perces, small pieces of ribbon.[2] The Corps had crossed Lolo Pass, already choked with snow, and they were in miserable shape, starving and frostbit. The Nez Perces fed them salmon and berries, and the corps proceeded on to a large village on the upper Clearwater for the first extended exchanges between the Nez Perces and whites.

It might have gone differently. The Nez Perces were unusually touchy. Most of their warriors had set off to the south only three days earlier to fight Shoshonis. Besides, the coming of whites was expected, and the anticipation was not all positive. The period between the first white influences and the whites' first appearance had brought benefits but also calamities—smallpox epidemics in 1780 and 1800. The unsettling changes inspired two conflicting prophecies, one predicting a new golden age, the other, heightened by a volcanic eruption and blizzard of ash in 1800, a horrifying end time—abuse of elders, child theft, rivers red with the people's blood.[3] Word that white men were approaching Nez Perce country forced the question: welcome this new presence, or snuff it out?

According to a recent telling of the tradition, a discussion was led by three prominent men, Twisted Hair, The Cut Nose, and Red Grizzly Bear. Kill the newcomers, some from the Salmon River bands argued. But others countered:

> Look at the things these strange people can do. They can make *kicuy* [kes-ooy; metal] and *qalanwn* [kh-la'wn; beads]. They make *timuni*

20

[tee-moo-nee; weapons] that kill at a great distance. We have six of these *timuni,* but we have no black powder which makes them work, and we have no lead balls that kill. Our enemies to the east and north have these *timuni* in great numbers and we don't. What can we do to get these many things that will make our life easier and help us to protect our families better?[4]

The decision turned on an elderly woman in the Clearwater village. Wat-ku-weis (Returned, or Returned From a Far Place) had been captured by Blackfeet or Atsinas as a girl, taken eastward, and sold to a French Canadian before finding her way home. Whites had treated her well, and tradition has it that as leaders discussed what to do, she testified "these are the people who helped me. Do them no hurt."[5] So the decision was made to spare the newcomers, who might also bring a welcome trade. "They are verry fond of our marchandize...and are glad to git anything we have," one of the men wrote of his first meeting, and the two sides swapped goods frequently while the corps rested and made canoes for their trip's final leg.[6] Lewis and Clark distributed gifts, including peace medals and two American flags, and then set off for the Pacific.

The following May, after a wretched winter near the mouth of the Columbia River, the Corps stopped with the Nez Perces for more than a month on their way home. This visit shaped significantly how the Nez Perces regarded the United States for the next seventy years, although Lewis and Clark seem not to have fully grasped its significance. It began with a council at the village of a respected war leader, Tunnachemoontoolt (The Broken Arm), who had been off fighting Shoshonis the previous fall. The corps arrived to see a good sign, one of their flags raised on a pole beside the lodge where they would meet, a structure a 150 feet long with two dozen fires down the center inside. Red Grizzly Bear, The Cut Nose, Twisted Hair, and others from their earlier meeting were there. The captains expressed their hope that the region's tribes would end their fighting so all could trade without fear at a post they said would be built on the Great Plains to the east, where the Marias River joined the Missouri. After withdrawing to deliberate, the Nez Perces, speaking through The Broken Arm, gave a pleasing response. They were "fully sensible of the advantages of peace," they said; "the whitemen might be assured of their warmest attachment," and from then on they would always "give...every assistance in their power." His people were poor, the warrior said, "but their hearts were good."[7]

Lewis and Clark took the council as a pledge of friendship and good-will. It was that, but Nez Perce tradition is clear that they considered it

**Figure 2.1** Weippe Prairie, with camas in bloom, where Lewis and Clark met the Nez Perces

something much firmer and with grander implications. The captains' plea for a regional peace struck an especially welcome chord. If these newcomers could bring the Blackfeet and Atsinas into line (and many Nez Perces were skeptical), their enemies would not use firearms against them. Even if a peace held only for a while, the Nez Perces could get weapons of their own during the interim.

Guns in fact were a recurring, teasing motif in the talks, along with Europe's other revolutionizing contribution, horses. The previous fall, Lewis and Clark had asked Twisted Hair to watch over their horses. Now, when he turned over some of them, they paid him back with a gun, two pounds of powder, and a hundred rifle balls, and they promised as much again when he returned the rest. Right before the council, the captains were given a fine horse. When they gave powder and balls in return, they noted that the Nez Perces "appear anxious to obtain arms and amunition," and during the talks the leaders reiterated that they would "come over and trade for Arms amunition &c." Two days later, Red Grizzly Bear and others approached the Corps camp singing songs of friendship, and when the chief presented the captains with a beautiful gray gelding, they gave back a handkerchief, two hundred balls, and four pounds of powder, "with which he appeared perfectly satisfyed."[8]

The Nez Perces were leveraging what they had most of to get more of what they lacked and embracing the chance that a widespread peace brokered by Lewis and Clark might give them power and material gain in a changing world. All indications are that they considered this an arrangement between equals calculated for the advantage of both. Future dealings presumably would be on the same terms—equality, reciprocity, and mutual respect. The agreement represented less a gesture of friendship than a new relation among peers.

The Nez Perces may well have thought it sealed by a personal bonding. When the captains learned that Lolo Pass would be blocked by snow for another month, they and their men settled into what they called Camp Chopunnish, near Twisted Hair's camp. Their tradition is emphatic that during the long stay there, Clark sired a son with the sister of Red Grizzly Bear. Such unions between influential whites and women of prominent native families were a nearly universal device to formalize a connection between whites and Indian peoples. Clark never acknowledged the parentage, although in context it seems more than plausible. Whatever his lineage, the child, named Halahtookit (Daytime Smoke), would live through the story ahead.

Nothing suggests that Lewis and Clark understood their arrangement to be quite so weighty, but they came away greatly admiring the Nez Perces. All in the corps who wrote of them agreed that they were handsome, dignified, cleanly, proud, cheerful, ethical, hardworking, open, honest, and above all welcoming. They were the "most friendly, honest and ingenious" of all the peoples of the journey, Patrick Gass told his journal, and Clark wrote that "to their immortal honor" they had performed "much greater acts of hospitality" than any people west of the Rockies.

Whatever qualms the Nez Perces might have felt when white men first walked into their world, they had chosen friendship and peace. They looked ahead to parlaying this new relation into a life of expanding promise.

The Lewis and Clark expedition had almost no short-term impact on westward expansion, with one exception: the fur trade. The captains' promised trading outlet on the plains never materialized, and after a nasty clash with the Blackfeet on the way home, neither did their brokered peace, but their reports of abundant game brought an immediate response. Even before the corps returned to St. Louis, a couple of the crew took off to trap the country they had crossed. Others from the East soon followed.

The fur trade plays prominently in the popular view of western history. The images of bearded and buckskinned hell-raisers at rendezvous are as familiar as those of cowboys and cavalrymen, but as with the others, the colorful impressions can trick us out of seeing what was really happening. The fur trade's larger-than-life central character, the mountain man, seems an American version of the German *Wildermann:* naturally feral, a hairy solitaire who has walked away from every constraint and convention of his mother society. As in modern treatments like the film *Jeremiah Johnson,* the mountain man seems one of our own who chooses to live against the grain, opposed to whatever the new nation was up to.

The reality was different. For practical reasons, of course, a trapper did go native in appearance and many practices, wearing greasy buckskins and beaded moccasins and maybe a feather in his long hair, learning Indian skills, and eating meals and adopting habits that would raise the gorge of most Philadelphians. Nonetheless, those bear-men were also point men in carrying national institutions into the West. Trappers were workers in America's biggest business, the equivalent of today's petroleum or computer industries. The fur trade, a major enterprise in the colonial era, was bigger than ever in 1805. It would soon produce the republic's first millionaire, John Jacob Astor, the immigrant fiddle-maker commanding the American Fur Company. In 1800, however, Astor and others faced a problem. Generations of trapping in the East had depleted the population of beavers, the mainstay of the business, and the hunt was on for alternatives. Lewis and Clark gave them one—the upper Missouri and Pacific Northwest.

Free agents quickly responded, and a few years later Astor launched a strategy of extraordinary brass. He sent men overland and by sea to establish a post near the mouth of the Columbia River, immodestly named Astoria. From there, furs taken by trappers he hired to work the Columbia's huge watershed were launched into a trans-Pacific trade that eventually linked Europe with the fabled Asian market. By the time Astor set this plan in motion, however, there was competition. England's North West Company had positioned itself with posts in present eastern Washington and western Montana.

The Nez Perces meanwhile had presumably been waiting for American agents who would follow up on Lewis and Clark's promises as they understood them. What they got was Donald McKenzie, the head of Astor's operation, who arrived in August 1812 to set up a post low on the Clearwater River near modern Lewiston. He brought a large load of goods, and the Nez Perce leaders he met were eager to deal—until he told them that he would swap only for beaver skins. The Nez Perces had no interest in trapping beavers; their annual round of fishing, gathering, and hunting left no time for it. McKenzie grew frustrated and angry; so did they. This was not the equal accommodation they had anticipated. Relations worsened when, after some young men raided McKenzie's caches of goods, he marched on the nearest village and held its people at rifle point while he searched the lodges. Meanwhile, another Astorian, John Clarke, was similarly trying to muscle the nearby Spokans to his terms, and while among the Palouses he hanged a man—as it turned out a visiting Nez Perce—for stealing a drinking cup.[9]

McKenzie finally came to tense and limited terms with the Nez Perces (a "rascally tribe," he thought) according to which they sold him horses and some food at inflated prices. By then he had learned that the United States and Great Britain were at war, and he soon sold Astoria to the North West Company and, with several other Astorians, hired on with the British. America's first ambitious commercial thrust into the Plateau was over.

The British built several posts in the Columbia basin east of the Cascades. They brought in teams of trappers and workers—English, metis (French and Indian mix), Iroquois from far to the east, and from farther west Hawaiians, also called Kanakans, who were hired on voyages to the Sandwich Islands. (The Owyhee River in southern Idaho is named for three of the company's Hawaiian trappers killed by Bannocks—a modern marker of how early the region was being bound to a wider world.) Some locals, notably the Cayuses and to a point the Spokans and Flatheads, supplied beaver pelts, clashing sometimes with the newcomers but taking advantage of what they offered.[10]

The Nez Perces stayed aloof, except for occasional visits to trade for horses and contact outside the homeland, and the British kept clear of them. They had no reason to cross Nez Perce country, cupped in as it was by the Blue and Bitterroot mountains, and every reason to avoid angering the region's most powerful people. They built Fort Nez Perces near where the Snake River met the Columbia, west of Nez Perce country. Its iron gate, rampart, cannons, and swivel guns suggested their worries about their neighbors.

Then the Americans, a dozen years after leaving, returned, this time without the officious behavior of Donald McKenzie and the Astorians. A party led by the young Jedediah Smith appeared among the Flatheads in 1827, offering friendship and generous terms to Indians who would supply trappers sent out from St. Louis. Smith was organizing the earliest of the famous rendezvous, annual summertime gatherings at some nicely pastured valley in the Rockies where American trappers, who had spent the year gathering pelts, would exchange them for goods and money brought by wagon caravans from St. Louis. After deals were made, plans were set for the next summer. A rendezvous was much like the trade fairs that had been part of the region's economy for centuries, and from the start the gatherings drew Indians, too. The style and tone was far more familiar than with the British, with plenty of socializing, gambling, and horse racing, stories swapped and tobacco smoked. The American practice of haggling, as opposed to the set prices of the British, jibed with the native bartering tradition, and something in the Americans' character and social converse, some looseness and congenial independence, appealed also to the Nez Perces and their neighbors.

The Americans, besides, were not asking the Nez Perces to do the scornful work of trapping beavers. They wanted horses. For that they offered better terms, and simply by providing an alternative option to trading with the British the Americans gave these Indians a chance to play both sides against each other. Dealing with Americans also made geopolitical sense. The Nez Perces and Flatheads were the peoples of the region who were located closest to the American approach out of the Missouri valley, which gave them first crack at this new source of wealth and put them in position to smooth or to disrupt the flow of goods to others. Here, it seems, was opportunity much closer to what the Nez Perces had expected after meeting Lewis and Clark. There were flashback moments. When a "venerable chief" first met a team of American trappers, it was by the guns-and-horses equation. The chief gave a beautiful young brown horse as "a mark of friendship," and when he was given in turn "a handsome rifle," he seemed "gratified by this outward and visible sign of amity."[11]

The Nez Perces began attending the rendezvous in 1827 and increasingly lived and swapped with Americans and guided them in their bid against their rivals, and when the British reacted by sending waves of their own men where their turf overlapped with the newcomers', the intensified competition only gave all Indians better leverage. The Nez Perces stood at the top of this food chain because they could offer the most and best of what both Americans and British had to have to make their enterprises work— horses. Peter Skene Ogden, a British trade captain, wrote in outrage of Americans buying "49 horses from the Nez Perces at an extravagant rate averaging $50," far above the usual price.[12] They also traded finely made clothes and wallets and the meat, robes, and saddle blankets produced from bison hunts. In return they accumulated not only guns, powder, and ammunition but knives, fishhooks, scrapers, tobacco and pipes, cloth and blankets, awls, ropes, and a range of factory goods, including beads, ribbons, paint, and other decorative stuff for themselves and their horses.

Here was the kind of advantage the Nez Perces had hoped for. They bettered their material lives, strengthened their position among both allies and enemies, and cultivated friendly connections with a distant power they might put to other uses in the future. Their dealings seemed entirely reciprocal. Nothing in them seemed threatening. What they missed—and how could they have seen it?—was that their new friends represented a presence far different from that of the British, and one that over time was infinitely more dangerous. The most obvious difference was contiguity. These trappers and traders were agents not of a nation an ocean and most of a continent away but of people massed scarcely a thousand miles to the east and whose western border, along the continental divide, abutted the Nez Perce homeland itself at the crest of the Bitterroots. That nation claimed not only the Plateau but all the Pacific Northwest to present-day Alaska, and although Great Britain did, too, by the time the Nez Perces started going to the rendezvous the odds were clearly tilting in America's favor, in large part because its people, from high business to common farmers, by then had developed powerful impulses of restless, confident expansion.

By welcoming American fur traders, that is, the Nez Perces unwittingly admitted an opening wedge of empire. The first fruits were profitable, or at least benign, but hints of aggressive and dominating influences came right behind.

Relations brought a cultural crossfertilization that was most obviously incarnate in children like William Clark's son Daytime Smoke, now in his twenties. Washington Irving, historian of a prominent trading captain, wrote of Nez Perce country: "Here, in time, the Indians and white men of every nation will produce hybrid races like the mountain Tartars of the Caucases." Village life increasingly displayed a blend of customs. The Bull's Head, a Nez Perce, was nicknamed "Kentuck" by trappers because he loved singing "The Hunters of Kentucky," the popular tavern ballad celebrating Andrew Jackson's victory at New Orleans.[13] The Nez Perce world, always connected to distant native peoples, was becoming part of a new continental continuum laced with European influences, including elements of higher culture that mountain men, counter to their image, helped carry in. The fur trade luminary James Clyman practiced a common cultural habit of the day—writing bad poetry, including a soppy tribute to the seasons: "The summer songsters left the trees / No more was heared the hum of bees." And a hymn to national expansion, including California's Bear Flag Republic: "And here the eagle first took flight / And spread his wings to mountain hieght / And strange to all it will apear / He took the form of grissley bear / For here was merican freedom born."[14]

Nathaniel J. Wyeth represented another expansionist figure, the commercial go-getter. While a Massachusetts hotel owner in the 1820s, he invented a combination sled and saw that vastly reduced the costs of gathering ice from frozen ponds. This made him a fortune and, with new methods of insulation he also pioneered, turned the ice trade from a local and regional to a national and then global business. By 1850, New England ice was sold in Calcutta and Persia. In 1832, Wyeth was trading among the Nez Perces and their neighbors. Here was opportunity as obvious as selling ice in the tropics—bringing the Pacific Northwest more tightly into the nation's economic orbit, gathering its furs, harvesting its salmon, and planting tobacco along the Columbia.[15]

American fur brigades could be more explicitly agents of national power. Captain B. L. E. Bonneville, the man chronicled by Washington Irving, was a West Point officer on leave when he arrived with a large trapping contingent and instructions from the War Department strikingly like Jefferson's to the Corps of Discovery—to meet and describe Indian tribes, to gauge the chances of trade with them, and to report on the region's natural history and its economic prospects.[16] He and others, in effect, were partnering with Washington in exploration, and more blank spots on the nation's maps were filled by mountain men following the smell of money than by formal government expeditions. The man who renewed relations with the Nez Perces, Jedediah Smith, spent three seasons looking for new beaver grounds in the far West. In the process, he became the first white to forge a southern route to the Pacific, to cross the Great Basin, and to travel California lengthwise. He had already made the effective discovery for non-Indians of South Pass, the broad saddle between the northern and southern Rockies that became the immigrant gateway to California and the Oregon country. Smith and Bonneville were essentially unsalaried government agents who provided information vital to later commercial and military expansion, including, from Smith, a crucial map, later lost, of part of the Pacific Northwest.

The popular image of mountain men is of runaways, borderline sociophobes turning their backs on everything behind them to embrace the wild life and its native peoples. A truer picture would have them carrying their society forward and drawing Indians into it. Fur trappers and traders were the first whites most Indians saw in the flesh. They built on the indirect influences that had preceded them, the tremoring of trade and the unsettling of native diplomacy, to reach into the lives of natives like the Nez Perces and to inoculate them with cultural and material influence. They gauged and reported how best to approach native peoples while connecting Indians tentatively to faraway centers of power. In turn, the Nez Perces and others did their own looking and gauging, got plenty of what they wanted, and asked for more. From the Nez Perces' perspective, the exchanges were between equal players on an even field. They were wrong.

The first shift in power came as the beaver trade gave way to the next step in national expansion. By 1840, the year of the last rendezvous, competition among trappers had reduced the beaver population to unprofitability. By then, however, there were other interests in the region—a few missionaries and soon the first sprinkling of farmers—and with that came a new kind of tension. White settlement was all to the west of Nez Perce country, along the fertile Willamette River on the other side of the Cascades, but clearly more immigrants could be expected. Missionaries came among the Nez Perces and their neighbors the Cayuses, and especially among the latter resentment grew toward the results.

More portentous was the coming of Elijah White. A medical doctor from New York, described as given to flattery and "smooth and slippery like glass," he had earlier worked with missionaries on the Willamette before returning East in 1841 and landing the job of the first government official in the Pacific Northwest: subagent to the region's Indians, salaried at $750 per annum.[17] The appointment was remarkable. The Oregon country did not belong to the United States; Great Britain also claimed it. By a joint occupation arrangement, citizens of both nations were free to live there until the two sides could agree on who owned what. Meanwhile, no military presence was allowed in what was a neutral territory. White, who by one account claimed virtually unlimited authority, was essentially operating on a bluff.[18]

Nonetheless, just by sending him there, Washington suggested that great changes were on the way. Dealing officially with Indians implied there would soon be something to deal *about,* which almost certainly meant significant white settlement. In fact, when White returned to Oregon with his commission, he came along with the first substantial overland party, about 125 farmers headed for the Willamette valley.

White's first official act as subagent was arguably his most consequential. For the Nez Perces, its importance over time can hardly be exaggerated. In late 1842, he traveled up the Columbia and Snake rivers planning to meet with native leaders. His goal was to convince them to accept basic rules meant to provide some stability, protect whites already there and those to come, and generally encourage settlement and development. His main concern was with the restive, unhappy Cayuses, but when he found none of their leaders available, he went on to the more numerous and

Figure 2.2 Elijah White tried to impose both laws and a social order on the Nez Perces

powerful Nez Perces. Twenty-two headmen met him with "civility, gravity and dignified reserve" and agreed to hear him out.[19] Among them was the ancient Red Grizzly Bear (Hohots Ilppilp), also called Many Wounds, who had taken a prominent part in dealing with Lewis and Clark nearly four decades earlier.

White's strategy was first to pitch himself as the protector against any future threats by whites. Assuring them of the government's "kind intentions," he said that any whites who intruded on their rights would meet "sad consequences."[20] This opened the way for his prime goal—laying down laws for protecting missionaries and other whites sure to come. His list ran to eleven:

A murderer would be hanged.

So would anyone who burned a dwelling house.

An arsonist of an outbuilding would pay for damages, get fifty lashes, and go to jail for six months.

Anyone who burned any property through carelessness would pay damages.

Chiefs would punish, as they felt proper, anyone who entered a dwelling without permission.

A thief would pay back double what he stole and receive twenty-five or fifty lashes, depending on the value of what was stolen.

Anyone who used a horse or anything else without permission would pay for that use and suffer twenty to fifty lashes.

Anyone harming crops or taking down a fence so livestock could come in would pay damages and suffer twenty-five lashes.

Only those who "travel or live among the game" could have dogs. If a dog killed any stock, the owner would pay damages and kill the dog.

An Indian who raised a gun against a white must be punished by the chiefs. If a white did so against an Indian, White "shall redress it."

"If any Indian break these laws, he shall be punished by his chiefs; if a white man break them, he shall be reported to the agent, and be punished at his instance."[21]

The headmen considered the laws and after some discussion agreed to them. Then White raised a second issue and made a second request, one that eventually had far graver consequences. As things then stood, he said, whites and Indians were in an "embarrassed relation" because of the "want of proper organization." In terms of power and identity, the Nez Perces were a collection of independent bands. How, White was asking, was his government supposed to deal collectively with this conglomeration? What was needed, he said, was a "high chief of the tribe" to speak for all Nez Perces, and beneath him subchiefs of each village, each with five men as "body guards" to enforce their commands. The arrangement he proposed would resemble a modern corporate flow chart with a head chief at the top.

The headmen seemed confused. If you want some one to deal with, they first told White, choose him and be done with it. When White refused, throwing the decision back to them, they consulted with the interpreters, discussed some more, and finally tapped a thirty-two-year-old minor chief to fill the role. White made some more comments, distributed medicines and fifty garden hoes, and then left.[22]

On their face, the two joined actions made no sense. White laid down laws without the slightest legal authority to enforce them. He pressed Nez Perce leaders to appoint a tribal authority who had no more power than he did. White's visit in fact had little consequence in the short run. The episode nonetheless provides a window into how whites and Indians thought about each other on the eve of momentous changes. And as the years passed and those changes got well underway, the seemingly pointless actions of 1842 became enormously important.

White's motives were obvious—protecting his newcomer compatriots. The emphasis in his eleven commandments was on threats to missionaries (arson, invasion of homes) and to property only whites had (crops, fences, outbuildings). The subtleties of his wording bound the Nez Perces more firmly than the whites. Indians who broke the laws "shall be punished," while whites would be reported to White and punished "at his instance"—that is, at his discretion. As for how much actual authority White thought he was investing in the head chief—who knows? He was "quite ignorant of the Indian character," a missionary wrote. Another contemporary more bluntly called White a "notorious blockhead."[23] Perhaps he believed the head chief would truly have the clout he meant him to have.

What significance the Nez Perces saw in the meeting is also elusive. They might have felt a little threatened. "Will you hear and be advised?" one interpreter asked as he introduced White: "If [you are] disposed to close your ears and stop them, they will be torn open wide, and you will be made to hear." The words had a "happy influence," White reported.[24] And yet the chiefs had never seen a soldier, and although the interpreter spoke of whites in the East numbering more than the heaven's stars or the leaves of the forest, the chiefs could not have imagined the population they were facing.

Probably the leaders understood basically what the eleven laws said and saw them as some protection from the white strangers they seen passing by their country, heading farther west. More generally, they likely considered them a general statement of friendship, particularized by ideals of behavior, offered by a messenger from the "great father" they had heard of years before. As for White's second act, pressing the Nez Perces for what he called a head chief, the headmen surely did not understand it as White did. Creating a figure with firm authority over all the bands would have overturned a social order seasoned for centuries. Doing that under any circumstance seems terribly improbable. Doing it persuaded by a man they had known for a few hours is incomprehensible. The chiefs probably thought they were appointing something like a liaison, a man who by language and social exposure was especially suited to communicate with whites. The man they chose, Elice (often called Ellis by whites), was young and of negligible social weight. He had, however, attended a Canadian missionary school, and he came closer than anyone to English fluency. He "can be ears, mouth and pen for us," Red Grizzly Bear said of him. Maybe the headmen went along with White for a far simpler reason. When White told the confused leaders to choose their great leader, he assured them that "if they did this unanimously by the following day at ten, we would all dine together with the chief on a fat ox at three."[25]

So the twenty-two headmen and Elijah White were talking aslant to each other. They left the council with quite different understandings of what had happened and different expectations of what was ahead. Their misunderstandings went beyond particulars to the assumptions behind them, the skeletons inside the respective words and thoughts.

Red Grizzly Bear, ninety or older, greeted White out of his memory of Lewis and Clark, "your great brothers." "They visited me, and honored me with their friendship and counsel," he recalled. Clark had ministered to the Nez Perce sick; the Nez Perces had provided guidance and supplies. Everything in the old man's memory, including his sister's bearing of Clark's son, assumed an equal and reciprocal standing. Now here was White, the first person sent by their "great chief" since Lewis and Clark, speaking of kind intentions and mutual protections. Except for the introductory threat of unstopping their ears, White said nothing to suggest a relationship different from the one promised by the captains thirty-six years earlier.

But the terms *had* changed. Lewis and Clark had come as the feeble touch of a distant government. Elijah White arrived a political evangel for a nation he saw poised to roll into the region and over its peoples. The day he was appointed subagent back East, he had strongly recommended a military post in the Northwest, equipped with artillery and war rockets. His reports from Oregon spent as much time praising the country and calling for its speedy possession as expressing concern with Indian matters.[26] White presumed a new order was about to happen, and because he did, he presumed that laws were needed to warn Indians away from the whites about to take command. He insisted on a mechanism, a head chief, that whites could use to carry out presumably the next step, putting the Nez Perces effectively into their subordinate place.

Elijah White acted by a kind of institutional reflex. At the time, the arrangement he thought he was making was an illusion, but when many others came into the country with the same mindset, acting with true power out of the same impulse, the relation he had presumed became increasingly real. Then the changes begun with the fur trade, fingers of influence from a new order, would enter a new stage, one that ultimately would demand from the Nez Perces their independence and their identity itself.

"Clark pointed to this day, to you, and this occasion," Red Grizzly Bear told White; "We have long waited in expectation."[27] What he expected, however, was not what he got. The old man could not have known how Clark's world had turned since their time together at Camp Chopunnish, or how his own people's world was about to shift under their feet.

## CHAPTER 3

# The Place of the Butterflies

A nother development was pulling the Nez Perces and their neighbors into the expanding nation, and like the trade in horses, guns and the rest, at first they welcomed, even courted it. Early in the fall of 1831, four Indians from the far Northwest arrived in St. Louis with an employee of the American Fur Company. They toured the city and visited William Clark, then serving as superintendent for Indian affairs, who said they had come in hopes that a missionary would be sent to teach their people about the Bible. Two of the four died in St. Louis and were buried in a Catholic cemetery. The others, after sitting for portraits by George Catlin, set off for home on board the steamboat *Yellowstone*. Before the *Yellowstone* reached Fort Union, another died, and the last joined a party of Nez Perces to hunt bison. He was killed by Blackfeet. His story of the trip, however, made it back to Nez Perce country, presumably sometime that year.

Meanwhile, a chance meeting back in St. Louis had produced a twisted account of the visit that soon exploded through the eastern religious community. William Walker, a white Ohioan well connected by marriage to the Wyandots, claimed to have heard from Clark a far more detailed version of why the travelers had come. (He also said he had visited the four, although the evidence is mixed.) According to Walker, the four said that a white visitor had explained that their way of worshiping displeased God, but assured them that whites "toward the rising sun" had a book that could tell them how to win God's favor and be welcomed to God's country after death. At a "national council," leaders had decided to send four chiefs to find that book and bring it back. A few weeks before the two surviving Nez Perces left St. Louis, Walker's account appeared in a Methodist publication, the *Christian Advocate and Journal and Zion's Herald,* with the exhortation "Let the Church awake from her slumbers and go forth in her strength to the salvation of these wandering sons of our native forests." Reprinted extensively and quoted in ringing sermons throughout the East, the plea of the Christ-starved "four wise men from the West" was an appeal to the missionary's zeal. "Who will go?" asked the *Advocate* in an editorial: "Who?"[1]

A better question was: What were the four men really after? Although Walker called them all Flatheads, three were Nez Perces: Wep-tes-tse-mookh Tse-mookh (Black Eagle), Heh-yookts Toe-nihn (Rabbit Skin Leggings), and Ta-weis-se-sim-ninh (No Horns). The fourth, Ka-ow-poo (Of the Dawn, or Man of the Morning) was half Nez Perce, half Flathead. They were partly after trade. The Nez Perces preferred commercial relations with Americans over the British, and if nothing else a St. Louis connection might give them bargaining leverage.

Clearly, the journey also had something to do with religion. Both Clark and St. Louis's Roman Catholic bishop, who visited the two dying men, said the four had asked that their people be given knowledge of the powerful book and the teachings they had heard were in the white man's possession. Just what the four meant, however, is not easily divined. Nobody in St. Louis apparently could speak Nez Perce or Flathead, and the sign language used likely could not communicate the subtleties of the conversations. Nez Perce religious life, however, and especially its changes during the previous couple of years, holds some hints about the mission.

Nez Perce religion differed profoundly from Christianity. As with all religions, however, both involved breaching the plane that separates humans from supernatural presences and forces. For Nez Perces, the vital connection across that plane was the *wey-ya-kin,* a person's guardian (tutelary) spirit, usually but not always taking the form of an animal.[2] A person learned of his or her *wey-ya-kin* during a spirit quest usually taken between the ages of five and ten, learning also an individualized song that invoked the spirit. It was a crucial moment in an individual's formation, one confirmed at the spirit dance held in winter, when the person first sang the song and danced in movements associated with the *wey-ya-kin.* With the help of a *tewat,* a person would spend several years honing an understanding of this spiritual relationship, including behaviors to be respectfully followed and actions and foods to be avoided. Power was also linked to a *ipetes,* a sacred package of power objects associated with the *wey-ya-kin* that was worn on ceremonial occasions and when enlisting the help of the tutelary spirit.

Supernatural relations were pegged directly to temporal success and failure. A person's talents reflected his or her guardian spirit's. People associated with elk, deer, wolves, and cougars were adept at finding game;

a man guided by a grizzly bear was ferocious in battle. On the downside, a crow as *wey-ya-ḳin* led to thievery, in which case it was best to seek another spirit. Neglecting obligations to a *wey-ya-ḳin* meant losing power, even getting sick; cultivating them would bring accomplishment and standing. Power might be gained as well through spirit quests, by working through a powerful *tewat,* and by ritual transference from someone else. Spiritual power thus was always on display, shown by someone's fortunes, and fluid, always able to be enhanced or diminished. The annual spirit dance was in part a series of competitive demonstrations to establish who among the villagers had the greatest supernatural influence.

Nez Perce religion, like its society, was also flexible and open to innovation, so their encounters with whites naturally raised provocative questions. The newcomers had remarkable things—guns and blankets and metal goods from pots to spear points, stuff that brought well-being— and because power and good fortune sprang from spiritual success, whites obviously had impressive supernatural connections, somewhere out there. Such spiritual heft could either threaten the Nez Perces or work much to their benefit. The question was how to respond.

The mission to St. Louis was obviously a positive response. Already, in fact, a modified Christian enthusiasm was sweeping the Northwest. While there had been no missionaries—an effort in 1798 had aborted— there had been religious exchanges between British agents and curious Indians, who sometimes paid for instruction. A Nez Perce gave a trader a good horse in exchange for "information about the forms of religion."[3] In 1825, British agents sent two sons of Spokan and Kootenai leaders to an Anglican school on Canada's Red River, near present-day Winnipeg.[4] The two returned four years later, bringing copies of the King James Bible, the New Testament, and the Anglican Book of Common Prayer, and they soon caused quite a stir. One, known as Spokan Garry, was especially well received as he read biblical passages, sang hymns, and told of Christian prescriptions for attaining heaven. Indians, including Nez Perces, came from great distances to hear him and carried their accounts back to their villages. By the mid-1830s, the revival's ripples had spread all the way to California and northern British Columbia.[5]

The four Nez Perces set off for St. Louis in 1831 just as this religious movement was gathering strength. The best guess is that they hoped the trip would be a double opening—to more direct access to trade and to a new supernatural influence, since the present religious connection was through the British and Spokans to Canada. Simultaneously, the Nez Perces hedged their bets by sending two of their own boys to the Red River Anglican school. One of them was Elice, whose English fluency on return made him a sensible choice for the head chief Elijah White insisted on. With more direct connections to the Americans, the Nez Perces might draw more fully on two traditional sources of strength, commerce and spirit. And with that they could hope for greater command of their immediate world, seen and unseen.[6]

As for how they would bring new religion into their lives—that was unclear. Plateau peoples had responded to Spokan Garry with a rich religious hybridization. They embraced some practices, such as Sabbath observance, while grafting other ideas and rituals onto their own traditions. A British trader found a religion grounded in Christianity but "accompanied with…heathen ceremonies." Captain Bonneville found the Nez Perces devoted to the Sabbath "like a nation of saints" yet mixing old and new into "a strange medley; civilized and barbarous," including a "wild fantastic" dance around a tall pole every Sunday.[7] Obviously, the response was no conversion in the sense of a rejection of old, false beliefs in favor of a new, true faith. The Plateau peoples did, however, seem ready to tap into what they thought was a new and potent source of power to expand the power they already had.

But the account crackling across the eastern religious network was of something else. The "four wise men from the West," it said, had come begging for someone to lead them away from their heathenish ways and onto the One Path, through Christ, to salvation. Presbyterians, Methodists, and other Protestants who heard what some called the "Macedonian cry" had another reason to answer it quickly. Looking westward, they felt the Papist breath on their necks. Roman Catholic authorities were planning their own missions, and soon they sent several Jesuits, among them Francois and Augustine Blanchet, Modeste Demers, and the remarkable Belgian Pierre de Smet, to minister to the region out of British posts. In this age of bitter enmity between Protestant and Roman Catholic, each saw the other as seducing natives down a Hell-bound path, as shown in a teaching device both used. Called a "ladder," this was a vertical panel with rung-like lines representing the centuries from Adam and Eve through Christ's resurrection and on to the End Time.[8] The Protestant ladder ended with a priest toppling head-first into Satan's inferno. The Catholic version had a gnarled and withered limb branching from the sixteenth century: Protestantism. In the years ahead they would help each other in the direst distress, but in normal times they did all they could to undermine the competition, and each strained with greater effort simply because the other was in the field.

The first to come were Protestants—Jason and Daniel Lee bearing credentials from the Methodist New England Conference to the Green

River rendezvous in 1834. The Nez Perces and Flatheads they met there at first were effusive—here were answers to their mission three years earlier—and then disappointed when they learned the Lees would pass through their country to settle in the Willamette valley. The next year brought better news. The American Board of Commissioners for Foreign Missions sent two Presbyterians, Samuel Parker and Marcus Whitman, to the Oregon country; at the 1835 rendezvous they were so impressed by the Nez Perce and Flathead interest and friendliness—the Indians treated Parker to strawberries and sweet currants and gave him a personal assistant ("Kentuck," the balladeer)—that Whitman returned home to organize another mission, taking along two Nez Perce boys he Christened Richard and John.

Whitman returned the next summer, with him Richard and John, a new wife, Narcissa, and another missionary couple, Henry and Eliza Spalding. Parker had sailed for home, so it was up to the Whitmans and Spaldings to establish the Presbyterian presence. When they found that both the Nez Perces and Cayuses clamored for attention, and after women of the two groups nearly came to blows over where the mission should be, the missionaries decided to serve both. The Whitmans settled among the Cayuses at Waiilatpu (in Cayuse, Place of the Rye Grass), south of the Columbia in the fertile Walla Walla valley.

The Spaldings followed the Nez Perces a dozen miles up the Clearwater River from its juncture with the Snake to where the valley narrowed, squeezed between thousand-foot rises, then up a creek called Lapwai (Place of the Butterflies) that flowed in from the south. The land widened as they moved up Lapwai Creek, and about two miles from the Clearwater they chose the spot to build their mission.

Henry Spalding's early life had been hellish. A bastard never acknowledged by his father and given up as an infant by his mother, he was driven from his foster home at seventeen, but by thirty he had worked his way through Western Reserve College, and three years later he and Eliza accepted Marcus Whitman's call to join him and Narcissa in the Northwest. Spalding was often his own worst enemy. In common sense, an evaluator for the Board of Commissioners wrote dryly, he was "not remarkable."[9] He could be rigid, petulant, hot-tempered, abrasive, and jealous. His personality darkened his relationship with the Whitmans. Some rumors had it that a few years earlier, Narcissa had rejected a marriage proposal from Spalding; later he doubted the Whitmans' prospects because, he said, "I question her [Narcissa's] judgement."[10] In a surviving photograph, the bearded Spalding has a wild-eyed look that fits his

**Figure 3.1** Henry H. Spalding, missionary to the Nez Perces

common reputation as a difficult man given to rages and slow-to-die grudges. Yet he was tenacious, brave, and devoted to his beliefs, and over the years he and Eliza forged a bond with some Nez Perces of affection, respect, and loyalty. Eliza, twenty-seven, was also courageous and utterly dedicated. She had answered the call despite frail health and her father's threat of disinheritance, which he carried out. Especially useful was her linguistic gift; within two months she had a working command of Nez Perce. Between them, the Spaldings seemed to have promise.

And they got off to a promising start. Henry built a spacious building as a home and meetinghouse, began religious services, and organized a school. Less than three months after his arrival, he wrote home that about a hundred Nez Perces regularly attended classes, while forty to sixty came to morning and evening worship and "a great multitude every sabbath."[11] In 1838 and 1839, Spalding spoke at well-attended revivals at home and in the Spokan country. He was soon convinced that his flock would respond best to the Word if it came in their own language, and he and Eliza adapted the alphabet to the Nez Perce and other area tongues.[12] With a printing press imported from Hawaii in 1839, they produced an eight-page book in Nez Perce, the first publication in the Pacific Northwest. Several other items were published over the next few years, including a Nez Perce version of the Gospel of Matthew.[13] They printed as well a list of Elijah White's laws that showed, in the boldest and largest print, the name "ELLIS" above the names of other headmen.[14]

In 1837 the Spaldings were joined by Asa and Sara Smith, he lately of Yale Divinity School, who settled sixty miles up the Clearwater near the Heart of the Monster, where Coyote had sprinkled the Monster's blood. Two other couples started missions among nearby peoples. Outwardly, the enterprise seemed to be going well.

By then, however, there was tension, and soon trouble. Part of the problem was personalities. Bristly and inflexible, Spalding flared up when crossed and took simple misunderstanding as willful opposition. As for Smith, in general likeability he made Spalding seem an Old World diplomat. He made no effort to understand his new neighbors on their own terms. Their purifying practice of the sweat lodge was "paying their devotions to hot stones." He watched men preparing for the hunt by purging and by pounding their legs to loosen them for running. His lesson: "Barbarous and cruel indeed are the customs of the heathen." Spalding, too, could be culturally tone deaf. For seriously broken rules around the mission he insisted on the biblical lashes, delivered by himself or other Nez Perces, although how much he used the whip is unclear. Public corporal punishment, as among most native peoples, was an extreme humiliation, and especially as relations worsened for other reasons, resentment grew, blow by blow. When a party sent back East in 1837 ended disastrously, with all its horses stolen and a Nez Perce and four Flatheads killed by Sioux, furious crowds reportedly kept the Spaldings besieged in their house for a month, shepherds penned up by their flock.[15]

The essential problem, however, was the gap between what Nez Perces and missionaries expected of each other. With their evolving, inclusive spirituality, the Nez Perces hoped to incorporate new sacred connections so they might heighten their own spiritual power. They might adopt some

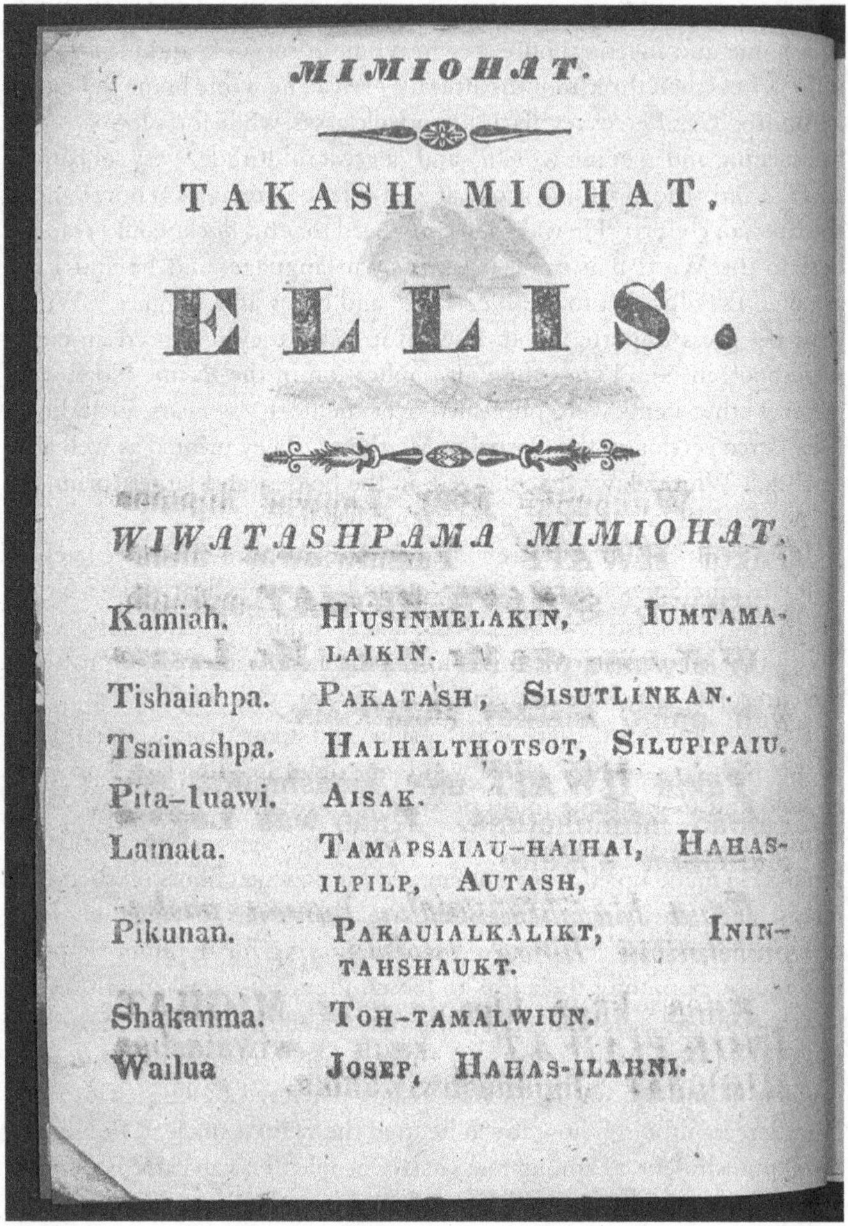

*MIMIOHAT.*

TAKASH MIOHAT,

# ELLIS.

*WIWATASHPAMA MIMIOHAT.*

| | |
|---|---|
| Kamiah. | HIUSINMELAKIN, IUMTAMA-LAIKIN. |
| Tishaiahpa. | PAKATASH, SISUTLINKAN. |
| Tsainashpa. | HALHALTHOTSOT, SILUPIPAIU. |
| Pita–luawi. | AISAK. |
| Lamata. | TAMAPSAIAU–HAIHAI, HAHAS-ILPILP, AUTASH, |
| Pikunan. | PAKAUIALKALIKT, ININ-TAHSHAUKT. |
| Shakanma. | TOH–TAMALWIUN. |
| Wailua | JOSEP, HAHAS-ILAHNI. |

**Figure 3.2** Spalding's published version of Elijah White's imposed arrangement

new rituals and customs, such as prayer meetings and Sabbath observance, and bend some old behaviors. They might even allow some whip-
ping of violators of new rules. But there were limits. Familial relations
like polygamy, the long hunts across the Bitterroots, living in beloved
places rather than moving close to missions—for many Nez Perces those
were fundamentals never to be compromised. Above all, the Nez Perces
expected the new spiritual presence to enrich their worldly well-being, to
make their good life better.

Spalding and his colleagues, however, meant them to be reborn out
of their old lives into utterly new ones. That was the supposed cry heard
from the "four wise men from the West," and that was what the missionaries demanded—to their frequent disappointment. Smith's great frustration was that the Nez Perces saw themselves as essentially good. He
insisted instead that they begin by accepting that they were irredeemably
corrupt, doomed by Adam's fall to roast in Hell (a concept with no basis
in Nez Perce tradition) unless they accepted their guilt and offered their
souls to a merciful Christ. The Nez Perces, not surprisingly, found this
unalluring. "My only hope is in giving them the pure unadulterated word
of God & enabling them to understand it," he wrote: "This & this alone
I believe will benefit them in this life & in the life to come." The great
impediment to his success, he concluded, was self-righteousness. He was
referring to the Indians.[16]

Some missionaries tried to bring their flocks along more slowly, but
in essentials they were no different from Smith. None questioned that
Indians had to accept "the great truth that all are under condemnation
& exposed to the penalty of [God's] law while in their present situation"
and that only by trusting in the full heartfelt embrace of Christ could
they be saved.[17] And repentance—literally turning fully about—went
well beyond that. To Spalding, Smith, Whitman, and the others, soul-
saving reached past spirit to the material. For Protestants at least, writes
the most authoritative historian of American Indian policy, Indians were
to be transformed into "copies of their white neighbors."[18]

There were five specific goals. Indians had to adopt Anglo-Saxon laws
and governmental principles. They must embrace the ethic of hard work
as good for its own sake, which shook out to mean turning from the hunt,
which seemed to allow much idleness, to the daily labor of the farm.
"While we point them with one hand to the Lamb of God which taketh
away the sins of the world," Spalding wrote, "we...point with the other to
the hoe."[19] Indians had to forsake collective ownership of land and things
in favor of private property and the accumulation of wealth. They must
strive to take on the outward appearances and trappings of Europeans,

such as dress. And finally, Indians were to submit to white education, starting with learning English, as the essential tool for accomplishing the first four goals. The idea was not that these changes would follow happily when Indians became Christians. Religious conversion and cultural transformation were parts of one process, fully entangled. They fed each other.[20] In the missionaries' minds, they together made civilization.

In the same minds, they also made a nation. Men like Spalding and Whitman saw little or no distinction between converting Indians and adopting them into the national family. Nor did officials back in Washington. The line between church and state was fuzzy in many areas of the youthful republic. In Indian policy, it never applied at all. The men in charge, besides thinking that Christianity was elemental to civilized life, thought that Indians could be saved from extinction only if they conformed culturally to certain behaviors they saw as binding all Americans into a common identity—farming, devotional labor, respect for law, nuclear and paternalistic families, a certain sort of rectitude. These, of course, overlapped exactly the Protestant agenda for full Christian conversion. Missionaries and officials agreed that as Indians became Christians they would naturally adopt lifeways that would make them Americans, and vice versa.

How predictable, then, that for decades before Spalding and Whitman, Protestant ministers were partners in the work of assimilation. They were not officially the government's bones and hands—not yet—but throughout the East they had lived alongside politically appointed agents, founding schools and promoting the agrarian arts while preaching the gospel. Church and state were not absolutely in sync. Ministers had been among the tiny minority of whites opposing Indian removal beyond the Mississippi, most famously in the case of Samuel Worcester, the Congregational missionary who went to prison to test Georgia's laws meant to bully the Cherokees into leaving the state. But disagreement was always about how and where assimilation should take place, not whether. On that, Protestant churches and the state were perfectly aligned: Indians' only alternative to destruction was to join the new nation, and joining required giving up most everything about them that was Indian.

When the inevitable followed—some conversions, some resistance, and a lot in between, factionalism within Indian groups and rising pressure from white settlement—the government's answer was not to question the process but to give it more time. The result was Indian removal—the displacement of Indians westward, beyond the Mississippi, close to what was then the far western edge of the nation, in what is today Oklahoma and eastern Kansas and Nebraska. A "permanent Indian frontier" of military posts was planned, to keep Indians on their side and whites on theirs. The assumption was that missionaries and agents, now cordoned off and protected, would have ample time (up to a century, some said) to finish the secular and spiritual metamorphosis that would bring Indians finally into national life.

Well before this scheme was being put in place, however, other developments, were undoing that assumption. Economic agents—fur traders the most obvious—were mapping the far West and blazing immigrant routes far beyond the "permanent" frontier, forging connections with western Indians, drawing them into an international market, and injecting elements of national culture into their world. Right behind these agents came the missionaries. Their goal was no less than to transform native peoples' identity, by imposing the Christian spirit world and converting them to the norms of national life. This, they fondly hoped, would bring western Indians and their lands inside the nation itself. Missionaries out West were subverting the arrangement their brethren were helping to make in the East.

Nothing makes the point better than the story of the coming of Christianity to Nez Perce country. President James Monroe formally proposed Indian removal in a special message to Congress in 1825, the year Spokan Garry left for the Red River school, and the year Garry returned, 1829, saw the inauguration of Andrew Jackson, strongest advocate of removal and its mailed fist. In 1830, as Spokan Garry's revival was starting to spread in the Northwest, Congress passed the Indian Removal Act. The first to go, the Choctaws, set off from Mississippi in October 1831, just as the four visitors from the Northwest arrived in St. Louis to ask for the white man's book; the Choctaw removal was finishing, with hundreds dead from exposure and cholera, as the two surviving Nez Perces headed home the next spring.

Over the next eight years, nearly a hundred thousand Indians were expelled from the East into what was now called Indian Territory, the area just west of Arkansas and Missouri. (When William Walker heard the story of the northwestern delegation and wrote his plea for their salvation, he was negotiating with William Clark about the Wyandots' removal from Ohio.) Resistant Creeks were crushed, and more than two thousand sent off in shackles in 1836–37, as the Whitmans and Spaldings headed to Oregon to set up their missions. In 1838, federal troops rounded up nearly sixteen thousand Cherokees, the most populous native people of the Southeast. As they moved to Indian Territory via their several Trails of Tears, Spalding was preaching to the Nez Perces and transliterating biblical passages into their language.

As the government constructed a "permanent" restraint at midcontinent against white expansion, the religious agents of expansion had already flanked that line and begun the work that would help undo it. And out where they were working, in the Oregon country, Indian peoples thought they had drawn out men and women whose power they might incorporate for their own strength and protection, while in fact they had invited in an enveloping force that was already eating at their independence and drawing them into a continental whole.

Pray God that the gospel's light would soon "dispel the thick darkness that broods over this vast region," Spalding wrote home in February 1837. When the cross was raised among every tribe, he predicted, the hearts of the saved would thrum "to notes of joy ... wafted over the mountains and vallies which now separate us and them from our dear native land."[21]

The Plateau's missionaries seemed to spend as much energy bickering with each other as in converting Indians, and when the Missionary Society heard through letters of their crabby jealousies, it nearly scuttled the whole enterprise. Smith was especially poisonous. In one nearly ten-thousand-word rant he accused Spalding of incompetence and lying, and in 1841 he recommended turning the missions over to the Methodists.[22] The next year, the Board of Commissioners ordered Spalding and Smith home and told the Whitmans to join another couple with the Spokans. The orders shocked the missionaries into a rare reconciliation, and Whitman quickly left on a desperate bid to plea for another chance. He crossed the continent on a hungry midwinter march, at one point eating his pet dog, Trapper, and in March 1843, ragged and malodorous and nearly penniless, he met the board face to face in Boston. They relented. Whitman and Spalding could continue their work at Waiilatpu and Lapwai, at least for the time being.[23] Meanwhile, the dyspeptic Asa Smith and his wife had left Oregon to harvest souls in Asia.

Now another factor complicated the missionaries' work. Whitman, coming home, helped bring it into play. In 1842, about 125 settlers had come out, Elijah White among them, and when Whitman arrived in Westport, Missouri, the next spring on his way back, he found about seven times that number, something between eight hundred and a thousand persons, about to embark with three to five thousand head of cattle and horses. The families were packed into more than 120 wagons. Horace Greeley, later one of expansion's great boosters, wrote that an overland party this size "wears the aspect of insanity," but they made it, guided by Whitman over the last rugged stage.[24] It was the first time wagons had made the full trip to Oregon.

The settlers kept going, drawn to the extraordinary Willamette River valley more than two hundred miles beyond the Whitman mission, but the sudden appearance of so many whites, even passing through, must have unnerved somewhat the Cayuses, Nez Perces, and others around them. This immigration equaled about 30 percent of the Nez Perce population. An equivalent for Bostonians would have been about twenty-eight thousand western Indians passing through the city toward settling on Cape

Cod, announcing that even more were sure to follow. In fact, the news that wagons could roll all the way to the Pacific was like unstoppering a bottle. In 1844, more than half again as many settlers came than the year before, and the next year the number rose to about twenty-five hundred.[25]

Oregon was feeling the early stage of one of the great folk wanderings of North American history. Over the next twenty years, roughly a third of a million persons would cross the continent to the Pacific coast. Fueling it all was a population growing at a rate that today would be among the highest in the world. When the Louisiana Purchase doubled the size of the United States in 1803, the average number of persons living on every square mile dropped from 6.6 in 1800 to 4.4 in 1810, but the nation was filling with people so rapidly that only thirty years later this figure had risen to 10.4, more than half again as much. The most rapid increase was in places like Illinois, Missouri, and Iowa, the nation's westernmost areas with enough rainfall to support the farming methods of the day. Missouri's population grew by nearly 600 percent between 1820 and 1840, Illinois's by more than 800 percent. Iowa had fifty white settlers in 1832, and more than forty-three thousand in 1840. The price of land went up correspondingly, and as the vicious depression of 1837–41 ended, the restless and cash-poor looked for alternatives. Partly by reading gushing descriptions in published letters from missionaries, they heard that if they were willing to move far enough, to the Pacific coast, they would find plenty of land so fertile that, in a phrase of the day, "if you plant a nail, it'll come up a spike."

In 1841, Senator Lewis Linn of Missouri introduced a bill offering a full section of land, 640 acres, to any citizen immigrating to Oregon. How the government would grant title to land where it had no jurisdiction, land in any case occupied by Indians, was unclear, but Linn was following a familiar strategy of westward boosterism: get settlers on the ground, and the government will find a way to follow. In 1842, Linn's bill had passed the Senate and only narrowly failed in the House. Its near success probably encouraged the crowd of immigrants Whitman found in Westport ready to make the leap into the new country.

The truly odd, underrecognized point about Whitman's famous journey to Boston is that having rescued the missions from his own bosses, he immediately turned his energy toward encouraging a far greater threat—pioneer immigration and settlement.[26] Even before leaving with the overland party, he wrote that "it is now decided that Oregon will be occupied by American citizens," something he had long hoped for. Within a year, he decided that this, "one of the onward movements of the world," would soon demand the best land. Indians and the missions would have to go. It was useless to wish it otherwise, he thought, for when had indolence and wastefulness ever stood against "money, intelligence & enterprise?" It was God's providence. Best to share the work of saving Indian souls with saving Oregon from England and the pope, and to that end: "I am happy to have been the means of landing such a large emigration on the shores of the Columbia."[27]

Not five years after the final removals of southeastern Indians behind that "permanent" frontier far to the east, Whitman was repeating the rhetoric of unstoppable white settlement. Once again, the missionaries' work was shifting strongly toward the project of national expansion. Only now the expansion was two thousand miles farther on, and the Indians in the way were not in Georgia and Alabama but on the Columbia Plateau.

And by now the missionaries were raising a smell among the Indians. Few if any improvements had come with the missions. Instead there had been growing pressure to abandon treasured lifeways, and then the disturbing first waves of settlers. More and more saw the invitation to the missionaries as a failed experiment.

Soon there were ugly incidents. Sometime in 1842, two men came to Eliza Spalding's school naked and painted with "the most horrible figures." When she complained, a crowd of several hundred threatened to seize and whip her, while a man held a cocked gun to her husband's head for twenty minutes. Church and school attendance dropped dramatically over the next few years, and once when Spalding tried to stop some men from feeding a fire with his cedar fence, they knocked him down and threw him into the flames. His heavy buffalo coat saved him from injury.[28] Around that time, Spalding wrote that while there was still great promise among his charges, he was sure that most of them would stand by indifferently to see his and Eliza's house burned to the ground and "our heads severed from our bodies."[29] The Nez Perces at least were buffered by geography from direct contact with immigrants, but the Cayuses watched the traffic run through some of their best lands, threatening both their pastoral and gathering economy and their position as trading middlemen for surrounding groups. They reacted accordingly. They openly insulted Whitman, pulling his hair and ears and once chopping open his door with an axe. It was these threats that moved White to lay down his eleven laws to protect life and property.

More ominously still, the prominent Cayuse Young Chief accused Whitman and the others of purposefully inducing the diseases that had spiked among Plateau peoples since the whites' arrival. The missionaries, he said, brought in "poison and infection" to eliminate Indians and take their lands and horses.[30] The Indians considered disease, like material success or decline, to be tied to spiritual power. They believed, Spalding wrote, that "death can be caused at any time, by the secret influence of some medicine man or woman," whether a native *tewat* or Christian clergy.[31] By offering medical treatment, missionaries inadvertently played to that belief. If a man could cure with prayers and pills, couldn't he kill through spiritual force and some malignance brought in a bottle?

Immigrants had indeed brought diseases, though not intentionally. The earliest, notably dysentery, ground slowly at Indian populations, but in the summer of 1847 something new appeared: measles. It killed quickly and massively, and it struck the children especially hard. And it came connected to another, particularly painful incident that would embitter feelings for decades to come.

In 1844, the son of a prominent Wallawalla, Peopeo Moxmox (Yellow Bird), had been shot to death while in California with a trading party. Back in Oregon, his father first called on Elijah White to punish the killer, as seemingly promised in the 1842 agreement, but White had no authority in Oregon, much less California, and when his posturing became clear, Peopeo Moxmox led a party of revenge back to California in 1846. California was in turmoil from the American conquest, and the raid came to nothing, but on their way back in 1847 the party contracted measles. Thirty had died by the time they made it home in August. The artist Paul Kane happened to be there as the names of the dead were called out. A "terrible howl ensued," he wrote. Women began tearing their hair and clothes, and messengers immediately set off to spread the dreadful news.[32] Probably they carried the virus as well.

Measles is extraordinarily contagious, with a 90 percent "attack rate" among the exposed, and while Old World peoples, having adapted over millennia, rarely died from it, New World populations were devastated. Its awful outward effects—hacking cough, raging fever, and an angry rash—were followed by pneumonia and encephalitis. A common native treatment of illness was to sit naked in a sweat lodge, enduring extreme heat as long as possible before plunging into a cold stream. However beneficial in other situations, the lodge's heat compounded the fever's effects while the icy water could send the body into shock.

The first cases hit the Whitman mission in early October. Virtually all the sick white children survived, but Whitman had little success treating the Cayuses, and the toll rose until, a survivor wrote, five or six persons, mostly the young, were buried daily. Spalding found as many as twenty-five persons in a single lodge, lying in their own filth, their suffering "inconceivable." He found it "most distressing."[33] Estimates of the dead ranged from thirty to nearly two hundred.[34]

Cayuse suspicions grew. A mixed blood from the East who lived among them, a man with a rancid antipathy to missionaries, spread the rumor that Whitman and Spalding had been planning a mass poisoning for two years. "How easy we will live, once the Indians are all killed off," he claimed to have heard the two men say, and of the prized Cayuse horses: "Our boys will drive them up, and we will give them to our friends."[35]

The situation snapped on November 29, 1847. Early that cold, foggy afternoon, several men came into the Whitman kitchen, demanded medicine, and then tomahawked and shot Marcus. During the melee that followed, Narcissa and a dozen men were killed. Forty-six whites were taken captive. Most Cayuses took no part in the killing, and many tried to help the survivors. Some Indian women "cried over us and gave us many things," one girl remembered.[36] After lying around for two days, the bodies were buried by a French Canadian employee of the mission. Narcissa had been decapitated, and when the remains were exhumed in 1897, it was found that the heads of both husband and wife had been cut in half with the doctor's surgical saw.[37]

Spalding barely avoided the Whitmans' fate. He had been at the Waiilatpu mission only a few days earlier to settle his ten-year-old daughter Eliza in Whitman's school and was returning there from a visit to Umatilla when a Roman Catholic missionary, Father J. B. A. Brouillet, intercepted him with the grim news. Instead of heading for the safety of Fort Walla Walla, he turned toward Lapwai and his family—a lucky move that threw pursuing Cayuses off his trail. After losing his horse and spending three frigid nights covering ninety miles, he made it home, battered and famished, his clothes frozen and feet swollen and bleeding. He found Eliza safe among some friendly Nez Perces but heard that others had looted the mission and taken its livestock. A few days later, protected by supporters, Henry and Eliza left for safe haven at Fort Walla Walla.

A month later, Brouillet and Peter Skene Ogden of the Hudson's Bay Company ransomed the survivors, young Eliza Spalding among them, for blankets, clothing, and thirty-seven pounds of tobacco. Spalding described his daughter as "a mere skeleton, and her mind as much impaired as her health."[38] The Spaldings relocated on the Calapooya River, a tributary of the Willamette, where Henry worked as a schoolteacher, postmaster, and pastor. But "I...have never felt at home among the whites," he wrote a friend in 1857, and he tried to return to the Nez Perces and finally succeeded.[39] Eliza's frail health worsened from the grueling winter trip to her new home, and early in January 1851 she died, age forty-three. Two years later, Henry remarried Rachael Smith, the sister-in-law of a local Congregationalist minister. He preached at his own wedding.

The Whitman massacre came eleven years to the day after the Spaldings' arrival at Lapwai, the Place of the Butterflies. By any apparent measure, the churchmen had failed colossally. When some missionaries are killed and another driven out after being tossed onto a bonfire, their reception cannot be called favorable. The longer perspective, however, is different. Some Nez Perce converts remained to become the core of support for a Christian reassertion in the 1870s. Today, Presbyterians and Roman Catholics are the main religious presence on the Nez Perce reservation.

Earlier, before things turned ugly, the missionaries had counted among their victories the baptism of a few prominent Nez Perces. For Protestants, baptism was not a step lightly taken. It meant full church membership, something extended only to persons truly thought to have fully accepted Christ as savior after a time of literal soul-searching, lengthy prayer, and, usually, some conversion experience. Spalding's two earliest baptisms, in November 1839, were of Tamootsin and Tuekakas, headmen of important bands. As was fitting for their rebirth into a Christian life, they were given new names. Tamootsin, leader of the Alpowa band living opposite the confluence of the Snake and Clearwater rivers, was christened Timothy. Baptizing Tuekakas was especially gratifying. He was head of the largest band of all, the one living south of the Alpowas in the area of the Wallowa and Grand Ronde rivers. Spalding gave Tuekakas the name Joseph.

There were a few other baptisms, notably of a leader among the upper Nez Perces along the Clearwater River. Named Hallalhotsoot, he was commonly called Lawyer for his talents at argument and persuasion.[40] He and Timothy remained faithful Christians, and both, Lawyer particularly, played prominent roles in the story ahead. Spalding had high hopes for Joseph as well. In services, Spalding told his diary, "Joseph speaks most affectingly, urging all present to give their hearts to Jesus Christ without delay," and soon Joseph moved many of his people close to Lapwai, presumably to take up a settled farming life.[41] By the time of the Whitman bloodletting, however, Joseph's commitment had cooled. He returned to the Wallowa country and the annual round of gathering, fishing, and hunting, and although keeping somewhat to Christian ways, he kept his distance, physically and in his loyalties.

Sometime during the year after his baptism, Joseph's wife bore him a son. He was baptized Ephraim, but with his father's move back to the Wallowa, the name did not stick.[42] His Nez Perce name was Heinmot Tooyalakekt, or Thunder Rising to Loftier Mountain Heights, and especially among whites he was called Young Joseph. Once he assumed his father's leadership, it was Chief Joseph. He was seven when measles ravaged the Cayuse children, some of them his cousins, closing one chapter and opening another in white America's reach into the Plateau.

# CHAPTER 4

# "God Named This Land to Us"

The measles epidemic that led to the killings at the Waiilatpu mission might seem a twist of historical chance. That it came when it did was happenstance, but in the history of conquest, diseases have played a recurring, ghastly, and enormously important role. They helped shape how empires fell out across the globe, including America's roll into Nez Perce country.[1]

Diseases are categorized many ways, but in the history of empires, one distinction stands out—that between contact and vector diseases. Contact, or "crowd," diseases pass directly from one person to another via body fluids like blood, fecal material, and the tiny droplets of moisture ejected by coughing and sneezing. Measles is a contact disease, as are influenza, tuberculosis, cholera, HIV/AIDS, and the common cold. Vector diseases are carried by an intermediary, such as a mosquito (malaria, yellow fever, West Nile encephalitis), flea (bubonic plague, hanta virus), or tick (Lyme disease). Most contact diseases are quite young, rarely more than five thousand or so years old. Vector diseases are much older. There's a geographical distinction, too. Vector diseases are more common in the tropics, where insects like mosquitoes and tsetse flies (carriers of tripanosomiasis, or sleeping sickness) survive year-round. Contact diseases are everywhere.

Both types of disease have one historical point in common: before Columbus, nearly all of them existed in the Old World but not in the New. The first immigrants to the Western Hemisphere passed through Siberia and over the Bering land bridge, frigid regions where most vector carriers could not flourish as they did in hot climates—and thus vector diseases apparently were left behind. Most contact diseases began when illnesses among other animals jumped to humans and then mutated into a variation humans could pass among themselves. Measles, for instance, evolved from rinderpest, an affliction among cattle. This occurred after humans started living cheek-to-jowl with cattle, horses, sheep, chickens, pigs, and other creatures. Except for dogs, llamas, turkeys, and guinea pigs, New World peoples had no domesticated animals—and thus far fewer contact diseases.

For thousands of years, that was obviously good news for someone in what is now Mexico or Nebraska. But there was a catch. By living with their diseases for such a long time, allowing evolution to winnow out those most susceptible, Old World peoples earned a resistance to them. A malady like measles became more a nuisance than a killer. They also developed protective mechanisms, like the sickle cell that exempts part of the African population from the worst of malaria. New World peoples, exactly because they avoided millennia of suffering, had no such advantages.

So when Europeans intruded into the Western Hemisphere after 1492, it was like bursting a protective bubble. They carried the accumulated epidemiological experience of one half of the planet to the other—an entire hemisphere vulnerable and primed for unimaginable calamity. Over a few decades, diseases that had appeared periodically and one by one over thousands of years in the Old World were injected among peoples who had little or no natural protection against them. The horrific direct losses from disease, taking not only the usual victims among the youngest and oldest but many in their prime, severely disrupted economies and produced a mix of panic and social malaise, which deepened the epidemics' impact and added to the death toll. Historians argue over the scale of the disaster. Estimates of the decline of native populations between 1500 and 1900 range from 50 to 95 percent. Whatever the figure, "virgin soil" epidemics killed tens of millions of people. As cultural disasters and in their toll of sheer human suffering and sorrow, they have a strong claim on being the worst thing ever to happen in recorded history.

The great killing flung open the door for all conquerors, but different combinations of diseases produced different patterns of empire. In tropical America, European contact diseases—along with social chaos, brutal treatment, and outright murder—essentially eliminated native populations in much of the Indies and parts of coastal South and Central America. When muscle was needed for the awful work of sugar plantations, the Spanish and later the French and English had to look elsewhere. They brought in African slaves, and by doing so they imported deep trouble for themselves. With the slaves came malaria and yellow fever and their mosquito vectors, and because Europeans had had less exposure to those diseases than Africans, the imported vector contagions hit European immigrants with a special ferocity. Because so many whites died of fever in the African interior, it resisted conquest until the medical breakthroughs of the late nineteenth century. By carrying slaves to tropical America, Europeans implanted the same conditions that had kept their own kind out of Africa. Europeans made of tropical America an empire that was largely unlivable for themselves, the imperialists. Demographically and disease-wise, the region became a kind of neo-Africa.

Because of the climate in temperate North and South America, vector diseases had far less of an impact there than in the tropics. From an imperialist standpoint, this was literally the best of all worlds. Europeans carried in contact diseases, which cut terrible swaths through Indian peoples, yet avoided the checks on their own numbers set by vector diseases, which nonetheless could take an especially heavy toll among natives. The resulting empires in the temperate Americas became neo-Europes.

Their double advantage goes a long way toward explaining why Europeans dominated so rapidly the temperate New World, as well as other neo-Europes like southern Africa and Australia. Carried by infected native peoples, diseases moved ahead of the main body of invaders. They became an epidemiological strike force that began the job of conquest. A terrible scourge around Massachusetts Bay in 1619, for instance, cleared out a village that the Pilgrims occupied and named Plymouth the next year. Across the continent, white explorers and early traders who told of thinly peopled areas often were describing the results of recent epidemics. Had Lewis and Clark ascended the Missouri only a quarter century earlier, they would have found the Mandan and Hidatsa villages where they spent their first winter far different—crowded with a population considerably greater than that of the St. Louis the explorers left in 1804.

The Mandans and Hidatsas had been ravaged by smallpox, the most voracious killer brought by Europeans. It arrived in the Pacific Northwest about the same time as among the Mandans, around 1780, perhaps introduced from Spanish ships but more likely coming overland, helped along by the horse revolution.[2] There are no firm figures for how many Nez Perces died, but informants later told Asa Smith of "very few surviving the attack of the disease."[3] A second wave around 1800 carried off perhaps 10 percent of the population.[4] Malaria struck in 1830, when an English ship brought it to villages around Fort Vancouver. According to the Hudson's Bay agent, three-quarters of the inhabitants died in three months. Over the next four years malaria ravaged the Columbia basin and California down through the central valley.

Soon another wave of contagion arrived by another means—the overland migration that began in 1841. Immigrants moved along trails that could hardly have been better designed to transmit disease. Persons from across the nation and the Atlantic world converged in crowded, filthy bivouacs, then moved along restricted travel corridors, sharing the same water sources and camping in each other's waste and refuse. By an appalling coincidence, the great rush of 1849 coincided with a national epidemic of Asiatic cholera, a terrifying disease that kills by diarrhea dehydration and soaring fever. Perhaps five thousand overlanders died of cholera that year, but the toll among plains Indians was far worse. Entire bands of the Cheyennes disappeared in what the survivors called the Year of the Belly Ache. Pausing along the North Platte River to celebrate on July 4, 1849, a party of engineers approached some Sioux tipis and found inside several decomposing corpses of cholera victims, including that of a teenaged girl "richly dressed in leggings of fine scarlet cloth" and wrapped in two fine bison robes.[5]

Cholera burned itself out long before travelers reached the Pacific Northwest, but more persistent ailments, notably dysentery, completed the trip and spread among the Plateau peoples. At Waiilatpu, it worked relentlessly among the Cayuses, priming their discontent before the onset of measles in 1847. Like cholera, measles completed its cycle during the first few hundred miles of the overland journey, so immigrants could not have introduced it. It arrived by the next stage of transmission. Once there were large concentrations of white population in the West, as in California in this case, there were enough uninfected bodies to support recurring introductions of ailments like measles. Towns and cities served as regional disease reservoirs where unlucky native visitors, like the Cayuses and Wallawallas who came looking for revenge in 1846, could acquire the disease and carry it home. Plateau peoples now were subject to the full range and brunt of contagions that migrated from the Old to the New World.

Indians responded to these onslaughts in various ways. They often consolidated their reduced numbers, leaving some villages—the ruins that became Plymouth was one case—and congregating in one or a few others. Near modern Bismarck, North Dakota, an extensive archeological site known today as Double Ditch (for its elaborate defensive perimeter) was one of several points noted by Lewis and Clark as vacated by the Mandans around 1779, when "the Small Pox distroyed great Numbers."[6] Captain George Vancouver in 1792 described many such sites along the Pacific Northwest coast, one with skulls and other human bones strewn among the weeds.

Another response was spiritual. Prophets appeared. In the popular sense, "prophecy" is often misused to mean simply prediction, but while

a prophet usually does speak of what lies ahead, he or she is better understood as one who describes great changes in the present, lays out with
painful honesty a spiritual crisis that has come with them, and offers
new teachings that will preserve traditional virtues and values in the face
(here's the predicting part) of even greater changes sure to come. Across
North America, indigenous prophets often appeared in times of great
change and stress, and the Plateau, convulsed not only by epidemics but
also by new trade and whites' other indirect influence, was no exception.
Some authorities say new prophetic movements appeared after the great
smallpox assault of 1780; others date them around 1800, when another
epidemic coincided with a volcanic eruption that coated the region with
ash.[7] At any rate, these movements' most notable feature was a new ritual
that came to be called the prophet dance.

Like most prophecies, the prophet dance promised to shore up its followers' spiritual well-being in the face of change, and the greatest change
of all, it was predicted, would be a new people who would come, very
soon, out of the East.[8] As for what changes they would bring, one version of the prophecy told of fresh material and spiritual power, another of
unparalleled calamity, even annihilation. The foretelling would resonate
with later events, notably when the prophecy incarnate, Lewis and Clark,
walked out of the mountains, and in 1831 when the mission to St. Louis
sought out good offerings from the East.

The prophecies were true enough. Times indeed were out of joint, and
the people were in spiritual upheaval. Whites would in fact bring opportunity and catastrophe. Thus epidemics, besides bringing mass death, also
reshaped Indians' perception of their world and by doing so helped make
their history. Smallpox indirectly opened the Nez Perces' arms and hearts
to Lewis and Clark. For the Whitmans and Spaldings, disease's role was
doubly ironic. Epidemics played a prime part first in their invitation and
later in their bloody rejection.

A final response of Indian peoples was the conviction that whites had
purposefully spread disease among them—that men like Whitman were
poisoners. The response was predictable on several counts. Whenever
whites came in numbers, so in fact did sickness that took a far greater
toll on the invaded than the invaders. By native tradition, besides, a holy
man like a missionary could use his powers to kill as well as to heal, and
the newcomers, after all, claimed as doctors to have special powers over
death.

Across the continent, the stories arose with the waves of contagion—
whites carried death in via gifted clothes, infected flags, shiny boxes. In
the Pacific Northwest, whites themselves planted the notion, hoping to

intimidate the locals. "The white men among you are few in number, it is true," Duncan McDougall of Astoria reportedly told local leaders in 1811, "but they are mighty in medicine." He then held up a small bottle, which he said contained smallpox. "I have but to draw the cork," he said, "and let loose the pestilence, to sweep man, woman, and child from the face of the earth." This earned him the name "the Great Small-pox Chief." In the wake of the malarial scourge after 1830, the story was told that the captain of the ship that brought it, angry with local Indians, "opened his phial and let out the 'cold sick'! [malaria]."[9] And so when measles struck the Cayuses, the claims that Whitman had brought it in and set it loose quickly took hold.

The claims were groundless. McDougall was bluffing. As for that ship captain letting loose the "cold sick," it would be sixty years before anyone figured out that malaria moved via the *anopheles* mosquito, and if Whitman had purposefully brought measles across the continent, he was twenty years ahead of Louis Pasteur in understanding the microbiology of disease and many decades in front of the technology of preserving and transporting contagions. Yet by 1847, the belief was well established that whites carried diseases in their arsenal, ready to unleash them at will.

The notion persists. The most common claim is of white authorities giving smallpox-infected blankets to spawn epidemics that would break the resistance of some troublesome tribe. The story has such mileage partly because it is based in fact. Although they had no idea how it worked, whites knew how to communicate smallpox over short distances and short time spans via crumbled scabs embedded in cloth. In the summer of 1763, during an especially bloody Indian war in the Ohio Valley and Great Lakes region, Colonel Jeffrey Amherst, commanding British forces, wondered to one of his officers: "Could it not be contrived to Send the *Small Pox* among those Disaffected Tribes" near Fort Pitt? The effort was made, although whether it worked is unclear.[10] Beyond that episode, however, there is no evidence to back up the recurring claims of germ warfare—not one credible case in the nation's history of whites intentionally passing smallpox to Indians. To the contrary, authorities frequently tried to prevent or stop epidemics. Lewis and Clark brought along the crude means of vaccination in case they encountered smallpox, although if they had tried it, it probably would not have worked. The first whites wanted to bring Indians into their orbit, to use and exploit them, not kill them.

On another level, however, the tradition is true. Stories of killer blankets and germ-full bottles speak with a mythic spareness about another threat. The nation was pushing its boundary to the Pacific. Invaders in overwhelming numbers were flooding in. The vast majority wanted only to sweeten their opportunities and make their life better, much like Indians encountering whites. Whites, however, came believing in their cultural superiority, beyond any doubt, beyond assumption. If they considered Indians at all, it was usually to set them mentally aside as exotic oddities. If they thought about how Indians might live around them—about how any like the Nez Perces might be part of their world—they assumed those people would have to adopt the lifeways being brought into their home country. If not, one way or another, they would have to go away.

Expansionist values in this sense were a cultural plague. Breathed into and circulated through the West, they struck directly and hard at what lay beneath Indian life—their bedrock identity, how they lived so as to give the world meaning.

Early in 1848, soon after the release of the hostages from the Whitman massacre, armed volunteers from the Willamette valley marched on the mission but found the Cayuses had scattered. Two years later, their leaders surrendered five men to authorities, and although all denied any role in the killings, an Oregon City jury convicted them after an hour and a quarter of deliberation. Before they were executed ten days later, they were baptized Roman Catholics and renamed Andrew, Peter, John, Paul, and James.

By then, the U.S. presence in the region had grown by orders of magnitude. The white emigration kept growing, spurred by the nation's yeasty population growth, and pushed Great Britain and the United States toward ending their arrangement of joint occupation and settling the question of ownership. Only part of the huge Oregon country was truly in dispute—that between the Columbia River and the Forty-ninth Parallel—and as American settlement just to the south increased, while the number of beavers in the contested area shrank, the logic of the situation tilted in favor of the United States. If his government did not resolve the boundary soon, an official of the Hudson's Bay Company wrote, "the Americans will soon leave nothing to settle."[11]

The election of both the expansionist James K. Polk as president in 1844 and a British government friendlier to the United States led to compromise and the Oregon Treaty of 1846. The new boundary would run along the Forty-ninth Parallel and then through the middle of the Fuca Straits, leaving Vancouver Island, the new base of the Hudson's Bay Company, in British hands. The United States got virtually all it wanted. Two years later, Congress created Oregon Territory, nudged into acting partly by the bloodshed at Waiilatpu. Scarcely forty years after the members of the

Corps of Discovery had been spared by the Nez Perces, the American state, its population more than tripled, was settling over the Plateau and its peoples.

With the Oregon Treaty and two other interconnected episodes, the annexation of Texas (1845) and the Mexican War (1846–48), the United States grew by 1.2 million square miles, or nearly three-quarters of a billion acres. An equivalent today would be the United States expanding southward to annex Mexico, Guatemala, Honduras, Belize, El Salvador, and Panama. This expansion began the Greater Reconstruction. It brought country into the young nation that contained dozens of cultures and some of the continent's most varied and challenging geography and richest resources. Expansion opened up stunning opportunities. It also raised troubling new questions in the West and deepened older ones in the East.

On the Plateau, the pace of change during the years just prior to the great expansion was breathtaking. Heinmot Tooyalakekt, or Young Joseph, was born four years after the first missionaries came to his people. He was two when Elijah White laid down his laws, six when the United States acquired Oregon, still only eight when it became a territory. The Nez Perces could hardly be blamed for not grasping what was happening and the implications.

In fact, to this point they felt few effects. Their neighbors and relatives the Cayuses were devastated. The Oregon volunteers had taken hundreds of their horses, their economy was in chaos, and immigrants streamed across their homeland. The Nez Perces by contrast had supported the government after the Whitman massacre and, protected by their mountains, now stood aloof from the overland traffic while dealing profitably with the travelers, swapping their splendid horses for guns, ammunition, oxen, and other goods. Immigrants allowed that the Nez Perces "could beat a Yankee on a trade."[12] No white authority had tried to use the top-down structure imposed by Elijah White—not yet—and the supposed head chief, Elice, had lost whatever interest he had had in the position. At the Whitman crisis, he was off on the Great Plains, hunting and following the old ways, and there he died, either from disease or fighting Blackfeet.

Elsewhere, the pressure built. Political organization gave the boosters a boost. Senator Linn's Oregon Donation Act (1850) gave a full section to squatters already there and offered a half section to those arriving during the next three years. That law, plus a modest gold strike on the Rogue and Umpqua rivers, brought a surge of immigrants from the East and California. The official 1850 population of about twelve thousand rose to probably almost twenty thousand by 1855, equaling or surpassing that of all resident natives.

The boom created a glaring problem. White newcomers could not legally settle anywhere in Oregon until Washington had dealt with the Indians on the land. The immigrants arrived already part of the way to legal possession. Under rules going back to the first European contact, the nation whose explorer saw a place first, before any competitors, gained sovereignty to it through the "right of discovery." If an Englishman saw Pennsylvania before a Swede, for instance, Indians on the Schuylkill River could not sell their homes to Sweden or anyone else but England. In 1823, Chief Justice John Marshall expanded that advantage hugely in *Johnson v. McIntosh*. Under the right of discovery, he wrote, Indians had not just lost their right to sell to anyone but the discoverer; they had lost ownership itself. All they had left was the "right of occupancy." Their legal prerogatives boiled down to the right to live where they lived.[13]

Whites still had to satisfy the right of occupancy, Marshall went on, either by paying for it or through conquest, presumably in a justified war, but he strongly implied that Indians eventually would have to give it up. Indians were not only "fierce savages" but an "inferior race of peoples," culturally retrograde because they lived by the hunt rather than farming. He was speaking for another assumption in international law of that time—that cultivation of the soil was essential to human progress. Any who resisted it at some point would have to give way to those who embraced it.[14] Marshall would have told the Nez Perces that they had a right to live where Coyote had put them. When whites arrived in numbers, however, they would be expected to join the new order or to make a deal and get out of the way. The alternative, Marshall had written, "was to leave the country a wilderness." And that was no option at all.

A few treaties had been negotiated in the region after the Indian Treaty Act (1850) authorized officials to open up tribal lands. Three years later, however, the Senate had approved none of them. Meanwhile, settlers simply took up whatever land they wanted, with a predictable rise in tensions. The problem was mostly west of the Cascades, in the rich country around Puget Sound. Although settlement was starting to creep up the Columbia, the Plateau, homeland to the Nez Perces and their many neighbors, so far felt little pressure. Things might have drifted for years if not for one of the story's more intriguing characters: Isaac Ingalls Stevens.

Stevens was a thirty-five-year-old engine of determination. His ambitions outmatched even his Victorian good looks: trim build, wavy hair, a goatee, and the intent stare of a stage tragedian. In 1853, he won an appointment as Oregon's governor, and to maximize his possibilities by making the territory the western terminus of the first transcontinental railroad, he got himself named head of the northernmost of three surveys the War Department was conducting to decide the best route. But bringing immigration via the rails would force the sticky issue of Indians. More than two score groups on both sides of the Cascades would have to surrender considerable land for the railroad's right of way and for the white settlement bound to follow. Stevens was in a position to accomplish that, too, since as governor he was also the territory's superintendent of Indian affairs. By a kind of triangulation, he coordinated the powers of his three positions in a bid to realize his audacious vision.

In 1853 and 1854, Stevens plotted a route from St. Paul, Minnesota, to Puget Sound that he argued was superior to the others, and although Jefferson Davis, the secretary of war, endorsed the southern route from New Orleans to San Diego, Stevens still hoped to encourage immigration by negotiating land away from Indians. He would try a new approach. Rather than remove Indians to some distant area of the territory, an approach they understandably resisted, he would confine them to drastically reduced remnants of their homelands. He would create, that is, what would be some of the nation's first reservations. But time was short. Pretty soon, Stevens wrote the commissioner of Indian affairs, he wouldn't be able to create Plateau reservations without displacing some white squatter.[15]

During 1855, Stevens made a run at forging a chain of treaties to open up a huge region from Puget Sound to the Montana plains.[16] He moved from west to east, starting in January and February with four treaties creating several small reservations for nearly all the Indians around Puget Sound. They were promised annuities and off-reservation hunting, fishing, and gathering rights where whites had not settled.

The situation east of the Cascades was different. There were more Indians, and group by group, they were much more powerful and less intimidated. They had heard of Stevens bullying the Indian representatives at the recent councils. Nonetheless, the Wallawallas, Cayuses, Umatillas, Yakimas, and Nez Perces agreed to gather in late May at a traditional council ground on Mill Creek in the Walla Walla valley close to the old Whitman mission. The first Oregon Territory had been split into Washington and Oregon territories. Stevens, now governor of the former, would preside, seconded by Joel Palmer, Oregon's superintendent of Indian affairs.

The twelve days at Mill Creek were the first official dealing between the government and the Plateau peoples since the expansion of the 1840s. The treaties themselves would shape profoundly the futures of all involved.

Just as significant was the tack Stevens took. He manipulated the Indians' social reality to fit his needs. In time, with the nation's force behind it, his bending of the truth would be made legal fact.

More than five thousand persons had assembled by the end of May 1855. How they greeted Stevens revealed a fissure in their ranks. The Wallawallas and Cayuses declined all gifts and refused to smoke with the governor—the equivalent of a white man declining to shake hands.[17] The Nez Perces, who accounted for about half of all attending, arrived in one great column. After sending ahead an American flag they had been given for their support against the Cayuses after the Whitman massacre,

> their cavalcade came in sight, a thousand warriors mounted on fine horses and riding at a gallop, two abreast, naked to the breech-clout, their faces covered with white, red, and yellow paint in fanciful designs, and decked with plumes and feathers and trinkets fluttering in the sunshine. The ponies were even more gaudily arrayed, many of them selected for their singular color and markings, and many painted in vivid colors contrasting with their natural skins,—crimson slashed in broad stripes across white, yellow or white against black or bay; and with their free and wild action, the thin buffalo line tied around the lower jaw,—the only bridle, almost invisible,— the naked riders, seated as though grown to their backs, presented the very picture of fabled centaurs.

After stopping and forming a long front, they again galloped forward, then halted as the several chiefs advanced to greet the commissioners. The thousand whooping warriors next charged in single file, firing rifles, brandishing shields, and beating drums, and as they drew near they broke and circled the knot of white representatives, "now charging up as though to overwhelm it, now wheeling back, redoubling their wild action and fierce yells in frenzied excitement."[18] Then about twenty of their leaders sat and smoked with the white agents. The Nez Perces' arrival was congenial in contrast with that of the others, but their full message was clear enough: We're your friends, but mess with us at your own risk.

Stevens and Palmer got down to business at midmorning on May 30. They sat on a bench under a small arbor facing ranks of chiefs sitting in long semicircles, with behind them one to two thousand persons "reposing on the bosom of their Great Mother."[19] Each day's talk ran six to eight

*Arrival of the Nez Perce Indians at Walla Walla Treaty May 1855*

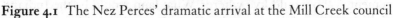

**Figure 4.1** The Nez Perces' dramatic arrival at the Mill Creek council

hours. As Stevens or Palmer finished a sentence, interpreters would translate both to the chiefs and to a pair of criers, who then would call out to the assemblage, one in Salish and the other in Sahaptin. Anything said by a chief was similarly translated and dispersed.

Everything said for the first two days was from the two commissioners, and except for some confused gabbling by Palmer, Stevens dominated. He used Elijah White's opening. Treaties would protect tribes from "bad white men," just as Cherokees and others at the opposite corner of the nation had been sheltered by being taken "across a great river into a fine country." Indians here would live on part of their own country, where "each man will work to have his own land," pasture his own cattle and horses, and enjoy grist and lumber mills built by the government. Parents would learn mechanical trades, and children would go to school and in time "be of some profession as a lawyer or doctor."[20] All would get annual payments of money and "blankets and cloth for leggings,...plates and cups and brass and tin kettles, frying pans to cook your meat." And in return? Stevens buried that in two sentences, one a day. Once Indians were put on the reduced parcels, "the rest [of the land will] be the Great Father's for his white children."[21]

Only on June 2 were the chiefs asked their opinions. Stevens and Palmer got an earful. Five Crows, Old Joseph's Cayuse half brother, took up a theme that others would echo—that the one "Father in Heaven" had created all people out of the earth and had given each people a particular place, where they should remain. A people's bond to their place could not be sold, Peopeo Moxmox (Yellow Bird) said: "Goods and the Earth are not equal....I do not know where they have given lands for goods."[22] If your mother was here suckling you, another said, and if someone took and sold her, "how would you feel then? This is our mother this country as if we drew our living from her."[23]

As for what Stevens offered, more trade goods were always welcome, but except for some Christian Nez Perces, few among the thousands at Mill Creek had any interest in a new life of fenced fields, grist mills, and schools. The Nez Perces' yelling, galloping arrival, literally running circles around the commissioners, embodied the ideal traditional life, passing the days as "fabled centaurs." Give that life up, Stevens had offered, and someday you can hope to be attorneys.

Besides that, he had given them no particulars about the proposed arrangement. Who would live where? What land would be the Indians' and what, in Stevens's words, "the Great Father's for his white children"?[24] Stevens got specific on the sixth day, June 4. There would be two reservations. The larger would encompass most of Nez Perce country. The Cayuses, Wallawallas, and Umatillas would be moved there. The smaller one, between the Columbia and Yakima rivers, would be home to the Yakimas and several bands and small tribes along and north of the Columbia.[25]

The testy mood quickly turned a lot worse. Except for the Nez Perces and Yakimas, the tribes were not being asked for some of their land; the commissioners wanted all of it. All groups would be crowded together and thus all asked to some degree to break or scramble the connections to homelands that were vital to the very meaning of who they were. Owhi, a Yakima, caught the consensus of most who spoke: "God named this land to us....I am afraid of the Almighty. Shall I steal this land and sell it?...Shall I give the land that are [sic] part of my body and leave myself poor and destitute?"[26] Other leaders answered Stevens with bitterness and sarcasm.

Only one leader spoke in favor of what Stevens offered: a headman among the upper Nez Perces known commonly as Lawyer. He had converted to Christianity early on, had remained a faithful, and now, with Timothy, was the most prominent among the Nez Perces leaning toward white accommodation.[27] After the death of Elice, Lawyer had assumed the role of head chief. As with Elice, his English fluency and experience with white culture made him an obvious spokesman and go-between in any government contact ("He was a great talker," Chief Joseph would say later), and Nez Perce tradition favored letting an especially able person take the lead in negotiations.[28]

As also with Elice, however, whether Lawyer had any authority beyond that is doubtful. His commitment to Christianity and white ways placed him well outside the beliefs and preferences of most Nez Perces, and nothing in their tradition gave him the kind of executive authority Stevens and the government would claim he had. Over the next dozen years, Lawyer would expand still more on this role and would play a vital part in the coming crisis.

With most headmen rejecting their offers, Stevens and Palmer, irritated and impatient, answered beside the point. To leaders who said that selling land was literally inconceivable, they answered that they were offering a good price. After chiefs like Owhi spoke of identities inextricably bound to places, Palmer gave them a pioneer's testimony of productive restlessness. He had left his birthplace "because it was for my good. I have come a long way."[29] The two sides were speaking past each other. It seemed an impasse.

Then came a breakthrough. On June 8, Palmer offered the Cayuses, Wallawallas, and Umatillas their own reservation, a smallish part of the Umatilla valley, instead of being crowded in with the Nez Perces. The government would supply the same support as on the other two reserves, including a house and salary for Peopeo Moxmox, and would pay a $100,000 in annuities over twenty years, plus $50,000 for construction, plowing, fencing, tools, and other materials. Peopeo Moxmox, speaking for his Wallawallas and for the Cayuse and Umatillas, agreed to the terms.[30] A relieved Stevens said the papers would be drawn up to be signed the next day. The bumping of wills and power seemed resolved.

But it wasn't. As the council was about the adjourn for the day, word came that a prominent Nez Perce, Looking Glass (Apash Wyakaikt, or Flint Necklace), was about to arrive. In an officer's words, this was "a new explosive element dropped down into this little political caldron."[31] Looking Glass was the elderly headman of the Asotin band along the Snake River. A non-Christian traditionalist and accomplished warrior and bison hunter, he was returning from the Great Plains. He and a few others rode up "painted and armed, singing a war song and flourishing on top of a pole a freshly taken scalp," a living display of the traditional life the Nez Perce stood to lose. After a few cool greetings, Looking Glass burst out: "My people, what have you done? While I was gone, you have sold my country. I have come home, and there is not left me a place to

Looking-glass
Apash-wa-hay-ikt
Chief of the Nez percé Indians

3½

Figure 4.2 Looking Glass, whose sudden arrival threatened to upset Isaac Stevens's treaty

pitch my lodge. Go home to your lodges. I will talk to you."[32] The next morning, June 9, Looking Glass first rebuked "those people who hang their heads and say nothing" and then asked Stevens why the president wished to disrupt his people's lives when "I do not go into your country and scatter your children in every direction."[33]

In the end, Looking Glass did not untrack Stevens's plans. The next day was Sunday, and during the recess Lawyer claimed to have secured from the other Nez Perce leaders their consent to their treaty. The final meeting on Monday, June 11, was anticlimactic. Two treaties had been finished on Saturday, with Peopeo Moxmox signing for the Wallawallas and Umatillas and Kamiakin and others for the Yakimas. Now the Nez Perces—Looking Glass and Old Joseph as well as Lawyer—signed or made their marks. Before all dispersed at around three o'clock, Palmer had the last word for the government: "We want you to have good hearts."[34]

So Stevens had his treaties. How he got them tells something about what power Indians and whites had at this crucial point in the story. It shows also how the perceptions that Indians and agents had of each other could be badly, dangerously distorted.

On one level, the two sides were assessing pretty accurately each other's power and playing their own against it. The chiefs understood that Stevens needed their names or marks on paper to get the land he needed, and they used that as leverage, most obviously when the Cayuses, Wallawallas, Umatillas and Yakimas kept a solid wall of opposition, forcing the offer of a third reservation, more annuities, and more support.[35] Interestingly, it was just when the parties were ready to sign *that* agreement that the disdainful Looking Glass rode up and threatened to undo the whole business. Some have argued that the timing was no coincidence but a ploy to squeeze even more from Stevens. In any case, the chiefs clearly knew how to play their recalcitrance against the governor's impatient ambition, and to a degree it worked.

Stevens had his own leverage. For all the commissioners' bluster and gas, native leaders had some awareness of how, as Peopeo Moxmox put it, "in one day the Americans [can] become as numerous as grass."[36] Somehow the Indian peoples would have to accommodate that reality. Stevens also played some groups against others. The Plateau's loose collections of villages and bands, groups the whites called tribes, had some common interests within themselves that differed from their neighbors, and wherever those interests diverged, Stevens had an opening. The Nez Perces were the key. They were the largest, the strongest, and the friendliest contingent at Mill Creek, and their spokesman, Lawyer, was most in line with what Stevens wanted. No surprise, then, that Stevens first proposed that the Nez Perces would lose only a small parcel of their traditional homeland. He was offering the most to the group that was the most powerful and the most compliant. That would drive a wedge between them and the others, who would feel the pressure to come into line with their powerful neighbor. When Lawyer spoke favorably of the first offer, Stevens presumably hoped the others would follow.

The other chiefs met Lawyer's words with withering sarcasm. If you can see the sense in this, Young Chief told him, then the rest of us are blind. Until now the Cayuses, Wallawallas, and others on the Plateau had been one with the Nez Perces, Five Crows said, "but this day we are divided."[37] That night, "everything seemed to be in violent commotion," an officer wrote: "The Cayuse and other tribes are very much incensed against the Nez Perces for agreeing to the terms of the treaty."[38] Whatever bargaining did or didn't happen during that row, the next morning Stevens and Palmer offered a third reservation, Young Chief turned more accommodating, and Peopeo Moxmox accepted the better offer.

The commissioners and the resistant chiefs had stared at each other across their differences, and neither had blinked. Each side had then given something up, come toward the other, and made a deal. They were like diplomats at a conference in Paris or London. At this level of understanding, all sides understood clearly enough the power in play.

On another level, the chiefs and commissioners were reading each other in wildly different terms, and much future mischief came out of these differences. The misconversation at Mill Creek measured the distance between two ways of thinking about how power was structured and exercised and who spoke for it. Stevens's way was a prime tool—and against Indians, a weapon—in binding the West and its peoples into the expanded nation.

The headmen understood that Stevens spoke for a distant leader of a people whose numbers were growing fast in their neighborhood. They knew that those settlers, and the soldiers they had seen, could be a considerable military threat. What they could not know was that Stevens represented authority extending over distances many times greater than any of them had ever traveled—authority that drew on resources they could not have imagined and could field warriors in numbers many hundreds of times their own. They could not know that that authority meant to bring their country, and all the West, under its control. They regarded Stevens in terms of their own profoundly different world.

Stevens, in turn, inscribed his world onto theirs. He assumed that their authority and identity cohered around discrete political units called tribes—the Nez Perces, Wallawallas, and the rest—that were roughly equivalent to nations like his own. He supposed that Lawyer, Peopeo Moxmox, and the other chiefs stood in relation to their tribes as he did in relation to the federal government, each speaking for his tribe and able to hold it to what was decided and written down.[39] He presumed the same set structure and leadership that Elijah White had presumed onto the Nez Perces he met in 1842.

Tribes as the government conceived them did not exist, however. Identity and loyalty were diffused, and chiefs couldn't commit the Nez Perces as a group to anything. Lawyer, called by Stevens the head of a "theocracy," was essentially part liaison and part traditional crier who announced news and coming events to a village.[40] Making things messier were lines of kinship threading across the Plateau. Old Joseph was born of a Nez Perce mother and Cayuse father. Lawyer's father was a Flathead. Umatillas intermarried extensively with Cayuses, Palouses, and lower Nez Perces. The resulting emotional bonds, linking villages hundreds of miles apart, could be as potent as those within a band.

Stevens got it doubly wrong. Identities and loyalties were at once more divided and more expansive than he reckoned, and the upshot was that when the government was in a dispute with any of the area's peoples, how a band or village or individual might react was, to put it mildly, unpredictable.

When Stevens wrung the treaties of 1855 from the Plateau tribes, his misapprehensions became legal writ. The most egregious example was the second of the three treaties. On paper, it was made with fourteen "confederated tribes and bands...who for the purposes of this treaty are to be considered as one nation, under the name of 'Yakama' [Yakima]." But the fourteen autonomous groups along or near the Columbia River had never formed anything like a confederation. Some spoke different languages. The treaty also said that the groups had authorized one man, "Kamaiakun" [Kamiakin], as head chief with full power to act on their behalf. No such position had ever been created or contemplated. Kamiakin did have some standing. He was a walking example of the Plateau's complex identities, connected by descent and marriage to the Yakimas, Nez Perces, Spokans, Palouses, and Klickitats. He had presence. Tall, dark, and dignified, with a large square face and "grave reflective look," he was widely admired.[41] He had plugged in well to the emerging economy and, like Lawyer, was known for friendly relations with whites and knew their ways well. But Kamiakin had no authority whatsoever to speak for the several groups listed. The commissioners repeatedly tried to draw him out to do just that. Repeatedly he turned them away: "I have nothing to say," and "What have I to be talking about?"[42]

And yet Stevens and Palmer finally maneuvered Kamiakin into playing that role. Simply by stating that he was acting for the fourteen groups, they put him in the crosshairs. If he kept insisting that he had no such authority, and if the others fell into line and signed treaties, his Yakimas and the thirteen other peoples would be shut out, alone, and vulnerable. Ultimately, that is, Stevens was threatening raw force against any holdouts. More than thirty-five years later, one of the council's interpreters, Andrew Pambrun, wrote that Stevens had announced that if his terms were not accepted, "you will walk in blood knee deep." After Kamiakin signed, Pambrun went on, he turned away "in such a rage that he bit his lips that they bled profusely." The scene could not have happened as described. Pambrun may, however, have caught Stevens's implicit threat truly enough.[43]

Agreeing to nothing, that is, risked losing everything, so Kamiakin signed. Or did he? By one tradition, he touched a stick to make a small mark, meaning only to promise friendship. A good guess is that in his head he was committing some close kin, some Yakimas and maybe some Palouses, to some sort of reservation. If he spoke for any others, it was out of an awful dilemma. He could deny a lie, or he could go along with it to better the odds for keeping people out of harm's way.

Kamiakin's lesson was one ultimately faced by all Plateau Indians, the Nez Perces included. As the government found the muscle to impose its will, not in legalisms but in flesh-and-blood consequences, it would effectively tell Plateau peoples who and what they really were as political and social creatures, just as missionaries told them who they were as creatures of God.

Less than two weeks after the treaties had been signed, in June 1855, an article "for the benefit of the public" appeared in the *Oregon Weekly Times* over the names of Stevens and Palmer and was quickly reprinted across the region. All land outside the newly negotiated reservations, it said, "is open to settlement."[44] In fact, no land could be legally opened until the Senate had ratified the treaties—another four years, it turned out. This act of stunning irresponsibility set off a rush of squatters east of the Cascades. Prospectors also crossed the country on their way to a modest gold discovery at Colville, often insulting and mistreating Indians and announcing that the land was no longer theirs.[45] Nothing could have more surely confirmed Stevens's disregard of the area's Indians and their interests.

Feelings already were running high among many Indians enraged by the Mill Creek treaties. Some, notably Kamiakin, claimed they had never agreed to the terms Stevens claimed they had. The rush of squatters and miners tipped the balance toward violence. In September 1855, six gold-seekers were killed; the Yakimas' agent had his throat slit; and when a hundred troops marched into Yakima country, they were badly beaten by five hundred warriors, Kamiakin among them. Then in November came a powerful counterpunch by a large army command under Major Gabriel Rains. Kamiakin asked for peace. Rains answered that he would fight "until not a Yakima breathes in the land he calls his own.... We are thirsting for your blood."[46] And blood there was after the Wallawallas' agent warned, with no clear reason, that the Wallawalla leader Peopeo

Moxmox was about to lead an uprising. A column under Colonel James Kelley came into the country and prevailed after four days of fighting. Peopeo Moxmox had greeted the Whitmans when they arrived at Waiilatpu. Even after his Christian son had been murdered in California, he had consistently worked for compromise, including at the Mill Creek council. Now he was arrested under a flag of truce and shot to death during the fighting. By one account, his body was flayed and his skin made into souvenir razor strops.[47]

The three years of fighting that followed might look like one more inevitable clash, with Indians bound to go down under the new order, but in the middle came an interlude suggesting otherwise. Commanding the Department of the Pacific was Major Gen. John E. Wool. He and Stevens were at odds. Partly it was personal, starting, preposterously, when Stevens questioned Wool's claim to have been the winning strategist at the battle of Buena Vista in the Mexican War, but the trouble here was over what had caused the current problems and how best to solve them. Wool blamed Stevens. He had opened Indian lands illegally, and by sending civilian volunteers to fight he had guaranteed the conflict would worsen. The best move now, Wool said, was to pull all settlers and prospectors out of the area, withdraw all volunteers, and send in regular troops to keep order and to keep out civilians. This of course put Wool at odds with the political order in both Washington and Oregon territories. Washington's territorial legislature resolved that the general's defense of tribal rights was a "high handed outrage" and a tyrannical act.[48] As civil authorities fumed, however, peace reigned for more than a year and a half.

Then Wool was replaced by General Newman S. Clarke, who, when tensions rose over rumors that two intruding miners had been killed, sent Colonel Edward J. Steptoe in May 1858 with 150 men into Spokan and Coeur d'Alene lands east of the Columbia River, country that so far had been free of fighting.[49] After being badly mauled, Steptoe's command escaped under darkness. They left behind twenty-five dead.[50] In August, Clarke sent in Colonel George Wright with more than seven hundred men on a final, punitive campaign. Armed with long-range rifles, Wright's dragoons and infantry routed several hundred warriors without a single death of their own.[51] Kamiakin got away to Canada, and when other leaders came in to treat, Wright had several men hanged, including four within sight of the negotiations. He especially wanted the Yakima Qualchen, son of the elderly headman Owhi. At Mill Creek, Owhi had spoken eloquently of the inseparability of his people and their homes ("God named this land to us"), but in the end had signed. Now Wright put Owhi in chains and sent word that if Qualchen did not surrender, his father would be hanged. "Qual-chen came to me at 9 o'clock this morning," Wright reported, "and at 9 1/4 A.M. he was hung."[52] Soon afterward, Owhi was shot and killed when trying to escape. The Spokans, Coeur d'Alenes, and Palouses were "entirely subdued," Wright wrote.

Why they and the others needed subduing is a question worth asking. All the fighting from 1855 to 1858 took place on land belonging to Indians. Peoples living there, far from posing any threat, seemed well adjusted to the new order of things. Wright told of seizing thousands of head of cattle and horses and of burning barns filled with wheat and oats as well as caches of camas, berries, and dried vegetables.[53] Whites had shown no significant interest in the land. "If any country in the world has ever merited the title of 'Indian country,' *this is it,*" the commander at Fort Dalles wrote in the 1850s, and another officer thought that if Isaac Stevens had not pushed his agenda, it would have taken three hundred years for whites to settle it.[54] Fighting came only after Stevens (called by his biographer "young man in a hurry") muscled through his treaties and then urged his own citizenry to break the law and enter the country, and even then there had been twenty or so months of peace when Wool had stopped the intrusions and enforced his keep-them-out policy. The chances of some mutual accommodation, one with adaptive Indians keeping their lands, seems quite possible.

As for the Nez Perces, they had stayed largely out of the fray. A faction led by Lawyer and Timothy sided with white authorities and provided some scouts and warriors, while some favored joining the other side, but most, while sympathizing with the resistance, stayed neutral. The basic reason was self-protection. Old Joseph's people, the largest band, lived perilously close to the area around Walla Walla where much of the fighting took place. Others, exactly because they were buffered and farther removed, saw no reason to court a fight.

Nonetheless, many felt a bitter resentment over the 1855 treaties and how their neighbors and kinsmen were treated. Old Joseph, speaking out of the solidarity of family ties and empathy, said he had never understood the treaties as Stevens now described them. The anger spilled out at a conference called by Stevens in 1856, during Wool's peaceful interlude. Several headmen lashed out at the governor. The Nez Perce Speaking Owl demanded to know whether Stevens would give back land he had taken: "That is what we all want to hear about." Stevens lectured on the treaties' virtues, then turned to Lawyer. Holding both the treaty and a government commission naming him head chief, Lawyer repeated the treaty's terms and said that all had signed or made their marks. And that, he declared as spokesman for all the bands, was that. Old Joseph, Eagle

Figure 4.3   Tuekakas, or Old Joseph, chief of the Wallowa band

in the Light, and others said no: they had been deceived, and Lawyer had acted illegitimately. Void the treaty, they demanded. At that moment of standoff, Kamiakin and a hundred hostile Yakimas rode up. Stevens broke off the council and left.

This abortive council came as close as anything to establishing a formal division among the bands. On one side were those who supported the treaty of 1855, on the other side those who denied it. In shorthand, the two groups became the "treaties" and the "non-treaties." Behind that split was a far deeper difference. The former group claimed that the Nez Perces spoke as one tribe through a head chief—said in essence that the Nez Perces had taken on a new collective identity; the latter group held to the traditional sense of who they were as social animals. The treaty faction essentially accepted the political order of a reconstructed America; the nontreaties didn't.

Ten years after the nation had expanded to the Pacific, the Nez Perces were still in command of their land yet were also troubled and vulnerable. All around them, the white settlement grew larger with each season of immigration. They could count on little help from their neighbors, who had been subdued while the Nez Perces either stood by or helped. Still, the Nez Perces were prosperous and powerful and reasonably secure, living behind their mountains in country Coyote had given them, out of the way of forces that were breaking the others and transforming the West.

That, however, was about to change.

CHAPTER 5

# Gold, Prophecy, and the Steal Treaty

I n the early fall of 1860, as Americans approached the most consequential election of their history, Washington Territory had its own excitement. The previous spring, a trader with Indians, Elias D. Pierce, had
panned some gold along the Clearwater River in the northern part of
the Nez Perce reservation. He found only a few flecks of dust, hinting of
much richer deposits higher in the mountains. In mid-August, Pierce and
ten others set off for a closer look.

They returned in October with big news. Staying outside and above
the reservation, they had crossed to the north fork of the Clearwater and
then struggled over a divide and through "the most dark, dense forest
I ever saw" to a promising stream they would name Orofino Creek.[1]
Newspapers quickly broadcast the discovery of gold that was "very
fine...rough and craggy when closely viewed—very heavy." It paid 5 to
15 cents a pan. It was found "in dry diggings as well as on the creeks," and
there was good quartz throughout the area. Pay dirt, interspersed with
small quartz boulders, lay two and a half to four feet deep over a bedrock
of decaying granite, and the strippings, about the same depth, were easily
sluiced.[2]

Translated, this said that placer gold—gold eroded from its mother
deposits in surrounding hills—was plentiful and accessible. It was there
in the creek beds and in the "dry diggings," the nearby gravel laid down
by ancient streams. Miners could easily wash away ("sluice") the two to
four feet of topsoil ("strippings"). Below that was a layer of earth well
permeated with eroded gold. A panful's yield of 5 to 15 cents meant a man
could likely make $5 to $10 a day. With a little luck, he could make a good
bit more. The prevalence of quartz, the usual medium of gold, meant that
deposits probably ran up and down the stream, by some reports as much
as forty miles. The bottom line: there was a lot of money there. By one
early estimate, it would take five thousand men a decade to take it all.[3]

The fact that editors assumed their readers would understand the mining shorthand said something. The gold discovered in northern California in 1848 had brought an enormous immigration. During the next dozen years, a rough understanding of mining had spread and percolated through Pacific coast society, but by the mid-1850s California's annual output had peaked, and its best claims had long been taken up. Thousands of California mining veterans, "yon-siders" savvy to the signs of riches, were on the hunt for new opportunities. In 1858–59, there were major new strikes at Virginia City, Nevada (gold and silver), and in Colorado's Front Range (gold), but except for a mild excitement around Colville, Washington, in 1855, the Pacific Northwest had been a disappointment. Pierce's discovery was bound to bring a rush of gold hunters.

He led about forty men back to Orofino Creek in early December and set up a raw camp they grandly named Pierce City. Eight weeks later, four of the party hiked nearly 150 miles back to Walla Walla, the first forty miles on snowshoes, to report that seventy-one claims had been made and several prospect holes sunk, all with excellent results. About fifteen thousand feet of lumber had been whipsawed and hammered into eight cabins, a three-mile sluice to carry in water to the dry diggings, and sluice boxes to wash the gold-bearing gravel. Several letters carried out by the couriers were uniformly sunny in their predictions. Editors quickly judged the strike equal to "the most palmy days of California."[4]

By the first week of March, the streets of Walla Walla were full of pack animals, and all shovels, picks and pans had been snapped up by men already headed for Orofino.[5] Within weeks, a horseback express service was operating, and soon afterward the first two head of cattle arrived in the camp as "a feast to the miners."[6] By the end of May, $41 bought the four-hundred-mile trip from Portland to within a few days' hike to the mines, all via steamer except for a jog around the rapids at The Dalles. Men lounged on deck, admiring the scenery while puffing Havana cigars, sipping champagne, and reading St. Louis newspapers barely two weeks old.[7]

The steamer stopped where the Clearwater River entered the Snake River. South of the junction was a flat, broad plain where a town appeared, soon named Lewiston. Because most western mining strikes were in mountainous high country, most needed transition points where goods and people could be funneled from and to the world beyond. Denver and Sacramento were born that way, and many smaller towns like Lewiston quickly became the mercantile, financial, governmental, and social hubs of emerging mining regions. In early summer of 1861, a crude wagon road was cut from Lewiston to Pierce City, and as traffic quickened to the diggings, Lewiston started to look pretty well rooted.[8]

**Figure 5.1** Lewiston early in the 1860 gold rush

As with nearly all rushes, however, this one was overblown, and hundreds of disappointed prospectors soon were looking elsewhere. The historian Hubert Howe Bancroft compared miners to the mercury, or quicksilver, they used to bond with and extract gold. "Dropped in any locality," he wrote, "[they] broke up into individual globules, and ran off after any atom of gold in their vicinity. They stayed nowhere longer than the gold attracted them." As early as May 1861, prospectors found more placer gold on the Clearwater's south fork, 125 miles below Pierce City, at what became Elk City. Seventy-five miles west of there, near the Salmon River, a party found deposits boasted as "the richest and most extensive...yet found north of California" and even "the richest diggings in the world." By fall, "there was a perfect jam—a mass of human infatuation, jostling, shoving and elbowing each other" to Florence, site of the new strike, and the next spring every road into the region was "one solid, moving mass of human beings and animals—a perfect column, moving forward, all coming one way." A correspondent claimed that Florence swelled by between six hundred and a thousand persons a day.[9]

It turned out, again typically, that the gold strikes around Pierce City, Elk City, and Florence were nothing close to the West's richest. By 1864, they had faded almost entirely, although Chinese workers squeezed out a bit more at Florence for a few years. By then, however, the rushes had played the role they would in westward expansion generally. A strike's long-term success or failure was, if not irrelevant, less important than that it happened in the first place.

A gold or silver discovery transformed its particular part of the West more than any other sort of event. Normally, a frontier is imagined as a line representing a people or an influence advancing incrementally into new territory. A mining frontier was different. It was more like an artillery shell lobbed far ahead of the army of an expanding society, landing with a terrific concussion that sent shock waves through its neighborhood. Thousands of wealth-seekers flocked to a place like Florence or Elk City, but that was just the start of it. As new routes were opened to some distant site, the areas along those corridors—up the Columbia, Snake, and Clearwater rivers and overland to the camps—were quickly and profoundly affected.

New service towns like Lewiston brought their own changes. Miners had to eat, so farmers and stock raisers soon occupied every feasible nearby site. The journalist Henry Miller predicted correctly that the upper Columbia and Snake river valleys were a sure thing for raising sheep, cattle, and horses to sell in the camps. Arable land and ample timber close to the rivers offered other opportunities.[10] By the time the mines began to fail, the towns, farms, and ranches had matured into their own sustained economies.

The role of mining rushes in sealing the nation's hold on the nation's new lands can hardly be exaggerated. For the Nez Perces, the jolt was especially damaging. Mining regions typically were in high, remote country that would likely have remained isolated for quite a while. The Nez Perces' homeland was a model case. Shielded by mountains, they had felt virtually none of the direct pressure that had crippled other peoples. The Orofino strike pulled in thousands through the only gate, up the Snake and Clearwater rivers past where Lewiston now was setting its foundations. The sheer numbers of miners meant their population was no longer the largest on the Plateau.

Access and numbers, however, were only the start of a rush's impact. A gold or silver strike brought with it the particulars of the society it sprang from—stage roads and road houses, steamboat lines and ferries, cornfields and fenced pastures, towns with their churches and general stores and liveries, courthouses and jails, milliners and tonsorial parlors. Within months, all this formed a tissue of development integrating a Lewiston or Florence or Elk City into an expanding national culture long before this would have happened otherwise. No wonder boosters greeted the strike with their lushest prose. Sleepy posts, an editor wrote, would become great commercial cities, "bustling with trade, and finding employ for a fleet of ocean, Sound and river steamers."[11]

For the same reasons, Indian peoples would come to mourn the news. A rush brought immediate friction that escalated more often than not into war. With few exceptions, every major Indian conflict in the far West between 1846 and 1877 had its roots in some gold or silver strike. James Marshall's find at Sutter's Mill in 1848 soon led to years of chronic assaults on California natives. Within five years of the Pikes Peak rush of 1859, Cheyennes and Arapahoes were at war with whites on the central plains. Relations with the western Apaches of Arizona were peaceful until gold was found in the Tonto region in 1863. The Sioux war of 1868 was brought on by discoveries around Virginia City, Montana, and that of 1876 by the rush into the Black Hills of South Dakota. And so it was with the Nez Perce War.

The discovery of flecks of gold in a few scattered spots in 1860 and 1861 brought almost instant confrontations, and then developments that ground steadily away at the Nez Perces' independence and traditional life. It took seventeen years after the strike on Orofino Creek, but the march to war truly began when Elias Pierce brought his news to Walla Walla in October 1860.

The gold rush was illegal, of course. According to the 1855 treaty, no unauthorized whites were allowed on Nez Perce land. Washington Territory's superintendent of Indian affairs predicted disaster for the Nez Perces, "that interesting tribe," and "rapine and blood" for the whole region. He ordered the Nez Perce agent, Andrew J. Cain, to block any attempt to follow up on Pierce's find, something easier said than done.[12] The moment Pierce found a dime's worth of gold in every pan, the center of power between him and the authorities shifted. After surreptitiously approaching in August, circling around through the back door, in mid-October he went home right through Nez Perce land, straightaway and cockily. No need to fear now: "We had the collateral."[13]

Cain tried to stop what he knew was coming. He posted a notice commanding prospectors to stay away and asked for promised military support. By the time troops arrived, however, deep snow kept them away from the diggings, and the next March a few miners brought a $1,000 in gold dust to Walla Walla and set it boastfully in a storefront window. The stampede that followed was far too great for the small garrisons to stop.[14] From that point on, no serious effort was made to keep miners away from the strike.

The Nez Perce response was mixed, falling along divisions already existing. The nontreaty bands were angry and alarmed, and the press was full of dire predictions that they would go to war.[15] Some in the treaty bands took advantage of the situation. The prominent Reuben (Tip-ia-la-na-uy-lala-te-skin, or Eagle that Speaks All) opened a ferry near Lewiston, and others chopped wood for steamboats now plying the Snake River.[16] Lawyer worked to accommodate. In April 1861, he and others signed an agreement meant to keep the mines and miners isolated on the northern fringe of the reservation. It didn't work. Within weeks came the rush to Elk City, and then the rush to Florence, and by midsummer miners were scattering all over the reservation. The later strikes were among the lower Nez Perces, the nontreaty traditionalists, and so were bound to cause trouble, and the traffic among the diggings, just by cutting through most of the country, demolished any hope of isolating whites from Indians. Lewiston, as the entryway to all the camps, took root and grew.

The strikes spun off their usual problems. The thousands of new horses competed with Nez Perce herds for forage. Miners pastured animals at the prime camas digging ground at Weippe prairie. Hunters depleted game populations. "Reckless men…[are] roving all over the country," an army officer reported, with predictable bad behavior. "It is very plain to me why whites and Indians are unfriendly," a California journalist wrote: "The Indian…does not relish the jibes and jeers with which low-bred white men often greet him." The trader and future agent Robert Newell wrote that many Nez Perces were "continually drunk" on whiskey sold just over the reservation boundary. When he lectured a Nez Perce man on the evils of strong drink, "he coolly informed me that he knew what was good as well as a white man," Newell wrote; "I caved, of course."[17]

An official wrote that the betrayal of their long friendship had roused some Nez Perces "almost to desperation."[18] The government's pitiful record in keeping other promises made in 1855 did not help. The treaty goods shipped in 1861 were an insult, the agent wrote, "geegaws and trifles," and instead of tools, the next year's shipment brought a couple of yards of cloth for each person and one blanket for every six.[19] Still, Lawyer and the treaty chiefs were willing to cooperate. There was money in the new trade—Reuben's ferry had made him almost landed nobility, a journalist wrote, with twenty-five hundred horses and a farm of several hundred acres—and the new diggings after all were to the south among the nontreaty bands.[20] At a council in November 1861, fifty leaders of the Lawyer faction said they were "perfectly content" with the mines at Elk City and Florence and the businesses at Lewiston—as long as all whites left after the gold was dug and meanwhile the government kept the miners in check and cleared out all whiskey sellers.[21]

There was not the slightest chance the army could meet those terms. It might have been able to stop the rush at the start, but now the door was open and unshuttable. A week after the council, Washington Territory's Indian superintendent predicted the next spring would bring twenty thousand miners onto the reservation, and "as a matter of course" many of the Indians' rights would be totally disregarded.[22]

Meanwhile, another development was unfolding. It was not about gold, pack mules, and ferries but the Earth Mother, the Man Above, and humanity's proper relationship to the divine. A "mysterious prophet" was fomenting an outbreak of "religious fanaticism," the *Olympia (WA) Pioneer and Democrat* reported late in 1860. This movement, the editor thought, was meant to stir up the region's Indians and to inspire in them the "courage and zeal for the struggle of the races."[23] Whether that was the intent was questionable, but all sides could agree that this spiritual stirring was something to reckon with.

The Nez Perce troubles stemmed from invasions, economic pressures, and environmental and social disruptions. The crisis was also spiritual. Nez Perce holy men played prominently in diplomacy and, once the war came, in the fighting. United States Indian policy was driven in considerable part by a muscular Christianity shared by the government's Indian agents in peacetime and, once the fighting started, by many military officers. Underneath it all, spiritual worldviews formed the basis from which Indians and whites acted. By broadening the term only slightly, the bloody events of 1877 can credibly be called a religious war.

The "mysterious prophet" the *Pioneer and Democrat* mentioned was a shaman of the Wanapam people of the Columbia River basin, a hunchback with a large head and short legs who had taken the name Smohalla (usually translated as "Dreamer" but sometimes as "Preacher").[24] His predictive powers had brought him a growing respect, while his dedication to traditional beliefs and ways of life had led him increasingly into conflict with those inclined to accommodation. In the late 1850s, he dropped out of sight after a vicious clash with a rival. Some said he had been killed or badly wounded, others that he had died of grief over a favorite daughter's death.

When he reappeared, Smohalla said he was returning from the dead. He now preached a collection of teachings he said were given him by divine power. Together they composed a creed he called Washani (Dancers). The creed's adherents came to be popularly known as Dreamers, reflecting their belief that the Creator communicated with them through dreams and trances, something denied to whites by their dawn-to-dusk laboring.[25] Smohalla taught that the earth, as divine creation, was perfect as people had first found it, and so people must live on it in their own perfect way, with perfect lightness, without injury or alteration. This intimate obligation was based in kinship, for humans were born of the earth. (By one account, Smohalla's original name translated as Arising From the Dust of the Earth Mother.) To adopt the life of white immigrants, he later explained to an army officer, Captain E. L. Huggins, was desecration, even matricide:

> You ask me to plough the ground! Shall I take a knife and tear
>     my mother's bosom? Then when I die she will not take me
>     to her bosom to rest.
> You ask me to dig for stone! Shall I dig under her skin for
>     her bones? Then when I die I cannot enter her body and be
>     born again.
> You ask me to cut grass and make hay and sell it, and be rich
>     like white men, but how dare I cut off my mother's hair?[26]

Subsistence, he preached, should rely strictly on the earth's natural bounty. Digging camas roots, for instance, was simply accepting "gifts that are freely offered," and because it did not interfere with the plant's survival, it was no more harmful than a suckling baby kneading a mother's breast. The white settler, by contrast, "tears up large tracts of land, runs deep ditches, cuts down forests and changes the whole face of the earth."[27]

To Smohalla, every white influence was baleful and virtually all white actions malicious. When Huggins pointed out that the Europeans had given Indians at least one good thing, horses, Smohalla answered: "O no, we had ponies long before we ever saw white people." That was true; horses had arrived via traditional trading routes well before any whites showed up. "The Great Spirit gave them to us," Smohalla went on; "our horses were swifter and more enduring, too, in those days, before they were mixed with the white man's horses. The Indian would be rich and happy if he had never seen the white man." His people's steady decline came from both pernicious influences and murderous assaults, he claimed, including the poison Marcus Whitman had brought in a bottle and loosed on the people. Illness and death had chewed at Plateau peoples ever since. The prophet himself had lost most of his family to diseases.

But there was hope. Smohalla said that in heaven he had been taught rituals, including a dance (Washat) performed to the accompaniment of

Figure **5.2** Early Dreamers, whose religion opposed changes brought by the white frontier

a bell rung by a young boy. If believers would follow those ways, reject whites' means of living and of transforming the earth, keep to the traditions, and patiently keep the faith, the Creator would reward them. He would bring back into the world the men and women and the abundant game that had passed into the hereafter, a great tide of life that would force the invaders out or in some versions destroy them. White colonization would be only an interlude. It "would fade away into a dim but horrible dream peopled by ghastly ghouls."[28]

The Dreamers represented one variation of the many prophet-inspired Indian religions that had been common in the United States since the colonial era. These movements combined older beliefs and practices with certain elements and even rituals of Christianity, while teaching their followers to limit or avoid contact with whites and white ways of life and to return to their own spiritual and material roots. Among the best known earlier movements were that of the Delaware prophet Neolin in the 1760s and that of the Shawnee Tenskwatawa forty years later, linked to the secular leaders Pontiac and Tecumseh, respectively. Tenskwatawa's vision included a vivid metaphor for Americans—a gigantic, hideous crab that had crawled from the sea at an especially revealing spot: Boston.[29] A dozen years after the Nez Perce War, another religion, the Ghost Dance, spread from the Great Basin to dozens of groups across the continent. Such "religions of the oppressed" also appeared in Europe's colonies in South America, Polynesia and Micronesia, Asia and Indonesia, and Africa in the eighteenth, nineteenth and twentieth centuries.[30] Most sprang up at about the same stage of the colonial experience: the tipping point, the moment like the one in Nez Perce country in the 1860s when the invader's grip was about to close beyond the hope of anyone wriggling loose.

The Dreamers were also rooted in spiritual traditions dating to the first indirect touch of Europeans, years of both fresh opportunities and the awful scything of smallpox and malaria. Cults had appeared, like the tuli-m, which also preached dreams of revelation and predicted the arrival of a strange people who had a book of special knowledge and a belief in an afterlife attainable by charity. This cult offered new ritual dances and foretold a divine day of reckoning, as heard in one early song:

> We look for him who children made [i.e. who made children]
> We are lonely and homesick
> He will descend, we will meet him
> The great chief above.
>     Hiya hi yi yi
> He will destroy those who are bad when he comes
> The great chief above.
>     Hiya hi yi yi[31]

Out of that spiritual milieu, Lewis and Clark were welcomed and the four emissaries sent to St. Louis in search of the white man's book. The earlier movements, that is, had drawn in the very changes Smohalla came to deplore, the people and influences he now said would be driven out if the new faith were followed.

Other prophets appeared in the 1860s, preaching Sabbath observance and telling of buckskin-clad angels standing on clouds. Some of the faithful died, visited heaven, and returned with still other new songs and rituals. What put a stop to such spirit travel, it was later said, was another pernicious white practice—embalming.[32]

Besides a few fundamentals—a kinship with the land, the value of dreams—the movements were not unified. Some Nez Perces invoked Smohalla's spiritual voice but strayed from his teachings. Young Joseph and his brother Ollokut, who turned toward the movement sometime in the 1860s, spoke passionately of the inviolability of the earth and wore their hair in the rearing pompadour favored by Dreamers. Yet they kept cattle. Smohalla condemned that, as well as the objects of white material culture that many of his sympathizers had in abundance. Upper Nez Perce bands with many Dreamers fenced their land and farmed—the reason, Smohalla would say, they lost the war. They "had good fields and gardens," he sneered; "I have no pity for them."[33] Some probably embraced Smohalla's apocalyptic prophecy of violent, God-driven liberation, but how much currency it had is not at all clear.[34] In all the later councils, no one, not even avowed Dreamers, ever alluded to it.

Nez Perce religion was like Nez Perce society—varied, decentered, fluid, and evolving. And as with the society, white authorities insisted on seeing the religion as something different from what it was. They would describe all spiritual resisters as Dreamers and would assume all Dreamers were alike. Beyond that, they lumped all Indians together as either Christians or non-Christians and linked ways of living to one category or the other. Farmers were presumed to be on the Christian road, while those who crossed the Bitterroots to hunt bison must be heathens. Hard lines were drawn over mundane details. Long hair carried spiritual heft among the Nez Perces. Missionaries insisted they cut their hair, partly to fit white culture's style but partly to make hair, the long or the short of it, a sign of being savage or civilized, which in turn stiffened the traditionalists' devotion to keeping it long. "If hair keeps people out of heaven," a mixed-blood Nez Perce thought, "God would have created man baldheaded."[35]

When agents considered Nez Perce society, they insisted it was a well-bounded tribe with one leader speaking for its several bands. It was part of an impulse to lay over the nation's new country an arrangement that was easily understood and dealt with. And so with religion. Nez Perces (and Indians generally) were said to be Christians or not, farmers or hunters, favoring long hair or barber-prone. This either-or division was considered also for-or-against. At this point, it's true, the government told the Nez Perces and others that they were free to worship as they wished. But Washington also made Christian conversion a prime goal and worked intimately with missionaries to make it happen. And in any scrape, any contest of power, if any like the Dreamers were to resist, in this case by teaching that breaking soil and making money were sins, they were called threats to national interest.

The nation's commitment to religious toleration, genuine enough toward its own spiritual traditions, never truly applied to Native America. When a challenge like Smohalla's ran against the need to bring comprehensible order to the new country, it became "religious fanaticism" that had to be resisted. Westward expansion became spiritual conquest.

Within two years of Pierce's discovery, the isolation of a good part of the Nez Perces' reservation had been utterly shattered. The pressure was by no means the same throughout their country. The lower bands were less affected, and those west of the Salmon River, including Old Joseph's people, were still entirely free of any white presence. It was the upper bands, in the Clearwater River watershed, that were overwhelmed. The white population there, virtually zero in 1860, soared in a year to more than fifteen thousand, a quarter more than all the whites in Washington Territory in 1860 and several times more than all the Nez Perces.[36] Boosters puffed this country beyond caution or common sense. Lewiston was called the "second Sacramento," and the agent to the Nez Perce reported, ridiculously, that gold was found everywhere east of the Salmon River. One official judged the Camas Prairie as fertile as the Missouri River's famed bottomlands, and another thought the reservation could easily feed more than twenty thousand miners.[37]

As the torrent of prospectors, and others hoping to mine the miners, came in from throughout the Pacific region, the supply center of Lewiston quickly became a dog's breakfast of log and canvas buildings that defied any usual terms of description. "Grab a handful of words and roll them in ink, and then scatter them on paper," a correspondent wrote, "and you will have a pretty fair description of the place."[38] Hundreds of hopeful farmers grabbed so many "little rich spots...all over the Reservation" that the agent thought "not...a foot [will be] left for its rightful owners."[39] The Nez Perces could only stand by, powerless, "except to complain, and behold with astonishment."[40] The white flood threatened their economic base, their horse herds. Besides constant thieving, scores of animals were traded daily to whiskey sellers, one head for two bottles of rotgut.[41] Invaders cut from the best stands of timber and seized huge amounts of driftwood fuel. In the late spring of 1862, Oregon's Indian superintendent wrote with only some exaggeration that "the entire wealth and resources of the country has been monopolized by our citizens."[42]

There were the predictable cultural abrasions. The crowds drawn to Lewiston were called "last scrapings of the earth," and the rush from there to the several scattered camps brought Indians into hourly contact with "the most miscreant and infamous violators of the public peace."[43] The worst problems centered on the "shebangs" that sprang up along every road and at every spring and stream crossing. All manner of conflicts and debaucheries were reported, including the prostitution of Nez Perce women. A sympathetic journalist found that a people always known for their friendship and generosity "now reap an abundant harvest of every species of villainy and insult."[44]

For help, the Nez Perces would have to look to Lapwai, the Place of the Butterflies, where Henry and Eliza Spalding had come and been driven out and where the nation's new authority had now reset itself. Lapwai was now the formal site of Washington's presence, its agency among the Nez

Perces. In time, its position would strengthen and its influence take on some heft. At this point, however, authorities were little or no help. Turnover at the Lapwai agency was high: three agents in two years. Washington Territory's superintendent of Indian affairs was disgusted by his time there. Employees gave most attention to seducing Nez Perce women, and the $60,000 paid out by the government so far to encourage farming had brought three tons of oats in a crude shed. He figured glumly that taxpayers were out $1 for each munch of his horse's jaw.[45]

Some troops were available, but by mid-1861 regulars had been sent back East—after all there was a war on—and many of the volunteers were from the California mines and as likely to join the trespassers as challenge them.[46] In overall command of Washington and Oregon volunteers was Brigadier General Benjamin Alvord. A scholar with wide interests—he would publish on topics ranging from grazing economies and geometry to the marketing of Christmas trees in Alabama—he had come to Oregon with one of the first overland parties and knew the region well. In 1862, he established Fort Lapwai where Lapwai Creek entered the Clearwater River, about two miles downstream from the agency, and assigned to it a cavalry and an infantry company. Several chiefs, including Old Joseph, reportedly were pleased at the hope of some protection.[47] Except for the area right around Lapwai, however, the military was only dimly felt.

Now everything that had happened—the surge of trespassers, the battering of the Nez Perce economy, the abuses, the pitiful floundering of authorities—was said to sum up to one conclusion. The Nez Perce treaty of 1855 was called untenable. Sticking to the 1855 agreement, it was said, would bring an "exterminating war." Whites would die by the thousands. Indians would suffer beyond measure. Promises had to be undone and tribal holdings severely reduced. As a correspondent put it, "the logic of events is stronger than parchment."[48]

From today's perspective, such talk, and that around Indian policy generally, seems deeply strange. The historian Richard White has called one rhetorical theme "inverted conquest." As whites rolled over and devastated Indian peoples, they described the *Indians* as the predators and themselves as set-upon victims, "badly abused conquerors."[49] Public talk of the Nez Perce crisis followed a different vein, just as odd, a flip-flop from inverted conquest. It might be called confessional conquest. White aggression and policy failures were fully, passionately admitted, but the lesson of all the mea culpas was not to reverse course. It was to push ahead and insist that Indians give up still more.

The overwhelming consensus in the press and official statements was that the Nez Perces were in the right. Their lands were being illegally invaded. The intruders were called human bilgewater—thieves, cheats, debauchers. In response, the Nez Perce were said to be models of patience and reason, as fit their unblemished record of friendship. In May 1862, Oregon Senator James W. Nesmith delivered an extended hymn to the Nez Perces to his colleagues in the U.S.Senate.[50] The Nez Perces were handsome, intelligent, and virtuous, faithful to their word and protective of American citizens. In return, they had suffered abuses and betrayals. Not that they were unique. From Maine to Oregon, Nesmith said, the government had consistently pledged what it could not deliver. Agents and missionaries had reduced Indians to "squalid thieves, vagabonds, and prostitutes." And now the old pattern was unfolding again. A corrupt and corrupting government was failing its responsibilities.

And Nesmith's conclusion? The Nez Perces must sign another treaty and give up more land. They had to be protected, and protection wasn't possible on the 1855 reservation. The only chance for protection was to have a much smaller reservation. Doing justice meant dealing with the results of botched policy by repeating what had been done in the first place, with the promise that the government would mend its ways, and right soon. First we buy some land from Indians and promise protection, Senator William Fessenden of Maine pointed out, then we buy the land we left them because we cannot protect it. "Where is this thing to end?" he asked. Without fundamental rethinking, the answer appeared to be that it woudn't.

Congress allotted $30,000 for the negotiation of a new treaty. A council was called for May 1863 at the Lapwai agency. Calvin H. Hale, superintendent of Indian affairs of Washington Territory, would head a delegation that included Charles Hutchins, earlier an agent to the Nez Perces, and another agent, L. D. Howe. The commissioners would have to forge a new treaty among bitterly divided bands, some of whom had never accepted the previous treaty. There would have to be a massive reduction of the reservation the government had promised to respect only eight years earlier. Several of the most resistant bands would have to surrender their home country and give up a tested way of life in favor of one they did not want and that showed little sign of supporting them. All Nez Perces would be asked to trust a government that was in default on virtually everything it had promised in the past.

"The obstacles in our way [are] numerous, complicated and difficult," Hale wrote his boss on the eve of the council.[51] But he would find a way.

Calvin Hale arrived at Lapwai on May 10, 1863, the day he had hoped the council would begin, but the only Indians around were the ones usually living there. A late planting season delayed some nearby farming bands, but many others were suspicious of what awaited them. Henry Spalding was there as an interpreter, but Lawyer and others also insisted that Hale wait for Perrin Whitman, nephew of Marcus and Narcissa, who was more fluent and was widely trusted.[52]

Incredibly, Hale had little idea of what his proposed new reservation would look like, and he used the next few days to ride around and plot it out. He proposed a five-sided block of land of about twelve hundred square miles. He would argue that the area, encompassing most of the Clearwater River and its tributaries, was best suited to farming, the new life all would be pressed to follow, but the choice was also a geopolitical stroke. Most of the upper Nez Perces, including all the treaty bands, already lived there and so would lose no land. He was offering the most to those who were most amenable, precisely as Isaac Stevens had done with all the Nez Perces at the Mill Creek council in 1855. The new reservation was also home to four nontreaty bands, those of Looking Glass, Eagle in the Light, Koolkool Snehee, and Big Thunder. By letting them keep their homelands, Hale was driving a wedge between them and the other nontreaties of the lower Nez Perces, the bands of Old Joseph, White Bird, and Toohoolhoolzote. They would have to surrender it all—their land, their lifeways, and their spiritual base. With this strategy, Hale might cobble together enough support, or at least quiet enough opposition, to claim the new treaty was valid.

He relied on the claim that the Nez Perces were one people, a tribe, with one spokesman for all, the head chief. That person was Lawyer. As a Christian and the leading advocate for assimilation, he was Washington's prime asset. At the present council, Hale said at his opening meeting, decisions would be made "for the whole Nez Perce nation, not for a part, but for every man who has an interest here." Lawyer would be "one of the contracting parties"—one of two, that is, the other being the government.[53]

By May 22, about sixteen hundred Nez Perces had arrived. None of the nontreaties had shown up, not even those living next door. Supplies for people and horses already were strained, and sickness, probably influenza, had appeared. A frustrated Hale decided to open the council anyway on May 25. For the first four days, only Lawyer's followers were there. Hale began by laying out the new treaty's basics—how the boundaries would be drastically reduced and everyone outside them would surrender their homelands, money and facilities would be provided, and the best of the reservation would be given out as individual farms protected from white intruders.

Lawyer spoke next. If Hale expected easy compliance, he got a shock. For three days the chiefs present, the friendliest of all the bands, spoke with anger and irony about the government's failures. Lawyer quoted

Stevens in 1855 saying that year's treaty would be "permanent and straight," yet here was Hale eight years later saying it was time to scrap it and making new promises when the old ones were still unmet—few payments made, their land invaded, no smithy or carpenter or wagoner shops, no hospital.[54]

Hale conceded that earlier obligations were unmet, but on the larger point he answered that the government had never considered the 1855 treaty to be set in stone. One of its articles, he pointed out, said the agents could survey lots and assign them to families wanting to settle them as farmers. He then argued, tortuously, that because the chiefs had agreed that some might settle someday on individual plots, they had tacitly said that eventually *all* would, which would leave much of the reservation unnecessary, which meant the Nez Perces should expect to sell land "which you could not use" and consolidate on a smaller reservation. That, Hale said, had always been the presumption. Gold had simply speeded things up. In had come so many "bad men who pay no regard to the law" that the army would need a hundred times the troops it had to keep them out. How can we protect you, he asked, "scattered as you are?" Shrinking their land might seem a betrayal, but in fact it was a reward for their faithful support. It is not for our benefit, Hale said, "so much as it is for yours, that we have proposed to make your reservations smaller."[55]

When the council reconvened on June 3 after a five-day break, and probably some deep breaths among the commissioners, the nontreaties had arrived. A couple of points stand out about the exchanges of the next three days. Statements from the nontreaties were terse to an extreme, and everything said was from their chiefs among the upper Nez Perces. From Old Joseph, White Bird, and others from the lower Nez Perces, the record has nothing at all.

It was the silence of stress. The council of 1863 would be the breaking point of tensions that had been at work among the Nez Perces for thirty years. The missionaries had divided the bands culturally along lines of religion and lifeways. The treaty of 1855 had deepened the split, as the converts supported it and the traditionalists opposed it. Revivalist movements like the Dreamers had made the rift deeper still. The division was partly geographical. All Christians were among the upper Nez Perces, along the Clearwater River, while the lower bands were all antitreaty traditionalists. Now Hale proposed that those most alienated, the lower bands, give up their homes, the very ground of who they were, and over time give up their way of life. He would ask them to crowd onto the land of culturally dissonant relatives, as if in an endless family reunion with hostile cousins and in-laws.

Figure **5.3** Lawyer, the Christian Nez Perce who was the leading advocate for the treaty in 1863

And when Hale asked for all this, who would answer for the bands? Hale put his hand on the shoulder of Lawyer—a Christian convert whose people would keep their lands, a chief who for years had called on the traditionalists to follow a life they didn't want, the man who insisted that eight years earlier he had bound them to another treaty, one they had rejected and still considered a disaster.

So on June 3, when the chiefs of the lower bands joined the council—a meeting that had started without them—they had little reason to expect anything good would come of it. And having little to trust, they had nothing to say. The next day Commissioner Hutchins tried pressure. They would not get such a good offer again, he told them, and they should accept it or be "utterly ruined and destroyed as a people, for the whites will come in as thick as grasshoppers and crickets." Two nontreaty chiefs of the upper bands, Big Thunder and Eagle of the Light, gave "haughty" answers, but otherwise "no replies of any importance were made," and the meeting of June 4 adjourned.[56]

The next twenty-four hours were crucial. Two things happened behind the scenes. Hale held a series of private meetings to work with more amenable headmen. Lawyer, despite his public criticism, was disposed to go along, and the leaders in his faction soon conceded, after some minor boundary changes and "items of further consideration"—the promise of improvements and $600 annually to Timothy.[57] The leading traditionalists among the upper bands, Big Thunder and Eagle of the Light, said they would not side with Lawyer publicly, but since they stood to lose no land, they told Hale in so many words, they would stay out of the way, neither accepting nor opposing the treaty.[58] Thus Hale sealed support among allies and neutralized some opposition. He made no effort, however, to meet with chiefs of the lower bands.

The other development was an all-night council of fifty-three chiefs representing all groups and factions. The ostensible purpose was to come up with a response to Hale, but its deeper one was facing the tensions and divisions that had pulled at the bands for three decades. By dawn on June 5, the Nez Perces had passed a turning point in their history.

By chance, an outsider attended and left an account. Captain George Curry and twenty cavalrymen had been sent by Hale to prevent any violence at what was sure to be a volatile meeting, but Curry found everything peaceful and was invited to sit with an interpreter. He later described an extended face-off between those opposed to the treaty, Big Thunder being the most vocal, and those inclined to accept it, led by Lawyer. Several headmen spoke with "dignified firmness and warmth." They considered the options. Finally, near dawn, the resisting side announced they would not accept the treaty "and then with a warm, and in an emotional manner, declared the Nez Perce nation *dissolved*." As the two sides shook hands, the resisters made their point all the plainer, telling the Lawyer faction "with a kind but firm demeanor that they would be friends, but a distinct people."[59]

From that moment on, whatever arrangement of power Elijah White claimed to have established in 1842, and it had been fuzzy and disputed from the start, was dead. The declaration of Lawyer's opponents, made in common council, ended whatever standing Lawyer had. Each band was politically severed from the others, as had been the case traditionally, and each spoke only for itself through its own leaders. The lower bands then stepped away from the whole business, and within hours they left for home. They presumed Lawyer would never claim to speak for them and that nothing decided would touch them directly.

Hale had to have known about the overnight meeting and, if nothing else, could not have missed that the chiefs of the lower bands were gone again, yet he never mentioned it in the record. The next morning, June 5, he pushed ahead and in fact turned up the heat. Hutchins told anyone resisting that if they refused to join Lawyer, "we will make [the treaty] without you. ... Your refusal makes no difference."[60] The elderly Big Thunder, who had spoken against the treaty at the council of chiefs but had told Hale he would not oppose it openly, asked a few questions and then, sick with whatever was sweeping the camp, left with his last words in the written record: "I am very sick, and spitting blood, excuse me."[61] Before Hale adjourned to draw up the formal treaty, Lawyer spoke in favor of it and asked the government to have pity on his children as long as the mountains stood above them.[62] Neither he nor anyone else mentioned the previous night's council or what had transpired.

On June 9, fifty-two Nez Perces signed the new treaty. With one possible exception, all were of Lawyer's faction. No one who signed lived on any of the land that was supposedly ceded. An account that appeared only in a confidential Senate executive report noted that "all the leading chiefs and head men of the friendly bands signed the treaty. None of the disaffected chiefs were present."[63] Curry was more blunt: "Although the treaty goes out to the world as the concurrent agreement of all the tribe, it is in reality nothing more than the agreement of Lawyer and his band...not a third part of the Nez Perce tribe."[64]

Hale was pleased. The Nez Perces had surrendered mining country on the Bitterroot slopes, "country...exceedingly valuable," he reported, and far more land to the west, the valleys of the Snake and Salmon rivers and the Wallowa country. That land, home to the lower bands, "will be found desirable and necessary for agricultural and grazing purposes." Everyone living outside the new reservation had a year to come on to it. The government would pay $265,000 for what was ceded, roughly 8 cents an acre, about half of which would pay for removal, fencing, and the first plowing. Much of the payment the bands would receive for their land, that is, would go toward getting them off. Another $50,000 would pay for tools and animals, with more toward schools, a hospital, other facilities, and "salaries" for compliant headmen.

Many tribal members today call this the "steal treaty." Just under seven million acres would be taken, nearly 90 percent of what had been guaranteed under the treaty of 1855. To imagine a similar loss for the United States in 1863, picture a north-south line drawn from Canada to Mexico through the centers of present-day Idaho and Nevada. The reduced nation would lie west of that line. All the rest, everything from Las Vegas eastward to the Atlantic coast, would be lost.

Calvin Hale had been part pettifogger, part bullyboy. His danceaway arguments and browbeating nonetheless summed up what the government had said for more than fifty years in taking control of hundreds of millions of acres of Indian land. There were echoes of *Johnson v. McIntosh* (1823), John Marshall's decision that left Indians not with true ownership but only a right of occupancy—the right to live where they lived. Washington might acquire it by purchase or conquest, but, Marshall said in so many words, when the time came, Indians would be expected to surrender that right. Progress demanded it. Indians were not using the land as it was meant to be used, Marshall said, and so did Hale. The Nez Perces should give up land "you do not use, and which you do not need," he said. They might have been drawing on their country in their own proven ways, feeding their families as they had for centuries on salmon, camas, bison, and the rest, but because they were not putting the land to white society's purposes, they weren't truly using it, and so they didn't really need it. It was up for grabs.

Americans, furthermore, were the destined grabbers. Hale said that the gold rush had left the government helpless to protect the Nez Perces. An unstoppable expansion, he said, had carried the prospectors into the country, and with them grocers and farmers and cattlemen, and with them the nation's institutions and power. He was echoing what was by then a familiar trope. For Indians in the Ohio valley, it had been flotillas of flatboats; for plains tribes, the great overland migration and then ranchers and farmers; for those in Arizona and Colorado, some other gold or silver rush. The claim was always the same. Events had made some prior arrangement obsolete. The Nez Perces, like dozens of peoples before them, would have to give up more.

In the government's eyes, the Indians' right to live on their homelands was like their practice of their religions. Both were officially recognized; both were expected to end at some point. Meanwhile, Washington would respect them both—unless, that is, either stood in the way of national destiny. That was the case now, Hale said. No one had sought the crisis. The resistant bands were about to be overwhelmed by the nation's rise toward greatness, fated since the birth of the republic. People weren't the Nez Perces' problem. History was.

And yet for Hale to be saying what he did *when* he did seemed historically out of sync. His superior air and bluff assumptions about national destiny might have struck some as, if not preposterous, much at odds with events of the day. Here was one more reason the Nez Perce story was a pivotal moment.

It was June 1863, the most uncertain weeks of the nation's history. As Hale spoke from a firm vision of an expanded union sure to dominate the continent, the union tottered on the edge of collapse as Confederate forces marched toward Washington. Here is a paradox essential to understanding midcentury America. After the expansion of 1845–48, events in the East built bitterly toward division and fratricide. Meanwhile, events in the West—the California gold rush and the great overland migration, silver and gold strikes in Nevada and Colorado and the surges they set loose, agrarian occupation of the Northwest—were a momentum of faith in a glorious future. Developments back East led finally to a war that threatened the very existence of the union. During that war, the union's embrace of the West became steadily more confident.

More in fact was done during the Civil War to incorporate the West than in any comparable period. Within six weeks in 1862, Congress passed and Lincoln signed three momentous bills widely expected to quicken western settlement. The Homestead Act (May 20) offered 160 acres of public land for a pittance to any adult willing to farm it and make a few improvements; the Pacific Railroad Act (July 1) allowed construction of a rail link between the Midwest and the Pacific coast; the Morrill Land Grant Act (July 2) promised to solve the riddles of farming in unfamiliar terrains and climates by pledging public land to finance agricultural education. An expanding infrastructure integrated the West ever more tightly into the nation. On July 4, 1861, the day Congress authorized the president to call half a million men to arms, crews near Omaha set the first pole for a transcontinental telegraph connection that was finished fewer than four months later, an astonishing nine months ahead of schedule. Government parties surveyed new roads across the Southwest from Arkansas to southern California, along the main overland route across the central plains, and through the northern plains and Rocky Mountains. The Mullan Road, laid out from Walla Walla in Washington Territory to Montana in 1858–60, linked the upper Missouri River to the Columbia and provided a much improved route to the doorstep of Nez Perce country.

The western white population grew prodigiously. California's increased by nearly half between 1860 and 1870 (and its Indian population shrank by 60 percent), and Nebraska's more than tripled. Gold strikes in the northern Rockies brought the steepest increases of all. Essentially no whites lived in Montana in 1860; a census in 1864 showed 15,812. Idaho in 1860 was the thinly peopled eastern edge of Washington Territory. A headcount in 1863 showed 32,342 persons, nearly three times the number in its mother territory three years earlier. As Union forces suffered setbacks in the East, western troops delivered devastating blows to Indian peoples. An uprising of Santee Sioux around New Ulm, Minnesota, in 1862 was crushed, and after thirty-eight Sioux were hanged in the largest mass execution in American history, nearly two thousand others were packed off to a bleak reservation across the Missouri River. The next year, California volunteers under Colonel Patrick Conner killed between 220 and 400 Shoshones along the Bear River in southern Idaho; the next winter, whites killed more than a hundred others in the region. In 1863, the famous guide Christopher "Kit" Carson, now commissioned a colonel, directed a devastating campaign against the prime native power of northern Arizona, the Navajos, destroying livestock, peach orchards, and other crops. The next year about eight thousand Navajos were marched three hundred miles to confinement in eastern New Mexico. The rush to the Colorado gold camps led to violence between whites and Cheyennes, Arapahoes, and Sioux in eastern Colorado, and then to the massacre at Sand Creek in November 1864. The fighting that followed broke the power of tribes that had dominated the central Great Plains.

These developments left America of 1860–65 sectionally divided along not one axis but two. We have kept our attention so sharply on the split between North and South, have been so mesmerized by its dreadful carnage and high drama, that we have missed almost wholly the other divide, that between East and West. In June 1863, if one had mentally split in half today's forty-eight contiguous states along the eastern edge of the Great Plains and then considered the general drift of events on either side, the tracks of the two halves could hardly have been more different. The East moved toward disunion, the West toward consolidation; the East more deeply into doubt about national survival, the West into an ever more confident vision of an expanded future.

The Union victory at Gettysburg on July 1–3 ultimately reconciled America along both of those axes. It preserved the union, turning the military tide against the Confederacy, and by blocking secession it confirmed that a national culture would continue to emerge and to pull the nation's parts into a whole as it rolled itself westward to the Pacific. The vision behind Calvin Hale's demands at Lapwai—that of national greatness and of conquest as irresistible as a sunrise—would win its day.

Meanwhile, the Nez Perces themselves faced their own crisis of who and what they were. On the night of June 4–5, a month before Gettysburg, when their leaders met and, in Curry's words, "declared the Nez Perce nation *dissolved*," they ended whatever gauzy bond they had made when prodded by Elijah White and when imposed on by officials ever since. Whites at the Lapwai conference, understandably given the context, read into this "nation *dissolved*" a parallel to events back east. The Sacramento *Daily Union* called Big Thunder's followers the Nez Perces' "secession element," and others wrote darkly that Jeff Davis's agents were at work to split apart the tribe, just as they were worming away at the national union.

The comparison essentially got it backward. It said the resistant chiefs were rebels trying to undo a well-rooted system; but the chiefs who stood against Lawyer and Hale were not challenging an old order, they were defending one. It was Washington that was demanding radical change—that all Nez Perces, and scores of other western peoples, conform to ideas and adopt lifeways and institutions alien to their traditions. The resisting chiefs refused, and in fact backed away farther than ever. That left them at odds with other bands, and it left them far out of step with the new America.

The Nez Perce War was still fourteen years in the future, but the trajectory toward it was set here, in June 1863. One flashpoint was immediate. When word arrived among the nontreaty lower bands that Hale considered the treaty of 1863 binding on all of them—that they would be expected to hand over their lands, to remove to the shrunken reservation, and to take up a new life of agriculture, white schooling, and Christian worship—Old Joseph was enraged. According to one story, he tore into pieces the copy of the Gospel of Matthew that Henry Spalding had given him at his baptism.[65] He vowed never to trust white men again and never to surrender the lovely Wallowa.

# CHAPTER 6

# "Conquering by Kindness"

T he Senate took four years to approve the treaty of 1863, and even
  when government agents took their place among the Nez Perces
they at first were almost comically inept. A later investigation found that
Idaho's governor and superintendent of Indian affairs, Caleb Lyon, acted
with "an ignorance unparalleled." He once provided the Nez Perces with
forty dozen pairs of elastic garters—but no stockings.[1] In a public dress-
ing-down in 1864, Lawyer said his support of Washington had left him
humiliated: "I stand here…naked."[2]

And yet there was soon a dramatic shift in the balance between those
supporting and opposing the 1863 treaty. At least two-thirds of the Nez
Perces had at first rejected it. By 1876, the opposition was well under half,
perhaps as little as a third. When war came the next year, a large majority
of Nez Perces remained neutral or supported the army.

There were several reasons for the change. One, paradoxically, was the
growing vulnerability of many Nez Perces. While the gold diggings had
mostly petered out by 1864, settlements spawned by the rush remained
and grew outside the reservation—Lewiston and the farms downstream
on the Snake River, more farms and ranches on the prairie to the southeast, knots of stores and homesteads around White Bird Creek and up and
down the Salmon River. The white American population in Washington,
Oregon, and Idaho exploded, from about sixty-four thousand to more
than four hundred thousand, between 1860 and 1877. Put differently, it
increased *each year* by a number roughly ten times the Nez Perce population in 1860. Here and across the West, native peoples would have to face
facts: national institutions and authority were there to stay.

The inevitable tensions were complicated by what must have seemed
the baffling mysteries of federalism. A card-game brawl among Indians,
probably Palouse–Nez Perces, in a village along the Snake River left one

man stabbed and dead. The agent at Lapwai had said that the village was still under federal authority and protection even though it was off the reservation, and when local whites, who also claimed jurisdiction, killed another man during an attempted arrest, the Indians demanded that the agent intervene. To make things messier, the incident happened in Washington Territory, just over the line from the Idaho locals who said they had jurisdiction for over crimes around the reservation. So the agent, who had insisted that he spoke for the Great Father who governed all, now had to say that he was not entirely sure who was in charge, not just because of lines around the reservation but also because of lines between things called territories that had their own authorities apart from those of the Great Father, whose power the agent claimed was paramount in the land—although, when it got down to particulars, not necessarily. No wonder the Indians were confused.[3]

And if confused and threatened, living on the reservation might seem the safest bet, especially as the situation there stabilized somewhat after the Civil War. First Robert Newell, an ex–mountain man who spoke Nez Perce, gave honest service as agent, and then John B. Monteith, a Presbyterian minister and a minister's son from the Willamette valley, took over in February 1871. Under his tenure, there were few charges of corruption and some genuine progress toward meeting some of the treaty's pledges. By 1875, fifty families were living in frame houses provided by the sawmill and carpentry shop, and despite drought and crickets, twenty-six hundred acres of plowed land produced enough grain and vegetables to feed the settled families, with some left over for sale. School attendance rose from twenty-five to nearly a hundred, and nearly five hundred Nez Perces had adopted white styles of dress.[4]

Even more striking was a surge in Christian conversions. The first missionary period of 1836–47 had left only a few prominent men as converts, and several of these, like Old Joseph, had fallen away during the interim. Then after 1871 came such a swelling of conversions that by 1877 a clear majority of Nez Perces were professing Christians, nine hundred of them Presbyterians. Partly this came from more vigorous missionizing. Agent Monteith worked in tandem (but not always in harmony) with Henry Spalding, who returned first as a teacher and then a full-time proselytizer. Roman Catholics and Methodists worked the field as well.[5]

The Nez Perces, however, had their own reasons. Whites were undeniably there to stay. Their presence and threat grew yearly—the farms and ranches, the roadhouses and vile whiskey holes. The reservation seemed to many to be the only remotely reliable source of security. This does not mean that the converts were insincere. Rather, in the Nez Perce way, they

saw no distinction between spiritual and temporal power, between supernatural commitment and well-being in the here and now. That equation
had been behind the journey of the "four wise men" to St. Louis in 1831.
It was behind the courtship and later the violent rejection of the early
missionaries. Now, in the present crisis, the same inclination was at work.
Some Nez Perces looked to holy men like Smohalla to turn spiritual force
against whites and their drive to domination. More, however, followed
the same impulse in the other direction, toward the Christians. That
seemed to be where the tides of power, seen and unseen, were running.[6]

In fact, when Nez Perces assumed a marriage of religion and power,
they were reading things right, though not necessarily in the terms they
thought. In the years after the Civil War, the several threads of national
policy regarding the West and its Indians came together more tightly and
coherently, and Washington worked much more vigorously to integrate
the land and peoples acquired in the great gulping of the 1840s. And in
that effort, an aggressive Christianity was an essential partner.

The Union victory in 1865 was a call for reckoning. The most obviously
pressing questions were about the South—how the defeated states were
to be readmitted to full political status and what was to be done with freed
slaves. Almost as obvious were western questions, especially regarding
Indians. Assuming they did not totter off into extinction, as some still
predicted they would, what would be their place in the confirmed nation?
How would they fit into what now was sure to be a rapidly expanding
white presence around them?

In 1865, a special congressional committee of seven, headed by Senator
James R. Doolittle of Wisconsin, toured the West to investigate the reasons behind the Indians' unrest and their deteriorating living conditions. The Doolittle Committee's alarming report led Congress to create
the Indian Peace Commission. Chaired by Nathaniel G. Taylor, commissioner of Indian affairs, it was composed of four civilians and four
army officers, including General William T. Sherman. They negotiated
two important treaties, Medicine Lodge Creek (1867) and Fort Laramie
(1868), meant to dampen conflict among the tribes, protect the overland
trails and transcontinental railroad, and open safe settlement on the newest farming frontier, in Kansas and Nebraska.

The commission's long-term goal was to devise the best strategy to
"insure civilization for the Indians and peace and safety for the whites."[7]
Its diagnosis of what it called "Indian problem" was a classic in the rhetoric of confessional conquest, echoing what James Nesmith (a commission
member) had argued to the Senate six years earlier when asking for a new

Nez Perce treaty. Recent conflicts had stemmed from the "aggression of lawless whites," corrupt agents, starvation and disease, and the government's utter failure to meet its obligations. There was no doubt where guilt lay. "Have we been uniformly unjust?" asked the Peace Commission in its report: "We answer unhesitatingly, yes."[8]

But as with Nesmith earlier, correcting injustice did not mean reversing course. It meant Indians submitting to a government that intended to stay that course but promised to do better. Washington should behave rightly and bear down on the job. It should strive, in the commission's phrase, "to conquer by kindness."[9]

This strange phrase summed up what was called Washington's Peace Policy. Peace was indeed its goal, but peace at Washington's dictation, like the peace imposed on the Confederacy. With the war won, a triumphant federal authority turned westward and took command. This policy was its blueprint. Its essentials could be summed up under three terms: mechanics, spirit, and national function.

Mechanically, Congress in 1871, only weeks after Monteith took over at Lapwai, took a hugely important step: it unilaterally ended treaty-making as the basis of its Indian relations. That year's appropriation legislation stated simply that tribes were no longer considered independent nations. From then on, Congressional law and executive orders, not negotiated arrangements, would say where Indians would live, how they would live, and what their obligations and the government's would be. The 1871 law was a breathtaking abrogation of a understanding going back to earliest contact, yet it also reflected the new reality. In the emerging new America, Indians would rapidly lose what political independence they had managed to keep before the Civil War.

As for particulars, the Peace Policy relied on reservations, precisely bounded areas where a particular native group would live and be assigned a government agent. Reservations were not new. They had first been tried in the 1850s, after expansion to the Pacific had left no place farther to push Indians out of the way, and several were operating by 1865, including those created by the Nez Perce treaties of 1855 and 1863. But the rigor and completeness of using reservations—*that* was new. Every tribe should be put on one, the commission said. The assumption was that much of the West would soon be tightly connected to the East and thickly peopled with new settlement. The need, authorities said, was both to protect white pioneers from "the terrors of wandering hostile tribes" and to save the Indians, who were sure to be "blotted out of existence, and their dust...trampled underfoot" unless they were somehow reconciled with the new order.[10] Reconciliation was a matter of Indians being taught to farm on individual homesteads and to practice basic mechanical arts, instructed in English and educational rudiments, introduced to national institutions, and converted to Christianity.

Indians were often told they could periodically hunt and gather elsewhere and could practice native religions, but reservations always were meant as factories of cultural transformation. The Indians' "haughty pride" had to be subdued, the commissioner of Indian affairs had advised as early as 1850, and their "wild energies" trained to civilization.[11] On the ground, this amounted to a relentless attack on indigenous identities—languages, family arrangements, dress and coiffures, spiritual practices, tribal loyalties, and anything else that would slow the pulling of Indians toward the cultural mainstream. Only then could they be "elevated in the scale of humanity," the secretary of the interior wrote in 1869, "and our obligation to them as fellow-men be discharged."[12]

The second key aspect of the Peace Policy was its spirit, described by the premier historian of Indian policy as "the old program rejuvenated by a crusading zeal."[13] Zealotry it was, and inspired by the cross. Senator Doolittle was an ardent Baptist who believed the United States was the chief agent of God's will. He considered the Declaration of Independence "the new gospel of man's redemption" and July 4, 1776, second in sacredness only to the day Christ was born.[14] Nathaniel Taylor, chair of the Peace Commission, was a sometime Methodist minister just as dedicated to a union of churchly efforts with federal programs to turn Indians into well-schooled farmers.

That union had been there from the start. Put into Indians' hands the primer and the plough, wrote Thomas McKenney, architect of policy in the early nineteenth century, and they will naturally turn to the Bible and then "leave the chase...and become useful members of society."[15] Conversion to Christianity and to national lifeways was all of a piece. A religious leader urged missionaries to employ "minor civilizing agencies...such as Base Ball, Croquet, &c." Without accepting Jesus, others argued, Indians would never develop insurance companies or chambers' of commerce, nor would they be truly in the faith unless they left their tipis for houses and "advanc[ed] the price of corner lots."[16]

What was new after 1865 was the level of passion for these ideas and how that passion was focused. The assault on slavery had gathered the moral energy of Christian reformers and increased hugely its wattage. What is often overlooked is how the slaves' plight was linked to that of Indians. Gerrit Smith in 1838 accused the government of twin abominations against "the two feeblest elements of our population—our aborigines and our colored brethren."[17] After Appomattox, with slavery abolished and freedpeople moving toward citizenship, activists looked more toward helping the other of Smith's "two feeblest elements" by bringing them "under the sway of Christian thought and Christian life and into touch with the people of this Christian nation." In one of the last issues of William Lloyd Garrison's *Liberator,* a letter appeared from "An Old Abolitionist" proposing that the American Anti-Slavery Society evolve into one "to promote the religious, moral, education[al] and personal good of the Indians."[18]

Congress acted out this social evangelism by creating in April 1869 the Board of Indian Commissioners, filled by the newly inaugurated president Ulysses S. Grant with ten prominent businessmen-philanthropists. All were dedicated Christian activists, and several had served on the Christian Commission, which had ministered spiritually to Union troops. Decrying the government's shameful record of deceit, corruption, murder, and broken treaties, this board in its first report called for the saving of the Indians through education, economic and cultural retooling, and especially "the religion of our blessed Saviour [which] is believed to be the most effective agent for the civilization of any people."[19]

Grant soon took the next logical step—formally marrying religion to the federal governance of the western Indians. Following a suggestion by a delegation from the Society of Friends (Quakers), he began replacing reservation agents, many of them political hacks, with missionaries. By 1872, nearly a dozen denominations had provided agents to more than a quarter million Indians on more than seventy agencies.[20] Methodists presided over more than fifty thousand persons, Baptists more than forty thousand, and Roman Catholics just under twenty thousand. Even the Unitarians had two agencies with nearly four thousand residents. The Presbyterians, with nearly forty thousand charges, were mostly in Indian Territory and the Southwest, but they had one assignment in the Northwest—Monteith's agency at Lapwai.

The third essential of the Peace Policy was how it meant to remake the nation. Once the eastern crisis of disunion was resolved, Washington was able to look more to the West, particularly to the thousands of Indians living far outside the generous circumference of American culture. Removal was no longer an option, short of loading them on ships, and it was obvious that whites and Indians would soon be rubbing shoulders, and cultures, in the remotest corners of the West. A few, mostly western locals, had a simple answer: kill them all. But true genocide, the formally sanctioned physical destruction of a people, was never remotely considered by anyone with any significant power. The answer instead was the Peace Policy. The goal was the "disintegration of tribes" and the birth of new identity, so that each separate people, imbued with patriotism and loving the flag, would "feel that the United States, not some paltry reservation, is their home."[23] The rhetoric was often redemptive. Richard Henry Pratt, founder of Carlisle Indian School, compared education there to full immersion baptism—saving the lost by holding them under until born again into higher life. Other metaphors were less benign. The renowned abolitionist Henry Ward Beecher wrote of common schools as the nation's stomachs in which the lesser were absorbed into the greater: "When a lion eats an ox, the lion does not become an ox but an ox becomes a lion."[21]

The Peace Policy overlay the victorious Union's answers to another problem—bringing into the national family another people, the newly freed slaves in that other troublesome region, the South. Emancipation left freedpeople in limbo, "neither citizen nor alien," as an agent later described Indians, and like Indians needing "to be civilized, citizenized, and made an integral part of the body politic."[22] Federal programs down South and those out West on reservations were paired efforts that used the same formula, education plus agrarianism plus religion, to integrate these two previously excluded populations into the new America.

The great difference, of course, was in the populations' response. Southern freedpeople wanted what the government was giving. They were already Christians. They welcomed schooling for their children. They hoped to work farms (their own, not someone else's). Some western Indians also reached toward what Washington was extending to them. Many, however, did not. They chose to stay with lives that had long sustained them, physically and culturally and spiritually.

The result was a deepening rift between those living by the old ways and those by the new. So it was in Nez Perce country. As the white threat became ever more obvious, and as John Monteith established the first effective federal presence, hundreds of Nez Perces converted to Christianity and turned toward the new life. Some surely acted on something like Monteith's terms, others out of the belief that a holy man's ability to shape events arose from his spiritual powers, so finding protection in the first meant aligning with the second. By 1876, those who held to traditional ways found themselves increasingly beleaguered. During the gold rush, they had seen the Nez Perces become a minority in their native land. Now they were a minority within that minority. They felt increasingly threatened, and for good reasons, for there was one option the government never considered—simply letting Indians alone to live as they wished.

In 1865, the government that had preserved the nation set out to create a truer union, one with the lumps smoothed out. Indians would not be allowed to arrest its progress, the Peace Commission assured Congress.

Cultural retooling was an order, not an offer. Violence, paradoxically, was always part of the Peace Policy. As Sherman put it, Indians would be treated by a "double process, of peace *within* their reservation and war *without*."[24]

John Monteith agreed. Soon after his arrival at Lapwai in 1871, word came of the first confrontations between whites and Nez Perces in Old Joseph's Wallowa valley. He would look for a peaceful way out of that and later conflicts, but Sherman's option was always in the wings, and Monteith was ready to bring down the whip of kindness.

And yet against the Nez Perces the policy of kindly conquest moved in stutter-step. Those in power pressed, then pulled back, then pressed again. It's hard to avoid the feeling that when it came to applying their grand principles to the particular people in front of them, they found themselves with doubts. Their erratic course toward a final showdown raises a nagging question: could things have gone differently?

Most of the nontreaty Nez Perces were in five bands.[25] The Alpowais lived among the upper Nez Perces along the Clearwater River. Their headman was Looking Glass, son of the man of the same name who had almost scuttled the treaty of 1855. Renowned as a hunter and warrior, he was also known as Alalimya Takanin—a name that referred to a benign "spirit-formed man" who rode a high wind, always east or west.[26] To the west of this group lived the Wawawai band, an amalgam of the Nez Perce and Palouse peoples, in two villages, one at the junction of the Palouse and Snake Rivers and the other upstream on the Snake. Their leader, Hahtalekin, lived in the first village, while another prominent figure, the great orator Husishusis Kute (Naked Head), lived with the second. To the south of these two, along a creek flowing from the east into the Salmon River, lived a large band known traditionally as the Lamatama, which in the 1870s more commonly took its name from its headman, White Bird (Peopeo Kiskiok Hihih; more accurately, White Goose). These three were the nontreaty bands in closest contact with whites—the farmers, ranchers, merchants, and squatters who had been drawn to the Clearwater, Snake, and Salmon valleys.

The other two bands were more isolated, and so less directly threatened. One lived between the Salmon and Snake rivers, in rugged mountainous country that held little appeal for whites. It was identified with its leader Toohoolhoolzote, a *tewat* whose name was probably a Flathead word meaning "sound" or "noise." The last band, the largest of the five, was identified with Old Joseph. They lived west of the Salmon and Snake rivers in far eastern Oregon. They spent the harsh winters in the sheltering canyons of the Imnaha River and in summer shifted to the west to the lush pastureland at the foot of the Wallowa Mountains.

Old Joseph's Wallowa country would turn out to be the sparking point of the war of 1877. At first glance, that might seem understandable. Rich in grasses from April to September, fed by the Wallowa and Grande Ronde rivers, graced by the lovely Wallowa Lake and above it mountains like ragged teeth, it was, and is, as beautiful as any place in the West. Seen only in summer, it would appear a rancher's heaven. In 1843 Henry Spalding had not seen but had heard of its splendid valleys, with sweeps of white clover and streams of cold, clear water—beautiful country, he wrote, and perhaps fit for farming, although he acknowledged it was surrounded by mountains and "may be frosty."[27] In fact, winters brought storms and deep cold. Living there in the white way, year-round on the same piece of ground instead of heading for canyons, was not impossible but was close to it, especially since the Wallowa was cut off from connecting points like Lewiston by canyons, rivers, and mountains. Nonetheless, the area's untested appeal guaranteed that at some point there would be strong interest.

After the treaty of 1863, Old Joseph had set up a makeshift boundary, marked by tall poles anchored in stone cairns, around his home country. Inside that perimeter, all his people had been born, Young Joseph remembered his father saying: "It circles around the graves of our fathers, and we will never give up these graves to any man."[28] By 1867, government surveyors had come in and laid out eleven townships ("the wigwam of the savage will…give way…[to] a thriving and busy population," their leader predicted), but four years later there were still no takers.[29] In the summer of 1871, a few whites finally breached Joseph's boundary to build cabins, pasture sheep and cattle, and put up wild hay.[30] That August, the old man died and was succeeded as headman by his son, now thirty-one. Eight years later Young Joseph, later known as Chief Joseph, told of his father's last entreaty:

> When I am gone, think of your country. You are the chief of these people. They look to you to guide them. Always remember that your father never sold his country. You must stop your ears whenever you are asked to sign a treaty selling your home. A few years more, and white men will be all around you. They have their eyes on this land. My son, never forget my dying words. This country holds your father's body. Never sell the bones of your father and your mother.

Young Joseph took the words to heart: "A man who would not love his father's grave is worse than a wild animal."[31]

But signs of change were quickening. More families arrived the next spring with large herds and wagonloads of house-stuffings, and with them came the first whiskey sellers. Joseph pledged his friendship to these people but insisted they had no right to the Wallowa, and when settlers called in John Monteith, recently arrived at Lapwai, the agent listened to Joseph and admitted to having grave doubts that whites had any right to be there. Nor, however, did he have authority to evict them. This was Joseph's first dealing with white authorities as chief of the Wallowas, and he finally agreed to allow some limited homesteading, "thinking then that we could have peace," he said later; "we were mistaken."[32]

The next five years, 1871–76, had to have been even more confusing than usual to Joseph and other nontreaty leaders. Authorities like Monteith, men utterly devoted to the idea that Indians must conform to white culture, still vacillated over whether the Nez Perces should be allowed to stay where they were. Soon after his visit, for instance, Monteith wrote Washington that the valley should never have been opened to whites and if possible even now it should be preserved for the Nez Perces. In March 1873, he and T. B. Odeneal, Oregon's superintendent of Indian affairs, advised buying out white settlers in the Wallowa, for "if any respect is to be paid to the laws and customs of the Indians," Joseph's people were not bound by the treaty of 1863. If any homesteading was allowed, they wrote, it should be confined to the lower (northern) portion of the valley. The Nez Perces then could have, unmolested, the upper (southern) part for summer hunting and pasturing.

On June 9, 1873, ten years to the day after the disputed treaty had been signed, President Grant issued an executive order that presumably set up that division. Except it didn't. Apparently, some blundering clerk essentially reversed the reserved grazing regions, putting the Nez Perces squarely in the most accessible area and giving whites the higher, colder, more remote country. The botched order could not have been better designed to displease everyone. For the first time, warriors and ranchers collided over summer pasture and drifting stock. And into the fray jumped politicians and editors in Oregon and Washington who railed against any thought of closing any Indian lands anywhere to settlement. In a widely published letter to the secretary of the interior, Oregon's governor, LaFayette Grover, demanded that the authorities reject "the caprices of untutored savages" lest the Wallowa be denied the fruits of cultivation. Claiming, untruthfully, that most chiefs had signed the treaty of 1863, he went on to say: *"Joseph's band do not desire Wallowa Valley for a Reservation and for a home."*[33]

This was clever cant. Joseph indeed was not asking for a reservation; he asked only to be left alone. And by long-established European standards, how his people lived there could not create a true "home" but could only, in Grover's terms, "gratify a wild roaming disposition."[34] The main punch of his argument, however, reminded readers of a double threat. In northern California the previous fall, the Modoc Indians had fought a costly, protracted war arising from a strikingly similar situation. Learn from that trouble, Grover argued, and force the issue here before it gets out of hand. Then came his most telling point. Joseph and the nontreaties argued that agreements made by other Nez Perce chiefs had nothing to do with them. But all treaty-making, Grover wrote, began with the assumption that Indians were grouped into tribes, each with one authoritative spokesman. Step back from that, admit that Joseph's band was independent, and a whole fabric of agreements would unravel, "for there exists hardly a treaty with Indians west of the Rocky Mountains in which all the sub-chiefs and head men joined, and against which they have not positively protested." Monteith had written that Joseph's band could not be bound by the treaty of 1863 "if any respect is to be paid to the laws and customs of the Indians." That was precisely why respect should *not* be paid, Grover answered. Admit this one case, and there will follow across the West "a general dissatisfaction." Rework this one treaty and the same "will have to be...carried out as to all."[35]

In September 1873, Monteith reversed his position. All nontreaties should be forced onto the reservation "at as early a day as possible," he wrote his superior. When Joseph warned of rising tension, he was bewildered to hear the agent upbraid the Indians for causing it. As more whites entered the Wallowa, younger men for the first time talked of armed resistance, but at a gathering of all nontreaty bands the headmen counseled patience. A tense peace continued. Stress increased in the spring of 1875 when word arrived that Grant had rescinded his order dividing the valley, thus opening it freely to white settlement. Once again the nontreaties met to consider fighting back, now with a few prominent leaders in support. Joseph and others again argued successfully to keep the peace.

Then came another reversal. In early September 1874. one of the story's central figures had made his entrance: Brigadier General Oliver Otis Howard had arrived at Fort Vancouver as the new commander of the Department of the Columbia. After long service and a mixed record in the Civil War, and losing his right arm at the battle of Fair Oaks, Howard had headed the Freedmen's Bureau in the South and then had served in the Southwest, securing the surrender of the Chiricahua Apache leader Cochise before being sent to the Northwest.[36] In the summer of 1875, Howard sent two companies under Captain Stephen Whipple to keep order in the Wallowa valley and to gauge the situation. Whipple found the Nez Perces to be "proud-spirited, self-supporting and intelligent," and several conversations with Joseph convinced him that his band was "a somewhat separate and independent community" unbound by the treaty of 1863. Wallowa winters were too cold for year-round pasturing, he thought, and local whites wanted mostly to be bought out. Howard listened. In his formal report, he advised Washington to "let these really peaceable Indians...have this poor valley for their own."[37]

Soon afterward, Howard told another aide, Captain Henry Clay Wood, trained in the law, to give an attorney's eye to Joseph's situation. Wood's remarkable report appeared as a pamphlet in January 1876. It not only dismantled Washington's claim for the Wallowa; it cut the ground from under the argument the government had used for more than thirty years to impose its will.[38] The Nez Perces were no tribe but a confederacy of bands, each with an identity rooted in its immediate area. There had never been a head chief until Elijah White had "virtually appointed" one in 1842, and the man now given that title, Lawyer, enjoyed only the "semi-assent" of a few bands. When the gold rush had brought a flood of "the very worst whites," the government had tried to control the crisis with the 1863 treaty, but the result instead was a "radical separation" between those for and against it.[39]

Still and all, given that the Nez Perces were now within a modern nation, shouldn't they all have to hew to what Washington said had been agreed? Here, Wood turned his government's argument back on itself. If the Nez Perces had fully owned their land, then like any "high contracting power" they would have to speak through one leader and all bands would have to go along.[40] But, as Washington had said for decades, Indians were not sovereign, only "semi-civilized" people with only a right of occupancy. According to the government's own terms, the rules for modern nations did not apply. Exactly because Washington had denied that the Nez Perces owned the land they lived on, Washington was obliged to respect the rules of their "semi-civilized" way of life, which left authority with the bands, not with Lawyer or any other fictional common authority. The conclusion was clear: "The non-treaty Nez Perces cannot in law...be bound by the treaty of 1863."[41] Legally speaking, every attempt to take Joseph's people out of the Wallowa should be null and void.

After leading readers through a dense legal thicket, Wood shifted in tone and topic to an impassioned assault on events unfolding elsewhere in the West:

In the Black Hills, with the Sioux Indians, the same policy of violated pledges is to-day having its inception. The wrongs suffered, the sacred treaty obligations disregarded, the insults, outrages, and

political crimes heaped upon the Nez Perces nation, are re-enact-
ing towards the Sioux. If our Government cannot keep its plighted
faith, even with the Indians, if it has no sense of honor left, the civilized nations of the globe will not be slow to find it out, and when
they do, there is a reason to fear a chapter in our history remains to
be written which mankind shall tremble to read.[42]

Six months later, in late June 1876, the Sioux crisis led to their crushing
victory over George Custer on the Little Big Horn. Simultaneously, in
the Wallowa valley, another confrontation began a chain of events that
led to war with the Nez Perces. A farmer named A. B. Findley suspected
(incorrectly) that the Nez Perces had stolen four of his horses. He and
another white, Wells McNall, approached a camp of Nez Perse hunters,
its trees strung with deer carcasses, and when a scuffle broke out between
McNall and the youthful Wilhautyah (Wind Blowing), McNall called
out for Findley to kill Wilhautyah (saying "Shoot the Son of a B———,"
Findley later told his son).[43] Findley hesitated, then fired and killed the
young warrior. By Nez Perce accounts, the slaying was unprovoked; by
white accounts, Findley feared being shot. With that, the two settlers rode
away.

   This was big trouble. Agent Monteith scrambled to assure Joseph that
Findley and McNall would be tried. Howard sent Major Wood to evaluate the situation. He met with Joseph and his younger brother Ollokut
(Frog), an esteemed warrior and Joseph's close confidant. When Joseph
said that the valley was "more sacred to him than ever before" and that
whites would have to go, Wood expressed his sympathy and pled for
restraint. Joseph kept his people in check, but after ten weeks without
an arrest, he and Ollokut announced that whites had a week to leave the
Wallowa. As the situation quickly escalated—white volunteers came
from the Grand Ronde valley and at one point warriors, stripped and
painted for war, laid siege to settlers in a cabin—Howard sent forty-eight
cavalry under Lieutenant Albert G. Forse to do what he could.[44]

   The war came within a wink of starting there. Joseph prevented it.
Little is known of him during his youth and how he might have been cultivated for the role of headman he assumed from his father. Yellow Bull,
a close friend who would deliver an oration at his death, later said that
he had once been "a drinking and carousing sort" and generally judged
less able than his brother Ollokut.[45] Whatever his earlier vices, however, at thirty-one he had matured into a leader of measured judgment
who clearly commanded respect. In the crisis of the moment, he faced a
dilemma he seems to have been coached on for years, "a heavy load on

my back since I was a boy," as he later put it. He knew that whites on the Plateau were so many that his people could not hold their own: "We were like deer. They were like grizzly bears." And yet as pressures and insults mounted, so did the odds for some flare-up. "Our young men were quick-tempered," he said, "and I have had great trouble in keeping them from doing rash things."[46]

The murder of Wilhautyah and the authorities' foot-dragging had pushed matters to the edge, and had Forse confronted the warriors with all his men, things might well have turned ugly, but on the morning of September 10, Joseph's deadline, Forse rode with only two guides to meet the headman. Joseph vented his frustration, but when Forse again promised that something would be done, he acceded and agreed to keep his people well to the south, away from whites, and at the end of the meeting he had his men form a single rank and empty their weapons as a show of faith. Forse sent away the white volunteers, positioned his men to keep the peace, and a few days later told Joseph that Findley and McNall had surrendered in the town of Union. Ironically, the trial came to nothing. McNall was set loose on grounds of self-defense, and Findley was acquitted of manslaughter after the two Nez Perce witnesses failed to show up. (Findley showed increasing sympathy for the Nez Perces, and by one account he later regularly hosted Walhautyah's widow at his house.)[47] As winter approached, the Nez Perces withdrew to the canyons of the Imnaha. Tensions eased.

In fact, Joseph's band and the other nontreaties probably felt hopeful that their situation might soon be settled favorably. During his visit, Major Wood had reported that Howard would ask for a government commission to resolve matters, and word arrived that fall that indeed commissioners were on the way for a council. Over the past two years, Wood, Whipple, and Howard had all concluded that the treaty of 1863 had no hold over the nontreaties and that Joseph's people were best left alone in the Wallowa. The resisters had heard the same even on the reservation. Monteith earlier had fired a minister and teacher who had repeatedly told nonreservation bands that the treaty had no force over them "but would allow them to remain where they are."[48] Now Howard was convening a council. Joseph and the others might naturally presume that it at least would seriously consider confirming their right to keep their lands.

But not so. Howard, like Monteith and others before him, had flipped his position. Just a year earlier, he had written in the public record that Joseph's band should "have this poor valley for their own." Now he was ready to say that they, and all nontreaties, had to concede. They must give up their homelands and their way of life and come into the reservation.

What flipped Howard? Part of the reason was probably timing. As the crisis in the Wallowa coincided with the humiliation at the hands of the Sioux in Montana, the predictable response was to stand very tough against any Indians, past friendliness aside. Another part of the reason was probably Howard himself. He had converted to a zealous, evangelical Christianity during the Seminole War and had followed that spiritual charge into the Civil War. As head of the Freedmen's Bureau, he had turned his religious zeal to ushering slaves out of bondage. Then he was sent West. "The Creator had placed him on earth to be the Moses to the Negro," his bitter rival George Crook wrote of Howard telling him, and now, having finished that job, "he felt satisfied his next mission was with the Indian."[49] Whether one sees him as dedicated or sanctimonious and prissy or both, it's clear that Howard felt called to press all Indians, dangerous or not, into lives he thought best for them.

There was also a deeper reason. As postwar Washington set out to consolidate the nation into a tighter, truer union, its efforts out West simply had no developed option that would leave room for people like the Nez Perces—historically friendly and utterly unthreatening but living by ways well outside the national mainstream—to live as they wanted while still being part of that new union. Some official like Howard might begin by saying some peaceable people should be left alone in some "poor valley," but then came pressure to open that valley up, and then some nasty business like the killing of Wilhautyah to force a decision. At that point, authorities had no structure of ideas to accommodate anything but pulling Indians onto some reservation. Language changed. "Sympathy" and "fairness" took on new meanings. Honest men and women, sympathizing with the deplorable things happening to Indians, insisted that they be fairly paid for their land and fairly supported as they built new lives. But whether Indians *would* surrender their land and change their lives—that was not in the discussion. When people like the Nez Perce resisters stuck to their claims, the reaction of authorities like Howard was to feel dismayed, frustrated, and, in a deeply strange inversion, betrayed.

This was the mood waiting for the sixty or seventy members of the Wallowa band when they rode into the Lapwai agency "with military precision and order" on November 13, 1876. Joseph was leading them. Supporters and opponents alike agreed that he was a striking figure in these years. At about six feet two inches, he was taller than most Nez Perces. Later, he would turn portly, but now he was strongly built with powerful shoulders and chest. He wore his hair long, braided on the sides and rising in a rearing sweep in front, the sign of his commitment as a Dreamer. Most would remark on his face—broad, with well-defined features, large dark eyes, and a high, candid forehead. It was a face that

**Figure 6.1** Heinmot Tooyalakekt, Chief Joseph, in 1877

conveyed calm and confidence, open and unthreatening yet revealing lit-tle—a diplomat's face.

Joseph and his delegation met with specially appointed commis-sioners—Howard, Wood, David H. Jerome, William Stickney, and A. C. Barstow. Jerome was nominally the chair, but neither he nor the other two civilians had any experience in Indian affairs, and none had ever been near Nez Perce country. They could be expected to follow Howard's lead, and they did. Their marching orders were clear. They were to settle all Nez Perces on the 1863 reservation, with orders straight from President Grant, Monteith's wife later recalled, "to 'make it final!' "[50] The one-day meeting was held in the agency church.

If Joseph had any hopes for a favorable hearing, they were immediately slapped down.[51] The commissioners took a position as extreme and rigid as any the government had ever taken. They claimed that the resistant bands were bound by the treaty of 1863, something both Wood and Howard had rejected less than a year earlier. Joseph stood firm. He showed "an alertness and dexterity in intellectual fencing" that the commissioners found "quite remarkable," and when stating his beliefs his "serious and feeling manner" was impressive.[52] He stayed calm. Rather than refute the claims point by point, he kept to higher, spiritual ground and spoke out of the Dreamer tradition. God's earth "should be allowed to remain as then [i.e., as first] made." He was content to live on its natural fruits and asked nothing from the government: "He was able to take care of himself." The "Creative Power" had made the land indivisible, and where he lived was "sacred to his affections," and so was inalienable. He was child to the place where he was born, and leaving it "would be to part with himself." The commissioners pressed him repeatedly, saying finally that in refusing he "placed himself in antagonism to the government, whose government extended from ocean to ocean." Again and again he replied that he would not, could not, sell the Wallowa.[53]

The meeting ended in such high tension that the Nez Perce translator feared a cross word might spark violence. Once safely away, the commission recommended that troops quickly occupy the Wallowa and that nontreaties be pressed to settle on the reservation (with due compensation). If they didn't agree within a reasonable time, the army must put them there by force. As their first recommendation, however, they urged that Dreamer holy men be quieted. Called wizards and magicians, they were said to spread "fanaticism," "pernicious doctrines," and "new-fangled religious delusion" incompatible with the government's plans.[54] The last point, at least, was right enough. The three prongs of the campaign to absorb the Indians—farming, schooling, and Christianization—were incompatible with Dreamer beliefs; as the commissioners wrote, the Dreamers viewed all three as "crimes from which they shrink." The impasse was as much spiritual as political.[55]

Early in January 1877, the secretary of the interior approved the commission's recommendations and ordered them enforced. Now the gun was loaded and cocked, but no one seemed ready to fire it. Monteith set a ridiculously early deadline and then backed off from it. Howard told two companies to get ready to occupy the Wallowa but gave no order to move. Do everything *"in the interest of peace,"* the secretary of war wrote him. Removal was the agency's job, he added, and the army's was *"merely protecting and aiding them."*[56] Meanwhile, Joseph and Ollokut stalled and probed for openings. Ollokut visited Monteith at Lapwai. He denied rumors that the Nez Perces were planning war. Again he pled that whites and Indians all could live in this country, each in their own way. The same being had created whites and Indians and had made the earth for them all. All could work that earth and grow happy. "I have eyes and a heart and can see...that if we fight we would have to leave all and go into the mountains," he told Monteith: "I love my wife and children and could not leave them. I have always been a friend of the whites and will not fight them." Monteith answered that the government wanted all Nez Perces to live on the reservation and "eventually get rich." And you, he told Ollokut confidently, "could plow as well as any Indian."[57]

Ollokut tried another move. He had heard that Howard was to visit Lapwai in early May. Could they meet then? Monteith raised the idea with Howard, who was pleased. Skittish about forcing a crisis, determined that "the Indian Bureau should take the initiative in dealing with these Indians," he welcomed the chance to meet with the resisters with Monteith on Monteith's turf.[58]

"I have been talking to the whites for many years about the lands in question," Joseph had said back in January, "and it is strange they cannot understand me."[59] The meeting at Lapwai would be the last chance to make the case.

Joseph and a contingent of Wallowas rode as a column into Lapwai's army post on May 3, 1877. The men wore brightly colored blankets over beaded buckskins. Their faces and the partings of their hair were painted red, and their hair was braided and tied with colorful cloth. Next came women, also in bright blankets and shawls. As they approached, they all began a song, a "wild sound...shrill and searching, sad, like a wail, and yet defiant at its close," Howard wrote, and they continued to sing as they rode around the entire fenced square of the post. The high-pitched chant was refracted by the buildings into "irregular burblings of sound." Howard was glad there were fifty of them, not five hundred.[60]

This meeting was to be with all five larger bands that still denied the 1863 treaty, and Howard and Monteith were determined to pull onto the reservation the four living off of it. Whipple had set off the day before with two companies from Fort Walla Walla to establish a post in the Wallowa, and that morning Monteith had written formally to ask Howard to round up any bands that resisted giving up their land. Whatever the nontreaty leaders might have expected, that is, the general and the agent were not interested in give-and-take, only take. They showed their muscle at the meeting site. The council would be in an enlarged hospital tent with the sides looped up, which allowed cooling breezes but also gave the visitors clear view of two neighboring buildings—the guard house and the barracks full of soldiers. Joseph sat down there with Howard and Monteith on May 3, but because the other resistant leaders had not arrived, he would not engage. They came the next day, and the serious talk began.

It began with a surprise. So far in the current crisis Joseph had taken the lead, partly because his land was most contested but also because his cool, measured skills made him the best choice. This time, however, the headmen had chosen as their spokesman Toohoolhoolzote, leader of the band living between the Snake and Salmon rivers. He was physically imposing, stocky and deep-chested and powerful (by one story he once carried two killed bucks home on his shoulders), with a deep, gravelly voice. He was a good bit older than Joseph. He was both a respected warrior and a *tewat,* a committed Dreamer. Joseph in council was firm but calm and smooth, a word-dancer who could frustrate his adversaries without confronting them; Toohoolhoolzote was brusque, and his emotions were much closer to the surface. He was more openly unbending, and when angry he radiated hostility. Howard later called him the "growler of growlers" and "an ugly, obstinate savage of the worst type."[61] Howard and Toohoolhoolzote did not get along.

Probably the nontreaties put Toohoolhoolzote up front because he would defend most tenaciously what they could not compromise—living on their home ground. By doing that, they also set up the clearest possible polarity of perspectives. In one account of the meeting, Toohoolhoolzote says:

> Howard, I understand you to say you have instructions from *Washington* to move all the Nez Perce Nation to the reserve. You are always talking about Washington. I would like to know who Washington is. Is he a Chief, or a common man, or a house, or a place? Every time you have a council you speak of Washington. Leave Mr. Washington, that is if he is a man, alone. He has no sense. He does not know anything about our country. He never was here.[62]

The inclination is to read this as intentional irony, the old Dreamer rhetorically pulling Howard's beard. But Toohoolhoolzote's band had been the most isolated of the Nez Perces, living in the rugged mountains between deep, swift rivers, country virtually unvisited by whites, and Toohoolhoolzote had taken little role in meetings with whites over the past few years. Whether or not he honestly puzzled if Washington was a man or a cabin, he was largely a naïf when it came to white ways of thinking. Just as Howard and Monteith were taking the government's most extreme position, demanding full Nez Perce submission to the new life, they faced the chief least acquainted with their world and most devoted to what opposed it.

The meetings were on May 4 and 7, a Friday and Monday. Joseph sat silent, and White Bird hid his face behind a feather fan. The exchanges were almost all between Howard and Toohoolhoolzote, and most fell along two lines. One concerned authority. Howard set down the standard claim—that all the bands were part of one tribe, and thus all were subject to the 1863 treaty, and so those still off the reservation would have to come in. Toohoolhoolzote answered that he had "heard about a bargain, a trade between some of these Indians [the reservation bands] and the white man concerning their land," but it had nothing to do with him and his people. Joseph later summed up his point in the simple language of the marketplace:

> Suppose a white man should come to me and say, "Joseph, I like your horses, and I want to buy them." I say to him, "No my horses suit me, I will not sell them." Then he goes to my neighbor and says to him, "Joseph has some good horses. I want to buy them, but he refuses to sell." My neighbor answers, "Pay me the money, and I will sell you Joseph's horses." The white man returns to me and says, "Joseph, I have bought your horses, and you must let me have them." If we sold our lands to the Government, this is the way they were bought.[63]

Howard's larger claim was that the Nez Perces, as part of that one tribe, lived as well inside one nation, a new structure of continent-wide power. "We are all subjects," he told Toohoolhoolzote, "children of a common government and must obey its requirements." This the old man seemed to find bizarre, and he bristled especially at the language. Children cannot think for themselves, he said, and we are no children: "The government at Washington shall not think for us."[64] Toohoolhoolzote in fact seemed to narrow his definition of authority to the individual level, as was traditional among Nez Perces, with no person ultimately given power over another. He spoke mostly in the first person and in one account proposed to Howard: "Let us settle the matter between you and me."[65]

The second line of talk was essentially religious. "His first remark was about the law of the earth," Howard wrote of Toohoolhoolzote's opening, and by that law "he belonged to the land out of which he came." Any arrangement that would surrender homeland and lead to farming, cutting into and profaning the Earth Mother, "*wasn't true law* at all." True law held that his people and their land were inseparable. Joseph had said something like this to the commissioners—that the earth had what the interpreter had translated as "chieftainship," meaning law, authority, or control.[66] The idea in both cases seems to have been close to the Greek term *logos,* for the fundamental order of all that is. For Toohoolhoolzote and Joseph, disengaging from that underlying order of things, the Earth Mother, went beyond self-destruction. It meant cutting loose from meaning itself.

Howard did not challenge anything Toohoolhoolzote said. He simply ignored it, as if putting up with someone tossing dust. Later he lumped and dismissed it all as a "flourish of words," "this sort of talk," and "the usual words." He considered it an extended stall against the inevitable.

Toohoolhoolzote repeated his position over and over in his raspy baritone. Howard repeatedly said the Nez Perces must come to terms and give up their lands. Each man grew increasingly frustrated. Howard also grew anxious. Looking Glass and White Bird were openly agreeing with the Dreamer, and even the reservation Nez Perces who looked on from outside the tent appeared edgy. Finally, on Monday afternoon when the old man invoked the law of the earth once again, Howard's strained patience snapped. "Twenty times over I hear that the earth is your mother," he said: "I want to hear it no more, but come to business at once."

Things quickly escalated. The *tewat,* "more impudent than ever," spoke again of the land and ridiculed the notion that white men could measure the earth and parcel out its parts: "What person pretended to divide the land and put me on it?" Howard answered: "I am that man. I stand here for the President, and there is no spirit, good or bad, that will hinder me." Then came the final face-off:

| | |
|---|---|
| Howard: | "Then you do not propose to comply with the orders?" |
| Toohoolhoolzote: | "So long as the earth keeps me, I want to be left alone; you are trifling with the law of the earth." |
| Howard: | "…the question is, will the Indians come peaceably on the reservation, or do they want me to put them there by force?" |
| Toohoolhoolzote: | "I never gave the Indians authority to give away my land." |

Howard:             "Do you speak for yourself?"
Toohoolhoolzote:    "The Indians may do as they like, but I am NOT
                    going on the reservation."[67]

According to another Nez Perce present, the Dreamer used a more vivid expression of manly independence: "I have a prick and I will not go on the reservation."[68]

Howard stepped forward. He upbraided Toohoolhoolzote for his "bad advice" and told him he would see him sent to Indian Territory "if it takes years and years," and then he and another officer each took one of the old man's arms and hustled him, unresisting, to the nearby guardhouse.

The other headmen sat and watched, seemingly cowed. Howard asked if they would now go to choose where they would live on the reservation, and after a few moments they nodded. The next morning, Joseph, White Bird, and Looking Glass rode with Howard, an interpreter, and a few soldiers up the Clearwater River to begin the selection. Looking Glass's band already lived in the reserve, and over the next few days the other two leaders chose land near him to settle their people. Placing the other two bands—those of the jailed Toohoolhoolzote and the Palouse along the Snake River, whose outspoken Dreamer Husishusis Kute (Naked Head) Howard thought showed "symptoms of treachery"—would come later.

The final meeting was on May 14. Toohoolhoolzote, wearing a white shirt given him by a soldier, was again there; Howard would not try to send him to Indian Territory. Now the general delivered a final, stunning order. Joseph's, White Bird's, and Toohoolhoolzote's bands had thirty days to move to the reservation; because the Palouse lived farther away, they had an extra five days. The deadlines were wildly impractical. Besides dismantling their lives and gathering belongings, and giving farewells to their homes, they would have to round up many hundreds of cattle and horses and, for two of the bands, somehow get them across the Snake and Salmon rivers at their highest, roughest time of year. But Howard wouldn't bend.

The next day, the bands set off for the homes they would have to abandon by June 15. What that move would mean, living day to day, they could not have known, although John Monteith had blocked out the specifics the previous November. Because of "their cruel habits in the slaughtering," he would issue them "beef on the block," already butchered, as well as flour and some other basics, but no coffee, tea, or sugar, "because the more they get the more they want." The men would get pants, shirts, and coats, but no blankets; the women shawls, stockings, and denim dresses, but no "fancy goods." Families pressed to farm would get hoes, plows, and other tools but no oxen, since they would only butcher them (no doubt barbarously)—only mules, branded so they could not be sold. Finally, Monteith wrote, he strongly favored undercutting any headmen who still commanded any authority. Any money should go not to them but to the agent, who would hire a "select police force [from among the Nez Perces] & detail them to make arrests and perform other such services as he may deem necessary."[69]

Five months before Howard gave the nontreaties their deadline, their future agent was setting out in detail how they would live—what work they would do, what they would eat and wear, who among their own would lead them and see that it was all done right. "I want to hear...no more" of the Earth Mother, Howard had said, "but come to business at once." This was the business he meant.

Howard left Lapwai thinking the council such a success, he wrote his brother, that he was inspired to force a similar arrangement on other "nomads & wanderers" among the Umatillas and Yakimas, "else the others will be discontented and think we do not tell the truth." Riding out with Joseph and White Bird to choose their new homes, he found them relaxed and cheerful, seemingly relieved that he had forced the issue by arresting Toohoolhoolzote. Looking Glass, he thought, felt "real joy" at how things were turning out.[70]

Nez Perce memories could hardly be more different. The showdown at Lapwai left them jumpy and fearful. They had clear standards of behavior for such councils. "Showing the rifle" by displaying weapons and talking of force was anathema, and by those terms Howard having soldiers and an armed guard nearby was a grave provocation. "General Howard was just pricking [us] with needles," Yellow Wolf said later. Actually using force, as when Howard seized Toohoolhoolzote and muscled him to his cell, was a breach far beyond the pale. "That was what brought war," Yellow Wolf recalled; "the arrest of this chief and showing us the rifle!"[71] When they next learned that troops had been sent to the Wallowa, they strongly suspected an immediate attack.[72]

When faced by "malignity and noisy opposition," Howard wrote elsewhere, "fearless sternness always produced the most wholesome and immediate consequences."[73] What he did at Lapwai did have consequences, and nearly immediately. Nobody, however, would call them wholesome. As the bands left Lapwai, heading off to uproot themselves from their mother country, it was with a mix of grief, rage, and despair. Their feelings were at a high simmer, close to a roil.

# PART II

# CHAPTER 7

# "It Will Have to Be War!"

During the first days of June 1877, members of all five nontreaty bands gathered near present-day Tolo Lake, about eight miles south of the 1863 reservation boundary. The place was called Tepahlewam (Split Rocks or Deep Cuts). It had always been a favored camping place in early summer. It had fresh water, good pasture, and ample camas bulbs for women to dig and dry—ideal conditions for congregating and socializing before fanning out over the country in the warm months ahead. Deep memories of abundance and free-roaming independence must have given the 1877 gathering a terrible resonance.

Eventually, about six hundred persons were there. The number is worth noting. Fewer than two hundred of these were men (the figure 191 is often given), and probably about half of those were of prime warrior age.[1] More would join as the war progressed, and in a crunch others, men not usually given to warfare and those older and younger than fighting prime, would take up arms. Still, at the peak of their strength, the Nez Perces' military punch would not exceed 250 fighters, and at most engagements it was far below that.[2]

The early summer gathering traditionally was a time when leaders of the bands met and consulted, and so they did now, but now the talk around camp was inflamed and quarrelsome, with much questioning of the decisions at Lapwai. Looking Glass repeatedly warned the other leaders to rein in the angrier elements in their bands. The question will always be open whether all the nontreaty Nez Perces would have bent to Howard's order—whether all, as they literally looked over the edge into a physically and culturally constricted life, would have traveled those last eight miles to the north and crossed into the reservation by June 15. A few points, however, are clear. Most nontreaties had left their homes and assembled just outside the boundary. (Looking Glass's band was already in compliance, having returned on June 10 to their home inside the reservation.) No leaders had openly said they would defy the agreement, Howard's later claims to the contrary, and Joseph and Ollokut, leaders of the largest band, showed every indication of keeping it. Yet the general mood was somber and tense, and many, especially among the younger men, were edgy and rancorous and feeling bitterly wronged.

That was the atmosphere on June 13 when White Bird's band held a *tel-lik-leen,* a ceremony in which men rode their horses in a circle around the camp as they recounted their triumphs in past battles. When whites learned of what they called this "grand parade," they feared it was in preparation for war.[3] The ceremony, however, was a traditional salute to collective history and to past and present warriors. In the circumstances, it may have been meant as a peaceful outlet for resentment and wounded pride. White Bird's band had the closest contact with white ranchers and merchants, and so had some of the angriest memories. Whatever inspired it, this *tel-lik-leen* provided the spark that set loose the greatest modern crisis of the Nez Perce people.

By tradition, two men on a single horse brought up the rear of the circling column, symbolically taking the precarious spot of possible attack. The two this time were Wahlitits (Shore Crossing) and Sarpsis Ilppilp (Red Moccasin Tops). At some point on the circuit, something happened. By one account, their horse stepped on some drying camas roots; by another, they frightened a child. Someone then taunted Shore Crossing and his honored place in the ceremonial train: "If you're so brave, why don't you go kill the white man who killed your father?"[4] Three years earlier, Tipyahlahnah Siskan (Eagle Robe), Shore Crossing's father, had been shot by Larry Ott, a settler along the Salmon River. A grand jury had discharged Ott, in part because Nez Perce witnesses would not take the oath before testifying. The insult at the *tel-lik-leen* brought back, painfully and publicly, the memory of the incident.

Overnight, Shore Crossing decided to right the imbalance.[5] Early the next morning, he, Red Moccasin Tops, and a young relative, Wetyetmas Wahyakt (Swan Necklace), set off for Ott's place well up the Salmon River. Ott wasn't home. Nearby, however, were others tied to old grievances. The three rode upstream to the cabin of Richard Devine, once an English sailor and now a prospector known to set his dogs on passing Indians. While Swan Necklace held the horses, the other two shot Devine in his bed. They doubled back to a ranch along the river, where they killed three men, one of whom had ruled in an inquiry in favor of a white man accused of severely beating a Nez Perce. After taking some horses, they came across Samuel Benedict, a storekeeper known for cheating Indians and suspected of killing a Nez Perce named Chipmunk.[6] A few years

**Figure 7.1** Nez Perce drawing of a tel-lik-keen like that at Tepahlewam

earlier, he had slightly wounded Shore Crossing. The men shot Benedict through both thighs before he managed an escape. With Swan Necklace carrying the news ahead of them, Shore Crossing and Red Moccasin Tops then returned to Tepahlewam.

Instantly, the divided feelings in the camp came to life. Some of the younger men rode through the camp encouraging more errands of vengeance, while what leaders were there (Looking Glass had already left, and Joseph and Ollokut were across the Salmon slaughtering a small herd of cattle) met in deep consternation to consider their options. None were good. They faced a two-edged crisis. Immediately, their dilemma demanded a practical answer to the threat at hand. More deeply, it played on tensions rooted in cultural fundamentals.

The army was sure to respond to the killings. The next day or two would likely decide whether the Nez Perces would go fully to war, and although no Nez Perce could have known what they were up against, they knew that war would be profoundly painful. What were their choices? They might try to negotiate a peaceful resolution. That, however, would mean surrendering the three involved with the killing, which invoked the other side of their dilemma. Young men like Shore Crossing and Red Moccasin Tops, like everyone else, were expected to hold the well-being of their people in the highest regard. They were to be ready to fight, out of their hearts, for family and band. To prime them for that, they were encouraged to perform acts of bravado that were meant to cultivate individual initiative and personal honor, which made a spontaneous foray against rivals or sometime opponents something to be praised, not criticized. That, however, raised an obvious conflict. Giving young men wide latitude for aggression might cultivate the spirit needed in the face of danger, and in fact Red Moccasin Tops and Shore Crossing would fight with courage and self-sacrifice in the weeks ahead, but it could also bring danger itself. Now, with the new white order firmly in place, danger was of a far higher order.

Leaders of the bands would have to plot a way out. They had their own problem, however. Their leadership was conditional. It relied on a fragile balance among three factors—the respect they commanded for their past decisions, their sensitivity to their people's views, and their nurture of a consensus. Their most recent decisions at Lapwai, to put it mildly, were much under question. Their people's opinions were deeply divided, both on the general situation and on how to react to what the two young men had done. That raised high the premium on finding consensus, which in turn called for time to cool passions and make a common ground. But now the leaders' ears told them that there was no time. Outside, young men were calling others to more raids, and from a neighboring lodge someone shouted: "You...are holding a council for nothing! Three young men have come from White Bird country, bringing horses with them! Horses belonging to a white settler they killed! Killed yesterday sun! It will have to be war!"[7]

Under the stress of events, long- and short-term, the Nez Perce system of leadership temporarily cracked. Events spun away from the chiefs' influence, and for the next forty-eight hours they could only react, not lead. When they next were in control, the choice would be not whether to fight but how.

Sixteen or so Nez Perces took up the call for more attacks. The next two days saw a horrific spasm of murder and brutality. All but one of the assailants were from White Bird's band, whose home along the Salmon River and White Bird Creek had felt the worst cultural abrasion. One of the first attacks was against Samuel Benedict's store. After being shot in both legs, Benedict had made it home and been put to bed by his wife, Isabella. Hours later, a party of Nez Perces rode up. Samuel crawled from a window and tried to escape, but the raiders shot and killed both him and a French miner taking refuge at the store. Isabella and her children were told to leave. They made their way to the nearby ranch of Jack Manuel.[8]

They found that raiders, probably the same ones, had been there as well. Manuel and his wife, Jennet, had heard of the earlier killings from a neighbor, James Baker, and with their two children, six-year-old Maggie and eleven-month-old John, they were traveling along with Baker back to his more fortified ranch when a Nez Perce party struck. Baker was killed and Jack Manuel severely wounded in the neck and hips. The Indians took his slightly injured wife and children back to their home (after raping Jennet, according to one account) and left them there with a warning that other parties might be less generous. There were two other men at the Manuels' house: Jennet's father, George Popham, and a passing miner named Patrick Brice. They were allowed to go after surrendering their rifle and remained in hiding in a thick stand of willows nearby. This was the situation when Isabella Benedict arrived in flight from her own family horror late on June 14.

Understandably nervous, Isabella and her children joined the two men in the concealing brush, but Jennet Manuel was adamant: with her husband Jack lying nearby, even if he were close to death, she and the children would stay in their home. After hiding in the thicket for another fear-filled day, the Benedicts struck out for Mount Idaho on the night of June 15. Popham and Brice remained. They helped the Manuels as best they could during daylight but pulled back into the brush as darkness fell.[9]

That night, some Nez Perces returned. What happened next remains one of the war's mysteries. The next morning, Brice heard whimpering as he moved through the willows. It was six-year-old Maggie Manuel, cold and in shock, shoeless and wearing only a sleeping gown. She told him that Chief Joseph himself had entered the cabin during the night and had killed her mother and infant brother.[10] All her life, Maggie kept to this story, giving gruesome details (her mother's pooling blood "oozed between my toes"). All other sources agree, however, that Joseph remained in camp far away. Maggie also said that she and Brice returned to the cabin and found the two bodies, but he reported that none were there, and later, after raiders had come back yet again and burned the cabin, investigators combed through the debris and ashes but discovered no bones, adult or infant. Brice would hide with Maggie for two days; Jennet and her son John never reappeared, and may have died in captivity.

Back at the Salmon River, a few miles above the mouth of White Bird Creek, Nez Perces attacked the store of Harry Mason, a former whaler and prospector whose relations with the Nez Perces had been testy. Recently he had bloodied two with a bullwhip. Now, learning of the outbreak, he, his wife, his brother- and sister-in-law, and a neighbor were preparing to run for Mount Idaho when warriors approached and fired a volley through a window that badly wounded Mason and killed his brother-in-law and the neighbor. The raiders stormed the cabin, killed Mason, and by some accounts raped the women before releasing them.

The violence washed out of White Bird valley northward into the Camas Prairie, close to Mount Idaho and Grangeville. Along the stage road connecting the two towns with Lapwai and Lewiston was Cottonwood House, a roadhouse like hundreds of others along western routes. Its owners, Benjamin and Jennie Norton, were there with their nine-year-old son Hill, Jennie's teenaged sister, and a hired hand.[11] On the afternoon of June 14, the freighters Lew Wilmot and Pete Ready pulled up for a meal and sleep before continuing with their load of supplies from Lewiston to Mount Idaho. Soon afterward, two others arrived. First, Lew Day rode in carrying a message of alarm from Mount Idaho for the commander at Lapwai. As he left to continue his errand, another wagon arrived carrying a farmer, John Chamberlain, his wife, and two young daughters on their way to Lewiston. With things clearly astir, the Nortons and Chamberlains tried to keep Wilmot and Ready with them for added firepower, but the men left quickly for their own families in town. Almost immediately, Day returned after escaping a party of Nez Perces, despite a gunshot wound in the back. With the rumors confirmed, all at Cottonwood House set off for Mount Idaho. Benjamin Norton, the hired man Joe Moore, and the wounded Lew Day were on horseback; the rest rode in a wagon driven by John Chamberlain. Several miles down the road, Nez Perce horsemen attacked, wounding Day and Norton and finally ending the chase by dropping one of the wagon's horses.

Then came an agonized siege. The party hunkered beneath the wagon and behind the dead horse and somehow managed enough return fire to keep the attackers at a distance. Day, Moore, and both Nortons were shot, Day half a dozen times, and all suffered terribly from thirst. As the night wore on, the Chamberlains chose to try to slip away toward town, but they quickly became lost. Benjamin Norton, blood pulsing from a severed femoral artery, told his son and sister-in-law to make their try; the girl shed her heavy skirt, and they left. The hours dragged. Norton died. Day slipped in and out of consciousness. Moore fired aimlessly into the night until his ammunition was gone, and then he fashioned and fired shells with powder but no shot in a faux defense. At false dawn the attackers left, probably for more ammunition, and Jennie Norton, though shot through both calves, crawled off in her own search for help. She had barely started when a horseman approached. He was from Grangeville—young Hill Norton had made it through, and several townspeople had immediately set off to help— but Jennie was so blood-soaked that the man nearly shot her as an Indian. Others from town soon arrived, but as they began to carry the survivors to the safety of the town, the Nez Perces returned for a final galloping pursuit, until more rescuers appeared in a classic cavalry-over-the-hill fashion.

Later that morning, searchers found John Chamberlain killed with his dead three-year-old daughter beneath his body. His younger daughter was alive. Wounded in the neck and with the end of her tongue apparently bitten off in a fall, in shock and primal terror, she tried to crawl beneath her father's legs for protection as her rescuers approached. Nearby, they found the child's mother stumbling through the brush. She had been shot with an arrow and repeatedly raped; she was hysterical and had to be surrounded and physically restrained before being taken in.

There was one last fatal incident. By now, other parties from town were fanning out to check on settlers. One party, approaching an abandoned ranch, saw three Nez Perces bolting for their horses. Two escaped, but the whites caught the last, Jyeloo, shot him with both pistol and shotgun, and smashed his skull. Other Nez Perces returned later and found the body, and then met an unlucky rancher on his way home. They ran him down and killed him.

Lew Day and Joe Moore lingered for a while after being rescued but eventually died of blood loss and infection. Remarkably, Jack Manuel survived. After several days lying paralyzed near the ruins of his house, he clawed his way to an outhouse, cut the arrowhead from his neck with a hunting knife, and subsisted on berries until soldiers found him nearly two weeks after he was shot.[12] Eventually he walked again, but he never fully recovered his mental bearings. John Chamberlain's wife and young daughter also survived; the mother's trauma and the child's night of cowering next to her dead father must have left severe emotional wounds. Days and weeks passed, then months and years, with no trace of Jennet Manuel and her son John or any sure account of their fate. Nez Perce testimony from much later suggests that Jennet may have been taken captive and during the bands' retreat either fallen sick and died or been killed in a quarrel between two men.

Assuming that Jennet and John Manuel died at some point in the raids or in the war, that left the final toll at eighteen whites and one Nez Perce dead and six whites seriously wounded. The Nez Perces raped at least one woman, probably three, and perhaps four. Especially on the Camas Prairie, there was considerable destruction of homes, crops, and livestock—more than fourteen hundred cattle, sheep, horses, and pigs were killed or stolen, according to later claims. Sympathizers with the Nez Perces have pointed out that what whites had done to them over the years wildly outweighed what they did at this time, that many victims had it coming, and that the worst outrages were by raiders deep into stolen alcohol.[13] The last claim is almost surely untrue, and some who were killed and most who suffered losses were guilty only of living where they did.[14] To whatever extent it was justified, the violence was a release of generations of building tension, intense and ugly and poisonous, less an outbreak than a lanced boil.

The events of June 14–16 were a double shock. Not only were the attacks the bloodiest by Indians on civilians anywhere after the Civil War; they came from people who had kept their promise of peace from Thomas Jefferson's administration to that of Rutherford B. Hayes. The Nez Perces had trusted that they could live peaceably yet with some genuine independence and in allegiance to cultural roots. The two together, the trust and the blood, pose the question about the Nez Perce story that will not go away: Could it have gone differently?

Joseph and Ollokut returned from the other side of the Snake River late on June 14. Only one young man from their band had gone with the raiders, but the rest of their people were panicked, and despite pleas to stay put, all but the two brothers packed up and moved north to another familiar camp on Cottonwood Creek. Joseph and Ollokut followed the next day, and on June 16, with danger heightened in the wake of the raids, all moved again, this time to White Bird Canyon, where the White Bird and Toohoolhoolzote bands also were gathering. Here, more than sixty miles from Lapwai, the band leaders could regroup over the night of June 16–17 and consider their options. The camp was aslosh in alcohol. Raiders had found barrels of liquor at Benedict's store, and with Wilmot's wagon they had taken another barrel of whiskey, a dozen baskets of champagne, and another dozen bottles of brandy. Most of the men partook enthusiastically and fell into drunken sleep.

Meanwhile, white settlers gravitated from farms and ranches into Mount Idaho, filling homes and public buildings, including the jail. Men strung wagons and logs as barriers across the streets, and as a bastion for women and children they built a "sort of fort" on a hill with trenches and log palisades. To calm crying babies and soothe anxious parents, a few women and men stood on sacks of flour they had stacked to absorb bullets and sang hymns of consolation ("Nearer My God, to Thee") and moral sturdiness ("Onward, Christian Soldiers") as well as popular ballads of spiritual sentiment:

> When heavenly angels are guarding the good
> As God has ordained them to do,
> In answer to prayers I have offered to Him,
> I know there is one watching you.[15]

Howard had arrived at Lapwai on June 14 to be on hand when the nontreaty bands reported. By then the killing was under way, but there was no outward sign of trouble. "Eventless," a sergeant wrote in his diary: "Not a thing to break the monotony, except mosquitos."[16] Howard's only inkling of trouble was a nervous note from Mount Idaho that warriors were trying to buy ammunition and seemed anything but compliant. Townsfolk asked that enough troops be sent "to handle them without gloves." On June 15, the day he expected the no-treaties at the reservation, Howard received a first brief word of the raids, then two more alarms reporting widespread assaults and an apparently imminent attack on Mount Idaho: "we are in the midst of an Indian war.... Don't delay a moment.... The Indians are in possession of the [Camas] prairie.... Give us relief, and arms and ammunition.... Hurry up; hurry!"[17] Howard's first thoughts, quite properly, were of the threatened settlers, but he had only the two companies of First Cavalry with roughly a hundred men under arms. Wiring Walla Walla and Portland for reinforcements, he ordered Captain David Perry to march the troops and several reservation Nez Perces fifty miles south to Grangeville and Mount Idaho. At about eight o'clock on the evening of June 15, they started down the muddy road toward the two towns. As they had three days' rations in their kits, the mission clearly was defensive.[18]

With daylight, the troops saw dead horses, burned haystacks and houses, and the looted wagon of Wilmot and Ready with cigars tossed about and a stove-in whiskey barrel.[19] At sunset on June 16, they were in Grangeville, presumably to collect and defend area residents; but now locals urged Perry to pursue and attack the bands they had seen moving that morning toward White Bird Canyon. Besides pressing for the return of stolen stock, these whites had a strategic argument. Below White Bird Canyon was a traditional crossing on the Salmon River. Once over the river, the locals said, the rugged, confused terrain would give the Nez Perces an enormous advantage and would open the way for an escape westward.[20] The most vocal spokesman for attack was Arthur "Ad" Chapman. A horse rancher and longtime resident with decidedly mixed relations with the Nez Perces, he assured Perry that the Indians could be easily beaten, and he offered to raise volunteers to help. The captain consulted his fellow officers, who agreed that the best course was to take the offensive. Chapman gathered ten other locals to go along with him, and at nine o'clock in the evening, as the men were just settling into camp, they were ordered back into their saddles for another all-night march.

Perry was not exceeding his orders, any more than Custer had almost exactly a year earlier at the Little Big Horn. A field commander should respond to threats and opportunities, and Perry had reasons to pursue. Reasons to hold back, however, were at least as good. Perry did not know

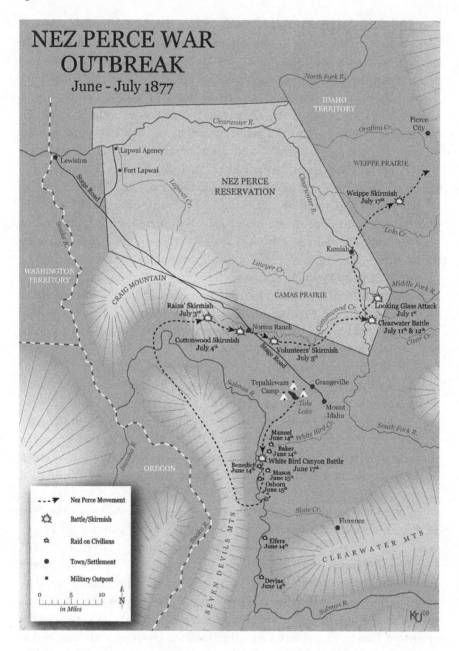

how many his opponents were or how well they were armed. He was not sure where they were. His own men were mostly innocent of battle, and his horses were fat and poorly trained. His troops had been awake for close to forty hours with little to eat, and if they attacked, it would be after another sleepless and foodless eight hours in the saddle. The problem of the bands escaping across the Salmon was compelling, but so was the danger of fighting under such uncertain circumstances. Perhaps Perry was influenced by the Nez Perces' history of persistent friendship. They had never opposed an American command, and at their most direct confrontation with the government, when Howard had threatened force some weeks earlier, they had backed down. If he now faced them and made that threat real, he might have wondered, how much of a danger could they be?

The command passed through the town of Mount Idaho and about midnight reached the head of White Bird Canyon, the entry to the valley to the south where the Nez Perces had gathered. The next stage of the approach dropped fully half a mile in elevation over two miles of march; before that steep descent, Perry ordered his men to halt until first light. They were told to rest, not sleep—but "I find many a tired trooper asleep," a sergeant later wrote, "and his equally tired horse lying down beside him."[21] At about four o'clock in the morning, the column mounted and started down a narrow defile. Suddenly out of the brush came a red-haired woman and two girls: Isabella Benedict with her daughters, famished and exhausted after hiding for the three days since their house had been attacked and Samuel Benedict killed. Isabella declined the chance to ride to Grangeville with one of the agency Nez Perces but accepted a blanket and some bread, while begging Perry to abandon an attack she said was sure to fail utterly. He promised to pick her up on his way back and continued down the narrows.[22]

Soon the trail opened into a broad valley. To the west, a massive north-to-south rise ran parallel to Perry's line of march. To the east, White Bird Creek drained along the valley toward the south. Directly ahead, lying east-to-west across Perry's path, was a rocky ridge with two knolls slightly east of it. Perry presumed the Nez Perces were far down the creek at its mouth, hopefully preoccupied by getting ready to cross the Salmon, perhaps even divided, with some on the far bank. In fact, the camp of about thirty lodges was just ahead in the trees along White Bird Creek. The ridge and knolls, however, kept it hidden.

The Nez Perces had posted four men on a nearby butte as pickets. One of them, Hand in Hand, spotted Perry's column as it moved into the valley. He cuffed the other three out of a drunken sleep, and one of them, No Feet (he had none), was heaved onto a horse and galloped to the camp yelling the inflected, cadenced whoop that signaled an enemy's approach.[23] Later, Howard wrote preposterously of Joseph coolly devising a battle plan while observing Perry through a glass. In fact, Joseph, Ollokut, White Bird, and Toohoolhoolzote decided hurriedly to seek a peace parley and, if it failed, to fight. Just rousing their men was a problem, since most were so stuporously drunk that not even severe whacking with quirts could awaken them. Eventually between forty-five and seventy warriors sobered up enough to defend the camp. Howard later reported variously that the Nez Perces outnumbered Perry's men by two or three to one. The true ratio was just the opposite.[24]

Perry advanced toward the ridge with F Company, followed by Captain Joel Trimble and H Company. Perry subordinate Lieutenant Edward Theller and eight men, including Ad Chapman, went ahead to reconnoiter. Accounts from whites are vague on what came next, but Nez Perce testimony is emphatic. As Theller's scouts topped the ridge, they were approached by a peace party of six riders led by Vicious Weasel. Chapman, the first to see them, immediately opened fire, and the Nez Perce party wheeled and broke for protecting timber.[25]

Thus began the war's first battle, a contest between hungover warriors and hungry, fatigued soldiers that almost instantly went calamitously wrong for the latter. Perry quickly moved his men up the ridge for a charge down the other side, but he paused when he saw well-positioned riflemen firing from trees along the creek. Besides, when he ordered his trumpeter to be ready to sound the charge, the man answered that he had dropped his instrument somewhere on the night march. Best to make a stand along the ridge, Perry decided. He sent the horses to the rear and spread his men out about three yards apart, with Trimble's company to his right. To his left, the terrain dipped to a swale and then rose to a knoll now occupied by the civilian volunteers.

About this time, Perry learned that a remarkable long distance shot in the first exchange had killed the other company's bugler.[26] Moments into the fighting, Perry had no way to communicate among his largely inexperienced soldiers, who were now arranged in a thin skirmish line with no reserves and were anchored to their left by eleven farmers and shopkeepers. Next, things turned doubly worse. Several Nez Perse warriors on a gallop flanked the line on its right. They were led by the two young men who had precipitated the crisis, Wahlitits (Shore Crossing) and Sarpsis Ilppilp (Red Moccasin Tops), and by Tipyahlahnah (Strong Eagle). Later, these were called the Three Red Coats because they tauntingly wore red blankets to invite the soldiers' fire. As Perry's right flank took several hits and began to falter, the volunteers on the left were already retreating. A handful of warriors behind the creek bank had fired on them, inspired by Lepeet Hessemdooks (Two Moons): "General Howard is upon us with his peace-talked rifle! The fighting is now here!" One of the civilians would later claim that Perry ordered the volunteers to withdraw, but clearly they panicked and fled on their own. Their first casualty, who either took an enemy bullet or shot himself while pulling his pistol and set his pants aflame, unnerved them, and with Ad Chapman in front, they fled on horseback via a cattle trail toward Idaho City.[27] (Chapman "was a great leader," a local cracked years later: "He had the lead going into the White Bird battle, and he was in the lead in going out of it.")[28] The Nez Perces quickly took the knoll and directed their shots at Perry's left flank. Six soldiers fell immediately.

Perry tried to compress the skirmish line by moving his F Company to the right, but some of his men already were bolting for their horses. By standard procedure, every fourth man had been tapped to hold the reins of four horses—no easy job as the untested mounts bucked and wheeled from the gunfire and shouts. As panicked soldiers ran toward the overwhelmed handlers of the terrified horses, the situation unraveled. A Nez Perce recalled the scene as "a bad mixup for the soldiers," ending as "a wild, deadly racing with the warriors pressing hard to head them off."[29] Trimble did his best to organize an orderly retreat and made one abortive effort to reestablish a position on the ridge, although the effect was only to isolate Sergeant Michael McCarthy and a handful of others, most of whom would die.

Now the survivors began a prolonged ascent of the steep grade, rising as much as one foot per five and a half feet, that they had marched down only moments before.[30] It was "the worst managed affair I was ever in," a veteran wrote—an increasingly chaotic scramble up whatever route seemed possible.[31] Perry, unhorsed for much of the retreat, commanded only the men around him, and those not too well. Trimble led others, as did his second in command, Lieutenant William Parnell. Theller, who had commanded the reconnaissance that had started the fight and who soon afterward was found wandering around in a daze, took seven men into a steep ravine full of thorn bushes; all were killed. Many others made their way alone or in knots and were washed over by their pursuers' momentum. With the last bullet of a shot-and-ball pistol, Wounded Head killed a soldier, took his rifle and cartridges, and left the older firearm on his chest "as a present." Yellow Wolf was saved when another warrior slew a cavalryman with a rock to the temple. A veteran on his fourth enlistment died several minutes into a long-range rifle duel. McCarthy, having broken out of his hopeless surround on the ridge, first raced away on foot, then had a horse shot from under him, then played dead as warriors rode past, then crawled into thick brush to hide, and finally walked bootless for two days back to Grangeville. He later received the Medal of Honor.[32]

At an abandoned ranch a couple of miles farther on, Perry managed a partial regrouping and more orderly withdrawal, although the Nez

Perces continued to press them a dozen miles more to Mount Idaho. By nine o'clock in the morning, all survivors but McCarthy were accounted for. Of the command of about a hundred, thirty-four were dead and two wounded. Perry was in semishock, at one point convinced that fourteen hours had passed instead of two.[33] No Nez Perces had died, and only two had battle wounds.

Back on the field, both men and women now stripped the troops of usable clothing. More useful were firearms and ammunition. In this first fight, the Nez Perces had been badly outgunned. Some, like Yellow Wolf, had gone into battle with bows and arrows, others with outdated arms, including muskets. Now they were better prepared, and in fact much of the firepower for the rest of the war came from what was taken from the army over the next weeks.[34] Three agency Nez Perces had been captured, but the next day they were released with the assurance that if they helped the whites again they could expect a lashing with hazel switches.[35] The victors also let three white noncombatants go their own way. Isabella Benedict's children had been taken up by fleeing civilians, and she had been given a horse, but in what must have seemed an endless nightmare, she had lost her seat and was found by Wounded Head. At the urging of Nez Perce women, she was set loose. (After the war, she thanked Wounded Head and gave him $6.)[36] At midafternoon, Patrick Brice stumbled out of some nearby willows, carrying the wounded six-year-old Maggie Manuel, and asked a young warrior, Whylimlex (Black Feather), if he was going to kill him. The pair had stayed in the brush for the two days since raiders had burned the girl's house and either killed or kidnapped her mother and brother. Now, fearing Maggie would die without a doctor, Brice came out of hiding and swore to his innocence in the Nez Perce troubles. After a short discussion, the two were allowed to go. They reached Mount Idaho the next evening.

# CHAPTER 8

# Maneuvering and Scrapping

The next three weeks were confused, even for a war that often seemed like men chasing cats in a dark room. Howard sent for troops from the Departments of the Columbia and of California to launch a wholly unanticipated campaign. Eventually, he would assemble nearly a thousand men—ten companies of cavalry, six companies of infantry, and five artillery batteries.[1] Officers closer by were quickly assembled. "I left Walla Walla at 2 hours notice," one wrote later, "just walked out of my house and left the Chinaman cooking dinner."[2] The assistant quartermaster scrambled to find mules and muleteers, blacksmiths, saddlers, and wheelwrights. Local liveries demanded and got sharp prices and ironclad indemnities. Government mules arrived, but "in a great measure worthless, from old age & service." Civilian packers and freighters signed on for good wages but chafed at army discipline and often quit, forcing the redeployment of enlisted men. Wagons were ordered and sent post haste. They arrived disassembled and in batches, some with all front wheels and none for the back, others vice versa.[3]

In approaching the fight ahead, Howard had plenty of military experience, having served from First Bull Run through Sherman's Georgia campaign. He became a corps commander relatively early and ended the war as commander of the Army of the Tennessee. His rise in rank might seem puzzling, however, since he was among the most criticized officers in the Union command. It was his position that was turned by Stonewall Jackson at the Battle of Chancellorsville, starting the rout at that stunning Confederate victory, and at Gettysburg his flank was turned again. In those and other engagements, his command suffered heavy losses. At some point his men gave General O. O. Howard a wry nickname: "Uh-Oh" Howard.[4] He may also have been especially distracted during the

**Figure 8.1** Oliver Otis Howard early in the Civil War

long fight now before him. His time as head of the Freedmen's Bureau had been roundly criticized and had left him with legal difficulties that would not be resolved until the following year.[5]

Most officers had known action and appreciated the risks ahead. Emily Fitzgerald, wife of John Fitzgerald, the post surgeon, wrote to her mother about the men gathering around her table "discussing the situation and all knowing they will never all come back." They asked her help:

> One leaves his watch and little fixings and says, "If one of those bullets gets me, send this to my wife." Another gave me his boy's photograph to keep for him, as he could not take it. He kept his wife's with him, and twice he came back to look at the boy's before he started off. One officer left a sick child, very ill; another left a wife to be confined [i.e., give birth] next month.

Caught between her government and those resisting it, Emily had little good to say about either. "What thanks do they get for it?" she asked about her friends' sacrifices. "No pay, and abuse from the country that they risk their lives to protect." As for the Indians, she "wish[ed] all ... in the country were at the bottom of the Red Sea. I suppose the country will have trouble until all are exterminated."[6]

One addition to the ranks of officers would play a crucial part in the story ahead: Lieutenant Charles Erskine Scott Wood, a recent West Point graduate who would become Howard's aide-de-camp. An aspiring writer who had never seen action, he kept a diary with a first-timer's impressions of moving ever closer to conflict. His regiment was en route from Alaska when they heard the "stirring news" of being called into the fight. As they ascended the Columbia, stopping at towns along the way, there was "Growing excitement, cheering remarks from citizens of—go in and kill 'em all boys. Don't spare the bloody savages. Confound [those] cusses— wish they were going to fight them instead of standing on a wharf and pat[ting] us on the back." He saw a "party of admiring damsels gaze on the defenders of the Country" and felt like staying with the prettier ones to allay "any sadness or anxiety on *my* account." Indians on the rocks of The Dalles "wave encouraging signals to us to go on and kill and be killed. Hard to tell which they prefer." As they neared Lewiston and debarkation, the mood turned more solemn: "peculiar nervous feeling of going to death."[7]

Wood arrived at Lapwai on June 24, the day after Howard took to the field with early reinforcements, leaving orders for the gathering forces to catch up. The general visited Mount Idaho and gave his sympathies to the wounded, including the wife of John Chamberlain. After new arrivals swelled his command to more than five hundred, Howard moved to the battle site, and on June 26 his men began burying the wretched remains of corpses that had lain for ten days in the summer heat. "Horrible stench," Wood wrote in his diary: "arms and cheeks gone, bellies swollen, blackened faces, mutilations, heads gone." Decomposed bodies had to be slid more than lifted into shallow graves dug with trowel bayonets. In camp that night, there was "singing story telling and swearing, profanity, carelessness,—accepting things—horrible at other times—as a matter of course."[8]

When scouts neared the mouth of White Bird Creek, they looked across the Salmon and saw Nez Perces "speckling the hills like ants," shouting insults, firing a few shots, and flapping red blankets when more troops arrived and raised a flag.[9] The bands had done what the settlers had said they might—crossed the river into the rugged country beyond—but not for the reasons suspected. The day after the battle, two renowned warriors, Five Wounds (Pahkatos Owyeen) and Rainbow (Wahchumyus), had returned from hunting bison across the Bitterroots. They had advised the move across the river. "I knew, we all knew, that was [the] one way to beat General Howard," Bow and Arrow Case (Phillip Evans) would explain. They would draw Howard across the Salmon, assuming correctly that he would think they were heading westward to the Snake River and to the Wallowa valley beyond, and then they would double back and recross the Salmon as their pursuers moved in the wrong direction through some of the roughest terrain in the region.[10] On June 19, the entire Nez Perce camp and its nearly three thousand horses crossed the river. Then they waited for a week for Howard, fired some shots when he appeared, and figuratively thumbed their noses before withdrawing into the timbered steepness of the Salmon River Mountains. Wood, at least, felt a powerful tug to give chase: "on hearing the shots nervous eagerness for the fight [and a] desire to be at the front, all thoughts of the future banished only want a crack at an Indian and no disposition to show any quarter."[11]

The maneuver was a bait and switch, and Howard bit. It took him three days to get his command across the Salmon and to begin slogging his way, through heavy rain mixed with sleet, more than three thousand feet up a path that was dubbed Dead Mule Trail after several animals stumbled under heavy packs and fell with "frightful velocity" nearly two thousand feet into ravines.[12] Only on July 4 did Howard learn that his quarry was not heading west but had passed back over the Salmon at another of their familiar fords, had moved eastward, and in fact was confronting an outmanned force at Cottonwood Creek.[13] He attempted to cross where they had, making a laughable effort to rig up a ferry using lariats and a disassembled cabin, before having his men retrace their miserable route and recross the Salmon at White Bird Creek. The irony was hard to miss. Howard was losing what initiative he had, falling ever farther behind the bands, because his movements were blocked by the Salmon, deep, swift, tumbling, and swollen to nearly a hundred yards across during *hillal,* the time of rain and melting snow. The Nez Perces, that is, were playing Howard against the very barrier he had refused to credit six weeks earlier when they had pled their case, telling him that in June the rivers became walls and that the floodtide would wash away their cattle if they tried to cross.

On July 8, after riding, trudging, fording, and freezing for seventy miles, Howard's troops were back where they had been two weeks earlier, at Grangeville, without having seen any Indians who were not shooting at or taunting them.[14] The larger situation had now changed dramatically for the worse. Before first crossing the Salmon Howard had sent Captain Stephen G. Whipple to the village of Looking Glass's Alpowai band on the Clearwater River on the southeastern edge of the reservation. Whipple's orders were to arrest Looking Glass and to confine the Alpowais, who numbered perhaps 150 persons, twenty to forty of them warriors, at Mount Idaho. Public rumors had it that Looking Glass was about to join the belligerent bands—for that matter there was common talk of a general uprising across the region—and Howard later claimed information that twenty Alpowais had already taken up arms.[15] A couple in fact might have been at White Bird, but there is no evidence to suggest that Looking Glass or other Alpowais intended to fight. To the contrary, before the outbreak he had warned the other leaders to control their young men, and after it he had remained steadfastly aloof, by one account calling the others fools for doing what could only bring disaster.[16] Although there were Dreamers among the Alpowais, this non-treaty band was the closest, culturally as well as physically, to the reservation Nez Perces. "We had a plow and raised good gardens," one of them recalled: "Potatoes, corn, beans, squash, melons, cucumbers, everything we wanted." They had rail fences to keep their dairy cows away from the produce.

Certainly nothing in Whipple's report suggests any hostility when he arrived early on July 1 with sixty-six troops and twenty civilian volunteers. As the Nez Perces tell it, villagers were puzzled and then alarmed to see armed men on a wooded rise across the shallow Cottonwood Creek near where it emptied into the Clearwater. Peopeo Tholekt (Bird Alighting) later sketched in what followed: Looking Glass sent him as an emissary to tell Whipple he wanted no trouble, only peace; Whipple replied by insisting on meeting directly with Looking Glass; Looking Glass sent his answer back with Bird Alighting and another man; halfway to the troops, the two planted a white cloth tied to a pole, then went on to repeat their leader's intentions ("We want no trouble....We ran away from war!") and to tell the troops to stay on their side of the creek.[17]

Whipple originally had planned to attack at dawn, but when he arrived too late for surprise, he presumably decided to seize Looking Glass during a parley and then secure his warriors. The Alpowai leader frustrated that move by refusing to meet, and the situation grew tenser by the minute. Bird Alighting said he suspected some whites had been drinking, and he told of one volunteer who thought he was Looking Glass and jabbed him repeatedly in the ribs with a rifle barrel. ("He did not hit easy!") Whipple, his control slipping, rode with a few others to the white flag and again demanded to speak directly with Looking Glass. Probably he hoped to press the issue before things fell apart. If Looking Glass came out of his lodge, Whipple might arrest him and make his bid for the others to surrender; if the chief called his bluff, he might call down his men, who outnumbered the village's fighters at least two to one, in a quick power play. But before either could happen, someone on the hill fired, and a Nez Perce man fell wounded. Immediately, troops and volunteers fired at will as Whipple and his companions whirled and galloped back.

Bullets tore through the village of eleven lodges, as the Alpowais ran either for their horses or into nearby brush. Few if any fired back, and the whites had no casualties—another hint that the villagers had never intended to fight. In the chaos, a few Alpowais were wounded, including Bird Alighting, who was shot in the leg. One died later. A mother and her baby strapped to her back drowned while trying to cross the Clearwater on a horse. The panicked villagers scattered up a wooded hillside, and when they returned hours later they found most of the lodges burned or otherwise destroyed, the gardens trampled, their belongings ransacked, their brass cooking pots speared with bayonets, and all their cattle and most of their horses, seven hundred head, driven off, in Bird Alighting's words, "by the robber enemy."[18]

"Of course this settled it," Bird Alighting said later: "We had to have a war." Howard had ordered Whipple to "arrest the Indian chief Looking Glass, and all other Indians who may be encamped with or near him." Whipple had arrested no Nez Perce, chief or otherwise, but instead had made real Howard's vague and probably groundless suspicions. As the general wrote later, "We thus stirred up a new hornet's nest." The Alpowais would add perhaps forty warriors to the resistance, among them Looking Glass, admired as a fighter and a strategist.

This attack would shape the story in other ways. Looking Glass was known as a skilled director of bison hunts across the Bitterroot Mountains and farther east in the Yellowstone River basin of the Great Plains. He was especially praised as the man who had fought in 1874 with the Nez Perces' Crow allies in a stunning victory over the Lakotas (western Sioux), again along the Yellowstone River. When he pushed Looking Glass into the conflict, Howard gave the New Perces a prestigious leader who had intimate knowledge of country where they would soon be headed. This headman's advice at crucial moments would influence, literally and physically, the direction of the Nez Perces' fate.

When the three bands already in the fight learned of the attack on Looking Glass's village, they moved eastward toward Camas Prairie to link up with the Alpowais. That route would take them past Cottonwood House, the road ranch the Norton family had abandoned to ride off to disaster. The site had been commandeered and renamed Camp Norton; Howard had ordered Whipple to take his men there from Mount Idaho to guard the road and to watch for any enemy movement from the west. Thus Whipple, having stirred a hornet's nest, found himself in the path of a swarm. The first indication came when two civilian scouts, probing to the west, met an advance party who gave chase and killed one of the two after his horse threw him. When the survivor reached Whipple, he called his men into the saddle and set off in the hope of saving the scout. First, however, he sent thirteen volunteers—Lieutenant Sevier Rains, ten enlistees, the surviving scout, and another civilian—to reconnoiter. Meanwhile, the Nez Perces prepared for a confrontation.

The next encounter was the first between fighters on roughly equal terms—not begun, that is, as the military's surprise assault—and Nez Perces warriors had time to prepare, singing their personal war songs softly and putting on their medicine objects to ensure their strength. As they rode out to meet what they assumed would be a full complement of troops, they saw Rains's advance party. Quickly they devised an ambush that killed some outright and forced the rest into a hopeless stand behind some rocks and pine stumps. Strong Eagle (Tipyahlahnah), one of the three young warriors who had led the first charge at White Bird Canyon, drew their fire, until others came up on the soldiers' blind side and cut them down. As they approached they saw one survivor, a soldier seated and leaning against a rock, shot twice in the chest and once through the forehead, washing his face with his own blood and clucking like a hen. They wondered at this "calling to his Power" and decided "He must be more like us!" They debated whether he was bound to die or whether "he can live if he wants to." After knocking him over with two more shots to the chest, they watched him pull himself back up, look around, and continue his clucking and his blood cleansing. With no *tewat* at hand, they finally took pity ("Poor fellow! He is suffering") and beat out his life with their war clubs.[19]

Whipple saw gun smoke from the fight and advanced, but he dismounted his men into a skirmish line after he topped a ridge and saw warriors well positioned and in superior numbers. The two sides traded fire for a couple of hours until Whipple, seeing no sign that Rains and his men had survived, pulled back to Camp Norton.[20] As the day ended, he had another concern besides a possible attack on his outnumbered command. He knew that Captain Perry and an even weaker force of twenty-nine were on the way from Lapwai with seventy-five mules packed with ammunition and supplies. They could be easily surprised and overwhelmed. At dawn on Independence Day, Whipple marched his men out to meet Perry and got them into camp without a fight, along the way discovering the remains of the Rains party. Now Perry was in command. He ordered rifle pits dug and a Gatling gun positioned for defense. In the early afternoon, the Nez Perces appeared. They surrounded the ranch, now dubbed Camp Rains, but kept their distance while mounted and crept closer to fire from within ravines and behind ridges. Neither side took casualties. The exchanges continued until dark and resumed around nine o'clock the next morning.

The Nez Perces' renewed firing was only to keep troops in place while a long train of their families and stock crossed the prairie to join the Alpowais about fifteen miles away along the Clearwater River. That might have ended the sparring, but two couriers arrived at Camp Rains with startling news. A group of civilians were pinned down about a mile and a half away. When word of the Rains ambush had reached Mount Idaho, seventeen volunteers led by Darius Randall had set off to help. As they drew close to the fight, some Nez Perces turned to meet them. Just how many warriors were involved is even murkier than usual—the civilians said 150; Nez Perce participants said twelve or fourteen—but the men, soon to be called the Brave Seventeen, were clearly in a fix.[21] They dismounted to make a stand, with little natural protection, until help arrived from Perry.[22]

But Perry didn't come. Later he argued that the group from Mount Idaho seemed beyond help, that he might be drawn into an ambush, and that he could not risk the enemy's taking his large store of ammunition. His thoughts are not hard to divine. Eighteen days earlier, the Nez Perces had thoroughly whipped and nearly annihilated his command, and just two days ago they had waylaid and exterminated thirteen men on an errand of rescue. There the situation might have stayed, if Perry had not been pushed by the men under him. In various accounts, a private yelled out sarcastically that in the future no one should expect help from *this* regiment, and a sergeant, a veteran of White Bird Canyon, went farther and called for a break in ranks ("If your officers won't lead you, I will") that aborted only when Perry threatened to charge him with insubordination.[23] Finally, after more than an hour, a civilian volunteer, George Shearer, by his own memory calling it a "shame and an outrage" to let the men die, rode off to help. Perry relented and sent Whipple after him with about sixty troops, and the Nez Perces withdrew without Whipple's men firing a shot.[24] Randall and another of the seventeen were dead on the field. A third died that night.

The incident brought to a head an understandable public frustration that took as its focus Perry and his performances at White Bird and Cottonwood Creek. He faced two courts of inquiry, one the following September and the other in December 1878. Both exonerated him. Within the ranks, however, opinions were at best divided (McCarthy wrote later that throughout his career "that coward" had "showed cold feet"), and among locals the judgment was scorching.[25] Lew Wilmot, whose liquor-loaded wagon had been taken earlier and who later had been one of the Brave Seventeen, was so vocal with his opinions that Howard called him in with Perry to confront him: Had he accused the officer of cowardice? When Wilmot "called him [Perry]] every filthy name I had in my vocabulary," Howard briefly arrested him for abuse of an officer. But Wilmot was only voicing the common public sentiment.[26] Howard especially was pilloried in the press for inaction and bumbling.

Behind this flare-up was a complication snarling the entire first stage of the conflict—and more generally western Indian policy. Relations between the military and the white citizenry were conflicted to their core. The army's essential job was to maintain order as the government consolidated its hold on the new country. That usually turned out to mean protecting Indians from white newcomers at least as much as vice versa. The military in fact often found themselves increasingly hostile toward civilians. In the current situation, at least four officers, Whipple, Albert Forse, Henry Clay Wood and Howard, at some point spoke out against local whites. When tensions rose, the situation cracked, and the fighting began, relations with civilians entered a newly contentious stage. Successful combat demanded a good knowledge of the field of operations, but compared to those soldiering in the East, an officer out West was running blind. The only alternative was to seek information and advice from white settlers, but bringing farmers and shopkeepers into the command could be double trouble. They might manipulate the situation to their advantage, as the townspeople had before the battle at White Bird Creek, goading Perry into rash action in hopes of getting back their livestock. And in the field, civilians were unpredictable and hard to control. Of the five clashes of arms so far in the story, three had begun with civilians acting on their own.

From a wider perspective, the tensions between civilians and authorities was one more angle on the problem of consolidation. The view from today is of the West being created by the government relentlessly taking command, but go back to the time, and events seem mostly out of its control. It was the locals, Indian and white, who usually determined the action. Howard and his officers and their counterparts were given the work of settling federal power across the West. They ultimately did, but in getting there they seemed less the commanders of events than their creatures.

In a great many ways, for that matter, the army was a study in frustration. Having given the muscle and blood needed to save the union, it was essentially gutted after Appomattox. Handed the work of overcoming physical resistance and bringing the West into the nation, the army saw its funds cut and what it was given reluctantly dribbled out, the number of its men capped at a shockingly low figure, and its basic supplies mostly pinched off.

Following the mass postwar demobilization, Congress between 1866 and 1874 reduced its standing army by half, from fifty-four thousand men to twenty-seven thousand. Because recruiting always lagged way behind losses from discharges, deaths, and desertions, the true number of enlisted men rarely rose above nineteen thousand.[27] As the military occupation of the South wound down, most of those were stationed out West. By the official count for 1877, taken seven days after the end of the Nez Perce conflict, 24,501 officers and men were in service. About 85 percent of them, just under eighteen thousand, were assigned to the West in the divisions of the Missouri, Pacific, and Arizona. The portion was hefty, but the numbers seem absurdly small. To manage militarily roughly half of the United States, the half by far the most difficult to traverse and where most outright resistance occurred, the government provided fewer soldiers than it had *lost* in the Battle of the Wilderness. Troops were scattered among so many posts and stations—about three hundred across the West in 1877—that a great many installations were essentially bluffs. Subtract the men needed simply to operate a post, and too few remained to take any effective action.[28]

While officers were nearly all veterans of the late war, the lower ranks were mostly recent enlistees. They were young—the average age of a

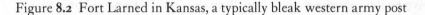

Figure **8.2** Fort Larned in Kansas, a typically bleak western army post

recruit at first enlistment was twenty-three—and close to half of them were foreign born, mostly from Ireland, Germany, and Canada, with a scattering from around Europe.[29] Some had served abroad. The last survivor at the Little Big Horn to see George Custer alive was his bugler, Sergeant John Martin (Giovanni Martini), who had fought in Italy under Garibaldi; Captain Miles Keogh, who died with Custer, had been an Irish mercenary fighting for the pope on the other side. Lieutenant William Parnell, who figured prominently at the battle of White Bird Canyon, was a rare survivor of the charge of the Light Brigade. Below the level of officers, however, most recruits had no experience. The ranks of those fighting the Nez Perces fit the general profile. More than four out of every ten soldiers in one crucial battle were immigrants.[30]

Base pay for a private was $16 a month until 1871, when Congress cut it to $13, or a bit more than $1.50 a day. Pay rose by ranks; first sergeants got $22 a month, and after 1872 the amount rose also according to time in rank. Obviously, an army career was not a money-making proposition, which raises the question of why anyone joined in the first place. Many immigrants probably found in the army a floor of security in a new life—room and board and pay—as well as a chance to head westward toward presumably better opportunities. The same reasons likely brought in many native born whose social demerits and lack of skills left them only marginally employable.

As an occupation, the military seemed for many a last resort, as is further suggested by conditions in western posts, which could not have been an attraction. At worst, Sherman would write, western troops "have lived in holes in the ground, in houses made from green cottonwood logs infested by vermin, in temporary shanties." At best, quarters were cramped, stuffy, and poorly built, with two and even four men in each bunk. Offenses to the nose must have been considerable. "I have been thirty-six years in service," wrote an officer in 1878: "I do not remember ever having seen a bath-house in any of our frontier-posts."[31] Officers' quarters were better, but not much. If space was available, and if they had the money, officers could sometimes live among civilians, but on the raw frontier that usually had its drawbacks. Alfred Sully, left behind in Lewiston when Howard took off after the bands, wrote his wife of the blistering heat at that "terrible dusty place." He stayed at Lewiston's best lodging, the Hotel de France (certainly not named for its food and coffee, he wrote), but he was worn down by the constant noise of squalling children and a neighbor woman's singing, "hawking and spitting," and all-night snoring.[32]

Recruits' uniforms were usually ill-fitting and their shoes and boots a shoddy construction of stiff, coarse leather and brass screws that "would wiggle up into the feet and cause all sorts of agony."[33] Rations rarely included fresh vegetables. Meat was frequently spoiled and mealtime a monotony, as declared in this barracks doggerel: "Of hash that's young, of hash that's old, / Of hash that's hot, of hash that's cold / Of hash that's tender, of hash that's tough, / I swear to God, I've had enough!"[34] Dried and compressed vegetables were introduced in the West as an experiment in the 1850s and used in the Civil War and afterward. These "desiccated vegetables," soon dubbed "desecrated vegetables," literally did not go down well. When a Union officer added water to his potatoes, he compared the result to a dirty brook full of dead leaves.[35]

Diet and living conditions contributed to a morbid health record. Isolation and a climate unfriendly to gardens sometimes left posts without citrus or fresh vegetables for months at a time, making scurvy an occasionally serious problem. Some doctors improvised. One found effective an oily goo made from boiling cactus, swallowable only with whiskey.[36] As for sanitation, soldiers living in the West's immense spaces managed to create around themselves some of the most densely concentrated islands of filth and putrescence imaginable. Outhouses and slaughterhouses were ill-kept shambles. Where the winters were the bitterest, men often went only a few steps outside buildings to relieve themselves and to dump manure, offal, and slops, all of which froze until the spring thaw brought clouds of flies and a stench that staggered the imagination and buckled the knees. An officer on the northern plains had to request formally the removal of a rotting bison from the outhouse—the carcass had been put there by the post doctor. Another reported that two dead mules beside the garden had become "extremely offensive" and recommended they be tossed into the river.[37] That remedy, all too common, promoted water-borne diseases from dysentery to Asiatic cholera, which swept through western posts in 1866 and 1867. Fort Harker in Kansas was especially hard hit in the latter year. A newly arrived surgeon discovered a large pit full of offal and rotting meat, a "hot bed of disease," only half a mile from the post.[38]

Occupational injuries included a remarkable number of gunshot wounds, the great majority not from combat but from defective weap-ons, jumpy sentries, hunting accidents, and stupidity. One trooper fatally shot himself in the face while striking a horse's head with his pistol butt. Another's rifle exploded after he failed to clear its barrel of a piece of pork he had used to grease it.[39] Exposure, especially while wearing poor uni-forms and thin boots, led to frostbite, freezing, and worse. Of 251 ampu-tations studied by the surgeon general's office between 1865 and 1871, the majority came after gunshot wounds, but one in six was from frostbite. One was a quadruple amputation on a trooper caught in a Dakota bliz-zard; he supported his wife and three children afterward with a pension and by selling photographs of his reduced self.[40]

Discipline in western posts could be harsh, degenerating often into bul-lying. The main goal was intimidation meant to ensure that field orders would be followed, something absolutely necessary, but as for any further training in what to do in a fight—that was minimal at best. Drills were rare, partly because of officers' slack, demoralized attitude and partly because troops were spread so thin. An authority estimated in 1878 half the western posts did not have enough troops to hold drills. At some posts, soldiers might fire their weapons on average once a month. Horsemanship was just as neglected. A doctor on the 1876 campaign against the Sioux found that cavalrymen "as a general thing are about as well fitted to travel through a hostile country as a puling infant" and were easy pickings for any Indian "who takes the trouble to lay for them behind the first conve-nient ridge."[41]

The frontier's chronic labor shortages and high wages made jumping into the job market a constant temptation. Mining rushes, like Idaho's in 1861, could all but depopulate the nearest posts. Depending on the denominator of calculation, between 14 and 34 percent of troops deserted every year between 1865 and 1891, with the worst hemorrhaging tak-ing place in 1872–73, right after Congress cut pay by nearly 20 percent. Higher ranking officers urged that something be done to stem the out-flow—Sherman was especially keen on providing libraries of good books and current newspapers and magazines—but serious reforms came only in the 1880s. Until then, talk was mostly in platitudes: recruit better men, Sherman advised, and make the service fit for them.[42]

Those who stayed coped as best they could. Many found bleak comfort with prostitutes among nearby Indians and post employees. An officer at Montana's Fort Custer reported that two out of every three men in the post hospital were there for venereal diseases, and a general commented on the common saying that post surgeons "had nothing to do but confine laundresses and treat the clap."[43]

Drinking was another common response. A soldier could buy liquor from a post sutler and in the saloons, usually the grimmest deadfalls, that sprang up nearby. Tippling was not confined to the posts. In the field against the Sioux in 1876, Colonel John Gibbon's officers tapped a keg of beer for an evening of "hitherto voiceless eloquence," singing, and "polemical contests of racy sort." As Howard's men first marched toward Lapwai, a month before the Nez Perce conflict began, a sergeant wrote in his diary that "one of the cooks drank too much Whiskey during our 10 minute halt and reposed under a tree all of the afternoon and night without blankets, blissfully unconscious of rain, cold or other annoyances."[44]

The long-term costs of drinking were considerable. During the decade after the Nez Perce War, roughly one in twenty-five regulars and officers was hospitalized for alcoholism—remarkable, given that only extreme cases were confined, men hopelessly compromised by stupors and the jim-jams. The longer in harness, the more likely someone was to slip over the alcoholic edge. Among those aged fifty to fifty-four, commitment for alcoholism was an astounding one in six.[45] Prominent officers, for example Brigadier General Frederick Benteen, who was involved in both the Sioux and Nez Perce conflicts, were disciplined for drunkenness, and devoted teetotalers like Howard still had to deal with the problem. At a critical point in the campaign, he was in correspondence with a past classmate asking for his help. After twenty-three years of service, the classmate, a major, was about to be drummed out because, as he cryptically put it, "I have got into serious trouble for drinking unexpectedly."[46]

Soldiers could ease their situation somewhat by spending their meager pay on better food, clothes, books, and amusements. They played some sports—foot races and baseball were particular favorites—and joined in group singing of popular music hall songs, sentimental ballads, and other songs composed from western experiences: "We wint to Arizona / For to fight the Injins there; / We came near being made bald-headed, / But they never got our hair."[47] Campaigning had a few attractions. Troops chasing the Nez Perces at one point had time for an especially impassioned pastime, trout fishing, and in June 1877, after General George Crook's column had a hard fight with the Sioux, soldiers refreshed themselves by catching thousands of cutthroat trout and playing baseball.

One of the few positive notes in the western army's wretched living conditions was the mateship that could grow from the shared misery among the common grunts. Some of the most poignant voices of the time are in letters sent by combat survivors to families of lost friends. "It becomes my painful duty to inform you that your poor Brother David is dead," a cavalryman wrote after the Nez Perce War's last battle. He described their attack on the camp and how he and David had been pinned down together. When his friend was shot in the chest, "he called to me at once and I crawled up to him and drew him in a hollow out of range of the firing. he say's Abe old boy if this thing kills me, write to my Mother with my love...after dark when I went to him he was dead. He was my fast friend. We were what in the Army is called Bunky's."[48]

The frontier army did its job. All significant Indian resistance was suppressed by the 1880s—ironically, the decade when modest reforms finally came to the military ranks. Success came partly from the army's persistence, from leadership that was at least competent and occasionally much better, and from enough soldiers' willingness to keep their lives on the line. Behind it all, however, was the nation's increasingly focused power. In this final twitching of nearly three centuries of conquest, the nation's numbers and resources dwarfed by orders of magnitude anything Indians could have put up, even if they had all united, which was never remotely possible.

The Indian wars after 1865 have drawn great attention, and for good reasons. Their campaigns and battles were at times exciting and heroic by the old standards—conflicts that were turned one way or another by a few men's courage instead of machines and massed bodies. Much of what happened to native peoples and to innocent whites who got in the way was heartbreaking and aroused strong feelings. The wars also reflected forces transforming the nation. But in the context of the Greater Reconstruction, the last native resistance was largely an irritant, and the force that dealt with it was less an army than an afterthought. The Indian wars were essentially a scrapping between two groups of the new America's underfed stepchildren.

# CHAPTER 9

# Ways of Life, Ways of War

After Perry finally relieved the Brave Seventeen, the bands moved northeastward down Cottonwood Creek to where it met the Clearwater River. Along the way, warriors raided farms and ranches, burning houses and fences and destroying crops. At the Clearwater, they were joined by Looking Glass and the Alpowais, raising the number in camp to around 750. Their plans at that point are uncertain, and probably were uncertain even to themselves. They could not expect to settle up on anything but punitive terms. If not that, what?

The army was about to force an answer. Civilian scouts found the camp on the Clearwater and decided to stay near it, concealed, until Howard could be notified and come up. When one of them spoiled the plan by accidentally firing his rifle, they withdrew to a flat-topped, rock-rimmed ridge and dug rifle pits. The Nez Perces knew the place as Possossona (Water Passing, because of a spring). Whites would dub it Misery Hill. Warriors assembled around it and with awful yells and hoots fired vigorously and crawled close, but they could get no clear shots and did no damage. They returned at night and stole more than forty horses, mostly mounts that whites had taken a week earlier from Looking Glass's village, and then fired again on the volunteers for a few hours before heading back to the river. Although one of the civilians later called the entire affair "a full-fledged, fizzling joke," others described a heroic defense against wave on wave of fanatical attackers. Yellow Wolf recalled it as a minor skirmish and a nighttime show ("It was just like fireworks cutting the darkness"). The Nez Perces' one casualty had his right index finger shot off.[1]

One of the men on Misery Hill was Lew Wilmot; he slipped off to tell Howard, back at Grangeville, of the bands' whereabouts. This was when Wilmot had his profane set-to with the general. After his arrest and release, he headed back to his friends in disgust rather than waiting to guide the troops. At seven o'clock in the morning on July 9, Howard set off on what he hoped would be a thrust to end the war. Finally he had a true bead on the enemy, and they reportedly were all together. A victory or even an especially punishing fight should force them to terms.

Then came one of Howard's more puzzling decisions. He did not retrace Wilmot's path to Misery Hill, an easy half mile from the Nez Perce camp. Instead, led by several locals, including Arthur "Ad" Chapman, the man who had started the fighting at White Bird, Howard marched to a bridge on the Clearwater River upstream from the bands, crossed, and on July 11 began marching downstream through rugged, difficult terrain. Besides putting a deep and swift river between him and his prey, Howard had his men marching along a series of high bluffs with little access down.[2] The bluffs also blocked the view below, and Howard had taken his men a full two miles past the Nez Perce camp, still at the mouth of Cottonwood Creek on the opposite side, before one of his reconnoitering officers noticed it. It was just before noon. Howard took a look and quickly set out to correct and attack.[3]

The battle that followed was unique in the war. It was not a rapid attack and rout, a siege, or a cat-and-mouse skirmishing, but a sustained confrontation in which each side had the strength to stand its ground and to maneuver. That made the Battle of the Clearwater especially revealing, showing something of both sides' strong and weak points and their respective ways of warmaking.[4] Those differences said something as well about the cultures and societies that faced each other, both here and across the West, as the new America emerged.

When the Nez Perces spotted the troops high above them on the other side of the river, they began running their horses to a safe distance and scurrying around to meet the threat. Howard first tried to build on the element of surprise by calling his howitzer to lob shells at the village from the bluff, but at that distance the aging piece managed only harmless airbursts. Having overshot the camp, Howard had to backtrack to put his men in position for an assault down one of two ravines that offered access to the Clearwater and the village. That delay gave the Nez Perces an opening. First, Toohoolhoolzote and two dozen men crossed the stream, rode up one of the gullies, found a protective rise, piled stones into barricades, and leveled a considerable fire at the arriving troops. The old warrior, humiliated when Howard had jailed him at the Lapwai council two months earlier, now blocked a thrust that might have taken the village and ended the war. A second group under Rainbow and Ollokut, after securing the horse herd and pulling families out of reach, ascended the second draw and fired from their own protected positions.

The momentum of the fight reversed. The Nez Perces now controlled the only ways down the bluffs. From the superior cover of trees and rock formations, they sent a heavy fire that stopped the army's advance and sent the attackers belly-flopping for their lives. Several fell dead or wounded. "Men were being shot on each side of me, the wounded were writhing and groaning and cursing," C. E. S. Wood wrote a few days later: "The red devils were 'yow-yowing' and war whooping and their bullets zee-zipping in the grass close to my head and I felt kind o' homesick you understand."[5] Although Howard's cavalry, infantry, and artillery together outnumbered their opponents' force by at least three and as much as five to one, Howard had to turn his full-throttle assault into a defensive deployment. He formed his men into a semicircle extending for about eight hundred yards across an open highland. With no natural concealment except tall grass and low swells, his men dug in as best they could, piling up stones pulled from the dry soil. Inside this crescent, Howard established his headquarters and a field hospital with a not-too-reliable bulwark of stacked packsaddles.

For the rest of the day, the Nez Perces kept up a heavy fire and made a few serious thrusts out of the tree line of scrubby pines they would call the battle ridge. "They gave it to us hot," a soldier remembered. The troops jabbed back, looking for weak points. Civil War veteran Captain Evan Miles led a vigorous charge that cleared warriors temporarily from one of their entrenched positions. A Nez Perce assault nearly captured the command's howitzer and Gatling gun; a counterattack secured the pieces, in the face of gunfire that took more lives in twenty minutes than were lost during the rest of the battle. Captain Marcus Miller led a push against the Nez Perces' densest concentration with an encouragement that must have struck a chord, given the events of the past weeks: "Men, get up and go for them; if we don't do something they will kill us all." They made some headway but faltered when hit by friendly fire.

By nightfall, neither side had accomplished much, although troops had found and gained a loose hold on a crucial resource, a small spring between the battle lines. Warriors had access to the river below, but most soldiers had only a canteen each to get through the day, choking on dust and baking in midsummer heat, their adrenalin-buzzed metabolisms burning their bodies' resources. With darkness the teamsters, hospital attendants, and officers, Howard among them, shuttled back and forth to the spring to help slake the thirst of men, horses, and mules.

The first day had shown one thing: both sides were brave. Infantrymen charged straight into precise and withering fire. When one howitzer battery lost four of its five men, the survivor, a cannoneer private, drove back the attackers by loading and firing the piece while lying on his back between the wheels. Knowing well the disasters of recent weeks, having heard inflated rumors of their own terrible losses, Howard's troops held their exposed ground despite exhaustion, thirst, and unnerving Nez Perce marksmanship. There were other unpleasantnesses. One private passed a bit of bravado to an officer—"this is a ticklish business"—and turned his head to see a rattlesnake at his elbow.

Staying put was quite a challenge in the face of the Nez Perces' own performance. Captain Eugene Bancroft, badly wounded in the fight, wrote later that they "fought like devils, and were brave as lions."[6] Another officer described the Nez Perce horsemen's distinctive and surely intimidating technique: "They ride up behind little elevations, throw themselves from their ponies, fire, and are off like rockets. Lines of them creep and crawl and twist themselves through the grass until within range.... They tie grass upon their heads, so that it is hard to tell which bunch of grass does not conceal an Indian with a globe-sighted rifle." Watching horsemen roll off their mounts to fire, McCarthy was equally impressed with the horses, which "remain[ed]...quiet and patient during the firing." The Nez Perces made their full charges "in regular daredevil style, nothing sneaking about it," McCarthy wrote later; "they were brave men, and faced a terrific fire."[7] Some made it almost to within a bayonet thrust of the soldier's rifle pits. Warriors sang as they rode and fought, "one of the bunch giving out the song, the others joining in the chorus." An artillery sergeant impulsively ran toward the enemy and was quickly cut down; an attendant journalist speculated he was so "weighed down with troubles" that he had chosen this death dash. Joe Albert (or Elaskolatat, Animal Entering a Hole), a Christianized Nez Perce serving Howard as a scout, learned that his father, a nontreaty Dreamer, had died in the scrapping at Cottonwood Creek. Albert flipped allegiances and galloped from the army line to the other, drawing fire from both sides. He changed from civilian to traditional clothes and later was shot in the thigh while taking part in a charge on the army's lines.[8]

During the night, many Nez Perces drifted down to the village and stayed there. The army wasn't attacking their families, some argued: Why keep up the fight?[9] Others stayed up top, some in comma-shaped stone forts built during the day. Across the field, the army cooks prepared the first food in more than twenty-four hours, flapjacks, which the troops ate while listening to chanting from their opponents' positions and women keening in the village below.

At dawn the exchanges of fire resumed—subdued from the Nez Perce side—and Howard decided on an offensive punch to get around his opponents' left flank. By three o'clock in the afternoon, he was ready to set it loose, when rising dust to the southwest signaled the late approach of a cavalry company and large pack train of supplies from Lapwai. This vulnerable train was at the opposite end of the army's perimeter from the artillery battalion that was about to strike, so the battalion's commanding officer, Miller, rapidly marched his men two miles and set them up as a protective screen. Then suddenly, to everyone's surprise, Howard included, Miller ordered his men to wheel and advance on the Nez Perce line at double time. Nearby infantry quickly took their cue and charged, and the Gatling gun and two howitzers were brought up to fire. Caught off guard, the remaining Nez Perces—by some accounts only a handful—held for a few moments, and then broke and fled down the ravine to the river and their village, "all skipping for their lives, for the camp!" as Peopeo Tholekt told it. Joseph rushed to warn the village. Terrified families took what they could, ran for the horses, and fled to the north up Cottonwood Creek. Retreating warriors followed the families as a rear guard as Howard shelled the camp as well as the battle ridge. Up in those fortifications, "rocks were showered and limbs of trees cut down," Eelahweemah (About Asleep), fourteen at the time, recalled: "Smoke from that gun was like grass on fire....I jumped out from there and ran!"[10]

Last to leave the ridge were Wottolen (Hair Combed Over Eyes) and Yellow Wolf. Wottolen, one of the older warriors, slowed to a walk, out of breath, but he was confident of survival: "I had promise from my *Wey-ya-kin* that no bullets would hit me." As the soldiers' fire kicked up dust around him, a man appeared on a loping white horse. It was a cousin, Weeahweoktpoo (later a Presbyterian minister, William Wheeler), who spurred the horse to a gallop as Wottolen grabbed the saddle horn and swung aboard. Yellow Wolf soon arrived in the village to find only a woman atop a wheeling, stamping horse. She was Springtime, Joseph's wife, who had given birth at Tepahlewam on the eve of the outbreak, and she was in a dilemma. Her baby girl was on the ground in a cradleboard, but if she dismounted to get her daughter, her nervous horse would probably bolt. She laughed with relief as Yellow Wolf handed her the child, and together they galloped off to catch the last of the fleeing families.[11]

Now the cavalry was at the Clearwater, but its leader, Perry, hesitated to cross the swollen river. He paused; finally he ordered two companies over, but instead of sending them in pursuit, he had them form a skirmish line in case the Nez Perces doubled back. There was further delay as the infantry was ferried across the river. Although it was barely late afternoon, Howard did not order a pursuit. Instead the command settled into the camp with its eighty or so abandoned lodges.

It must have felt like sitting down where a family had run out on an errand. Cooking fires still burned under simmering meals. There were vast amounts of supplies—food, utensils, weapons, and hides—as well as personal possessions. More was found buried as caches under the lodges. Presumably, the Nez Perces anticipated being gone a long time, perhaps even now were planning to run eastward across the mountains, and had stashed underground their most treasured, least portable items. But the civilian packers and other locals ("it was marvelous how many citizens seemed to arrive" as soon as the firing stopped, an officer remembered) proceeded to prospect the soft ground with ramrods and to dig up troves of jewelry, gold dust, fine clothing, and silver tableware thought to date from the Hudson's Bay trading days. When the looting was finished, the rest was burned.[12]

Howard would claim twenty-three Nez Perce dead—fifteen killed in the battle and eight more found along the route of retreat—and twice as many wounded.[13] How he came up with these numbers is a mystery. Although one body was found on the battle ridge, no participants on his side claimed to have seen for certain any deaths during the fighting, and no other sources mention corpses found along the trail. The only other officer to address the point, Captain W. R. Parnell, wrote that the number of enemy losses was unknown, "as they carried their dead and wounded with them."[14] Nez Perce testimony is unanimous that four died and six were wounded, only one seriously. The army and its civilian support suffered thirteen dead during the fighting and twenty-seven wounded, two of whom died later.

Two facts about the army's casualties are startling: the high number of officers and sergeants (nine out of forty) among them, and the one-to-two ratio of dead to wounded. In the initial clash, young Yellow Wolf was firing furiously at the advancing soldiers when an older warrior, Otstotpoo (Fire Body), approached him: "Dear son, we are going to die right here! Do not shoot the common soldier. Shoot the commander!"[15] A lieutenant was hit in the thigh, then hit in the arm holding the tourniquet he had applied. The toll of dead and wounded in later battles suggests that many Nez Perces again might have singled out commissioned and noncommissioned officers.

Whether aiming at privates or generals, warriors still had to hit their targets, and clearly they were superb marksmen. About a third of the shots that found their marks were fatal, although most were fired from a great distance. In several, non-fatal wounds the difference between death and survival was millimeters. A bullet took a sergeant's eye cleanly out of its socket, not even touching the bone; he finished the campaign wearing a green eye patch. A rifle ball hit a private near his right ear, bounced around the back of his head, staying between skin and skull, and stopped by his left ear. It left a black, hairless path. Anything exposed and offering the slightest target was vulnerable. A trooper died from a bullet to the brain when he poked his head slightly above his cover; another had his canteen shot through the neck as he raised it to drain its last drops; another took a shot in the heel when he squirmed in his shallow trench and raised his foot for an instant above the rim.

This ability, in addition to the Nez Perces' horseback charges and their shimmying through the grass, sum up a lot of what can be said of their military strengths. A closer look shows their weaknesses as well. Army observers were sure they operated under coordinated direction. McCarthy, who knew plenty about fighting, wrote of mounted warriors in groups of three or four attacking independently but in "excellent" formations and of maneuvers executed through signaled commands: "A chief on some point out of range directed the movement by waving a blanket or circling his pony." Howard also wrote of a man who "paraded himself in plain view.... He would dance around and leap up and down in a strange way with arms outstretched, waving a red blanket."[16] The Nez Perces did indeed show an uncanny sense of strategy. At White Bird Canyon, their flanking of Perry's right side and their seizure of the civilian's hill were the ideal maneuvers to unhinge the army's attack. At the Clearwater, their quick moves up the ravines and their choice of positions at the top threw Howard instantly on the defensive and left his superior numbers exposed, off-balance, and vulnerable. McCarthy and Howard naturally assumed their opponents fought by some leader's shrewd direction.

But the facts were different. The moves that were so effective at White Bird and the Clearwater were spontaneous. Each began when someone took the initiative—the "Three Red Coats" and Two Moons in the first battle, Toohoolhoolzote and Ollokut in the second—and several others joined in. Once the fight was joined, there was a loose leadership of men respected for past performance, but they led by exhortation and advice, not command. In his recollection, Yellow Wolf calls Wottolen "one of the commanders" at the Clearwater, but his leadership consisted of striking Yellow Wolf with a whip and telling him to kill some soldiers before they killed him. A few pages later, Yellow Wolf calls Wottolen "my partner," who discovered the two were alone at the battle's end and called out: "Nobody here! We will quit!" Another participant, H-wow-no Ilpilp (First

Red Feather of the Wing), related that when troops were first sighted on the bluff line, someone "made [the] remark" that they should go up and meet them. So they did. After a while, Two Moons "gave the remark that [we] must quit again for a while," which they did, and then fought later elsewhere. "The next morning I heard some young men...[say] that we might as well quit the fighting," he continued; "We quit."[17]

As always, a leader's power was "more advisory than mandatory," as a white confidant of the tribe put it. A leader could not demand any action of any warrior.[18] The common good was always the end, but personal impulse was the means. An episode at the Clearwater made the point. A man who "had no good name" wished to acquire a brave one and so spontaneously galloped toward the troops and raced nearly the full length of their line before turning back. In the storm of bullets, one finally struck him in the back and exited his breast. With a friend, he went down to the river and submerged himself in the icy water for cleansing. His *wey-ya-kin* was in the male bison, so he emerged on all fours, pawed the ground with his fists, and rumbled from his chest like a bull in rut. Clots of blood fell from his wound, and after his friend dressed it, they returned to the battle. He earned his name: Kipkip Owyeen (Wounded Breast).[19]

The premium in battle was the same as in everything else—a mix of individual initiative, respect for proven experience, and a commitment to the collective good. The problem was that disagreement about the third (collective good) combined with doubt about the second (proven experience) gave such wide latitude to the first (individual initiative) that things could rapidly fall apart. The chances of that increased considerably if the fighting lasted more than a few hours. "They are so strongly fatalistic," according to Edward S. Curtis, the legendary photographer who knew many of the participants at the Clearwater, "that if a battle cannot be won in the first grand rush, they begin to question the medicine power of the leader and think it better to fight at another time and place, where the spirits may be with them."[20] Once this tendency kicked in, there was no countervailing authority to hold warriors in place—nothing like the iron command the army tried to ingrain in every recruit. As a consequence, Curtis wrote, "Indians rarely, if ever, have won a serious conflict which continued to a second day."

The Battle of the Clearwater might seem an exception, but in the end it proved the point. Their common effort was cracking by the end of the first day, and halfway through the second it crumbled. When Teeweeyownah (Over the Point) and several younger men called for a do-or-die charge against the troops, an argument started. The others were cowards, he said, and he vowed to die soon as a free man, and then he abruptly called for a end to the fight, and he and his friends rode down the bluff and away from the action. Soon afterward Miller led his impromptu charge and ended the fight. Command, obedience, and perseverance trumped individualized courage and skill, as they would time and again in the Indian wars.

If art can imitate life, so can war. The Nez Perce way of war, paradoxically, was intensely communal yet trusting in free-flowing inspiration and responses—a "remark" about one move or another, a momentary incitement, and the call or silence of unseen spirits. That could produce stunning victories, as Perry found at White Bird Canyon, but there was no ordered authority to hold it all together. The strength of Howard's command, like its society, was so elemental that it was easy to miss. It was a regimented order. Troops were part of a structure that could focus decisions from Washington, D.C., St. Louis, or San Francisco into actions in Georgia, Texas, or Idaho. A campaign might be hobbled by bad luck and poor performance. It might be poorly supplied and slowed by jealousies and conflicts. But the point remained: the army, as a mechanism, was a persisting presence, whether occupying a region for years or staying in a fight for days. Everyone in it, from division commanders to grunts in the field, worked in general obedience. Add to that the nation's overwhelming numbers and resources, and the odds were beyond prohibitive. The Nez Perces—and the Apaches and Sioux and any other Indians—might sting the army and temporarily escape it. What they could not do was win.

Native leaders could not be expected to grasp a social order and mental arrangement so utterly different from their own. The misapprehension was two-way. Many western commanders, and certainly Howard, seemed never to understand how their enemies were ordered and how they worked.

This mutual misapprehension was the context for the most enduring misperception of the war. Howard and whites generally assumed Joseph was in firm and sole command.[21] Howard even claimed to know his enemy's conversations. In *Nez Perce Joseph* (with its subtitle referring to *His Murders* and *His War*), it was Joseph and Ollokut, not Hand in Hand and No Feet, who spied the soldier's dawn advance at White Bird. "'Hu-hugh!'" Ollokut says; "'Horses!'" After peering through a "white man's glass," Joseph barks out his orders: "'Get the people ready.... White Bird, take your men and turn the Bostons [whites] when they get to this ridge.'"[22] Later C. E. S. Wood, Howard's aide, wrote in the *Century* that at the Clearwater Joseph directed every maneuver with "fierce calls." He "was everywhere along the line; running from point to point... wholly reckless of himself."[23]

JOSEPH, THE NEZ PERCÉS WARRIOR.—[From a Sketch by an Army Officer.]

**Figure 9.1** Fanciful drawing of Chief Joseph as stern commander of the Nez Perces

All nonsense. Howard knew nothing of what happened in the camp at White Bird, of course. As for Wood, by the time he wrote his article he knew Joseph well, but at the time of the battle he had never met him. How, then, did he recognize Joseph from hundreds of yards away across a dusty plateau—and, as it turns out, suffering from badly inflamed eyes?[24]

Hyperbole and purple prose aside, putting Joseph at center stage made sense at the time. He had been the primary spokesman for the nontreaty bands during the months leading up to war, and in the show-down at Lapwai he had been the conciliator after Howard had arrested Toohoolhoolzote. Wouldn't he then be in control when peace gave way to war? To the Nez Perces the answer was obvious: no. Leadership was situational. When talk turned to war, it shifted from Joseph the natural diplomat to gifted warriors like Ollokut, Toohoolhoolzote, Five Wounds, Rainbow, and Looking Glass, and they took charge. Joseph showed plenty of courage every time he was in battle, but he never took the lead. At the Clearwater, he was never mentioned as participating in the fight up top but only as rushing into the village at the end to tell the people to run—a role he would play again.[25]

The most intriguing question is not why Howard made Joseph into a commander but why anyone looked for a commander at all. Maybe it was out of a narrative need for "heroes and scapegoats"; Edward Curtis wrote: "commonplace men make dull history."[26] Perhaps. But Howard was also following the line the government's agents had taken for more than thirty years: pulling the Nez Perces into the national embrace, projecting onto them a single identity with one man at the top. It was what the government needed and expected. Now, in war, the natural impulse was to see the same projection as a structure of command.

Howard's Joseph—pulling a "white man's glass," sending subordinates this way and that, the dashing inspirer riding down the line—might have been Lee or Longstreet, Grant or Chamberlain, a model leader who fit the very state-making the Nez Perces had bet their lives against. Eventually, once the war was finished, the real Joseph showed his true brilliance and greatest leadership by playing on that misapprehension and using it to his people's benefit.

At the end of the Battle of the Clearwater, Howard had his own brush with the top-down, knit-together structure he was helping to establish: he nearly lost his job. Local press accounts, describing his performance before the Clearwater as even worse than it was, were splashed across the eastern press. According to one rumor, residents of Lewiston had burned him in effigy.[27] With the Associated Press reporting that the cabinet was

calling for Howard's replacement, President Hayes ordered Captain
A. D. C. Keeler, sent by Howard's immediate superior, Irvin McDowell,
to assess the situation. He arrived at the Clearwater just in time to see the
end of the battle and wrote a short, glowing message that reported Joseph
in headlong retreat and Howard master of the situation: "Nothing can
surpass the vigor of General Howard's movements and action."[28] Quickly,
Howard seized the advantage. Wood, now Howard's aide, telegraphed the
president directly to report the victory and to pass along Keeler's words.
Howard sent the War Department his inflated number of enemy casualties and claimed he "was in fine condition ... to make a thorough work"
of his adversaries. He soon reported that he had "pretty much cleared this
part of the country of every hostile Indian" and thanked his troops for
"surely bring[ing] permanent peace to the Northwest." McDowell, while
miffed at Howard for wiring the president on his own, still wrote that
he was "infinitely relieved and rejoiced." Howard's critics backed down
from their demands that he be sacked.[29]

It was a nice save, but in fact Howard's position was hardly what he
claimed. He had passed up his best chance of the entire conflict for a fatal
blow and had given the Nez Perces a great unearned opportunity. As
the bands had begun their disorderly flight at midafternoon on July 12,
Howard had been closer to them than he ever had been or would be until
the end of the war. He knew which way they were going—north, downstream. Their path, he knew, was toward what was suddenly a strategically critical point, the base of the Lolo trail. From there, he knew, they
could take that traditional passage, the route taken for plains bison hunts,
eastward and escape into Montana. He knew also, however, that the bands
were running down the west side of the Clearwater, across from the Lolo
trail, so to reach the escape route they would have to march to a usable
ford, then swim their horses and ferry their people across—a process of
many hours. Once across, they would be out of immediate danger and be
much harder to catch, but while still on his side of the river, they were
highly catchable. Clearly the call was for a rapid and aggressive pursuit.

But Howard stalled. It was late afternoon by the time he got all his men
across the river and into the Nez Perce camp, but this was high summer, and
there were hours of daylight left. His men were tired, but so were the bands,
and they were only a couple of hours ahead of him, slowed by the burden of
their elderly, their children, their large horse herd, and what possessions they
had kept. Instead of taking up the chase, Howard put his men into camp and
the next day spent all morning getting his Gatling gun and howitzers down
the bluffs and across the river.[30] Meanwhile, the bands reached the ford of
the Clearwater River at Kamiah, and around midday on July 13, as Howard

was just starting after them, they began crossing the river in saucer-shaped bullboats of made of hides stretched over willow frames.

By the time the cavalry arrived at the ford, fully twenty-four hours had passed since the battle. All the Nez Perces had crossed the Clearwater and were safely making camp, with their horses grazing on a distant hillside. Spotting the approaching column, warriors hid in the riverside rocks, and as the cavalry drew within range they opened a heavy fire that sent some riders galloping for safety and others jumping from their saddles to hide in a wheat field. The shooters laughed and jeered—one warrior later called this a "fun-war"—and Howard later admitted that the humiliation was "a fierce delight to our foe."[31] The hoots continued as the army's howitzers lobbed shells harmlessly toward the new camp. This was the moment, as he was taunted by an enemy he had let out of his grip, when Howard wrote so confidently that he was about "to make thorough work" of the hostiles and quickly bring them to heel.

His best chance now was to make up what he had lost by somehow getting himself across the river and behind the bands, between them and Lolo Pass, and after losing another day considering his poor options, he left much of his command in camp ("Rest for the weary sole," Wood punned)[32] and made his try. He feinted one way, and then led a column down the Clearwater, planning to cross by ferry and then head back upstream by a trail that would put him at Weippe Prairie, at the base of Lolo Pass.[33] He had barely started on the forty-mile march, however, when he learned that the bands had packed up and were heading to Weippe, sure to get there long before him. He turned around and returned to camp.

If Howard had given the Nez Perces a temporary reprieve, their troubles still ran far deeper than his. True, their immediate situation seemed positive. They had scored lopsided victories and outmaneuvered their opponents. They had killed eight enemy combatants for every man, woman, and child they had lost. In their hasty retreat, they had left behind tipis and supplies, but they had lost few men and had kept most of their horses. Yet the terrible truth was that all their success only highlighted how desperate their condition was. The lesson of the Clearwater was that they could not stand up to sustained confrontation, either for forty-eight hours of fighting or for weeks of maneuvering around their home country. There were only so many places to go, so many rivers to put between themselves and the army, so many ways to jog onto so many unpredicted routes. Worse, leaders had to make these military moves while seeing to the basic needs of several hundred persons of all ages and conditions and, equally important, about two thousand horses, the irreplaceable living tools in both war and peace. They could expect no help. Local whites talked anxiously of others joining the fight, but the other Nez Perce bands were firmly against the resisters, and the region's other tribes had seen their own power broken earlier, when the Nez Perces had stood apart and let them go down alone.

Their basic problem was that they had long ago lost command of what had been their home and now was their military theater, which left them in the fix common to all Native America: How do you sustain a way of life without controlling that life's stage and its props? Their enemies moved as they wished and ultimately controlled most needful things. Given that, anything the Nez Perces did, no matter how brilliant and star-blessed, could only postpone disaster.

Opinions differed on what to do. Joseph reportedly was indecisive and depressed. His band was the farthest from home, and the odds of ever seeing it again ("Think of your country," the dying Old Joseph had told his son) seemed remote. Apparently, he weighed ending the fight. Right after Howard heard that the Nez Perces had decamped, he got other startling news. Joseph was considering surrender. The next day, July 15, an emissary crossed the Clearwater to visit the general, who said that Joseph could expect a fair hearing with a military tribunal, but only if he surrendered unconditionally. Howard was so confident that the end was at hand that he selected Miller to receive the chief and his arms, but July 16 came and went without any sign of Joseph. Howard later wrote that Joseph had snookered him, using the surrender ruse to keep the troops in place while he got a head start—a line of thinking that once again assumed that Joseph, the master strategist, was in sole command. More likely, Joseph honestly considered giving up but stayed the course because others pressed him to and because of what might happen to his people at the army's hands. Leaders of other northwestern wars, most recently Captain Jack of the Modocs, had been hanged, an especially horrifying death in those cultures. Given that Howard had not exactly built up a reservoir of trust, hearing "unconditional surrender" must have been worrisome.

Others persisted in their hostility. A council was held at Weippe Prairie on the night of July 15. The mood must have been a mix of anger, frustration, jumpiness, and defiance. No one spoke for surrender. Some called for a thrust westward back to the wild, rough country along the Snake River, but more argued for heading in the opposite direction, east over Lolo Pass to Montana. The trail was familiar, with steep inclines and heavy timber ideal for defense, and on the other side were more horses and their longtime friends the Flatheads. Still, crossing Lolo Pass was a sobering commitment. The face-off with the government had come down to two issues: living independently and keeping their homelands. Start up that trail, the leaders knew, and the one might be possible, but the price would be giving up the other for an indefinite time.

Looking Glass tipped the balance in favor of leaving. This was the strange fruit of Whipple's attack on his village a week earlier. Before that ill-advised and botched move, the chief had cautioned restraint and had stayed out of the fighting, but once in, he took a prominent role and now argued strongly that the bands would find sanctuary by crossing the Bitterroots and pushing on to the Great Plains. The Crows would take them in, he said. For many years, they had welcomed them into their lodges during the long hunts on the plains. According to Thomas LaForge, a white who had married among the Crows, intermarriage between the two peoples was so common that only through personal acquaintance could someone know who was of what tribal stock. Just three years earlier, Looking Glass had done his legendary work against the Sioux ("Ah, but there was a man!" LaForge recalled of that day), and by traditional diplomacy he was owed a debt the Crows would pay by giving sanctuary.[34]

Thus, the decision was made that began an American odyssey and made the Nez Perce experience unique in the western wars. Other Indians, facing similar facts, had chosen between two options—keep fighting and finally lose, typically at terrible cost, or give up and surrender independence sooner than later. The Nez Perce tried a third way: they ran to someplace else. On July 16, seventy-two hours after Howard had declared virtual victory, the enemy he said he had whipped took their leave while the army sat and waited on the far bank of the Clearwater.

This part of the story had a sad but somehow fitting epilogue. On July 16, as Howard waited for Joseph to surrender, some Nez Perces did in fact show up. The group—seventeen men, the most prominent being Red Heart, with about twenty-five women and children—had recently returned from a Montana hunt and had been in Looking Glass's village when Whipple had attacked. Determined to avoid trouble, they had withdrawn to Weippe Prairie as Looking Glass and his people had headed in the opposite direction to join the hostiles. They were still there when the retreating bands arrived after the fight on the Clearwater. Having tried to keep out of the way, they found themselves squarely in it, and as the bands started up Lolo Pass, they once more moved in the other direction, this time to the army to say that they wanted none of the fight.[35]

Howard arrested them, took their horses and most of their possessions, and sent them sixty miles by foot to Fort Lapwai. The "horrible hot stifling march" over an "open scorching prairie" was so brutal, Wood wrote, that the accompanying troops had to dump packs from the mules to carry the fainting and the sunstruck.[36] Soon afterward, thirty-three of

Figure **9.2** Red Heart, imprisoned with his band in 1877, at a happier time in later life

the group were sent in irons to Fort Vancouver. Emily Fitzgerald, the wife of Howard's surgeon, watched them as they readied to leave. Certain that they would be hanged, they keened and wept and cut beads from their clothes to leave as mementos mori for family left behind. It would be nine months, without a hearing, before they were finally freed.[37]

Howard never mentioned this episode directly in his public writings; his only reference was oblique and disingenuous. To his bloated claim of Nez Perce casualties at the Clearwater (twenty-three dead, nineteen more than the truth, and more than forty wounded when there were only four), he added that there were forty prisoners.[38] A reader would assume these were captives taken at the time of the battle. In fact, none were. The forty were Red Heart's bunch, noncombatants who walked conveniently into Howard's camp four days later, just as his predicted victory was dissolving and he was facing public ridicule for his lack of results.

As Howard was arresting Red Heart, the other Nez Perces were starting their passage up the Lolo Trail. They might well have looked at their surroundings through deep memory. Kamiah, where they had crossed the Clearwater and thumbed their noses at Howard, lay close to the Heart of the Monster, where Coyote had sprinkled the blood that sprang to life as the Nimiipuu, the Real People. The trail they ascended was the one Lewis and Clark had taken down into their country, and Weippe Prairie, where they had just made their decision to leave home, was where Nez Perces had seen their first white men in 1805. There the Nimiipuu had spared the starving explorers and fed them salmon and berries.

It was also at Weippe, on the return trip, that William Clark had sired a son, Halahtookit (Daytime Smoke). He was among the nontreaties. Now seventy, he moved up the Lolo Trail with a family that included Clark's granddaughter and great-grandson. Together, they reversed the steps his father had taken to set in motion the forces now sending the Nez Perces out of the homeland Coyote had given them.

CHAPTER **10**

# Leaving Home

The Lolo trail ran about a hundred miles north and east from Weippe Prairie over the Bitterroot Mountains. It began at three thousand feet above sea level and rose in places to well above twice that. Sherman wrote later that it was "universally admitted.... [to be] one of the worst *trails* for man and beast on this continent."[1] On both sides of the divide, it was no straight incline but a series of peaks and troughs that sometimes dipped or rose more than two thousand feet in a mile. Parts of the twisting path were rocky and barren, parts muddy and slick in wet weather. Thick timber closed in for much of the way, and in places it was scarcely a footpath along the rims of canyons hundreds of feet deep. During the summer, it was bisected by dozens of freshets. A dependable road was not built over the pass until 1962.

The threat of ambush was made clear even before the army started its pursuit. On July 16, as the Nez Perces started up the trail, Howard sent Major E. C. Mason with cavalry, some civilians, and Nez Perce scouts to reconnoiter. When signs of an Indian presence increased, Mason sent the scouts ahead of him to feel out any threat of concealed attack—a good thing, as a Nez Perce rear guard fired on them from thick timber, killing one and wounding two. Mason and his horsemen abandoned the scouts with their casualties and scampered back to camp.

Howard's first plan was to avoid the pass entirely and take his men onto a long looping route twice as long as the Lolo Trail but so much easier and faster that, he thought, he could be waiting for the Nez Perces at the end of their crossing. From Lewiston, he would move north to the Mullan Road, one of those government projects that had begun to stitch the West together on the eve of the Civil War, and follow it eastward across the Bitterroots to Missoula City, a short march from the trail's eastern terminus.

Again, local concerns spoiled his plans. There were dark rumors that other Plateau groups would rise up as soon as the troops left, and some feared that the bands' move up the Lolo Trail was only a feint before roaring back once Howard was gone—a threat that seemed real when some Nez Perce raiders hit the reservation settlement near Kamiah and made off with about four hundred horses. The raiders had only doubled back briefly before rejoining the others up the trail, but the strike threw locals into "consternation scarcely equaled by the Caracas people in an earthquake."[2] Pressured by civilians, perceiving enemies literally left and right, and worried about being outmaneuvered yet again, Howard decided to wait for help. Troops were coming north from Fort Boise, and in a dramatic demonstration of the nation's expanding infrastructure, ten companies of the Second Infantry would soon arrive, having come all the way from Atlanta via railroad and steamboat in only sixteen days. Meanwhile, Howard gave arms to civilians and commercial travelers, put a strong guard around Lewiston, and kept his men in a defensive posture.

Howard's new plan broke his increased command into three parts. The first stayed in Idaho to tamp down any new trouble. The second moved west, discouraging Plateau peoples from joining the resistance, and then took the Mullan Road, following Howard's original plan, and waited at Missoula. The third—the main column—Howard led in pursuit of the bands over the Lolo trail. He hoped he could still catch them or trap them between his own men and those at the other end.

On July 30, Howard set off up the Lolo trail with battalions of infantry, cavalry, and artillery, fourteen companies in all, with more than seven hundred officers and enlisted men, along with civilian volunteers, Indian scouts, and packers hired for a train of 350 mules bearing supplies and rations for nearly three weeks. In a steady rain, men, horses, and mules trudged through a sop of mud. The trail steepened and tapered to a path through thick underbrush, tangled vines, and a forest of white pine and spruce. The men were "climbing one mountain for miles, only to plunge again into a deep gorge," an officer wrote home; "most tiresome work."[3] The trail sometimes widened onto vistas, sometimes passed through marshes, sometimes funneled into a narrow track blocked by fallen trees. The climb was difficult and wearing—they found several dead horses left by the bands ahead of them—but the two-mile-long column still traversed up to twenty-two miles a day and passed the summit on August 6.[4]

By now, Howard knew something of the Nez Perces' whereabouts, and the news was not good. They had left earlier than he had thought, made good time, passed the summit, and reached a traditional camping spot by some hot springs around July 23, a full week before he had left.

Long before Howard's other troops might arrive to plug their exit, they were off the Lolo trail and pushing toward the Crows in buffalo country along the traditional route that ran southward up the Bitterroot River. By August 6, as Howard topped the Lolo summit, they had traveled the length of the Bitterroot valley and ascended the next range of mountains. They were at least 150 miles ahead. An officer would note dryly that it was still possible to overtake Joseph "by the time he reaches New York."[5]

Events along the way had been both confused and revealing and, at moments, almost comic. Word had leaked to Montana that the Nez Perces might be headed that way, and whites at the eastern end of the Lolo trail were understandably nervous. The nearest railhead was the Union Pacific at Corinne, Utah, the nearest telegraph was at Deer Lodge, nearly seventy miles away, and the closest troops were two undermanned companies under Captain Charles Rawn at Missoula City. On July 18, Rawn sent a party up the trail to check for approaching Indians. By their later report, they went well past the Lolo summit and back yet found nothing to worry them, which meant they somehow managed to pass more than seven hundred persons, two thousand horses, and hundreds of dogs along a narrow path without noting anything amiss. Then they came across four persons—three Nez Perces and a mixed-blood then living in the Bitterroot valley—who told them of the bands descending toward Montana.

This word threw the settlements in a near panic. Governor Benjamin Potts wired General McDowell for help; McDowell asked whether Potts could arrest the Nez Perces; unlikely, Potts answered testily, since Washington had denied him permission to raise a militia. Then he raised one anyway. Missoula's newspaper sent out the call "HELP! HELP! COME RUNNING!" At Stevensville, the town nearest the Lolo trail outlet, locals shored up a crumbling trade outpost with fresh sod bricks and built two more defenses at Corvallis and Hamilton to the south. The first they named Fort Brave; the others, in bleak self-deprecation, they called Fort Skidaddle and Fort Run.[6] Other communities spontaneously formed units of armed volunteers that now moved toward the Lolo outlet.

On July 25, Rawn took his tiny command of about thirty-five men up the lower reaches of the trail. About four miles up, where the canyon narrowed, his men began felling trees for an emplacement to block the way out. It was audacious on the face of it, with the warriors outnumbering his troops by more than six to one, but he had the advantage of a defensive position, and citizens were starting to gather, about fifty at the time with more coming in. By the next day, their numbers roughly equaled that of the Indians against them. On July 25 and 26, soldiers and civilians worked the site into a rude fortification with walls of two or three stacked logs atop a mound of dirt pitched from a trench dug with trowel bayonets.[7]

Meanwhile, Rawn was in dialogue with Nez Perce leaders. Of all the episodes of the war, accounts of this exchange are the most garbled and contradictory, which is saying something. There was one meeting, or two, or three. Rawn's first (and last?) parley was on July 25, 26, or 27. It may or may not have included White Bird and Joseph, and if there was a second meeting, Governor Potts may or may not have been there. The most important confusion regards what was said and how the parties responded. Rawn seems to have begun by demanding an unconditional surrender of arms, ammunition, and persons. Looking Glass, who was definitely at the parley(s), may have offered up ammunition as a sign of peaceful intent, but guns were not negotiable. "When a Chinaman travels he carries no arms," one account has him telling Rawn: "Do you think I am a Chinaman?"[8] Looking Glass also stressed that his people had no quarrel with Montanans and hoped to pass through without conflict. Let us by, he told Rawn, past your stockade and through the Bitterroot valley, and no one need be bothered.

The key uncertainty is what Rawn's ultimate response was. He wrote in his official report that he had insisted on full surrender while also stalling in the hope that reinforcements were close by. After pressing his point, he said, he returned to his log blockade, expecting the Nez Perces to attack in full force. There he did indeed find movement. The volunteers were leaving. Once they heard of the Nez Perce promise to do no harm, Rawn reported, they saw no reason to rile them. "Things seemed to get quiet," a participant remembered, "and then we discovered that our citizen contingent was getting much smaller all the time."[9] At some point, probably on July 26, Governor Potts had appeared, although his role in negotiations, if any, is unclear. Now he left, too.

Some Nez Perces would agree that Rawn made a rigid demand. They responded with distrust, worrying again about being hanged. One account has the young warriors Red Moccasin Tops and Rainbow calling for a fight to the end. These accounts, like Rawn's, sound like a standoff. Yet Joseph wrote later that when Rawn told them that they could not get past the soldiers and citizens, they answered that they would, peaceably or not, and that "we then made a treaty with these soldiers. We agreed not to molest anyone and they agreed that we might pass through the Bitterroot country in peace." Howard also claimed that the Nez Perces had "negotiated their way" past Rawn.[10]

Whether Rawn would have fought turned out to be moot. On July 28, the bands started down the canyon, and then turned north on an alternate path, unknown to Rawn, behind a crest that shielded them from any hostile fire. A few men stayed behind, perched in some rocks, and fired occasional warning shots at a steep angle to keep Rawn in place. A few miles down the canyon, the bands emerged into the Bitterroot valley and made camp several miles to the south. Rawn withdrew to Missoula to wait for help.[11]

Some Montana editors ridiculed Rawn and his command as imbeciles and cowards and "useless as boys with popguns."[12] Their log emplacement became an artifactual jibe, dubbed Fort Fizzle. It is hard to imagine, however, what else Rawn could have done. By the time the Nez Perces made their move, his force had shrunk to a number that would surely have been overrun or, at best, blown by in a confrontation. He could only have angered the warriors, not stopped them, which in turn would only have endangered white Montanans, not protected them.

In fact, once past the barrier, the Nez Perces could not have behaved more peacefully. They joked with a few volunteers who followed them, and on July 31, the day after Howard started over the trail, some of them came into the town of Stevensville looking for supplies, especially flour. Store owners Henry Buck and his brother found that the Indians had plenty of gold coin and promised to pay for everything, although the Bucks had little flour and the party proceeded to a nearby mill to buy some. The next day, a much larger group came to town, the "finest looking tribe of Indians I have ever seen." Buck counted 115 warriors; the only hint of trouble was when a few younger men bought whiskey and turned rowdy. Older leaders quickly controlled them.[13] The townspeople, too, were reasonably cordial.

Many among the pursuing troops were in a rage when told of these exchanges. "These are the 'hardy frontiersmen' the eastern papers talk about," Mason wrote to his wife: "it is for such cattle that we risk our lives."[14] The press railed at the "avaricious wretches" and claimed, apparently without foundation, that they had trailed the bands with wagons of goods in pursuit of more profits.[15] Townspeople, however, were only selling what probably would have been taken anyway, perhaps violently, and some of them knew the Nez Perces who came often to hunt and visit in the area and considered them friends.

During the next few days, as Howard's command labored toward the Lolo summit, the bands moved up the Bitterroot valley at a leisurely pace, bothering no one and apparently buying more supplies from white residents. They added slightly to their numbers. A few weeks earlier, a small band of a dozen or so had returned from a hunt on the plains and were on their way over the Lolo trail when they heard of the troubles in Idaho. To avoid the fighting, they turned back to Montana, and now they joined the procession up the valley. One of them, a mixed-blood named Lean Elk, had arrived limping from an accidental leg wound, and jittery whites had reportedly accused him of being a war refugee. Lean Elk would turn out to be an important addition. Called Poker Joe by whites, he knew the mountains between them and the buffalo country in exquisite detail; he soon emerged as a natural leader.

The events between the time the Nez Perces left home to when they were easing up the Bitterroot valley toward buffalo country have more import than just the fiasco at Fort Fizzle. They hold hints about a puzzle with revealing answers. The puzzle is what the Nez Perces were thinking when they decided to leave Idaho. The answers say something about their thinking generally, and that of other western Indians, and about how that thinking now was calamitously out of sync with a transformed America.

Back home, the Nez Perces had taken a dozen and a half civilian lives and had inflicted humiliating defeats on the army, while killing nearly sixty officers and men. Now they apparently reasoned that simply by crossing the Bitterroots from Idaho to Montana they would be in the clear, and then by taking one step farther, into buffalo country, they would find safe refuge among their friends the Crows. They did apparently consider heading north, directly for Canada, a place they called "King George's land" or, in reference to Queen Victoria, "the old woman's country," but the main drift of their discussions was about the choice they saw as simple: stay in Idaho to fight or cross the mountains to get away from fighting.[16]

The reasoning seems breathtakingly naïve. It makes sense only when one tries to reimagine their perspective. Like most Indians, the Nez Perces lived in a small-radius world. They knew whites had come from far away, and they knew of Washington (but was Washington a man, Toohoolhoolzote had asked? A house?). They knew that the settlers who had come through and into their country were connected to others to the east, and they knew that whites close by and far distant had power, economic and spiritual. What they seemed not to grasp was how that power even then was of a concentrated scope far beyond anything they had ever known. And why would they have known? At the time of the war, no leader among the resisters had ever been back East, or for that matter to any sizeable center such as Portland. None had ever dealt with anyone who had invoked anything but the most ephemeral authority, some reference to some president and Congress and a constitution. No white leader had ever come up with more than a few hundred troops to make that authority real.

What they did know well was their local world. They understood the threat of local whites, but they had also learned to use them. They had integrated white material culture into their own—witness the silver place settings and brass kettles cached at the Clearwater campground—and had learned the ropes of economic exchange well enough to amass considerable cash, which they now used to buy flour and other supplies from merchants at Stevensville. They understood local power, at least as far as it had been revealed. It rested mostly with ranchers, farmers, and businessmen and with John Monteith, who was enough of a force that the majority of Nez Perces had come into his orbit for protection.

As for that distant power of the never-seen "Great Father" and his government, it had to have been a mystery—promising this now, that later, threatening and then reversing, all the while never showing much of a real presence. Then, when things turned nasty, there had been the army. Soldiers with rifles were indeed a worry, but the Nez Perces had no knowledge of military force beyond their own country and could not possibly have grasped how troops were being funneled in from as far away as Georgia. The only soldiers they had seen so far were ones they had known already. To say the least, they had handled them well.

This was the context of their decision to leave home. By one account, some leaders wanted to stand their ground. The question, one said, was whether in their home country, the land where their fathers were buried, "the white man or the Injun has got to die." Stay, he urged, "and drive the white man away from our land." Others answered that too many whites were there, with more coming all the time. In neither prospect, however, was anything beyond the immediate vicinity even considered. In the end, the decision was that the combination against them, the army and civilians and the reservation bands, would allow them no refuge. The only real choice seemed to be to go east, to "the land where the buffalo stay." They saw that place as another, separate small-radius world. The whites there were friends; once they knew that "we will do them no wrong...[they] will be only too glad to let us pass quickly...and go on our own way." There were soldiers east of the mountains, but there "are not many," it was thought, and so not worth much worry.[17]

Next came the confrontation with Rawn. He tried to explain. "The soldiers of the west side and those of the east side were brothers," he said, "all under one great chief, and when [Indians] fought with one they had to fight with the other." But that did not seem to register. The headmen stated their grievances with the Idahoans and their hatred of Howard—they "would fight the one-armed chief wherever [they] met him"—but over and over they stressed that they wanted only peace and friendship with the soldiers and their longtime white friends east of the Bitterroots. In one version of the council following the talk with Rawn, Looking Glass said that crossing the Bitterroots had freed them from any future pursuit: "If the officer [Rawn] wishes to build corrals for the Nez Perces [a sarcastic reference to the log fort] he may, but they will not hold us back. We are not horses. The country is large. I think we are as smart as he is and know the roads and mountains well."[18] Rawn, that is, and only Rawn, was the problem they faced, and they could handle that "little bunch of soldiers from Missoula." The bands could take their time ("We had best take the world as easily as possible"), he said; "we are not fighting with the people of this country."[19] Local Montanans seemed to agree. Once convinced the Indians were peaceful, they left Rawn on his own.[20] Being welcomed into the shops at Stevensville would have sealed the Nez Perces' impression that they had passed from hostile to friendly country. Tension evaporated. Rawn's fort became a fizzle.

From the Nez Perce perspective, finding safety and peace simply by crossing Lolo Pass was perfectly sensible. In fact, of course, that thinking was calamitously flawed. Crossing the Lolo divide, they passed as well the boundary of their understanding into a new reality they could no more have comprehended than they could have imagined subways. In time, they would have to learn of it, and how to manipulate it, if they were ever to return home.

A crucial gap in the Nez Perces' knowledge was technological. They were largely oblivious to the revolution in transportation and communication that was helping create the new nation. No one among the resisting bands had ever seen a locomotive or a railroad. One account has Rawn telling the headmen that Howard soon "will talk on the clack-clack with the great white chief far away," but nothing suggests that any of the resisters had ever seen a telegram.[21] They had no notion of how a new infrastructure was binding the union together, consolidating its power, and shrinking its distances to replace scores of small-radius worlds with the one of the century ahead.

They would soon begin to find out. Back on July 21, General Philip Sheridan, head of the Division of the Missouri, had wired Colonel John Gibbon, commanding Fort Shaw on Montana's Sun River, to be ready to defend Montanans should the Nez Perces head their way. Gibbon telegraphed orders to Forts Ellis and Benton for units to join him, and on July 28, spurred on by news from Lolo and a wire from Howard, Gibbon set off for Missoula with several companies of the Seventh Infantry. He arrived there on August 3 and the next day started south in pursuit of the bands with 17 officers and 149 enlisted men. With rapid marches helped along by mule-drawn wagons, they gained ground steadily. By August 6, Gibbon's men had gone the length of the Bitterroot valley and were climbing into the mountains, at most two days behind the bands.

The telegraph—nothing illustrates better the unifying power of the new order than how information traveled during the war, in this case putting Gibbon close behind the bands. Howard, back in Idaho, had asked for help in a message sent from Lewiston through San Francisco to General Alfred Terry, head of the Department of the Dakotas, headquartered in St. Paul, Minnesota, who had passed it on to Gibbon in Montana. Governor Potts had asked for, and been denied, permission to recruit citizen volunteers through messages that had crackled over the wires among himself, Sheridan, and the secretary of war in Washington. General William Sherman oversaw it all from wherever he happened to be. The effects of the "talking wire" were not limited to the upper ranks. Troopers like Theodore Goldin in eastern Montana tracked events from the first raids and battles in Idaho to the opera bouffe at Fort Fizzle. They would follow the war more closely as it moved their way.[22]

The public, too, plugged into the informational flow. Facts and rumors flew over the wires, agitating settlers nearby, piquing the interest of readers across the continent, and complicating military politics. News from the Northwest spawned eastern editorials that nearly unseated Howard, who took the lesson and made sure his version of the Clearwater fight was the first one telegraphed to Sherman and the public. Even as the story unfolded, electronic transmissions gave the primary players faces and personalities, created heroes, goats, and martyrs, and made a kind of instant history that crystallized not over months and years but in days and weeks.

Telegraphy, that is, by essentially collapsing time and space, sped up the mythical integration of the West into the new nation. The point had been made dramatically the summer before. George Custer met his end on June 25, 1876. Two days later, John Gibbon's command discovered the carnage. It took another three days for his column and their travois of wounded to reach the steamboat *Far West* on the Missouri River, and it was nearly six more days later—close to midnight on July 5, ten days after the last stand—that the *Far West* reached Bismarck. Bismarck had a telegraphic connection. Its operator, J. M. Carnahan, spent the next twenty-two hours sending out details, but the essence was set loose across the nation within moments, and across the world within a few hours, virtually simultaneously with the republic's centennial. Information might still

THE ARMY TELEGRAPH—SETTING UP THE WIRE DURING AN ACTION.—[Sketched by Mr. A. R. Waud.]

**Figure 10.1** Civil War soldiers string out the wire that would help unify the continent

move slowly by the old ways, by foot and horse and river craft, but once it tapped into the new system, it really got down to business.

The primary inventor of the telegraph, Samuel Finley Breese Morse, had conceived the idea during a dinner conversation about electromagnetism when he was returning by ship from Europe in 1832, disappointed in his modest success as a painter. He reasoned that with some minimal control over an electric current, "it would not be difficult to construct a SYSTEM OF SIGNS by which intelligence could be instantaneously transmitted" over great distances. He worked on the idea for more than a decade, with the help of his collaborator, Alfred Vail, and some of the nation's leading scientists, and eventually he received congressional funds to build a prototype to operate between the national capital and Baltimore. The first formal message was a short biblical passage: "What hath God wrought?" Generations of schoolchildren memorized these words in honor of the great moment.

The demonstration was on May 24, 1844, the eve of America's great territorial gobbling. Six months later James Polk was elected president, and less than four years later the nation, at least on paper, had reached the Pacific. By 1877, as the West was coming sharply into focus, the telegraphic system had achieved a remarkable level of sophistication and had spread across the nation and world. The same could be said of America's rail system, which grew in those years from just over four thousand miles of track to just under eighty thousand, much of it in the West. Building an infrastructure of rails and wires and birthing the West as a distinct region—the two developments played off one another, grew up together. They were historical twins.

The telegraph was linked to the West in one more way. Samuel Morse's father, Jedidiah Morse, a leading Congregational minister, was also the nation's most prominent geographer and one of the earliest proponents of the doctrine that became known as Manifest Destiny: the belief that the American republic was fated to expand to the Pacific and to dominate all the peoples and cultures of North America. He predicted the United States would require at least a century, and probably much more, to establish its dominion. His son's invention helped reduce the conquest to barely two generations.

The Morse telegraph was adopted faster and more widely than any other technological innovation of the nineteenth century. It was cheap to build. Its sending and receiving devices were elegantly simple, as was the code Morse and Vail devised, and operators quickly learned that they could easily translate the code's dots and dashes by ear, streamlining the process still more.

The main reason the telegraph caught on so quickly is simple: it separated the man from the message.[23] Before it, with a few impractical exceptions, information could move only as fast as the people who carried it. Now it was carried by electricity, which travels at virtually the speed of light, roughly 670 million miles per hour. Railroads moved people and things up to ten times faster than the fastest wagons. The telegraph sped up information tens of millions of times. There was still the time needed to send and decode and to relay through hubs where lines converged, and there were delays from the traffic of thousands of messages, but the advance was still easily the most dramatic in the history of communication. By the early 1870s, nearly fifteen million messages a year were traveling over more than 150,000 miles of wires inside the United States. Through connections and cables, someone in Silver City, Idaho, or Wickenburg, Arizona, was potentially in touch with Tokyo and Calcutta.

At first, most telegraph and rail construction was in the eastern third of the country where population was densest. It was obvious, however, that both technologies were beautifully designed for the West, because they could move their cargoes (news and people, respectively) efficiently across vast distances and could tie together scattered points of human concentration. By 1850, some were calling for a rail line to the Pacific, while others, for example a St. Louis editor, predicted that a "streak of lightning" soon would allow "instantaneous and constant communication" between his city and the far coast.[24] The problem was that railroads and the telegraph, while nicely suited to western geography, were terribly *un*suited to attracting the money needed to build them. Their risks seemed enormous, and the same western conditions that made them such a natural fit—relatively few people sprinkled over a great big place—meant that returns at first would probably be small.

The answer was a partnership between the national government and corporate capital, and there is no better example of how the two defining events of the mid–nineteenth century, westward expansion and the Civil War, made a new America. Expansion created an undeniable need for hugely expensive projects for the public good. The war made it terribly urgent to bring the West truly into the union. The double crisis of distance and disunion pushed government and business into an unprecedented marriage that was crucial to remaking the nation.

The telegraph came first and showed the way. The Pacific Telegraph Act of 1860, passed just two months and six days after the attack on Fort Sumter, in effect was a prototype for the law that two years later provided for the first rails across the continent. Both laws gave financial support and provided public land for rights of way, and both gave contracts to two companies that would build from East and West and meet somewhere near Salt Lake City. From the start, the two technologies were as twinned miracles compressing space and time and bridging the nation's parts. Telegraphy especially seemed pure wizardry. A California poet marveled at the device ("Hark, the warning needles click / Hither, thither, clear and quick") that seemed to have command over elemental restraints on human effort: "Here again as soon as gone, / Making all the earth as one. / Seems it not a feat sublime—/ Intellect has conquered Time!"[25]

For the West especially, the importance of rails and wires would be hard to exaggerate. Railroads provided the means for moving everything from families to mining machinery in and everything from cattle and wheat to bullion out. The telegraph told speculators and jobbers the going price of longhorns and shovels and drew investors from Liverpool to Berlin into hungry western markets. The greatest influence was so obvious it is easy to miss: the telegraph and railroad went a long way toward making it possible to think about the West at all. With the land acquired between 1845 and 1848, what most people would come to call the West was about half of the nation. Far larger than any other region, the West-to-be was also far more diverse—geographically, climatically, culturally. How, then, could it be considered one thing, the West? Why not several regions: "Pacifica," say, for California, Oregon, and Washington, "the Desert" for the intermontane interior, and "Greater Montana" for the Rockies? By redefining practical distance and time, telegraphs and railroads reduced a vast and varied area into something mentally manageable. They shrank the West into being.

More widely, they tied together the new America. The metaphors were obvious. Oliver Wendell Holmes called the telegraphic web a "network of iron nerves which flash sensation and volition backward and forward to and from towns and provinces as if they were organs and limbs of a single living body." Railroads, in turn, were "a vast system of iron muscles which...move the limbs of the mighty organism one upon another."[26] Holmes was writing early in the Civil War; his was the body military. What was a New England regiment southbound by train, he asked, "but a contraction and extension of the arm of Massachusetts with a clenched fist full of bayonets at the end of it?"[27]

After the war, the fists and biceps were turned toward the West, with especially doleful consequences for Indian peoples. Western railroads, the secretary of the interior wrote in 1869, had "totally changed the conditions under which the civilized population of the country come in contact with the wild tribes." Instead of settlement slowly advancing on native ground, "the very center...has been pierced."[28] All Indians must quickly be confined to reservations. Fourteen years later, Sherman credited soldiers and settlers with doing their part in "the great battle of civilization and barbarism" but added that in bringing peace and order, "the *railroad*...has become the *greater* cause."[29] The same mix of cant and reality might have been said about the telegraph.

As the Nez Perces entered the mountains from the Bitterroot valley, they had no inkling of this weapon and what it could do. An early historian of the war noted Looking Glass's failure to appreciate the telegraph: "Poor misguided savage! He deemed himself the wisest and most cunning of his kind; yet little did he know of the ways and resources of the white man."[30] The comment is overripe, arrogant, and condescending—and essentially on the mark. The moving bands could not have known it, but a copper net that extended across a hundred thousand square miles of mountains and plains was starting to settle around them.

As the Nez Perces saw things, all was well. Local whites showed no sign of hostility as the Indians moved up the Bitterroot valley. Scouts reported one man heading for the river with his fishing pole on his shoulder, obviously unconcerned, and Yellow Bull traded his horse with another man, getting $20 with the swap, which he used to buy some flour.[31] Lean Elk (Poker Joe) and his band apparently also thought that the war was over. A few weeks after quickly backing away from fighting, they now joined the bands they thought were bound for a peaceful hunt in Crow country.

Nez Perce headmen were probably a bit rattled by the response of their longtime allies the Flatheads; their leader, Chief Charlot (or Charlo) refused support, avoided contact with the bands and even contributed warriors to Rawn at Fort Fizzle.[32] There were other unsettling moments. The second camp after the Lolo trail was at the Medicine Tree, a tall yellow pine that had a huge mountain sheep's horn embedded at its tip about eight feet above the ground. Native peoples of the region had long revered the tree for its spiritual power. Perhaps because of the place's spiritual energy, some began to have unsettling premonitions. They seemed out of danger, yet not. Yellow Wolf remembered the mood: "No more fighting! We had left General Howard and his war in Idaho." Nonetheless, there was a feeling "none of us could understand." One morning, a young man with medicine power rode about the camp to tell of a dream the night before: "I will be killed soon! I do not care. I am willing to die. But first I will kill some soldiers. I shall not turn back from the death. We are all going to die!" This was Shore Crossing (Wahlitits), one of the three whose killings on June 14 had begun the war and one of the "Three Red Coats" who had begun the rout of the army at White Bird canyon. Lone Bird (Peopeo Ipsewaht) also rode among them and warned that his "shaking heart" had told him that unless they hurried ahead, "trouble and death" would catch them: "I cannot smother, I cannot hide what I see."[33] But Looking Glass, given a rare collective authority during the crisis, kept the bands on their leisurely pace up the valley and into the mountains.

On August 7, they made camp at a beautiful spot that hunting parties often used for rest and replenishment on the long and wearing trip to the plains. There was plenty of grass for grazing, open space for lodges and horse racing, and a willow-lined stream for water and bathing. Hills, some well timbered, rose up on the west side of the stream. To the Nez Perces this was Iskumtselalik Pah, a Salish phrase referring to the many small rodents nicknamed "picket pins." Whites called it the Big Hole. In trapper patois, a "hole" was a high mountain valley, usually a hospitable one, like Wyoming's Jackson Hole, and in previous decades the Nez Perces and their allies had traded and socialized here with mountain men, including such luminaries as Jim Bridger and Jedediah Smith.[34]

After the leisurely pace of the last week, the Nez Perces now stopped. Looking Glass wanted to spend a few days fattening the horses and making lodge poles. All the previous poles had been left behind and burned at the Clearwater, and since then everyone had been sleeping in the open or in small brush shelters. On August 8, the women cut pines on the hillsides and skinned them of their bark, and that night all once again slept in the comfort of their hide tipis. The plan was to spend another couple of days resting and letting the poles dry and season a bit before resuming the journey to the Crows.

Several men, however, were still edgy and suggested sending scouts with swift horses back along their route to make sure they were not being pursued. Looking Glass quashed the idea. Later, it was said he acted out of cockiness or even an oblique allegiance to Montana whites whom he thought might be insulted or feel threatened by Indians doubling back to check on them. The respected warrior Five Wounds also argued for sending scouts but finally threw up his hands: "All right, Looking Glass. You are one of the chiefs! I have no wife, no children to be placed fronting the danger that I feel coming to us. Whatever the gains, whatever the loss, it is yours."[35]

Meanwhile, Gibbon had made good time. At first, he had been convinced the bands would break north, not south, so he had hurried to Missoula to block them, covering the 150 miles from Fort Shaw in only a week. When he learned the truth, he immediately started up the Bitterroot valley. At least one officer thought the pursuit quixotic. At a party before the march, Lieutenant James Bradley had predicted to Gibbon that the Nez Perces would move south, (Now, he wrote to his wife, "I feel like saying to him 'I told you so,' but I guess he'll remember it.") Surely, he thought, the Indians wouldn't lose such a lead, but Gibbon was determined to chase them, and "there is no telling how far a useless pursuit once begun might be carried."[36] Luck was with Gibbon. With the bands dawdling and his men being hauled in freight wagons, he covered roughly two miles for the Nez Perces' one and rapidly narrowed the gap.

At Missoula, Gibbon had added Rawn's two companies and another one called from Fort Ellis, and was joined by a company of mounted volunteers from the valley town of Corvallis. These volunteers initially numbered about seventy-five but dwindled finally to half that; men left because— like the group's first captain, John Humble—they disagreed with Gibbon's tactics and also thought much along the same lines as Looking Glass: the Nez Perces had not bothered their families, and once the bands were out of the valley, that good behavior should be honored.[37] The thirty-eight who stayed chose as their leader J. B. Catlin, who had risen to major in the Civil

War. Gibbon "had no use for the citizens," Catlin wrote, but he kept them with him—one more necessary union of army with locals. Gibbon had only nineteen horses, while all the volunteers were mounted. The men in Catlin's company also knew the route over the divide, as well as the various trails the Nez Perces might have taken.

The ascent proved slow going—near the crest, they covered only two miles in six hours, hauling their wagons upward by dragropes—and the frustrated Gibbon sent Lieutenant Bradley with the mounted troops and volunteers to locate the bands.[38] If they caught up and had the chance, they were to steal or scatter the Indian horses, leaving the bands foot-bound and ready to round up. Some had worried that the Nez Perces might turn back west into Idaho, but the scouts confirmed that they had moved east toward the Big Hole, and Bradley located the camp early on August 8. In daylight, there was no chance to stampede the horses, so he pulled his men back a few miles and sent word to Gibbon. Then he and another lieutenant drew close enough to the camp to hear axe blows and the voices of women cutting lodge poles. The two climbed a tall tree to get a full view of the encampment (it's worth asking what they would have done if the women had picked it as a pole) and then returned to wait for Gibbon, who was still seven miles behind when Bradley's message reached him. Gibbon reached Bradley about sunset. The wagons arrived a few hours later.

With Bradley's clear and detailed picture, Gibbon planned his attack. His men would follow the trail to the Big Hole, but before crossing the river into the grassy open space where the bands were camped, they would turn left onto a narrow trail, move along the base of the hills, and form a battle line directly opposite the camp and somewhat above the stream. That would put the river between them and the enemy, but they would also be between the enemy and their most vital possessions, the horses that grazed on the hillside above the soldiers. As soon as light permitted, the command would fire volleys into the camp and then cross the river for a direct assault. With 149 regulars and 35 volunteers, the attackers would be outnumbered, although not badly, and surprise was crucial. Just as important, all parts of the line would have to overrun the camp quickly and at about the same time. Anything else would give the warriors the time and a place to regroup. If the Nez Perces were kept scattered and confused, they would have to surrender or be destroyed.

Each man was issued fifty rounds of ammunition for his belt and forty more in his haversack. Just before midnight, they set off to cover the last few miles down to the Big Hole. Because the trail was so blocked by trees, the howitzer and a mule carrying two thousand more rifle rounds were to wait until daylight to start. Noise was an obvious concern, but except for a brief spooking of the Nez Perce herd near the end of their approach, Gibbon's command was in place, undetected, by one o'clock in the morning on August 9. Six companies of regulars formed the right flank and center. On the far left were Bradley and his troops, now afoot, and the volunteers.

The night was clear and starlit. Gibbon took heart from one point of light: "Old Mars is smiling upon us tonight, that's a favorable omen."[39] Most of the men had left their coats behind to make the marching and fighting that much easier, and although it was high summer, many shivered in the mountain air as they sat and waited for first light. About 150 yards to the east, they saw the soft glow of fires inside the tipis, flaring occasionally when fuel was tossed on. Now and then, Gibbon could hear a human presence: a woman talking, the sleepy crying of a fretful baby.[40]

## CHAPTER 11

# Big Hole

Much of the press would celebrate the battle of the Big Hole as a shining triumph of the army and a crushing defeat of the Nez Perces. In this, "one of the most desperate Indian fights on record," the *San Francisco Chronicle* sang, Gibbon's force ("only a handful of men") struck "a fierce and telling blow" against the Nez Perces, "such a blow as they never before had received."[1] Official reports heaped praise on Gibbon and his men; Sherman wrote that if the colonel had only had another hundred troops, "the Nez Perce war would have ended right there." Five years after the fight, Gibbon himself would write an epic poem saluting the troops who had stormed the village: "The stream now running red with human gore / Is passed in triumph, and the teepees gained, / Whilst shouts of victory, louder than before, / Give promise that the victory's more than feigned." A year later, the battle's first historian called it "one of the most brilliant, heroic, and desperate pieces of work known in the annals of Indian warfare," "a glorious achievement" on a par with "the charge of Balaklava or the battle of Bunker's Hill."[2]

A more balanced perspective is suggested by the terse entries in the diary of Second Lieutenant Edward E. Hardin:

August 9. Fight
August 10. Ate horse.[3]

However portrayed, those two bloody days impacted hugely the course of the war. They changed its tenor. The Nez Perces suffered losses they could not afford and counted dozens of women and children among the dead. If that was not enough to leave them bitter, the punishment began with a surprise attack led by some of the Montana citizens they had trusted to keep the peace. When they came across civilians in the weeks ahead, the gloves were off. The battle also shifted their strategy. They learned the painful lesson that they had gained no safety simply by putting a couple of hundred miles between themselves and Idaho, and although they might not have grasped their full predicament, they knew that the chase was very much on. As for the army, Gibbon's defeat gave even greater urgency to the pursuit. The fight at the Big Hole came uncomfortably close to being a repetition of the Custer disaster barely a year earlier. Now messages snapping over the telegraphic net would begin to position soldiers stationed across the sprawling Divisions of the Pacific, the Platte, and the Dakotas to find and corral the roughly seven hundred survivors moving away to the south.

Once Gibbon had his men in place, he ordered Companies D and K to move slightly ahead of Companies A, G, F, and I.[4] With the first two leading as a skirmish line, these six companies would punch hard into the south and center of the Nez Perce camp as Lieutenant Bradley's Company B with the volunteers, the army's left flank, would strike the north end. At precisely four o'clock in the morning, the colonel gave the word to advance. On the far left Catlin and some civilians led, but before they reached the river they had to wade through a slough and push through thick clumps of willows. As they emerged from that brush, they looked up and in the dim light saw a Nez Perce horseman coming slowly toward them. He was Wetistokaith, up early to check on the unguarded horse herd on the slopes behind the attackers. Old and nearly blind, he noticed nothing before he was blown off his saddle by four or five rifle shots.

With that, troops all along the line fired furiously and low into the lodges. The few horses that were picketed in the camp died in this first fusillade. "Bullets were like hail on the camp," Young White Bird remembered, nine or ten at the time: "the noise was like Gatling guns, as I have since heard then...I heard bullets ripping the tepee walls." He and his mother ran first to a slight depression in the ground, and when a man called out that troops were now in the village, she took his right hand in her left and they ran. A bullet took off her index finger and his thumb before they jumped into the river as, they hoped, a refuge.[5] Other women and children also dashed for cover to the river and its bordering willows, although some women and older sons stayed to fight. One private told of having to fight his way out of a tipi when attacked by women and boys with knives and hatchets. Presumably, he had entered the lodge to kill those inside; a lieutenant wrote of "the dingy lodges...lighted up by the constant discharge." It was "a regular melee," he remembered: "the

# Battle of
# BIG HOLE

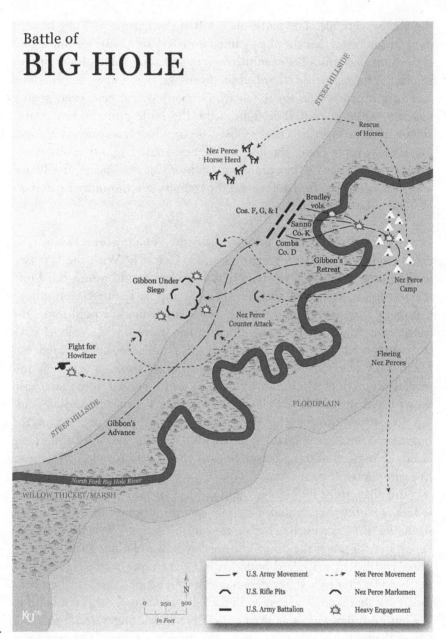

ground is covered with the dead and dying, the morning air laden with smoke and riven by cheers, savage yells, shrieks, curses, and groans." The Nez Perces' heaviest loss of life came in these first moments, especially at the south end of camp, where the regular troops made it quickly across the river and marsh and among the lodges.

Soldiers were doubtless guilty of some atrocities. A woman had given birth during the night in a maternity lodge on the southern edge of the camp. She and her elderly midwife were found dead, as was the newborn, its skull crushed as if by a boot heel. The mother's other two children died in a nearby tipi. About Asleep (Eelahweemah), twelve, was put in a shallow gully by his father when the firing began. With him were his mother, younger brother, and four other women. Some troops soon saw them and began to shoot: "I saw one woman killed—my mother, Tumokult (I Block Up).... Then I looked around. All the other four women lay dead or bad wounded! I said to my little brother, 'We must get out of this place!'" Soldiers fired on them as they ran, but they escaped. Other troops showed restraint. Down in the river, where Young White Bird and his mother had fled with several others, troops made as if to fire, but when his mother raised her hand and called out, "Women! Only women!" the men lowered their rifles and turned away. One of them waded into the water and shook the women's hands. White Bird's wife had the courage to approach the advancing soldiers with her infant; an officer waved her through the line.[6]

Many women and children who died likely were killed at the outset in the storm of firing into the camp. Outside a tipi, Corporal Charles Loynes saw a dead woman lying on her back and on her breast a baby "crying as it swung its little arm back and forth—the lifeless hand flapping at the wrist broken by a bullet." Josiah Red Wolf's mother grabbed him and his young sister and started to run with them; but, he remembered eighty-eight years later, "a single shot passed through the baby and her. She dropped down without saying a word." When he refused to leave the body, his father covered him with a bison robe and told him to be still, which he did ("I tried not to cry"), and he was found later.[7]

There were surreal moments common to all combat. In the middle of the closest fighting, a soldier was seen sitting beside a tipi and writing a letter; soon he was shot. Five Fogs (Pahka Pahtahank), only thirty years old but with "an old-time mind," was baffled by rifles, so he shot arrows from his hunting bow at the charging troops, who fired back from close range, repeatedly missing him as he danced about. Finally they killed him. At the height of the fight, a private walked up to Lieutenant Charles Woodruff with a practical question: "Do you think I will live?" Woodruff looked at the bubbling blood he was breathing out of his lung wound, checked how the ball had left his back, and said he would live if he had the courage. (Two years later, the private, now a hotel runner in St. Paul, grabbed Woodruff's valise as he left a train and shook his hand, with "You see, I had the nerve.")[8] Yellow Wolf saw a soldier standing beside the river bank, his head cocked and staring north. He started to fire at him but sensed something was wrong: "He could see me, but did not move. Then I understood. *That soldier was dead!* ... He was the only dead man I ever saw standing." An elderly man sat smoking his pipe throughout the battle. "He was shot many times!" Yellow Wolf reported: "He did not get up.... He did not move." No blood, only steam-like vapor, came from his wounds. He "just sat there smoking as if only raindrops struck him!" A young boy, Pahit Palikt, dashed from his lodge carrying his blanket and hid below the stream bank with his brother. When his brother was killed, he realized something else was missing: "I thought, 'Where is my blanket?' I had dropped it while running for the bank. I ran back and got [it]."[9]

There was little resistance to the initial assault. The first impulse of most warriors was to get their families to safety, off to the north end of the village. A few, however, tried to make a stand. Several died. An early casualty was Shore Crossing (Wahlitits), whose morning errand to avenge his father nearly two months earlier had started the war. Running from his tipi, lying in a shallow place behind a log only as "thick as a man's leg," he waited for the enemy. The men of A Company, led by Captain William Logan, burst out of the river willows just fifteen or twenty strides away. Shore Crossing killed one man, but as he raised his head to look for another, he in turn was shot, by Logan himself, according to Nez Perce accounts. His wife, many months pregnant and already wounded, took his rifle and killed a soldier, perhaps Logan, before she in turn was killed.

The tentative opposition slowed the assault enough to permit a withdrawal to the northern edge of village. There the survivors found relative safety, for the left flank of Gibbon's battle line had failed in its prime assignment, to overrun that part of the camp. After the civilians had opened the fight by shooting Wetistokaith from his horse, Bradley had led them and his own men in a charge out of the thick willows along the river, but he had gone only a few steps when he was shot in the face and killed instantly. Bradley, the first white who had seen Custer's dead thirteen months earlier, was the first white to die at the Big Hole. His leaderless command did not push forward but drifted southward along the river toward their more successful counterparts. That left the north end of the camp in Nez Perce hands.

The warriors regrouped. In Nez Perce accounts, it was White Bird who turned them around with a mix of shaming and exhortation:

> Why are we retreating? Since the world was made, brave men fight for their women and children. Are we going to run to the mountains and let the whites kill our women and children before our eyes? It

is better we should be killed fighting. Now is our time; fight! These soldiers cannot fight harder than the ones we defeated on Salmon River and in White Bird Canyon. Fight! Shoot them down. We can shoot as well as any of these soldiers.[10]

Meanwhile, amazingly, troops at the other end were not pressing their advantage but instead were trying to burn the lodges. With their green, newly cut tipi poles and tipi hides wet from dew, some only smoldered, but others were ablaze. Some parents had hidden children inside tipis under clothing and blankets, and now some of these boys and girls burned alive. "We heard them screaming," Wounded (Owyeen) remembered; "We [later] found their bodies all burned and naked."[11]

Nez Perce warriors used this pause to find protected positions on high ground and soon were shooting into the camp they had just abandoned. Now it was the soldiers who were exposed and vulnerable; now the willows and brush that had given them protection during their attack left them blinkered and disoriented and gave shelter to warriors moving in for closer shots. Gibbon later remembered that with every rifle shot from the perimeter one of his men fell, and Catlin wrote dryly of his men's frustrated efforts to burn the tipis: "We soon found we had more important work on hand."

The tide turned. Gibbon took a wound in the leg in a shot that crippled his horse, and soon afterward, realizing he might soon be surrounded, he ordered a withdrawal. First sending Rawn's company as a skirmish line against the brush where most of the firing was coming from, he led the rest of the command back across the river and southward toward a timbered tongue of raised land. Advancing warriors took rifles from fallen soldiers and with this added firepower pressed the retreating soldiers hard. There was a near panic when the troops threatened to break and run, and if they had, the result probably would have been a reprise of the Custer annihilation. But Gibbon took hold of them. Did the moment feel familiar? As a commander on Cemetery Ridge at Gettysburg, badly shot through the shoulder, he had commanded the Second Corps, which had held the point where Pickett's charge broke and fell back. Now Gibbon shouted that if his men bolted, he would "stay right here alone." His men held their places and followed him in an orderly withdrawal. Corporal Charles Loynes and two companions were among the last in the camp:

My Company what was left had already gone, probably two minutes before my captain and one soldier passed by me and entered

**Figure 11.1**  At the Battle of the Big Hole, John Gibbon barely avoided George Custer's fate

the creek, the captain telling us, Sgt Hogan, Corporal McCaffrey and my-self, to get right out of there. The captain had not gone a rod before McCaffrey was shot. He fell forward and with his right hand on the ground, his left on his chest where he was hit, says don't leave me here. We tried to hold him up, one of us on each side, when instantly Sgt Hogan was hit and then I found myself alone. The command had gone. I did not know where. Then I entered the creek and as I crossed I could hear the ping of bullets around me. In about ten minutes I was with the rest and there we remained till relieved by General Howard.[12]

There were several other casualties, including three officers wounded, but the survivors stayed together and reached the place Gibbon had chosen for a defense.

This wooded bench about a half mile south of the camp gave the men elevation, cover, and spots to dig in, but it still was vulnerable. On one side there was higher ground, and there Nez Perce marksmen set themselves among the rocks as other warriors probed and pushed up from below. Gibbon's men hacked out shallow trenches that gave them a protected angle against the riflemen above.

By now, the Nez Perces were walking through the carnage of their reoccupied camp. Yellow Wolf remembered:

> It was not good to see women and children lying dead and wounded.... Wounded children screaming with pain. Women and men crying, wailing for their scattered dead! The air was heavy with sorrow. I would not want to hear, I would not want to see, again.... The chiefs now called to the warriors to renew the fighting where the soldiers had hidden themselves.

Gibbon heard that "wail of mingled grief, rage, and horror" and above it the call for attack "and the warwhoop in answer which boded us no good."

At this point, two booms were heard to the south. The howitzer had arrived. Its crew of six soldiers and two civilians had left their camp at dawn, and arriving at the mouth of the canyon where the troops had begun their final approach hours before, they moved the twelve-pounder to a bluff with a fine view of the valley. That first pair of shots, however, were all the crew managed before about thirty warriors overran their position. They quickly killed one soldier and a mule. Two privates immediately took off, and four of the others managed only a brief resistance before fleeing. That left one man alive, a fifty-six-year-old private in his seventh enlistment who was pinned and tangled in the fallen mule's harness, but he cut himself loose and also escaped. The Nez Perces made no use of the howitzer—varying accounts report that they dismantled it, or they ditched it purposefully over the bluff, or it took off on its own down the slope as they puzzled what to do—but they did gain a major prize, a packhorse carrying two thousand rounds of ammunition. Once again, artillery so laboriously hauled over such difficult terrain proved worthless. The two shots fired did no harm. Apparently the crew, rattled, had failed to put fuses in the cannonballs.

The howitzer did provide one help—it deflected some of the warriors' pressure against the retreating, entrenching troops. Even so the fire was terrific. The only surviving horse, after Gibbon's, was Woodruff's. Gibbon had declined it for the retreat and had put one of the wounded in its saddle, but that man was shot again and killed as the animal approached the defenses, and the horse was so badly wounded it had to be put down. As the men began digging their pits and building breastworks, and as Gibbon stood by discussing their predicament with his officers, "a shot was heard," the colonel wrote later, "and Lieutenant English, standing by my side, fell backward with a cry. A bullet had gone through his body." A private carried English inside the breastwork and as he laid English down was himself hit in the shoulder. That fire was from only a few hundred yards away across a gulch, where riflemen had climbed yellow pines into perches high enough to allow them a downward killing angle. They wounded one civilian in his rifle pit, and then finished him off with a bullet that passed through him and badly hurt his trench mate. Other Nez Perces maneuvered up from below, some as close as fifty feet to the perimeter. One, shielded behind a fallen tree, killed four men in a pit before he was shot.

Gibbon's command had no medical supplies; the closest thing they had to a medical officer was a green officer with some seat-of-the-pants training, and because he had been shot through both legs above the knees, through a hand, and through a heel, the men were left mostly to care for each other. The uninjured did what they could to help, ripping up uniforms to bandage wounds, but as the afternoon wore on, everyone's suffering increased. "Their groans were very trying," Woodruff remembered.[13] His horse was partly butchered and served to those who were interested—the meal Hardin mentions. Worse than hunger was thirst. Most canteens were long since empty, and the men waited impatiently for the cover of night so a party could try for the nearby stream. The injured suffered piteously. As Charles Loynes fired over the breastworks, a fatally wounded musician lay at his feet, occasionally speaking of his mother and "[crying] for water for gun-shot wounds create a thirst."[14] Water was not all that was running short. The day's ammunition, ninety rounds for each man, was so diminished that it was doubtful whether the command could hold off a well-executed charge.

That threat loomed suddenly in late afternoon when the Nez Perces tried a new tactic. "It looked bleek [sic] for us here," Woodruff would recall. "The Indians set fire to the forest and kept up a fire from the brush and the hills, their idea was to follow up the fire and charge us."[15] For Gibbon, it was a grim recognition. The previous year, Looking Glass, on his way home from a Montana hunt, had visited the colonel's camp and had demonstrated exactly this maneuver to amuse the officers.[16] Now the flames advanced with a strong west wind, and as the smoke thickened, Woodruff later wrote his wife Louise, "I began to fear that I should never see you again." As the able among the soldiers prepared for an attack and some of the wounded covered their heads and waited to die, Woodruff prayed, thought of his wife and young son, and readied two revolvers in hopes of killing some of the enemy before they took him, but "Our Heavenly Father was on our side and the wind changed and blew away from us....I never knew how much I loved you until I thought [we would never] see each other again."[17]

This effectively ended the battle. A few Nez Perces fired occasionally to keep troops in place while the rest of their people took their leave. During the afternoon of August 9, the survivors in the camp took stock of their losses, tended to the wounded, packed their belongings, and laid the dead in shallow graves. The bodies of several who had died in the river had washed against a crook in the streambed; the bank was broken over them as a makeshift burial. Survivors worked amid the moans of the injured and the women's keening, a sound described as like "nothing...in heaven, Earth or Hell."[18] Smoke hung in the air and with it the stench of dead, scorched horses. The mood was of shock, rage, and sorrow.

For the first time, there was also a touch of despair. The day had claimed four of the Nez Perces' best warriors. Shore Crossing fell in the first moments of the attack. Later it was Red Moccasin Tops (Sarpsis Ilppilp), Shore Crossing's friend and partner in the killings that began the war. After he learned of his friend's death Red Moccasin Tops led an assault on the entrenchments but was shot in the neck and killed. The fatal bullet cut a necklace of protective beads from around his throat.

Still more disheartening was the loss of Rainbow (Wahchumyus) and Five Wounds (Pahkatos Owyeen). This pair were renowned not only for their courage and skill in a fight but also because they were "strong in planning battle," gifted with a sense of tactics and a strategic intuition. On joining the bands after the battle of White Bird, they had recommended crossing and recrossing of the Salmon River, the feint that had left Howard chasing his tail. Later, Rainbow had led one of the two companies of warriors that had halted Howard's first attack at the Clearwater. Close as brothers, the two had vowed to die on the same day. Rainbow's *wey-ya-kin* promised he would not be killed in battle as long as the fight was in sunlight. The predawn attack left him vulnerable, and as he moved to meet the skirmish line in the opening moments, a tall white man emerged from the willows. Both men raised their firearms. Rainbow pulled his trigger first, but his rifle misfired, and his opponent shot him dead through the breast. By the time the soldiers had been driven from the camp, word had spread, and Five Wounds, devastated, came to his friend's body, wept, and announced that he, too, would give his life. He swigged a little whiskey from a captured canteen and with several others made his way to where the troops were digging in. At the base of the hill the others stopped and began firing, but Five Wounds continued, walking into the open, and was killed.[19]

Sometime after midday, most of the survivors left the valley and made off to the southwest as warriors kept up their pressure on Gibbon's beleaguered command. White writers later claimed that more than two hundred were killed at the Big Hole—a number far above the truth. Gibbon reported finding eighty-three dead in the camp and six more in a nearby ravine. Nez Perce estimates of fatalities ranged from forty-three to a hundred, the majority of them women and children. There were many wounded. As the departure began, those hurt the worst lay on travois; others sat painfully on horseback. Several of the injured died during the next few days.[20]

The battle was not a total disaster. The bands had saved most of their possessions and supplies, and from fallen troops and the howitzer incident they had gained a good number of firearms and a large store of ammunition. Some of their best warriors, including Ollokut, Toohoolhoolzote, and Yellow Wolf, survived, and in the weeks ahead, other leaders would show that their strategic sense could be as sharp as ever.

The Nez Perces' most significant accomplishment was easy to miss, since it took place away from the fighting. In his approach, Gibbon had carefully placed troops and civilians between the camp and the two thousand horses grazing on the hillside to the west. His purpose was obvious, and even before the fight he considered sending several men to drive the herd back toward his wagons, out of his enemy's reach. A later story has it that a civilian scout talked him out of it: "General, you had better keep your command together, you are not fighting the Sioux now." He did send a group to grab the horses as soon as the firing began, but before they could do so, Joseph and No Heart (Teminisiki) ran and herded the animals out of the reach of the attackers.[21] It was a defining moment in the story.

Horses, paradoxically, were both recent arrivals and longtime residents of the West. About fifty millions years ago, the rabbit-sized *Hyracotherium* appeared on the Great Plains. By the Pleistocene era, after a typical branching and rebranching into mostly dead ends, the modern horse, *Equus caballus,* had appeared on the plains. Eventually, it migrated across an exposed bridge of land connecting what is now Alaska and Siberia. When the Ice Age ended, horses disappeared in the Americas, along with dozens of other species, but their cousins flourished in central Asia. People there had domesticated them as early as about five thousand years ago and had begun an experiment with the man-horse partnership that would continue across much of the world until the coming of the industrial age. Horse cultures spread across Asia, to the Middle East and northern Africa, and to Europe. From Spain, one of the more polished types, a mix of Moorish and European traditions, crossed the Atlantic and rapidly conquered the Indies and central Mexico. From there the Spanish moved northward, settled in what is now New Mexico, and pushed into the continent beyond that, as far as modern Kansas, Colorado and Utah. They came riding horses.

*Equus caballus* had come home, a circumnavigator and native child, but it arrived changed, not so much physically as culturally. Not only had people adapted horses to their purposes; horses had also bonded intimately with the animals on their backs. Domesticated horses relied for their basics on people, who relied on horses for their transformed life. For humans, this made for two vulnerabilities. They had to do whatever it took to give their horses what they needed, and if they had adapted fully to the new way of life on horseback, losing their horses would leave them with no options. Nevertheless, horses offered such seductive advantages—greater military and economic power, an expanded range of influence, a new sense of time and space and human potential—that it was natural to overlook the vulnerabilities.

Over time, however, western Indians had to face some facts. Providing food could be a problem. While much of the West was grassland, much also got only limited rainfall that varied greatly over time. Finding enough pasture throughout the year, year after year, turned out to be a challenge. Winter storms drove everything warm-blooded from higher and more exposed terrain into stream bottoms and canyons offering shelter and fuel, like those that made Nez Perce homeland prime horse country. There were just so many of those sheltering enclaves, and over time the winter concentration wore heavily on them. By winter's end, an army veteran wrote, Indian ponies usually were "wretchedly poor, and unable to bear their masters on any extended scout or hunt." Many did not survive.

This wintertime crunch gave western warfare a distinctive seasonal pattern. The situation throws light, too, on the Nez Perce War. Because they

**Figure 11.2**  A Nez Perce drawing of the animal that revolutionized Native American life

had to hunker down in the cold time, Indians were vulnerable to attack. Cavalry mounts were mostly corn fed, and when accompanied by wagons of feed were much freer to travel during winter. The army had only to locate a camp, plan and pounce. For months, the Indians' ponies "can't live out of the cottonwood bottoms," the wife of Howard's surgeon explained to her mother, and so they were easily found: "that is our advantage. In the summer, the advantage is on the other side."[22] That warm-weather advantage could be considerable. The Indians' most famous victory, against George Custer on the Little Big Horn, came on June 25 along the river the Sioux called the Greasy Grass, where rich summer grass beds permitted an almost unprecedented gathering of people; their horses were fat and feisty and ready to turn back and overrun the Seventh Cavalry.

It was the following June, just ten days shy of the first anniversary of the debacle, when the Nez Perce war began. Howard was chasing the bands at their most mobile. Besides that, he could not afford to take along the wagons of corn used in winter travel—his march, already falling behind, would have slowed to a creep—so his cavalry mounts had to get by on grass. Now his horses were on their opponents' dietary turf. Bred and chosen for their heft to throw against an enemy, they soon began to weaken. Indian ponies, smaller and faster and raised on natural pasture, fared far better. And the very fact that they were being chased gave the Nez Perces first crack at the horse fuel that both sides had to have. Lieutenant Wood wrote that the Nez Perces, "the best mounted Indians in the world," had left little behind but crumbs. "Where their animals grazed ours starved; where they had a horde of fresh horses to replace their exhausted stock, we found only the useless ones they had abandoned."[23] Where the route was restricted, as on Lolo Pass, there was "little else for the horses to feed on than leaves from the brush," another officer wrote. By the far side they were "in wretched condition, hardly able to move a leg."[24]

The army had other advantages, of course. It fought by both the old ways and the new. It fought as men had for centuries, pursuing and fighting on horseback, while also bringing to bear the flexibility, technology, and coordinated power of a modern state. Since the army had both the old ways and the new and Indians had only the old, the logic was obvious: use the combination of the two to cripple the one. In the field, this shook out to what became a truism in western Indian wars—grabbing horses was at least as important as killing Indians. Six and a half months before the fight at the Big Hole, Colonel Ranald Mackenzie's troops had routed Dull Knife's band of Cheyennes from their camp on Montana's Powder River, killing about forty persons. The capture of about six hundred Cheyenne ponies was a prime reason for the band's surrender shortly afterward. Two years earlier, Mackenzie had surprised a large camp of Comanches and Kiowas at Palo Duro Canyon in the Texas panhandle. Most of the Indians escaped, but the troops seized nearly all of their mounts. Between 550 and 1,800 were shot. The screams of those animals, more than their owners' retreat, marked the end of Indian resistance on the southern plains.[25]

Thus Gibbon's anxious thrust for the herd at the Big Hole. If he had managed to drive most of the horses out of practical reach, the bands would have been left afoot, and thus at Howard's mercy, even if Gibbon and every man under him had died. The war would have ended then or shortly afterward. But Joseph and No Heart stepped in front of disaster.

The reprieve was temporary, of course, which gives the Nez Perce story some of its poignant weight. Far western horse cultures were arguably the final flourish of a phenomenon that had been moving across the planet for more than five millennia. From the Asian steppes to China, the Sahara, and Iberia, peoples had cultivated the horse's possibilities and found in them a burst of affluence and power. The Nez Perces, blessed with country perfect for sustaining this revolution, took it farther than most. Then, after only about five generations, the forces that were reconstructing the nation hobbled that expansive life, and the Nez Perces were told to dismount into one more constrictive than they had ever known. In 1877, they made one last try to keep the old way alive. Ultimately, the government brought its strengths to bear, but during most of the chase itself, the army and the

Indians still faced off as warriors had for so long, as horseback peoples. On those terms, until their final fight, the Nez Perces never lost.

The Big Hole was the closest they came along the way to losing that freedom. Joseph and No Heart saved them. For all the later misguided belief in Joseph as master strategist and *uber* war chief, this moment, spooking the herd out of harm's way, was equal to anything done by anyone else during the war. The Nez Perces kept their horses, and by doing that, they kept what every hopeful option depended on—the power to move. By the end of August 10, the Nez Perces had filed away with more than two thousand head. Gibbon's men carved up their only mount, Woodruff's sorrel, and ate it.

# CHAPTER 12

# Toward Buffalo Country

Meanwhile, Howard was camped at the upper end of the Bitterroot valley, three days and a hundred miles behind. On August 6, when he was at some hot springs on the eastern side of Lolo Pass, a courier had arrived with Gibbon's plan of pursuit and a request that Howard come ahead with cavalry support. Howard told his infantry to hurry along behind him, and during the next three days he and two hundred mounted men covered about seventy-five miles. "We live on hard bread, bacon and occasional potatoes, one wrote."[1] On the tenth, as Gibbon's men were dug into their thirsty bench land staving off disaster, Howard cut loose with twenty of his best horses and seventeen Indian scouts and made fully fifty-three miles, camping over the divide at Ross Hole, less than twenty miles from the Big Hole.

That night, seven refugees from the battle stumbled in and reported that Gibbon was barely hanging on. Howard sent word for his cavalry to catch up quickly, then set off before dawn on August 11 to find Gibbon. Around ten o'clock that morning, he arrived to find the Nez Perces gone and the survivors "all right & cheerful." Able men were bathing and washing clothes as the injured awaited treatment. Gibbon had sent urgent dispatches for medical help, which had missed Howard but had reached the cavalry behind him, and the next day the doctors Charles Alexander and John Fitzgerald would arrive after riding through fifty-three miles of mountains without rest. Now, however, Gibbon lay crudely bandaged and resting. Howard greeted him, asked for a pair of slippers, and settled in for a talk.[2]

Twenty-three troops and six citizens had been killed, thirty-four officers and men and four civilians wounded. Seven of seventeen officers were killed or injured. Two of the wounded, one of them English, would die in the days ahead. With a casualty rate approaching 40 percent, judging the battle a victory would be a stretch. (In 1915, J. B. Catlin, leader of the civilian volunteers, was invited to take part in a celebration of the battle. "I don't know what we'd celebrate," he reportedly answered. "The Indians kicked the hell out of us.")[3]

As troops buried their dead, Howard's Bannock scouts dug up Nez Perce corpses, mutilated and scalped them, and that night performed dances with the trophies. The remains were left on the field. It was "a dreadful sight…more squaws were killed than men," one of Howard's officers wrote to his wife; "I have never been in a fight where women were killed, and I hope never to be."[4] Stevensville merchant Henry Buck recognized a woman "sitting up in her grave half covered" and wearing a dress made from calico cloth he had sold her only days earlier.[5] Wolves and grizzlies later pulled out and fed on bodies from both sides.[6]

Gibbon turned over fifty of his uninjured infantry to Howard and on August 13 set off with his wounded for Deer Lodge. On the way, they met a large civilian party coming to ease the troops' troubles with bandages, medicine, and wagons full of chicken, mutton, cases of jam, oysters, sardines, whiskey, and brandy.[7] Howard restarted his pursuit the same day. Three or more days behind his quarry, he followed the southeasterly trail of trampled grass and grooves left by the travois that bore the wounded. The Nez Perces now moved as fast as was feasible, caring for the wounded as best they could. Several died during the first few days and were buried at night camps. Following custom, some of the elderly dropped out so not to slow down the rest. Howard's scout, John Watermelon Redington, found an old man who sang his death song and asked to be killed; Redington instead gave him half his bread.[8]

Howard had a dual concern. The direction of flight would take the bands very close to the town of Bannack City, Montana; given their probable mood, that could mean serious trouble. He was also unsure where they might go next. They might curve westward back toward their home country; if so, he hoped to catch them between himself and troops left in Idaho. Or they might go east toward the plains; if so, he might catch them on his side of the mountains. If not, they might be met by forces across the Rockies and perhaps be squeezed from behind by his own men. For now he had to be in position to move in either direction.

There is no evidence to suggest that the Nez Perces considered shifting the direction of their march, but the terrible bloodletting at the Big Hole led to a change in leadership. With their faith in Looking Glass shattered, his place was taken by Lean Elk (Poker Joe), who had two things going for him. He knew intimately the country they were traveling and that of the projected route and so was ideally suited to steer the bands through what was bound to be many traps and pitfalls. And as a mixed-blood who had joined the column only in the Bitterroot valley, he was not associated with any particular band, was outside any rivalries, and so was more likely to be widely accepted. He set a disciplined schedule of march—on the move by dawn, four hours of midday rest, then back on the trail until ten in the evening—that covered good distances even while the injured were being cared for.

The Big Hole had shaken up more than the Nez Perce leadership. Now none could believe that leaving Idaho had taken them into a safer world. They were in hostile territory, and the civilians they had thought were their friends had proved to be something else. Later, their most withering opinions were leveled at locals they considered despicable liars who had betrayed them when they saw some advantage for themselves. The lesson from the Big Hole was simple: all whites were against them.[9]

That frame of mind, along with the needs of what was obviously going to be a very long journey, helps explain the bloody episodes of the next few days. The bands crossed a divide into another pastured valley, Horse Prairie. Most of its panicked families had gathered in Bannack City in a fort built in the middle of the main street and inside the courthouse, with feather beds at the windows to catch the bullets.[10] A few men had stayed at their ranches, and warriors killed five. Besides revenge, the warriors were after the valley's considerable number of horses. They would need them, and they needed to deny them to the pursuing troops. They grabbed about two hundred head.

The taking of those horses had a haunting historical echo. On August 13, 1805, seventy-two years to the day before the raids on the ranches, Lewis and Clark had entered this valley and had their first encounter with the Shoshonis. Here they had met the chief Cameahwait and witnessed his famous and improbable reunion with his sister Sacagawea. Cameahwait had provided their most desperate need, the horses they would ride (and eat) on their final push to the Pacific.[11] Now the Nez Perces, after leaving Weippe Prairie, site of their first encounter with the Corps of Discovery, were following in reverse the route Lewis and Clark had taken in coming. Like Lewis and Clark they passed through Horse Prairie in search of animals. Like them, they moved toward an undetermined end. Their course, however, was toward not expansion but exile.

They proceeded southward, crossing the continental divide a second time and entering the country of the Lemhi Shoshonis, whose chief, Tendoy, offered no help and pressed them to keep moving. Other Indian groups went farther, volunteering against them. Besides the Bannocks already with Howard, Bannocks and Shoshonis from Fort Hall and

Shoshonis from the Wind River reservation stood ready to take arms against the Nez Perces. The circumstances argued for making for buffalo country as quickly as possible, either to find friendlier reception among the Crows or to move from there to Canada.

The bands bypassed a stockade of frightened settlers (making a mock charge before breaking around the fortification and riding away, laughing) and headed along the base of the mountains to the south and then east. Along Birch Creek, they came across some unlucky teamsters hauling whiskey and other materials to Salmon City, Idaho. The meeting at first was friendly, but younger warriors were on a short fuse, and something, probably a refusal to turn over some horses, sparked a flare-up. The warriors shot, stabbed, and bludgeoned five men to death but let two Chinese passengers go. One teamster managed to escape. Once they tapped into the whiskey, the Nez Perces turned violent again, this time against each other; Stripes Turned Down (Ketalkpoosmin), who had helped seize the howitzer at the Big Hole, was shot and died a few days later.[12]

Howard arrived at Bannack City on August 14 to the accolades of relieved locals, which he couldn't resist contrasting with the brickbats suffered in Idaho and in the Bitterroot valley. Like a young girl in the town of Gettysburg who had waved her hanky to passing Union troops, he wrote later, so did Bannnack's ladies cheer his men with their smiles and welcome words, "such as before and afterwards...we did not often have the privilege of enjoying."[13] By this point, two treaty Nez Perces had convinced him that the bands would not return to Idaho but would make for Crow country to the east. Howard wired McDowell that with help from Sheridan and commands on the eastern side of the Rockies, "[we] may yet stop and destroy this most enterprising band of Indians."[14] There remained one chance to catch the Nez Perces before they crossed the mountains. Instead of following along, keeping in their wake, and trying to catch up, his men might cut southeastward over the divide at Monida Pass and reach the bands' expected route before they arrived. For the only time in the pursuit so far, Howard had a chance to cut a corner and come out ahead.

Once again, local interests undid the opportunity. George L. Shoup, commanding volunteers from Salmon City, sent urgent word that the citizens at the Junction stockade were in imminent danger. Going there meant once again following the Indians' trail, and Howard knew that "my pursuit of them by a stern-chase would be hopeless," but under public pressure he agreed anyway. Early on August 16, however, he got word that the settlers were safe and the Nez Perces were moving rapidly eastward. "Relieved of my embarrassment," Howard could return to his first plan; but next he learned that volunteers from Deer Lodge had pushed ahead and were hoping to intercept the bands on their own. The general, aghast, rushed Wood out to ask them instead to move to his far flank, out of harm's way.[15] The particulars of Wood's journal capture the frustration of a western commander's relations with the civilians he was charged to protect. Howard "begs them not to go...as were they to get into trouble it would necessitate his helping them, and thus act as a diversion in favor of the enemy." He would prefer them to help on his terms, "but would not order them to do so, only begged them to desist from their present line of march."[16] Eventually, the men neither helped nor hindered; they just went home.

At last, Howard could make his move to intercept the Nez Perces. He had two options. The Nez Perces were moving west to east across the broad plain of the upper Snake River to the south of Howard. The Centennial Mountains, running east and west, separated him from the bands. He could cross the mountains over Monida Pass via a stage road, marching north to south; if he moved fast enough, he would be waiting for them when they reached the road. Or he could stay north of the mountains and proceed eastward, hoping to stay ahead of the Nez Perces' parallel march on the other side, until he reached Henry Lake. That spot was strategically crucial. The Nez Perces clearly were now headed into the mountains immediately to the east. The terrain there was high, rugged, and baffling to move through, and a chase there would be a greater challenge than anything so far. To reach that high country, the bands would have to pass by Henry Lake. Stopping them before they did would end the war. Letting them pass by would complicate things hugely.

On August 18, as Howard's men and horses rested and he considered his options, he learned that the bands once again had moved faster than anticipated. They were camped twenty-six miles to his south, already at the stage road, just where he had hoped to be in order to block them. They would surely press ahead before he could get there. His first chance at interception was gone.

By his own strategic logic, Howard should have taken his second option and marched his full command eastward to Henry Lake. Looking back, this was his last reasonable shot at ending the war himself. But he did not take it. Instead, he led most of his men down the stage road to where the Nez Perces had already crossed and once again fell in behind them, proceeding "by a stern-chase." He did not give up entirely on getting ahead of them. He sent Lieutenant George Bacon with forty cavalry and some Bannocks to the area of Henry Lake to look for Nez Perces. Howard's choice was puzzling. Maybe he thought he could quickly catch up with his enemy—by moving via the stage road, he would be closer behind the bands ever before—and if he should gain ground, Bacon might slow their advance and allow him to catch up. But if Howard should fall even farther back, as he so often had, Bacon would be on his own. What then? Bacon's command, outnumbered nearly five to one, would be destroyed if he engaged the Nez Perces. Probably Howard was again bowing to the locals. The stage road superintendent, an agent, and others pushed him to use that route as the most expedient way—a move that also, of course, would best protect their stations. "They thronged me," Howard wrote.[17] Whatever his thinking, he later put the best face on his situation. Late on the night of August 18, after he had moved down the stage road to its intersection with the fresh trail of the bands, his Bannock scouts reported his quarry was less than twenty miles farther on: "How confident I then felt!"[18]

His confidence was quickly dashed. The Snake River plain was a wide east-west corridor that was easily traversed but undulated with disorienting lava ridges. The trail was easy to follow. Besides the path of hooves and travois poles, fifty yards wide, the Nez Perces had piled large cones of horse dung at each resting spot, signs of contempt for the inept pursuit.[19] Howard camped on August 19 where the Nez Perces had been the night before, a rich pasture called Camas Meadows. He had gained no ground that day—"We could see their dust miles and miles away," an officer wrote—but his fighting strength had grown by yet another group of volunteers and, more promising, a company of sixty cavalrymen under Captain Randolph Norwood.[20]

As Howard's horses fed on the lush grasses and his soldiers pulled trout from Camas Creek, the Nez Perces were making their own move. It started with a vision that came to a warrior wounded at the Big Hole. According to one account, it was Black Hair; according to another, it was Grizzly Bear Youth, whose *wey-ya-kin* was the Air Bird, a gigantic creature that alighted only on clouds, never in trees or on the earth. In both accounts, the vision's message was the same: Cut-Arm (Howard) was camped at Camas Meadows, and warriors would double back over their route and return with many of the army's animals.[21] When their leaders learned that Howard was indeed camped at the meadows, they took the vision as a sign and a chance to add again to their herd and to slow their enemy's pursuit. A large party set off at sunset on August 19 to fulfill the prophecy.

Just before dawn, they drew near Howard's camp. He had posted a heavy guard—Wood felt safe enough on retiring to take off his pants for the first time in many days—but some warriors were able to creep among some grazing animals. At this point, a man toward the rear prematurely fired his rifle, either out of nervousness or petulance. ("Always Otskai was doing something like that," Wottolen said later: "Crazy actions.")[22] With that, a "reveille of musketry" brought troops and civilians out of their blankets. For the only time in the war, the army received a surprise attack, and the result was chaos. Men scrambled for clothes and weapons (often finding neither), and the night was filled with the screams of horses and mules, the falsetto yells of the attackers, the buzz of bullets, and rifle flashes that seemed "a magnified imitation of a swarm of fireflies flitting in the alders."[23] The volunteers were especially terrified. Some ran and fell into the creek. Their commander tried to pull a hat onto his foot as a boot. In the end, there was only one grazing wound, probably a ricochet, perhaps because most troops had kept down, while the civilians, camped in the lower drainage of the creeks, were well below the line of fire.

Almost as suddenly as it had begun, the attack was finished. The mounted Nez Perces had charged close and fired blindly into the camp, while those afoot had stampeded the herd back toward the trail. There had been talk of infiltrating to kill Howard and his staff, but once the

**Figure 12.1** An English view of O. O. Howard's "pursuit"

attack was sprung, the warriors contented themselves with the theft of the horses. Or what they *thought* were horses. As they tried to hurry the animals to their camp, they were puzzled by their slow gait. Daylight explained it: mules. Howard had ordered the cavalry mounts picketed along a strong cable anchored with iron rods. The bell mares had been hobbled. Only the pack mules were set out to graze, and only these, along with some of the volunteers' horses, were taken. Some horse cultures, like the Comanches, had a high affection for mules. But not the Nez Perces. Their feelings were summed up later by Yellow Wolf: "*Eeh!*"[24]

Just as they discovered their error, they realized they were being chased. Mules were essential to Howard's heavily laden column, and he immediately sent three companies of cavalry under Major George Sanford to retrieve the pack animals, numbering roughly a 150. Meanwhile, Howard prepared his infantry for another possible attack. He apparently assumed the Nez Perces would leave the mules and run once they spotted the pursuit, but instead they sent the mules ahead and, about eight miles from Camas Meadows, deployed behind some low ridges. When the cavalry came within a thousand yards, they opened fire.[25] The three companies in turn dismounted, sent their horses to the rear with handlers, and found their own cover. In the first exchanges, the young bugler of the company farthest to the right was shot through the heart and killed. Some long-distance dueling followed, and after about an hour, some Nez Perces were able to dodge through the broken terrain and begin to fire at close range on the left end of Sanford's line. Afraid he might be outflanked, Sanford ordered everyone to fall back, but as the withdrawal began, the warriors began to turn both the left and right flanks, and with that, the companies at each end retreated so quickly than the one in the middle, commanded by the newly arrived Norwood, found itself suddenly alone. He led his company in a dash to a stand of aspens on a lava knoll, where they frantically stacked pieces of loose lava into more than a score of small breastworks. They faced in every direction, assuming a surround.

When Howard heard of the fight, he hurried with reinforcements and met the two retreating companies and Sanford, who said he had chosen to "draw back a little" in face of opposition. Howard asked the obvious: "But where is Norwood?" "That is what I am trying to find out," Sanford answered, begging the question of how he would locate Norwood by running away from him.[26] Howard turned the companies around, and by the time the combined forces reached Norwood's beleaguered company, the Nez Perces had broken off and returned to their camp several miles farther on.

Norwood's cavalry had endured four hours of sharpshooting, some from warriors who had moved within fifty yards. Eight of his men were wounded. Two would die—three if the count includes a corporal who later killed himself after chronic pain from two cartridges that were driven from his belt into his hip by an enemy bullet.[27] For Lieutenant Henry Benson, his wound was poor payment for a determined effort to do his duty. He had been on leave back East when he read that his unit, Gibbon's Seventh Infantry, had been set to the chase. After traveling by train, steamboat, and wagon to Fort Shaw, he had set off on his own to catch up, arrived too late for the fight at the Big Hole, but persuaded Gibbon to assign him to Howard. He joined Howard on August 18. Two days later, lying behind some low rocks during the initial encounter, he was shot through the buttocks. The next day, he and the other wounded were sent to Virginia City.

Remarkably, the Nez Perces who stayed in their camp remained there throughout the day's long combat instead of using the time to put more distance between themselves and Howard. Even stranger, Howard did not press on to attack them. The opportunity would seem too good to pass up. When he reached Norwood's company, he was less than ten miles away, closer than he had been since the fight on the Clearwater and closer than he would be until the end of the campaign. He had about two hundred cavalry and infantry and a howitzer. Except for Norwood's company, the command was nowhere near exhausted, and there were hours of daylight left. The Bannocks urged him to fight. Yet Howard took his men back to Camas Meadows, buried the young bugler, and gave orders to fortify the camp, in case the Nez Perces, who had ridden thirty-six miles and fought a battle during the past twenty-four hours, rode another eighteen miles and attacked *him*. Howard appeared shaken and cowed—a mood likely felt by the whole command. "I candidly think Joseph could whip our cavalry," a journalist wrote from the camp, "and cannot blame General Howard for not giving him battle."[28]

That evening, Howard's infantry caught up with him. He had last seen them way back at the hot springs on Lolo Pass when he had taken off to help Gibbon in his pursuit. With a considerable train of civilian wagons, they had labored their way up the Bitterroot valley and over the divide to the Big Hole, and then pushed methodically on in the cavalry's wake. They were still behind by two or three day's normal marching when a courier brought news of the raid at Camas Meadows. Immediately they surged ahead, the infantry alternately riding in wagons and marching at quick time, and at sundown they arrived at the meadows. They had covered a remarkable forty-six miles in a day.[29]

For the first time since leaving Idaho, Howard's command was united, and the next day, August 21, they traveled eighteen miles and camped about where the Nez Perces had been the previous day. They followed the trail another two days, through "the most tangling mass of lava that one could imagine," before learning that the bands had passed Henry Lake and entered the mountains through Targhee (then called Tacher) Pass.[30] The quarry was loose and off into the high country. "What a disappointment!" Howard later wrote.[31]

He linked his dashed hopes to Bacon's errand to the area of Henry Lake. Four years later, in *Nez Perce Joseph,* Howard wrote that when he had dispatched Bacon back on August 18 it had been specifically to Tacher Pass, the gateway the Nez Perces would use to enter the park. It had become "evident to my mind," he wrote, that the Nez Perces would go that way. But the lieutenant had arrived too early, Howard went on, and seeing no Indians, had turned back, thus missing the bands by two days. His command's "tedious work" might have been finished, Howard wrote, "if only Bacon could have known!"[32] Much later, in 1907, Howard took a much tougher shot at the young officer (who by then was dead and unable to defend himself). He wrote that Bacon had been at Tacher Pass when the bands showed up, "but did not have the heart to fight the Indians on account of their number," and so let them "go by and pass through the narrow gateway without a shot." If not for Bacon's cowardice, he was saying, the war might have ended right there.[33]

This is the most egregious case of Howard's postwar dissembling and self-serving, if only because of its unfairness to a loyal officer. Howard's orders to Bacon surfaced decades later. They show that he had sent Bacon and his forty men not to Tacher Pass at all but to Raynolds Pass, fully fifteen miles away. Bacon was "to exercise prudence and caution." His orders were not so much to block the Indians' advance—how could he?—as to harass them if possible and above all to tell Howard where they were. His mission, that is, was essentially reconnaissance, not combat. Finally, Bacon was told to spend no more than forty-eight hours in his search and to come straight back if he had not found the bands by then.[34] Bacon obeyed these instructions perfectly and consequently never had a chance to be the coward that Howard would call him. He never saw any Indians because he was sent nowhere near them and because he left the area when told to, after two days.

That was on August 20, when the Nez Perces were engaging Norwood's company and when Howard, after that fight, was choosing not to push ahead only ten more miles to confront the Nez Perces in their camp. Later, Howard wrote that on learning that the bands had gotten away into the park, he felt "like a poor dog watching the hole from which the badger had just escaped."[35] But in retrospect, it was Howard, not Bacon, who seemingly "did not have the heart to fight the Indians."

Howard reached Henry Lake on August 23 and ordered an indefinite halt. In twenty-six days of hard marching since leaving Idaho, his command had traveled about five hundred miles; those who had chased the bands back in Idaho had covered much more than that. For days they had lived on rice, coffee, and fried dough. Their writings suggest they were not so much exhausted as thoroughly frustrated and looking longingly over their shoulders. Everyone was sick of the "fruitless pursuit of these Indians," Fitzpatrick wrote to his wife, and Wood thought that "the command is pretty much—I might insert 'tired' there—but rather homesick I imagine." There was no doubting the toll on their appearance. Howard's chief of staff called them "dirty, ragged and *lousy*." Most had not bathed or washed their clothes, or even taken them off, for more than three weeks. Wood described himself as "artistically and picturesquely ragged…clothed in dignity and a pair of buckskin patched pants out at the knees and fringed at the bottoms, with the wreck of a white slouch on my head and a tattered blouse fluttering on my back." He resembled nothing more than "a living scarecrow."[36] The problem was more than sartorial. The next leg of a pursuit would take them into high mountain country during a season of rapidly cooling weather. Already, their water buckets had a layer of ice each morning. Each man had only one thin blanket, and unless the troops were supplied with overcoats, socks, and more covering, one of Howard's surgeons wrote, they would soon be slowed or stopped by illness and rheumatism.[37]

While his men rested, bathed, and laundered their clothes, Howard rode sixty miles to Virginia City, the nearest settlement of any size. To refit his men, he picked the town's outfitters nearly bare and bought more than two hundred horses and mules to replace stock lost by attrition and raids. Virginia City also had the nearest telegraph terminus, and Howard wired McDowell and Sherman about his next move.

Sherman happened to be nearby, at Fort Shaw in west central Montana. Only a week earlier, he had been much closer than that. He was spending much of the summer touring western posts, and in early August had decided to see the area's more impressive sights. During August 6–17, Sherman and a small entourage visited the mountains in northwestern Wyoming where the Yellowstone River had its head, a spectacular country of waterfalls, hot springs, and geological oddities. They enjoyed it hugely. They also sat squarely in what was about to be the Nez Perces' path, which raises the war's most intriguing "what if" possibility. When Sherman entered the area, there was no hint of trouble there. He took only four soldiers. "I do not suppose I run much risk," he wrote. The Nez Perces were far away.[38] Then, as he was seeing the sights, out of touch, the Nez Perces were moving south from the Big Hole to the Snake River plain, and then heading rapidly eastward. Sherman was the army's commanding general, the nation's highest ranking officer except for the president. What if the Nez Perces had found him and his party around some campfire, sipping whiskey and frying trout? They might have taken him hostage. More likely, they would have killed him as just another soldier. Whatever the outcome, it would have eclipsed by far the hoopla around Custer's defeat. It certainly would have shifted the course of the war. Such a turn was avoided when Colonel Nelson Miles sent a party on a rapid ride from the Tongue River cantonment, and Sherman ran into a few tourists who told him of brewing trouble. He left the area on August 17.[39]

Now, out of harm's way at Fort Shaw, he heard from Howard in Virginia City. Things were at the sticking place, Howard wired. Should he stay the course, or should he turn over the campaign to others across the mountains in buffalo country? His feelings, to say the least, were divided. He "has changed his plans three or four times," Mason wrote. Howard was disposed to press on, "disappointed at not reaching a brilliant end," yet in the previous sentence Mason told of Howard making arrangements to carry on "unless he can get permission to return," implying a quite different attitude.[40] Fully ten days earlier, back at Bannack City and before the trouble at Camas Meadows, Howard had told officers that unless he caught the Nez Perces in the next day or two, he would notify McDowell that he was quitting.[41] Now he wired Sherman: "I cannot push [the command] much farther." He had heard that colonels Nelson Miles and Samuel Sturgis were somewhere ahead of the bands. If they could only head them off, he said, he would give it up and proceeded slowly back to Boise.[42]

If he hoped to be taken out of the game, he was disappointed, and doubtless humiliated, by the response. McDowell replied that Howard was closer to the Nez Perces than anyone else in the army, and everyone—Sherman, the War Department, the nation—expected him to push ahead aggressively "to the very end." Stop worrying about what others might do, McDowell added "in all kindness," and look instead to your own resources and strategies.[43] Sherman agreed. Howard's force "should pursue the Nez Perce to the death, lead where they may." Then came what must have stung: "If you are tired, give the command to some young energetic officer" who could get the job done. Howard was back at Henry Lake when he heard from Sherman. He quickly replied: "You misunderstood me. I never flag." It was just such energetic young officers who were fagged out, not himself, and Sherman and McDowell shouldn't fear for the campaign or "doubt my pluck and energy." The next day, Sherman wired that he was "glad to find you so plucky." Units farther on would stand ready to help, he added, but he suspected that the Nez Perces were lurking somewhere close, probably in the Big Horn Mountains, in hopes that Howard would break it off so they could head to Montana.

The next day, the chastised Howard led his men up the trail the Nez Perces had taken six days earlier. It took him into Yellowstone National Park. In one sense, it was one more stretch of difficult terrain. In another sense, he was entering another realm.

# CHAPTER 13

# War in Wonderland

A lmost exactly five and half years earlier, on March 1, 1872, President Grant had signed the Yellowstone Act. It withdrew more than two million acres from the public domain, most of it in northwest Wyoming, with a bit lapping into Idaho and Montana. As the rest of the West was being sold, homesteaded, or devoted to some other developmental purpose, this corner was to be saved as "a pleasuring-ground for the benefit and enjoyment of the people." Yellowstone was the world's first national park.[1]

It was a volcanic plateau on average between seven and eight thousand feet above sea level.[2] Its name came from the river that rose there and flowed north and then east across Montana to join the Missouri River at the North Dakota border. The river was named for the colored rocks farther down its course. The river flowed from a huge glove-shaped lake and as it sped down toward the plains it had cut canyons so deep the water's roar was hardly a whisper at the rim. Along the way, the river shot out over two great waterfalls, one higher than a modern football field is long. Other magnificent sights awaited in what its promoters called "Wonderland," after the fantastic world that Lewis Carroll's Alice found only a few steps away from the ordinary.

The Yellowstone Plateau is the latest creation of a geologic "hotspot," a weak point in the earth's crust where magmatic material squeezes close to the surface, gathers pressure, and every so often lets loose in an eruption of unimaginable violence. The Pacific Northwest has felt the force of three such events during the past 2.1 million years. Each time, billions of tons of the underearth was blasted into the stratosphere and cascaded into the surrounding region as pumice and clouds of superheated shards of glass. Spewed ash from the eruptions fell as deposits as far away as California and Louisiana. Each blast left a roughly circular depression called a caldera. Meanwhile, the floating tectonic plate that is North America was moving southwestward over the hotspot, which left the geological remains of these periodic eruptions trailing behind it, appearing to run northeastward. Earlier cataclysms created the Snake River plain, which the Nez Perces and the army traversed; during their siege, Norwood's men built rifle pits out of pieces of remnant lava. The most recent cataclysm formed the Yellowstone caldera, thirty-five by fifty miles, at the heart of the plateau.

That was 640,000 years ago, but the basic processes are still at work. Molten material seethes just below the surface. As rainfall and runoff seep downward, they return to the surface as burbling mudpots, vented steam, more than five thousand hot springs, and more than two hundred geysers, including the largest anywhere. Yellowstone Park, America's "Wonderland," is a hissing bomb, with more hydrothermal activity than in the rest of the world combined.

While its weather can be spectacularly beautiful, Yellowstone's altitude, topology, and distance from moderating seacoasts can make it at best inhospitable and at worst unlivable. Some years, it freezes every night. Winter lasts from mid-October until April or May. Above seven thousand feet, there is snow on the ground about 250 days of the year. Storms sometimes whip the plateau with frigid winds approaching the force of hurricanes. Temperatures sometimes sink to fifty degrees below zero. Summers bring warm days and cool nights, but on the most pleasant days, the area might be struck by terrific thunderstorms.

Nonetheless, people have been using Yellowstone for at least ten thousand years.[3] Probably its weather limited year-round habitation—only small numbers of Sheepeater Shoshonis were living on the edges of the high country when the first whites showed up—but its broad, lush grasslands made it a superb hunting ground. There were also outcrops of obsidian, formed when lava had flowed into water and cooled quickly into a black glass that fractured smoothly into edges so thin that some eye surgeons today prefer obsidian to steel for their scalpels. As the raw stuff of points and blades, Yellowstone obsidian must have been highly prized, for it was traded over a good part of the continent. In the nineteenth century, as the spread of horses lengthened the reach of Indian peoples, the ancient comings and goings quickened. Bannocks, Crows, Blackfeet, Shoshonis, Nez Perces, and others came to the high country both to hunt and to pasture their horses on their way elsewhere. The fleeing bands of 1877 were moving along some of Yellowstone's many well-worn trails. The most heavily trafficked, the Bannock trail through the northern part of the park, had been well traveled for at least half a millennium.

Now this place was being set on another historical path and dedicated to other purposes. How that was happening tells a lot about the larger course of events in the West and America. Yellowstone National Park reflected three powerful forces creating and defining the West. The first was an aggressive effort to describe the West comprehensively and inventory what it held. After the Civil War, the national government sponsored four great surveys, led by John Wesley Powell, Clarence King, Lieutenant George M. Wheeler, and Ferdinand Hayden, that covered much of the western half of the map. These surveys dovetailed with other efforts the government at least partly supported, such as Powell's celebrated descents through the inner gorge of the Grand Canyon in 1869 and 1871. The most straightforward goal was to map the West more fully, with both topographical mapping of the region's landforms and what might be called deep mapping—a geological survey of unprecedented scope and intensity and the gathering of information on phenomena ranging from butterflies, snakes, and cacti to fossilized plants, Anasazi ruins in Mesa Verde, and the first comparative studies of native languages. Every scientific endeavor also considered how to put the West to use. Wheeler mapped the best routes for military movement; King probed the Comstock Lode; Powell studied how to dam rivers for irrigation. Hayden was the most enthusiastic. His reports touted every positive possibility, including, disastrously, the theory that "rain follows the plow," proposing that by planting trees and crops in the semiarid West, settlers would increase its annual precipitation. In Hayden, the tireless scientist shared mind and body with the passionate promoter: "Never has my faith in the grand future that awaits the entire West been so strong."[4]

His boosterish faith helped birth Yellowstone Park. Only in 1870 did an expedition by several prominent Montanans describe the plateau in some detail; after hearing a lecture on the findings, Hayden immediately shifted his summer exploration there for 1871. His report, more than usual a mix of science and exaltation, included images of the wondrous sights by the West's most celebrated photographer, William Henry Jackson, and sketches by the romantic landscape artist Thomas Moran. When Hayden recommended setting the place aside for public enjoyment, the project moved with astonishing speed. A bill was introduced in December 1871, passed in February, and signed in May. When Hayden returned that summer for a second reconnaissance, it was to a national park.

A second force creating the park were western railroads. Jay Cooke's Northern Pacific Railroad was building westward out of Bismarck, North Dakota, up the Yellowstone River valley. The private expedition into Yellowstone in 1870 that had piqued Hayden's interest had been hired by

Cooke as a strategy to make Montana as attractive as possible in order to better market construction bonds. When Hayden returned from his first Yellowstone visit, he found a letter from Cooke's office manager suggesting a national park.[5] Hayden complied, using the man's language almost verbatim in his report, and in periodical articles he stressed that via the Northern Pacific, citizens on the Atlantic coast would be only three days away from the geysers and grizzlies of this American wonderland. It was one more instance of railroads and Washington partnering to tap western resources, in this case by pioneering a new business: tourism. The government did its own boosting. Military reconnoiterings turned out reports that read like promotional copy. Yellowstone Canyon was "the finest piece of scenery" on earth, an officer wrote in 1875. With rail connections, the park would be "thronged with visitors from over the world."[6]

A third force had to do with what those throngs would expect on arrival. As the West came into focus as part of a reconstructed America, it showed two separate but linked identities. One reflected the old vision of a wilderness turned garden. Its value lay in development, and its purpose was to provide the stuff of individual advancement and national greatness. The other identity was newer—a vision of a wilderness kept forever. The value here was in protecting wild landscapes for their own sake, exactly because they were *not* developed. This notion appealed to anyone caught up in the nineteenth century's Romantic tide. In Yellowstone, England's earl of Dunraven wrote after his visit in 1874, human concerns and conflicts become only "the slight creaking of machinery" within an infinitely grander scheme, an "all-pervading Something...a great awful Oneness."[7] The appeal had a nationalistic edge. Wild landscapes set America apart from an overcivilized Old World. One way to maintain America's uniqueness was to keep those places apart, to preserve the wild places from the very changes first vision celebrated. The vision of wilderness kept forever gathered momentum as the public's eyes were opened to extraordinary landscapes contained in the expansion of the 1840s. As a new America emerged, it was easy to believe that these wonders—the yawning chasms, vast deserts, towering mountains, a wildness long vanished in Europe—made America different. The Old World had Rome's Colosseum and the cathedral at Chartres. We had the Grand Canyon and Yellowstone.

Government exploration, corporate expansion, and a nation's need for timeless sanctuaries came together to produce Yellowstone National Park. Easing the way was the area's isolation and climate, which left it largely unusable by ranchers, farmers, or others who might have objected.[8] Just what Congress meant by describing the park as the people's "pleasuring-ground" was unclear. Suggestions included a zòo, a hydropathy institute, a racetrack, a swimming school, and a national observatory. Whatever its final meaning, Yellowstone Park reflected the impression that the American nation, expanded and redefined between the 1840s and 1870s, found some meaning in its wilderness.

"Wild," however, presumably meant mostly apart from human influence, which would have been an odd notion to Crows, Bannocks, and Nez Perces as they moved along trails through country that other native peoples had used five thousand years before Moses. Senators had assured each other that the park would bring "no harm to the material interests of the people." But which people were those? Some, like the Nez Perces and Shoshonis, would feel a definite bump when they arrived ready to hunt elk, only to find crowds of train-borne tourists picnicking, geyser-gawking, and searching for an "awful Oneness." Early promoters occasionally brought in Indians as living, romanticized displays, but real natives, the ones who thought the national park was their neighborhood, simply did not fit. Helen Hunt Jackson, the most famous Indian advocate of the time, was disgusted by the Indians she met in Yosemite, people "half-naked, dirty beyond words," who viewed the valley's incomparable beauty dully, through darting "soulless eyes." Yosemite's most impassioned advocate, John Muir, thought the Mono people he met there "seemed to have no right place in the landscape."[9] Indians did not fit the vision of wild untrammeled spaces innocent of history.

Consequently, Indians were banned from America's wild cathedrals and written out of Yellowstone's story. Philetus Norris, an early superintendent and prominent shaper of the park's image, cultivated the preposterous claim that the region's tribes had stayed clear of the area out of "superstitious awe" of its geysers and sulphurous vents. He would use the Nez Perce War to claim that Indians, "painted vagabonds," came there in his day only to hide after massacring white pioneers. To Norris, the true purpose of Yellowstone, "nature's crowning temple," was as a refuge for "the overtasked businessman." It was America's gift from God, "who created it for His own wise purpose [and] preserves it for our enjoyment and benefit."[10]

In August 1877, however, the recasting of Yellowstone had barely begun. The Nez Perce bands that filed into the high country were following very old, persistent paths of meaning that were about to intersect with others just being laid down.

Within a day of the Nez Perces entering the park, its older and newer meanings collided. First the bands met John Shively, acting out the traditional hope of a land of riches by prospecting along the Firehole River. He had found no gold, but now the Nez Perces found him, and rather than kill him, as some wanted to do, they enlisted him to help them locate an eastward route different from the one they usually took. Given the options, he agreed.[11]

Next, the Nez Perces came across some walking, breathing examples of the area's new definition: tourists. Seven men and two women were also camped along the Firehole: George Cowan, an attorney, and his wife, Emma; her brother and younger sister, Frank and Ida Carpenter; and four friends and a young teamster. A stifling summer and a grasshopper plague had sent them off to the high country to see the sights in the lower geyser basin. They had heard the Nez Perces were coming in their general direction, but several days earlier they had been assured by no less than William Sherman's guide that they would be safe. By August 23, they had seen enough and planned to head home the following day.[12]

The next morning, as they were crawling from their tents to cook breakfast, Yellow Wolf and several warriors rode into their camp. Some apparently were inclined to kill at least the men in the party, but after a gift of flour and bacon, the Montanans were taken to join the Nez Perce column. Probably the scouts realized something that was to become a concern of Nez Perce leaders. They had chosen a route they hoped would throw Howard off the scent. If the tourists were set loose, they would likely point him in the right direction and undo any advantage. In the main Nez Perce camp, the tension rose another several degrees. After the Big Hole, many younger warriors especially were ready to kill any whites within rifle range. The tourists found sympathy, however, among some leaders, including Poker Joe. As most of the party's possessions were being seized, their wagons dismantled, and the wheel spokes taken as quirt handles, two of the men managed to slip away into the woods, and the others were given two decrepit horses for Emma Cowan and Ida Carpenter and sent on their way. Their freedom was brief. Yellow Wolf had cautioned that the Nez Perces were "double-minded" on sparing any whites they met, and the seven tourists had barely started away when several young warriors began following them, menacingly, and soon ordered them back to the main body of Indians. They started to obey. Then, the Cowans later recalled, "two Indians came dashing down the trail from the front, and, stopping their horses within about fifteen feet of Mr. Cowan, one of them raised his rifle and fired, the ball passing directly through Mr. Cowan's right thigh." When another aimed at his head, he slipped from his saddle to the ground.[13] As Emma Cowan bent over her husband, another Nez Perce asked George if he had been shot in the heart, and when he said not, the man drew a bead on his head. Emma shielded him; the man pulled her away just enough for a second warrior to shoot him in the forehead. When Emma saw others hurling rocks at George's bloodied head, she fainted.[14]

Three of the remaining men were attacked and chased, and one shot in the mouth, but all managed to make it into the brush and hide. All three later found their way to Howard's column. Frank and Ida Carpenter and Emma Cowan might well have been killed had not Poker Joe and several others come to save them, having noticed that the group of younger men Yellow Wolf called "the bad boys" had circled back to waylay them. The three captives stayed with the bands that night and most of the next day as the procession continued eastward and camped after crossing the Yellowstone River. Emma later wrote that Joseph, "sombre and silent…grave and dignified," seemed concerned with their plight. There were kindnesses. When it began to rain, a woman draped some canvas around Emma's shoulders.[15] Years later, a Nez Perce woman, Three Flocks on Water, remembered as a girl meeting Emma and the freckle-faced, shivering Ida. Both were given moccasins, and a woman tied up Ida's torn shoe. At her mother's prompting, the girl gave Ida a shawl and whittled a wooden pin with which to clasp it around herself. They gave Emma camas to eat on the trip ahead and "wanted her to take more but she couldn't understand."[16]

After a council decided to set them free a second time, the three siblings were accompanied for half a mile by Poker Joe and some warriors to make sure they got away unmolested. Poker Joe delivered a final long, repetitive discourse on not wanting to fight Montanans, neither civilians nor soldiers, and exhorted them to ride "'All Night, All Day, No Sleep'"; then he wheeled his horse around and led his men away. Emma, Frank, and Ida set off down and across the Yellowstone and then to the northwest, in the opposite direction of their captors' march, and the next day met some army scouts out of Fort Ellis. Gathering with some other tourists at Mammoth Hot Springs, they soon left the park for Bozeman. Emma, who had marked her second wedding anniversary shortly before her capture, was "worn out with excitement and sorrow" and haunted by images of her husband "dead and unburied, perhaps dragged and torn by wild beasts."[17]

A week later, friends came to her door with an extra edition of the local newspaper: "COWAN ALIVE. He is with General Howard's Command.… This news is reliable." Probably because of damp cartridge powder, the bullet to George Cowan's forehead had lodged under the skin without piercing the skull. When he had regained consciousness, he had managed to stand with a makeshift crutch, only to be shot again by a Nez Perce lagging behind the others. Now with three gunshot wounds, the newest from his hip through his abdomen, he had spent four days pulling himself along with his elbows roughly a dozen miles to the party's last campsite. There he had rested and drunk some weak coffee before continuing down the Firehole River to its mouth. The crawl had taken his last reserves, but as he lay against a log, resigned to death, some of Howard's scouts suddenly appeared. They gave him blankets and built him a fire before leaving, counting on his being discovered by the troops following them, but Cowan was still alone when he awoke from an exhausted sleep to find his clothes on fire. He rolled to the nearby river and quenched the flames. Soon after that, the soldiers found him, his "ghastly paleness" a vivid contrast to his inky hair.[18]

Yet another case followed of ill will between the army and white civilians, this one grimly comic. Although some felt sympathy for the battered lawyer (Mason wrote that when Cowan learned his wife was safe and free, "his joy...was most touching"), others, including Fitzgerald, the surgeon, seem to have disliked him immediately. Fitzgerald got the bullet out of his forehead but would not treat his other wounds, and Cowan later accused the doctor of purposefully rough treatment. The quartermaster refused to sell him replacements for his filthy, bloody underwear. Cowan, in turn, was generally cranky, occasionally insulting, and often demanding. He pressed unsuccessfully for an escort back to Henry Lake, in the opposite direction of Howard's march; Howard instead had him carried, jolting, over what the injured, feverish man later claimed was "the worst road ever passed over by a wagon," and then sent him to Mammoth Hot Springs.

Meanwhile, his wife hurried toward the park. Once the couple were reunited, exactly a month after she had last seen him, shot in the head and presumably dead, they quickly set off for medical treatment in Bozeman. On the way, the wagon flipped over a precipice, tossing Cowan and the others onto the road. In town, he was taken to a hotel, where, as a friend worked on his wounds, his bed collapsed with a great crash. This "nearly finished him," Emma recalled, and Cowan reportedly called for an artillery strike to end his misery, but he was seemingly indestructible, and after some recuperation the couple made their way home to Radersburg. Thus ended what was surely the worst vacation in American history.

There were other even bloodier encounters with tourists. On the west side of the Yellowstone River, not far north of where Cowan was shot, a party of eight men from Helena had spent several days lounging and admiring the river's great falls. After spotting a party of Nez Perces

**Figure 13.1** Members of the Cowan party of Yellowstone tourists after their ordeal

they tried to stay hidden, but the next day warriors discovered them and attacked. One man, Charles Kenck, was killed. Another was badly wounded, but all the survivors managed to scatter to safety, and as two of them made their way back toward Howard and eventually to Virginia City, the other five of their party reassembled at Mammoth Hot Springs. Two of them set out to retrieve Kenck's body and look for their missing friends, only to run into more warriors and barely escape after losing their horses. Back at the springs, they found that yet another group of raiders had attacked there.[19] Richard Deitrich, a young German immigrant who had settled as a music teacher in Helena, had been standing in the doorway of a cabin that served also as the area's first hotel when about half a dozen men, including Yellow Wolf, had approached. Chuslum Hahlap Kanoot (Naked-footed Bull) remarked that his sister and three brothers, none of them warriors, had been killed at the Big Hole, and "it was just like this man did that killing." Best to shoot any white man, he said, rather than risk him becoming a soldier. With that, he and another shot and killed Deitrich. The others in the hotel escaped into nearby woods. One, an African American cook, had a special reason to be thankful. The man chasing him later reported that he wanted his scalp because "colored men's hair is good medicine for sore ears."[20]

Nez Perces also attacked the Henderson ranch, several miles north of the Springs, outside the park's boundaries, and engaged in a two-hour firefight with the residents. Just as they were starting back to the south with some stolen horses, a contingent of cavalry appeared and gave brief chase. This was the command of Lieutenant Gustavus Doane. Nervy and ambitious, he had taken advantage of ambiguous orders from both Miles and Gibbon to ascend the Yellowstone into the park on the chance of meeting the Nez Perces leaving it. With a single troop and some Crow scouts, he would "not have been a mouthful" for the combined bands if he had found them all together, an officer wrote later, but the party he surprised was small, and after this short encounter Doane's command went on to Mammoth Hot Springs, where they paused to bury Kenck and Dietrich, the latter in an old bathtub.[21]

This all happened between August 23, the day the bands entered the park, and August 31. The final tourist toll was two dead, three seriously injured, and fourteen more badly frightened and subjected to various degrees of suffering. What the Nez Perces thought of the vacationers is hard to say. They surely knew nothing of Yellowstone's emerging status as part national curiosity, part wild shrine. Most of them likely felt something along a spectrum from sympathy through indifference to hostility, with many tending toward the latter end. "These people were not soldiers," Yellow Wolf said of the Cowan party, "but all white people seemed our enemies."[22]

For their part, the tourist accounts are strange and dichotomous. In her reminiscence, Emma Cowan gives considerable space to the pleasures of her trip, the fine sights of "Wonderland," and evening sing-alongs and hijinks before she shifts into the story of her physically and emotionally wrenching ordeal.[23] The men, too, gush at the scenery. "What a sight!" Andrew Weikert of the Helena party wrote of the lower falls of the Yellowstone: "Anyone that would say they were not glorious, ought to be shut up in a dungeon and never see the light of day." In describing his Nez Perce encounter he takes the ironic, derring-do tone common to the bluff heroic accounts of the day. When his horse stopped after being shot by pursuing Indians, Weikert writes, he said " 'Goodby Toby, I have not time to stay, but must make the rest of the way afoot.' "[24] Cowan's and Weikert's remembrances, written twenty-three and twenty-five years later, retell the details of 1877 in the terms of the mythic image that most of the nation and the world held of the West by 1900. By then the West, especially its showpieces like Yellowstone, had become a three-dimensional canvas of the sublime where Americans met the wild, brave women persevered, and stalwart men made daredeath escapes while tossing bon mots to their horses.

Even then, in fact, real time was blurring into showtime. Among the tourists Emma Cowan met at Mammoth Hot Springs was the earl of Dunraven and his guide, John B. "Texas Jack" Omohundro. An outrageously handsome ex-Confederate and respected plains cavalry scout, Texas Jack in 1872 and 1873 had shared the stage in eastern cities with William F. "Buffalo Bill" Cody and James Butler "Wild Bill" Hickok in *The Scouts of the Prairie,* the dreadful play that had launched Cody's career as celebrity. Omohundro was determined to follow Cody's trajectory. Soon after leaving Yellowstone, he would star in his own version of *Scouts of the Prairie* in New York City, and already he was the lead character in several Ned Buntline dime novels. Now he tried to pull his current brush with history onto those pulp pages. On the trip to Bozeman, he told Emma and the earl that he had spotted a band of marauding Nez Perces. He rode off to meet them alone—white womanhood would be protected!—and returned at a gallop after a miraculous escape from a reported hail of gunfire. All were impressed until someone noticed the bullet hole in his stirrup had to have come as a shot from the saddle.[25]

The Nez Perces had no illusions about Yellowstone or about their predicament. But the picture of what exactly they did there, and when and why, is especially confused. A central question is: Were they lost? John Shively, the captive prospector, said they were. In a story told to a Montana editor soon after escaping, he said that the chiefs initially enlisted him to show the way to Crow country. Shively went on to say that when a "Snake chief" claimed to know the route, he was put aside as a guide but kept close at hand. By Shively's account, the bands next drifted around, confused, for several days. Finally they asked him again: Which way to Crow country? He pointed out a route and during the night slipped off toward Mammoth Hot Springs and Bozeman. Shively's firsthand account has dominated histories of the war, at least until recently.[26]

The Nez Perce version has always differed. Their accounts of these weeks, although unusually sketchy, say that the bands were only briefly disoriented. On the second day in the park, Yellow Wolf said, they left their usual trail and looked for a southern route to the Crows. They became "partly lost for a short time. Not sure of their way." For that reason, they sought Shively's help, and he guided them for "half of one sun."[27] That would have ended his involvement on August 24, barely twenty-four hours after the tribe entered Yellowstone. Nothing in their memory suggests any confusion between then and their exit from the park more than two weeks later.

The lost-or-not argument is more than a minor historians' quarrel.[28] For one thing it touches on a nagging question: Why did the Nez Perces stay so long in the park? They were there about two weeks, as long as it had taken them to travel all the way from the Big Hole to Yellowstone. What had been a confident march, Shively was saying, turned into a bewildered creep. The disagreement speaks to larger issues, and not only about the Nez Perces and their situation. The idea that they were ignorant of the area reinforced the reasoning behind creating the national park. It fit the claim that fearful and superstitious Indians had always avoided the high country, which in turn left the impression that Yellowstone was the nation's virginal wilderness, untrod and free of anybody else's claims. As it turns out, the argument also touches on persistent misunderstandings of the Nez Perces' society and how it operated.

Where the bands went for the first few days is clear. There are several accounts by whites—those of Shiveley, of the captured tourists, and of a recently discharged soldier who was also grabbed and kept for several days before escaping. Finally, the bands were being trailed closely by Howard's advance scouts, about forty Bannocks captained by Stanton Fisher. Fisher, who had ridden with the Bannocks from Fort Hall and had joined the troops immediately after the fracas at Camas Meadows, would figure prominently in the story over the next few weeks. Howard later praised him as the finest scout of the campaign, and he proved his worth right away. When Howard rested his command at Henry Lake, he sent Fisher and the Bannocks ahead to keep track of the bands, and they were able to stay with the trail until close to the end of the month.[29]

After entering the park along the Madison River on August 23, the Nez Perces camped along its southern tributary, the Firehole. The next day they took Shively and the tourists captive, ascended the Firehole's east fork, continued eastward (George Cowan was shot along the way), and camped between the Madison and Yellowstone watersheds. This was an awful passage along a narrow trail so densely timbered that pack animals often became wedged between trees. Women bellowed at the animals and whacked them on their heads to back them out so they could try again. Fisher and his scouts found many dead horses and trunks of lodgepole pines smeared with the blood of animals that had pushed their way through.[30]

On August 25, the bands crossed the Yellowstone River and made their third camp. There Emma, Frank, and Ida were set free. Next, the bands moved up the river (southward) and camped near Lake Yellowstone. From there, raiders set off for the Helena tourists. Probably the captured soldier, Irwin, had told them of that group, and probably the warriors also were probing down the Yellowstone River to scout for troops. On August 28, the bands turned eastward again, ascending Pelican Creek, a vigorous, broad-valleyed stream that drained into the lake, and then crossed from its watershed to the upper reaches of the Lamar River. This river flowed northward about thirty miles before joining the Yellowstone.

The uncertainty at this point concerns where the Nez Perces went next and, more intriguingly, their thoughts and evolving strategy. William Lang has taken the closest look at these questions and has given the most convincing answers. The bands, he writes emphatically, were never lost, at least not after that initial brief confusion. For one thing, they were probably resting. They had been on the move for two and a half months. They had paused at two traditional resting places, but neither had been much help. In late July, they had stopped at Weippe Prairie but had soon left when it became clear that Howard was pressing them. The stop at the Big Hole had turned nightmarish after only two days. Now, in wide valleys lush with summer grasses, knowing that the stretch ahead was bound to be grueling, the temptation to pause and rest must have been great.

The bands likely separated to take best advantage of forage and game. In that they would be following social protocol. Living separately was their inclination, their social default. During a journey they moved as one, and under one leader, but this was a pause. Stopping to rest and recoup, they likely would have broken into their natural constituent parts, which also helps explain the different, conflicting reports of their location.[31]

They were also jockeying for the way out of the park that best fit their needs—needs that kept changing. Basically, there were three feasible routes. The first option was northward down the Yellowstone River and onto the plains around what is now Livingston, Montana. The Nez Perces had typically used that trail on their hunting trips to the plains. But not this time. Had it been their first choice, they would have turned north soon after entering the park to take the well-worn Bannock trail from the Madison River to the Yellowstone. Instead, they had moved in the opposite direction, southward up the Firehole and then east to the lake.

They were headed for the second option, a trail southward out of the park to either the Shoshone (or Stinkingwater) River, which flows onto the plains at modern Cody, Wyoming, or to the Wind River. Their strategy at this point was to find aid and sanctuary among the Crows, and this southern pass was the most direct way to that end. This second route, however, was far less known to them, which explains why they used Shively, who had worked in that area, to point them correctly.

Then, apparently, came bad news. Although the evidence is fuzzy, about the time they were camped near Yellowstone Lake, the Nez Perce leaders seem to have made contact with the Crows, who made it clear that they were unwilling to help. This would have had a twofold effect. The Nez Perces would now have little interest in leaving to the south to the Shoshone River, especially if the Crows had indicated there might be soldiers in that area. Worse, the Crows' rejection cut the ground from under the overall strategy they had followed since leaving Idaho—the plan, advocated by Looking Glass, to find a safe haven among their friends in buffalo country. Now they knew there would be no such sanctuary.

That would have pushed them back toward their first option, the trail northward down the Yellowstone River. Not only was that way easier and most familiar; it also had them moving in the right direction, because if sanctuary with the Crows was out of the question, their last hope was to head for Canada, and if they left the park to the north, following the Yellowstone River, they would be that much closer to the international border.

On the last day of August, a few days after the Nez Perces apparently heard from the Crows, warriors struck the Henderson ranch and the tourists at Mammoth Hot Springs. Both sites were on the traditional trail to the north. These raiders sometimes have been described as renegade marauders, and obviously they took advantage of what whites they found, but more likely they were scouts sent to see whether the old northward trail, now the preferred option, was open and safe. Chased off by Doane's command, they would have returned with a second piece of bad news. Now this option seemed closed.[32]

Only one option was left: heading east. That meant leaving through the Absaroka Mountains that rose along the park's eastern boundary. This granite range was the highest in Montana, with several peaks over twelve thousand feet and its tallest, the highest point in the territory, nearing thirteen thousand. It had glaciers and permanent snowfields fed by snowfall that in some winters surpassed twenty-five feet. Even to enter the mountains, the bands would have to ascend the Absarokas' western flank, thickly forested and cut by steep canyons, some of them thoroughly clogged by washed-out timber. Compared to the relatively easy passways out of the western, southern, and northern sides of Yellowstone Park, the Absarokas rose like a great imposing wall.

There were openings. The best was up Soda Butte Creek and over a divide to Clark's Fork of the Yellowstone River, then down that river to the plains, but that would mean passing by a settlement later named Cooke City, a collection of white gold miners with a small smelter. Going that way meant sure trouble and, even worse, alerting their pursuers to the route they had chosen. The other passes were higher and more difficult, even for smaller hunting parties, and the challenge would be far greater for a moving village with a huge horse herd. Still, if the bands had any chance to break out, it would have to be by some route through those peaks.

All this probing and maneuvering—and capturing, raiding, and killing—took time. By the time the Nez Perces were settling on an eastern exit, they had been in Yellowstone between ten days and two weeks. Howard, meanwhile, had been moving through the park, Fisher and his Bannocks scouting ahead of him. He had ten wagons with him, and the thick woodlands and steep divides, terrain where Indian horses had gotten wedged between trees, were by far the greatest challenge his teamsters had faced.[33] It was slow going. Fisher told his journal he was "becoming tired of trying to get thee soldiers and the hostiles together. 'Uncle Sam's' boys are too slow for this business."[34] A unit of civilian laborers under Captain William Spurgin, nicknamed the "skillets" for their skill at building bridges and cutting roads through the densest timberlands, now showed their stuff. They hacked out a crude road, the one the agonized George Cowan called "the worst...ever passed over by a wagon," and on one sharp descent "about as steep as the roof of an ordinary house," they belayed wagons to the bottom with a hundred-foot rope tied to the rear axle of each and looped around a series of strong trees. The spot took the name Spurgin's Beaver Slide.[35]

Howard's advance faced another threat—military politics. Less than a week after Sherman expressed renewed faith in Howard, he encouraged him to step down. He wrote from Helena that Howard's force had "not much chance of a fight," given that the Nez Perces were so far ahead, and as Sherman was heading next for Walla Walla and Howard's Department of the Columbia, it would help to have Howard on hand for consultation. If Howard wished, he could head home "with perfect propriety" and turn his men over to the bearer of the message, Lieutenant Colonel Charles C. Gilbert. Gilbert, commander of a plains outpost, Camp Baker, had come to Helena ostensibly to check on an order for flour. He likely also used the situation to jockey for a field command and a chance to push his career.

Whatever was behind it, the possibility of Howard leaving the story never came into focus. On September 3, Gilbert met Lieutenant Gustavus Doane at Henderson's ranch. Doane had been there since his brush with the Nez Perces a few days before, and now he urged the obvious next move, to push farther into the park upstream along the Yellowstone and look for Howard. If Gilbert had done that, he would have met Howard in a couple of days and presumably taken command. Instead, to Doane's astonishment and frustration, Gilbert took an utterly nonsensical route, backtracking with Doane's men by a long, looping trail to where Howard had first entered the park on the west side. Having pushed his command hard to place themselves five days behind, he then pushed them again to catch up via the same brutal route Howard had taken. When Gilbert finally arrived back on the Yellowstone River, close to where he had started, Howard was long gone, his own men were exhausted, and his horses were reduced to shambling bonebags. He abandoned the chase and went home.[36]

During Gilbert's ridiculous march, Howard had moved down the Yellowstone. Perhaps sensing the possible humiliation of being replaced, he issued a field order giving a stirring, and occasionally outrageous, account of his men's performance and assuring "a war to the death with the savage foe."[37] With Fisher's help, Howard had concluded correctly that the Nez Perces would move east over the Absarokas. The bands made their move on September 5. Again, their exact route is still debated. They probably moved in two groups up the Lamar River and Miller Creek, a tributary of the Lamar, and rendezvoused at Hoodoo Basin, a place of fine pastures and fabulously eroded rock formations. From there they moved eastward, quickly passing across the new park's boundary, topping the Absaroka crest and gaining the watershed of Clark's Fork of the Yellowstone River. Their next goal was to find their way to where Clark's Fork emerged onto the Great Plains and to follow that stream to its juncture with the Yellowstone proper.

Very soon, however, they would learn that the eastern gate, too, seemed to be closed and locked. Army strategists had been frustrated when the Nez Perces had escaped into the high country, but the two weeks following had allowed them to marshal their forces and position them into what appeared to be a foolproof array. The park that had first offered a refuge now seemed an inescapable box. Any observer would have predicted that the remarkable running escape would end here. In fact, the Nez Perces were about to accomplish their most brilliant maneuver of the war.

CHAPTER **14**

# "The Best Skirmishers in the World"

D uring the sojourn in Yellowstone, telegraphic dispatches had kept the public informed, and there was a gathering confidence. A Montana editor found the situation "in the highest degree gratifying." Sherman, "the lion in him roused," had his quarry boxed into the high country: "We wait now hopefully for news that the Nez Perces have been struck hard and fatally."[1]

Sherman had indeed been busy. Working through the heads of the Departments of Dakota and the Platte—Brigadier Generals Alfred Terry and George Crook, respectively—Sherman prepared for all contingencies. The Nez Perces most likely would come down out of the Absarokas via one of the two rivers, Clark's Fork of the Yellowstone or the Stinkingwater (or Shoshone) to the south. Sherman sent troops to cover those possibilities. Another escape route, via the Wind River, was much less likely, but Sherman dispatched more cavalry there, just in case. On the west side of the Absarokas, Howard had cut loose from the wagons that had slowed him like an anchor and proceeded with pack mules toward the mountain crest. He moved by the fastest route, the one the Nez Perces had rejected to avoid the gold miners along it. So as the Nez Perces were crossing the Absarokas, hundreds of troops were waiting for them on the far side, while others under Howard were pressing from behind. There seemed no way out.

And then the Nez Perces escaped. How they did can be explained by a combination of timing, chance, the military's errors, and a gamble by the Indians, outrageous on the face of it but gracefully, remarkably executed.

The force sent to cover the unlikely escape down the Wind River was the Fifth Cavalry, eleven companies with about seven hundred men riding up from Wyoming. They arrived too late to play any part. Near the

Stinkingwater on September 17, they came across a broad trail of other cavalry heading north toward Clark's Fork, and when they arrived there they found evidence that something big had occurred, some convergence of forces, before everyone involved had headed down Clark's Fork toward the Yellowstone.[2]

The trail they had seen at the Stinkingwater was from the Seventh Cavalry, part of the remnant from Custer's debacle the year before. Its commander, Colonel Samuel Sturgis, had been in the field for nearly a month, having been sent first to the central Montana plains, well to the north. Many had thought the Nez Perces would head to Canada to join Sitting Bull's Sioux, and there were even rumors that the famed chief had come back into the United States to join the fight. Sturgis was to set himself near a key point, Judith Gap, and block the Nez Perces if they should break for the border. Then, when it became clear that the bands were moving not north but east over the Absarokas, Sturgis moved with his 360 men to plug the exits.[3]

He reached Clark's Fork on September 5, just as the Nez Perces were about to head his way. He was positioned where the river emerged onto the plains, exactly where the Nez Perces would come down from the Absarokas and where Howard, right behind them, would come out as well. With the three groups about to converge, it seemed the army would finally run its quarry to ground.[4]

Doing that, however, required coordination. Howard and Sturgis would each have to know where the other was and where the Nez Perces were heading. To press their advantage, that is, they had to know they *had* the advantage. But as the commands drew close together in the forests, mountains, and canyons of Wonderland, the speed-of-light communication that had helped put them into position, the telegraphic zipping that had kept the public attuned and ready for the trap to be sprung, did them no good. Now information walked or rode, and things happened by intuitive maneuvering and luck. The army and the Indians were back on even terms.

Howard and Sturgis had certainly tried to stay in touch. Way back at Henry Lake, Howard had sent a company of cavalry and two of artillery to Fort Ellis, at Bozeman, and to the Crow Agency. They were told to load up with eight thousand rations of bacon and hardtack and be ready to march to wherever the Nez Perces broke out of Yellowstone. Once Howard was sure the Nez Perces were heading east, he ordered those companies, under the command of Captain Henry Cushing, to find Sturgis on Clark's Fork and relay the plan: "Indians are between me and Sturgis, and I hope we may entrap them this time."[5] Just then, however, word came that Howard might be replaced by Gilbert, and Cushing was told to wait for orders from the new commander. He would sit there for weeks, forgotten, hearing nothing.

Meanwhile, Sturgis was reaching out for Howard. He hired three scouts to assess the situation in the mountains and warn any miners of impending danger, and when they found Howard about to march eastward, they delivered good news and bad. Sturgis was in perfect position, but he had no clue where Howard was or what he planned to do. Howard immediately sent two of the scouts back to fill Sturgis in. Neither made it. The Nez Perces were killing any whites they ran across, in part to keep their pursuers as blind as possible. Besides killing at least five miners—one by means of a pick driven through his neck into the ground, according to one account—they killed another scout Sturgis sent to find Howard, and when they met the two returning couriers, they killed one and left the other near death.[6] So while Howard knew where Sturgis was, Sturgis was in the dark. For all he knew, he was going to face the Nez Perces alone, if in fact they were coming his way.

Sturgis camped on a tributary of Clark's Fork near the base of Heart Mountain. Not a true mountain but a gigantic chunk of Paleozoic carbonate, it had broken from the east face of the Absarokas about fifty million years earlier and made an incomprehensibly slow half-somersault to land, upside-down, twenty miles onto the plains. This was an ideal location for Sturgis to observe the two possible exits, the valleys of Clark's Fork to the north and the Stinkingwater to the south, and to position his men to engage the Nez Perces or hold them until Howard came from behind. But Sturgis didn't *know* Howard was coming. He had been told that Doane would join him with enough troops to cover both exits comfortably, but Doane was on the other side of the mountains, first dealing with the Nez Perce raids and then traipsing around with Gilbert in his bungling effort to find and replace Howard.[7] Feeling isolated and shorthanded, Sturgis was increasingly anxious, which in turn may have clouded his thinking.

Sturgis had plenty of campaign experience. When barely out of West Point, he had fought and been captured in the Mexican War, and in the Civil War he had been at Wilson's Creek, Antietam, Fredericksburg, and Brice's Cross Roads. He had field experience against Comanches, Kiowas, Cheyennes, and Apaches. The current campaign, however, had to have been highly charged. After the Civil War, he had been assigned to command the Seventh Cavalry, but in the summer of 1876 he had been kept back at a desk in St. Louis while his subordinate, Custer, led his regiment to disaster at the Little Big Horn. Sturgis became perhaps Custer's harshest critic, and he had special reason. Among

**Figure 14.1** Samuel Sturgis, outmaneuvered by the Nez Perces outside Yellowstone Park

the dead around Custer, so mutilated that he was identified only by his bloody underwear, was Sturgis's son, Second Lieutenant James G. Sturgis, just out of West Point. Now, fourteen months later, the colonel faced another group of warriors with a history of humbling the army. They were somewhere over the mountains, coming at him by some route he did not know, and he had little idea of what support, if any, he could expect.

The Nez Perces had proceeded from the Absaroka divide down Timber and Crandall creeks to Clark's Fork. They could not simply follow the river out, however. Below them it funneled into a hopelessly narrow canyon where the swift river swept along sheer walls hundreds of feet high. They had to move upward by a trail along a bench above the canyon, and then up again, around a rise later named Dead Indian Hill for an elderly, abandoned Nez Perce who was killed and scalped by Fisher's scouts. From here, on the eastern foothills of the Absarokas, the usual way down was a trail southeastward to the Stinkingwater, but with their first clear view of the plains below, the bands must have seen Sturgis's command barely ten miles ahead near the base of Heart Mountain. They knew Howard was on their tail, and now knew someone else was at their head. Barring some remarkable turn, it was over.

Down below, Sturgis's men had been fishing. They had been given only individual issues of flour, and once in camp they gorged on trout caught with grasshoppers and the lines and hooks most kept in their shirt pockets and hatbands. A sergeant remembered the trout as "like the manna in the wilderness were to the Children of Israel."[8] While his troops went angling, Sturgis worried that only he was there to cork up the two exits. "It will be readily observed," he wrote later, "that I felt a great responsibility resting upon me, and that I was liable to leave Clark's Fork at any moment, depending altogether on what information might reach me from day to day."[9] That information came from patrols he sent to observe both the Stinkingwater and Clark's Fork approaches. Their reports were crucial to what followed. The first found the two couriers who had reached Howard, but one was dead and the other so badly wounded that he did not tell of Howard's presence. Their unspoken message, given that they were on the trail to the Stinkingwater, put Sturgis on the scent toward that river. The other patrol reported, first, that the access to Clark's Fork was so rough and treacherous that the Nez Perces could not possibly get down to that river. Second, they told of seeing "what appeared to be the hostiles, moving on the Stinking River trail, and that they had disappeared behind a range of mountains, going in the direction of the Stinking River."[10]

With that, Sturgis committed to the south, to the Stinkingwater. On the afternoon of September 8, his men were hurriedly reassembled with bugles and rifle shots. An officer arrived at a gallop with five strings of trout heads strung from his saddle horn, their bodies having jolted off during the frantic ride.[11] With what daylight was left, Sturgis marched his men farther along the base of Heart Mountain, and the next night they camped among the sulphurous fumes that gave the Stinkingwater its name. He would first establish himself where he thought the Nez Perces would debouch, then move up the trail he thought they were coming down, so he might engage them or turn them back on Howard, whom he hoped was following them. He found no one on the river, so on September 10 he led his troops up his quarry's presumed oncoming route, a rough and steep trail that had has men puffing and lightheaded in the thin air of the high Rockies. Still no Indians.[12]

Around Dead Indian Hill he finally found their tracks—headed away from him toward Clark's Fork. Instantly, he understood. He had moved away from the mouth of Clark's Fork precisely as the Nez Perces had moved toward it, descending through what Sturgis had thought was impassible terrain. The next day, his men found an abandoned horse carrying a brand of one of Howard's units, showing that Howard had come through here chasing the Nez Perces while Sturgis was making his wrongheaded march. Later that day, Sturgis came upon Howard's camp below the mouth of Clark's Fork canyon.[13] The Nez Perces were nowhere in sight. The bands had been caught between two forces; they had gotten past one and had stayed ahead of the other and now were miles ahead and loose onto the Great Plains.

What had happened? First of all, Sturgis obviously had bad information. There *was* a way down and out via Clark's Fork. All the options were so difficult that the cavalry patrol and its white guide might understandably have given it no chance, and Sturgis, besides, had been told by Crows that they had never heard of anyone crossing the Absarokas that way.[14] Sturgis also had made a critical strategic blunder: he had committed more than necessary. His decision to move away from Clark's Fork down to the Stinkingwater assumed that he had to choose one exit or the other. In fact, by staying near the base of Heart Mountain, with scouts feeling out in both directions, and allowing his men to rest, he would have been in prime position to move rapidly either way in time to meet the bands, whichever way they came. Nervous about being out of communication, with fewer men than he had hoped, told that his enemy could not leave by one of the exits and was headed toward the other, no doubt concerned with restoring the reputation of the Seventh Cavalry and perhaps a bit intimidated by a foe who had whipped the army consistently, Sturgis moved before he had to, and he moved by what he thought was most likely, not by what he knew.

What seemed likely was, obviously, wrong. For that, the Nez Perces themselves were most responsible. Their exact movements after they spotted Sturgis below them on September 8 are not known, but the general outline is. Stanton Fisher, Howard's scout, arrived at the spot and puzzled out what had happened. The Nez Perces first started down the trail toward the Stinkingwater. When Sturgis's patrol saw them and reported they were headed away from Clark's Fork, Sturgis made his choice and led his men off to the south. The bands then reversed course, back toward Clark's Fork. Before that, however, they "milled" their horses, rode them around in every direction. Having feinted Sturgis out of position, they took pains to confuse Howard coming behind. Their stratagem was not to conceal their trail; rather, they made the trail seem to go everywhere at once. To find its true direction, Fisher had his scouts explore the area in widening circles around the "mill." At last he stumbled on it and returned to Howard with the news.

The bands reached Clark's Fork about two miles below where it emerged from its gorge at Devil's Gate, a thin slot between stone walls hundreds of feet high. They came down by one of a few small, steep canyons. There's a cavalry adage that a horse can go anywhere a man can go without using his hands, and according to those terms, these canyons were all passable. But when one remembers that not only two thousand horses descended but also people of all ages carrying the essentials of an entire village, simply reaching the valley floor seems an extraordinary feat. Just as remarkable were the maneuvers that led to their escape. While Sturgis had himself partly to blame, it was the inspired combination of feint and confounding, the jog to the south followed by the "mill" and the audacious descent of the close and steep defile that opened the door onto the plains and that slowed the pursuit.

Who thought of those moves is unknown. Nearly forty years later, the Nez Perce No Feather told an interviewer that a young man "said he had been all through that part of the country and he knew how to dodge the soldiers, so we let him guide us." His name translated as "Bad Boy" or "Rough Customer."[15] Wherever they got their information, the Nez Perces' decisions had to have been hurried and spontaneous, and so all the more impressive. Back in Idaho, they had done something similar when they drew Howard into a fruitless, slippery chase from White Bird Canyon into the mountains across the Salmon

River, but that idea had been hatched over days and with the help of seasoned strategists who now were dead. This tactic was conceived in the moment, at most over a few hours, and it sprang them from a far tighter bind.

It left the military frustrated and embarrassed—but also with a growing admiration that, interestingly, had always been there.

"I'll tell the world the profanity that filled the air was deep and hearty!" So wrote one of Sturgis's soldiers of the moment when he realized that the Nez Perces had come out of the hills only a few miles from where the Seventh Cavalry had left only four days earlier. Howard looked "much dilapidated," he added, and an embittered Sturgis reportedly offered a cash-starved officer's ultimate remorse: "Poor as I am I would give $1,000 if I had not left this place."[16] Yet Howard later would praise the "consummate generalship" and "quick wit" behind the Nez Perce ruse and would commend their people's "hardihood" in slipping down the canyon to "break the almost impassible roadway."[17] To a point, Howard was being the magnanimous victor at a time (1881) when Joseph's public image was becoming especially polished. His praise also reflected a deeper ambivalence felt by many in the military.

In the popular image of the Indian wars, the army appears sometimes as heroic, sometimes as villainous, but always the soldiers and Indians are separate and utterly opposed. Their only apparent contact comes while shooting at each other. Otherwise, they face off across a cultural chasm, almost like alien species. In fact, the military was likely to have more contact with Indians, and contact more varied and intimate, than most other whites in the West. The fullest exchange happened around frontier posts and in the field, where the cultures most closely blended and abraded. The military's impressions, what they took in about Indians and what they made of it, can be especially revealing. It is a mixed and intriguing picture.

Most surviving impressions are from officers, who generally had more education and longer military experience than those under them, and thus more exposure under more circumstances with native peoples. Often they wrote for publication, and so were more likely to reflect prevailing notions, or at least were less likely to offend them. Their opinions varied, not only among writers but sometimes within the pages written by any one of them.

Some patterns nonetheless stand out. Observers measured all cultures by the same standards—literacy, Christianity, and what they considered higher thinking and advance institutions, meaning of course their own.

One thing, however, was clear: set next to European-Americans, Indians did not nearly measure up. What passed for reason among them, Colonel Richard Dodge wrote in *Our Wild Indians,* was scarcely instinct, and in fact their "ordinary mental activity...may be estimated at zero." Some thought native peoples were bound to vanish, either through wars or by a sort of undefined evaporation as they confronted a superior civilization.[18] Asked by a special congressional committee why Indian populations were declining so badly, General James Carleton cited wars, intemperance, and various diseases but ended with the divine will "that one race of men—as in races of lower animals—shall disappear off the face of the earth." Just as mammoths and giant sloths had vanished, so also "the red man of America is passing away!"[19] Many, however, thought Indians could change and survive. Dodge was one of many who believed all cultures were engaged in one great march of progress, and as Indians advanced from savagery toward civilization, in time they might at least come within sight of the white society. He found the typical Indian much like a "mere animal...modified to some extent by reason," but still "far ahead of many tribes and people."[20]

There was universal agreement that the new order of whites was destined to prevail and the old order doomed. The death of indigenous lifeways was considered as inevitable as a sunset. Along the way, officers found things to admire; typically, these were virtues held up as a contrast to clichéd notions of the costs to whites of cultural progress. If civilized whites could be jaded and harried, Indians were called happy and carefree and easily amused. They "made merry" over white men's bald heads and each other's pratfalls, Oliver Howard wrote, and while cruel in war, they were free of modern man's acquisitive passions and oily hypocrisy. Someone once asked Howard whether Indians were treacherous. "No," he answered, "not so much as the Anglo-Saxon."[21]

On points like these, observers were no different from scores of Victorian Romantics. Things got more interesting when they wrote of their closest contacts in war and peace. Indians' courage would "always command the admiration of the soldiers who conquered them," one wrote, and others marveled at their marksmanship, skills as horsemen, command of terrain, and sense of strategy.[22] At the Big Hole, Gibbon wrote, "we could not compete" with warriors Howard judged were "like the cossacks of Russia, the best skirmishers in the world." Dodge praised Indians' "magnificent riding" and "superb drill" and found them superior to whites "in every soldierlike quality" outside of discipline and raw courage.[23]

In peacetime, observers' on-the-ground impressions ran the full spectrum from being nauseated and appalled by native habits and appearance to being shamed by their generosity and humbled by their character. The range of impressions alone told of seeing beyond platitudes to ordinary humanity. Most intimately, some officers were involved sexually with Indian women beyond a pay-as-you-go arrangement, although predictably details were hidden, and any influence on attitudes is impossible to gauge. Howard's aide, Charles E. S. Wood, who later became an outspoken critic of Indian policies, had at least one Indian lover. So, reportedly, did George Custer. There is more of a record of respectable social contact between Indian men and army officers, their wives, and their families. One young wife at Fort Laramie was surprised when Sioux guests to her home sat in the parlor "as if they had been born there." She took to inviting the prominent Red Cloud to lunch and found him "very polite, and dignified in all respects, and when he smiles I never saw a sweeter."[24] Anson Mills and his wife, Nannie, also invited Sioux men to their home. She was put off by the obsequious No Flesh but was taken with Spotted Tail's "engaging manners" and "liked [him] at first sight."[25]

In those moments, "the Indian problem" took on a human face. "They came to be real people to me," an officer's wife wrote of the men and women she met, people with a life of their own being overwhelmed

Figure 14.2 As with these Crow warriors, soldiers and Indians often met on close but peaceful terms

by aliens, of whom she was one.[26] Some officers developed a nuanced appreciation of tribal cultures. An obvious example was John Gregory Bourke, who saw much action in the Southwest and on the Great Plains and rose to the rank of captain, but was more notable as an accomplished early ethnographer. During a dozen years of fieldwork, especially in the Southwest, he compiled several vocabularies and filled forty notebooks with observations of native life. Later he was chosen president of the American Folk-Lore Society.[27] Lieutenant James H. Bradley, who served in both the Sioux and Nez Perce campaigns and was the first attacker killed at the Big Hole, showed a hungry curiosity about native life on the northern plains and the Columbia Plateau, gathering material on horse cultures and interspersing his account of the Sioux campaign with sections entitled "Indian Hieroglyphics" and "A Bit of Crow History."[28]

When soldiers got a close look at what was called progress, many were critical, and some outraged. Edward Wynkoop had called for the annihilation of Indians when he first came West, but he came to call the government's treatment of Indians a "damnable infamy" and a "disgrace to the country and a blot upon our flag." If the present course continued, he wrote, "I'll be damned if I don't desert my country [and] forswear Christianity."[29] Few went that far, but many would have agreed with Dodge that for all their diversity, native peoples had a few points in common: "all are savage, all are swindled, starved and imposed upon."[30]

Different groups of Indians were regarded differently, of course, and the peoples of the Pacific Northwest were especially complimented, none more than the Nez Perces. In the decades before the war, they were praised as handsome, cleanly, dignified, honest, and loyal and as masters of horsemanship. In the field, even as military losses and frustrations mounted, they won a grudging admiration. Shortly after they slipped the trap outside Yellowstone, Howard's surgeon John Fitzgerald wrote his wife: "Poor Nez Perces!...I am actually beginning to admire their bravery and endurance in the face of so many well equipped enemies." At the war's end, Colonel Nelson Miles would write his wife that "the whole Nez Perce movement is unequaled in the history of Indian warfare."[31] As for the causes of the conflict, one officer compared Isaac Stevens's forcing of the treaty of 1855 to "something like the Highwayman, who with his hand on your throat, and a pistol at your head, requests your small change."[32]

None of this means that officers and soldiers generally were a great reservoir of sympathy and goodwill. They could picture Indians as cultural knuckle-walkers and unspeakable brutes. Dodge called them "savage fiends" and left a rare description of gang rapes of white women captives. When Edwin Mason, Howard's second in command, heard from survivors the story of the attack on the Cowan party in Yellowstone Park, he wrote that the Nez Perces "should be killed as we kill any other vile thing."[33] These charges of corruption and abuse might be read as the same rhetoric of confessional conquest heard from sanctimonious agents and gaseous politicians. Even their compliments could be self-serving. To say that warriors were courageous and worthy opponents was to say that the victorious army must be even better and braver.

The very muddiness of judgment, however, is revealing. Writers seemed caught on a divide. Their faith that their own society should prevail was the cultural air they breathed. Yet as the men most directly engaged in making that faith real, they saw what it meant in fleshly terms. The Indians whom they believed were doomed to conquest, maybe to extinction, sipped tea in their parlors, patted their children, warmed to their families. The ways of life the white men called inferior some came to know as also richly endowed, full of beauty, and wonderfully expressive. Some soldiers found that simply keeping the peace boiled down to smoothing the way not only for honest settlers and people like their own families but also for bummers, whiskey-sellers, and political hacks.

Living on that divide must have been especially wrenching for some. Bradley, the curious ethnographer and collector of native plains lore, was the first white to find the blackening corpses of George Custer and his men. General George Crook, whose command was badly handled by the Sioux and Cheyennes and who saw plenty of Apache depredations in the Southwest, wrote of having to witness injustices against native people he called friends. And then, he said, "when they were pushed beyond endurance and would go on the war path, we had to fight when our sympathies were with [them]."[34]

The dilemma is poignant, simply as one of people of conscience drawn into a bad place. In the context of the nation's remaking at the midcentury, it becomes more telling. Virtually all western officers had fought to preserve the union. Now they were on a second mission—to pacify its new western reaches. In one sense, the fighting back East and the fighting out West were part of the same purpose. Both were confirming, unifying, and consolidating a nation. In another sense, the two missions grated against each other. The Civil War ended by giving freedom to more than four million persons; the army's job in the West was to take freedom away from thousands of others. This moral dis-chord was at the heart of the new America created by reunion and expansion. Others, farther away, could gloss it over, but western soldiers, living in the grit of direct, sustained contact with Indians, found it harder to ignore.

Some of the most mixed and conflicted reactions came from those in the thickest action. In September 1878, Gibbon dined with John Gregory Bourke on a train from Montana to Washington, D.C. In June 1876, Gibbon's command had rescued survivors and buried the dead at the Little Big Horn, and then thirteen months later he had led troops and civilians against the Nez Perces at the Big Hole. That near disaster had hurt his career, and he still felt the leg wound he suffered there (his career's only other injury had come repelling Pickett's charge at Gettysburg). But in Gibbon's opinion, "as in that of all army officers," Bourke wrote in his diary, the war "was an unjustifiable outrage upon the red men, due to our aggressive and untruthful behavior toward those poor people."[35]

How far down the ranks those opinions ran, and how these men managed their snarl of feelings, nobody knows. But there are hints. McCarthy barely escaped a field of dead friends at White Bird Canyon. ("It looked so still, not a soul moving on its surface.") Yet leading up to that day he had witnessed and written about Nez Perce families being bullied off their lands and generally humiliated. A few days after being nearly killed at White Bird, when he was safe among the civilian victims of the Nez Perce raids, he told his diary of their broken lives and their dazed, lost looks. When he looked back on the troubles, he found whites wholly to blame. "I could not for anything be the apologist of the Indians," he wrote, "but I could not shut my eyes to what I saw and close my ears to what I heard." Later he crossed out the words, as if his thought had never happened.[36]

## CHAPTER 15

# Toward the Medicine Line

It was September 11 when Sturgis and Howard finally linked up on Clark's Fork. Four days earlier, they had had the Nez Perces trapped between them. Now the Nez Perces were fifty miles ahead. Howard assumed command and the two men "entered into mutual explanations," Sturgis wrote dryly, "and had the poor satisfaction of exchanging regrets over the untoward course events had taken."[1] A year after its tragedy on the Little Big Horn, the Seventh Cavalry had managed a farce, and Sturgis, clearly embarrassed, was determined to make it up. His horses' "elastic tread" contrasted with Howard's tired mounts, and Sturgis proposed a series of forced marches to try to catch the Nez Perces. Howard agreed and contributed fifty of his freshest cavalry and two mountain howitzers on mule-back; the command set off before dawn on September 12. The weather was miserable: cold, wet, and windy. "I'll sure never forget that...day's march," a trooper recalled: "For breakfast we just sinched [sic] our belts one hole tighter." By late evening, they had covered more than fifty miles.[2]

With the bands loose and well ahead and running, however, Howard had to hedge all bets. Presumably, they would head for the Canadian line to join Sitting Bull's Sioux, who might come across the border to meet them. Both the Nez Perces and the Sioux had humiliated the military during the past year, and from the start of the present campaign the thought of the two joining forces had preyed on the minds of the officers directing it, especially after the Nez Perces had headed east out of Idaho.[3] After they broke out of Yellowstone, the western press flared up at the thought of the linked Indian forces bringing "frequent and murderous raids" and "fire and murder" throughout the northern plains. By one claim, in fact, Joseph *was* a Sioux. When the Minnesota Sioux had been removed westward in 1863, he supposedly had taken off for Idaho and now hoped to rejoin his kinsmen.[4]

Only one other command might catch the Nez Perces short of Canada. Colonel Nelson Miles was at the Tongue River cantonment—today's Miles City, Montana—where the Tongue River joins the Yellowstone, roughly 150 miles downstream from where the Nez Perces would cross. If Miles left right away and moved rapidly on a northwesterly tangent, he might still intercept them. Orders sent both by boat and horseback urged Miles to take to the field immediately.[5] He received them on September 17 and the next day set off on his long-shot mission.[6]

The bands still had to clear one last barrier in their run for the border. At the end of the Clark's Fork's twisty course, they entered the broad valley of the Yellowstone River. It was a grand corridor easily traversed—as long as the traveler moved along the river, upstream or down. Getting out of the valley was another matter, especially for anyone moving north, as the bands wanted to do. A natural palisade rose to the north: a rimrock, four hundred feet tall, that ran parallel to the Yellowstone for many miles in both directions. Above those cliffs, the land was an open sweep. If the Nez Perces could get up top, they were free, but if they couldn't, they might easily be caught.

There was only one break in this barrier. Canyon Creek (an inflated name this time of year for a series of stale, alkaline pools) sliced through the rimrock several miles below where Clark's Fork entered the Yellowstone. This canyon offered easy access to the plain above, and its boulders and narrow turns made it ideal for a rearguard defense. This gateway was well known to the Nez Perces, and they made directly for it.

On September 13, as they made their bid for that doorway toward Canada, they clashed sharply with the pursuing military. The episode is usually called the battle of Canyon Creek, a term that subtly distorts the facts in two ways. It was less a battle than a serious skirmish, a running fight that lasted several hours. Human losses were light on both sides, and in their accounts of the war the Nez Perces scarcely acknowledge the affair, at least insofar as it involved the army. To them, the incident was a rankling episode in diplomacy involving other Indians—their old allies the Crows. They scarcely mention the army.

Montana promoters predicted that the Yellowstone valley, "as large as one of the larger New England states," would soon blossom into one of the continent's finest farming regions, and in fact it did become a prosperous pocket of the northern plains, but when the Nez Perces came through this stretch it had only a few ranches, a timber camp, and the town of Coulson: several tents and a saloon.[7] The main Nez Perce column moved downstream a few miles from Clark's Fork, crossed at the mouth of Canyon Creek, and started up that dry streambed toward the opening that would spring them loose onto the plains. A couple of raiding parties went farther downriver. They burned Coulson's saloon—all in town had fled—and surprised and killed two trappers in a camp. They also burned the houses and haystacks of a couple of ranches, one of which was also a stage station. There might have been more deaths there, but neighbors rode up with a warning just as a stage was pulling in with two passengers, a dentist and a popular mining camp entertainer, Fanny Clark. Everyone dashed into some nearby brush to hide; when an accompanying dog wouldn't stop barking, they cut its throat. Raiders fired the house, and then took off with the stage, tossing behind them Fanny's clothes, some mail, and sets of false teeth and "tools of torture" from the dentist's valise.[8]

After his fifty-mile day, Sturgis had made it to the Yellowstone, but with no Indians in sight he assumed they were out of reach, and by mid-morning he was ready to call a halt. His men were bone weary and close to famished. Provisions from Fort Ellis had yet to catch up, and for several days each man had gotten by on of a pint of flour, a cup of coffee, and a slice of bacon "half the size of your hand."[9] Troops were just starting to unsaddle their horses when scouts, after spotting the dragooned stage speeding toward the main column, reported that the Nez Perces were just ahead. Sturgis immediately ordered an attack.

The lead squadron was under Colonel Wesley Merrill, who had been part of the command that had come up from the south and joined Sturgis and Howard at Clark's Fork. After five minutes of tightening their horses' girths, they formed a skirmish line and set off on a lope. After several miles, they topped a rise and saw the bands hurrying toward the mouth of the canyon. Warriors on horseback were doubling back to provide a covering fire.

The goal now was to stop the Nez Perces and their horses from reaching the canyon gateway, which seemed to call for a dual strategy. As Sturgis tried to catch the column with a quick pursuit from behind, other cavalry would make a fast, oblique approach to the mouth of the canyon before the Nez Perces reached it. It was a condensed version of the campaign since leaving Idaho: try hard to catch up with the bands while looking for shortcuts and the chance to head them off. As with every step of the war so far, the lay of the land proved crucial.

Howard later described that plain as "the most horrible of places—sage brush and dirt and only alkaline water and very little of that!"[10] In fact, it was typical of this part of the river's long basin—dry, brush-covered, and rock-strewn. Sturgis ordered Merritt's lead battalion to pursue the column hurrying up Canyon Creek. A bit later, a battalion under Captain Frederick Benteen set off on a gallop toward the canyon's mouth. Feeding

**Figure 15.1** The reading public kept up with the war and battles like that at Canyon Creek

into Canyon Creek from the west, the direction of Benteen's approach, were several deeply gouged arroyos that now lay across his most direct line of advance. His battalion took a slightly roundabout way, skirting the heads of the worst of those gullies, and ran for the canyon.

As they were maneuvering toward the canyon, however, they received a heavy fire from the bluffs ahead. Warriors had gotten there first; securely perched among the rocks, they "rendered our position open to decided objections," a trooper recalled.[11] The cavalry dismounted and traded fire for a while, then made a move to get atop the bluff and into better position. They finally did, only to find that the Nez Perces had pulled back into the lower portion of the canyon. By then, the bands' noncombatants and most of their horses were into the passway and on their way to safety.[12]

The Nez Perces were able to reach the canyon so quickly in part because Merritt's lead battalion never worried them much from behind. As Benteen's men rode ahead toward the rimrock, one of them looked back to see "the Sturgis outfit FIGHTING ON FOOT" as their opponents rode rapidly away from them.[13] Instead of having Merrill's cavalry charge on horseback, Sturgis had ordered them to dismount and establish a firing line. He may have expected the Nez Perce warriors to mass and stand against him—expected, that is, that they would treat this as a pitched battle—but they wanted only to provide a covering fire. When the troops dismounted and began firing from about five hundred yards, the Nez Perces stayed mounted and fired back for a time, as usual with each man acting on his own, and in time rode off by individual whim. "We had our warrior ways," Yellow Wolf explained; "We did not line up like soldiers. We went by ones, just here and there."[14] As the Indians withdrew, the troops advanced on foot for about three miles before Sturgis finally told them to mount.

By then, all initiative had been lost. The exhausted cavalry rode to the canyon and joined Benteen's battalion, but the two officers wisely chose not to press into the canyon. The Nez Perces called this place Te-pah-le-wam Wah-kus-pah, or Place Similar to Split Rocks, referring to the site near Tolo Lake where the bands had camped on the eve of the war.[15] It was ideal for defense: its wide opening narrowed to an upward path with rocky sides that formed, a soldier wrote, "a perfect line of breast works."[16] Sturgis later described his troops driving their enemy up the canyon "from gully to gully and from rock to rock" until darkness ended the action.[17] In fact, small numbers of warriors easily held off pursuers. After the column had passed, some had felled trees and rolled rocks into the passage. Trying to push through that clogged gauntlet would have turned a frustration into a disaster.

Artillery had again been brought into play, and again was useless. Howard had sent along two mountain howitzers carried on mules, but the overly excited young officer in charge of one placed it in a ravine where he could not even see the enemy. Fisher the scout "left him in disgust."[18] Howard's son, Lieutenant Guy Howard, commanded the second piece. Rather than taking it off the mule, he swung the animal around, rammed in a shell, "and let drive, nearly turning his mule a summersaut." When the round fell short, he shot off another, and "this time the old mule had all four legs spread out and was braced for the recoil." The barrage-by-muleback then was abandoned.[19]

"Our Colel I think showed very poor generalship and by it the herd was allowed to escape," a private wrote that night in his diary, thinking, like most, that Sturgis had thrown away his chances when he ordered Merrill's men off their horses; "In fact the Officers give him a rather hard blast for his day's management."[20] Sturgis himself observed everything through binoculars from half a mile away, and he held so many cavalry in reserve that a scout thought that fewer than half the available force was ever engaged. Sturgis held back, he said, because he mistook an approaching group of friendly Crows for Nez Perces and feared for his pack and ammunition train back on the Yellowstone. Perhaps; but some thought he was so haunted by his son's death under an overly rash commander that he became overly timid. In any case, the rapid marches of the past two days had come to nearly nothing, or as Redington the scout put it, the "forceful energy of troopers and troop-horses" ended with a "forceful failure."[21] A pursuit up the canyon the next day never got close, and that night a courier brought orders for Howard's fifty men and their scouts to return to the Yellowstone. Sturgis could only plod ahead and hope for a break.

Three troopers had died, and eleven had been wounded. Sturgis claimed sixteen Nez Perces killed in the fight and five the following day, a ridiculous inflation that his own scout rejected. His report of between nine hundred and a thousand ponies taken that day and the next was also far above the facts.[22] The Nez Perces would say they left behind some lame and worn-out mounts and lost few of any value to the army.[23]

They did, however, lose some good horses to an unexpected foe—the Crows. Canyon Creek was barely twenty miles east of the Crow agency, the largest concentration of the tribe on the plains. About fifty warriors had joined Sturgis on the Yellowstone and apparently had helped scouts locate the Nez Perce column. They took no part in the fighting that day, instead hiving off some Nez Perce horses and trying to get some of the army's.[24] A much larger contingent, about two hundred, appeared later and troubled the sleep of the weary troopers by dancing and "shouting and singing all night." Before dawn on September 14, they and some of the army's Bannock scouts took off in pursuit of the bands.

Above the rimrock, the Nez Perces made good time across the rolling prairie, and the Crows and Bannocks on their fresh horses did even better. Yellow Wolf was guarding the rear of the column when he saw some strange Indians coming on: "Eeh! Crows!" He and others, among them Ollokut, kept them at a distance for the rest of that day and part of the next, and in the end only one warrior was killed, and an elderly couple who had lagged behind. The Crows made off with thirty or forty head of good stock before heading home.[25]

This trouble with the Crows, not the fight with Sturgis, stands out most in the Nez Perce memory. They had long considered the Crows allies, and that friendship had been the center of their strategy in leaving home. Even after the calamity at the Big Hole, they had thought they might trust the Crows to help them to Canada. When they learned in Yellowstone Park that this hope, too, was misplaced—that the Crows would give them no outright support—they still had some assurances. The Nez Perces say, and Crow tradition agrees, that prominent Crows promised that any Crow warriors who were with the soldiers would only feign a fight and shoot over their friends' heads. They even contributed some ammunition for the days ahead.[26] Then came Canyon Creek and the running raid the next day. It seemed the ultimate betrayal. "Many snows the Crows had been our friends," Yellow Wolf remembered; "But now, like the Bitterroot Salish, [they had] turned enemies. My heart was just like fire."[27]

Maybe the horse raids were a caprice, maybe a concerted assault. Whatever the Crows' motives, they were acting out of a new diplomatic reality. Seventy years earlier, Lewis and Clark had come into a world ruled by an ancient diplomacy, one of evolving connections among many centers of Indian power. Europeans complicated that world—horses, guns, and other goods raised the stakes and invigorated the action—yet Indians still dealt with whites at least as equals and often with the upper hand. Early on, new influences like diseases began to eat away at that power, but it was the expansion of the 1840s that was its great undoing. The stuff of diplomacy is leverage. It might come from offering what others want, but the new economy of white settlement, farming and ranching and mining, left Indians with nothing to bargain with. Leverage can mean threatening other players, but by 1865 most western Indians were a small minority in their own homelands, no more threat to national dominance than Nepalese Ghurkas. Always before, Indians had leveraged advantage by working various players against one another. Playing one side against another, however, requires some "other" to play the "one" against. Now one player ruled the field.

In the final flickering of the old system, some Indians were able to gain an edge by helping the new rulers against the last opposition. In 1876, the Crows had scouted and fought with the army against the Sioux. It was partly to protect their own land. Although Custer often is pictured as invading Sioux turf when he met his end, the Sioux were the invaders; by the treaty of 1868, the Little Big Horn was Crow country. But by helping the military defeat their enemies, the Crows made themselves diplomatically irrelevant. If the Little Big Horn was Custer's last stand, the war around it was the Sioux's, and once the last of them had surrendered or fled to Canada, no one else was resisting white control. The Crows lost their last leverage. Success was failure. They had insured their own subordination.

Then the Nez Perces came down from Yellowstone Park, and briefly the game was back on. This was only a denouement, however, a recurrence signaling the end, and the Crows clearly knew it. Once more, the government played its role. In a flurry of correspondence, Miles, Doane, and Sturgis worried about handling the Crows. Doane, working most closely with them, was told to be discreet and to use a familiar trump card: "provided the Crows assist in the work, the [captured Nez Perce] ponies and ammunition may be given to them.... You can withhold any ammunition or rations until this is accomplished."[28]

Guns and horses: an echo across seven decades, one more negotiation in an old diplomacy now in its final twitch. Perhaps the running fight for the Nez Perce herd was impulse, perhaps part of a deal with the army, but whatever it was, the Crows worked from an understanding that was now dawning on the Nez Perces. Whites in the new America were neither allies nor enemies. They were commanders. Horses and guns, and all other means of living, ultimately were theirs to give and take away.

By breaking north, the Nez Perces acknowledged the new realpolitik. The lines that mattered now were not boundaries among friends but borders between nations, and the only genuine diplomatic maneuvering involved playing one nation against another. The only possible sanctuary was with traditional enemies, the Sioux under Sitting Bull, now potential friends because they were some of the few who were still resisting the new structure of power.

Two commands chased the Nez Perces, one known to them and the other not. Howard was following their trail. Colonel Nelson Miles was coming on a diagonal from the southeast. The two pursuers were quite different. The often hesitant Howard was derided by Joseph and others as "General Day after Tomorrow." Nobody would jibe like that at Miles, a New Englander who had joined a volunteer unit in the Civil War, fought in some of its bloodiest engagements, suffered four battle wounds, and steadily moved up in rank to become a brigadier general and, at twenty-six, a division commander in the Army of the Potomac. After the war, he had married well (the niece of William and John Sherman) and with the rank of colonel took command of the Fifth Infantry out West. He was a field commander in the Red River War (1874–75) that finally broke the power of the Comanches and Kiowas on the southern plains. In the aftermath of Custer's disaster, Miles had led the winter and spring campaign that hounded and finally subdued the Sioux and Cheyennes. Indians called him Bear Coat after the heavy garment he wore in the wintry field, a name tinged also with respect for a fierce fighter. He was a ferociously ambitious self-promoter, vain and pompous, equally good in pursuing enemies in the field and making them among fellow officers; but no one could question his courage and relentless drive against whatever he was set against.

Miles's work against the Sioux and Cheyennes was scarcely over when he was told to chase the Nez Perces. Between the two efforts, he directed fourteen months of nearly continuous campaigning. A trooper present for only the last eight called it "the roughest times I have ever experienced in my life in the army or out of it."[29] With Howard's order, Miles nonetheless set off like a hound from hell. The present circumstances—a well-publicized enemy who had embarrassed and eluded colleagues of higher rank—offered a grand chance to win the general's star he so coveted.

Still, catching the Nez Perces was a long shot. Not only would Miles have to cover a lot of ground quickly; he also had to anticipate the bands' trajectory, much like a skeet shooter aiming at his target, and end up at the right point to catch or block them. He would need luck.

The Nez Perces had their own problems. To reach Canada, they would have to travel about 150 miles across the northern plains. Popular notions aside, this country was not flat but was an expanse of rolling grasslands punctuated by mountains that were not as lofty as the Rockies but still formidable barriers. Directly north were two ranges close together, the Little Belt and the Big Snowy Mountains, separated by a stretch of plains called Judith Gap. (It took its name from the stream draining northward, the south branch of the Judith River, which William Clark had named for the woman he would marry.) Here was one more gateway where the army might have blocked the bands' advance. Back when it was feared

**Figure 15.2** Nelson Miles, "Bear Coat," led the final pursuit of the Nez Perces

that they were heading for Canada instead of Crow country, Sturgis and Doane had been sent there, but both had been pulled southward, leaving Judith Gap unguarded.

A second barrier was the Missouri River. For a long stretch of Montana, it flowed through the Missouri Breaks—tall, rugged bluffs and broken terrain that extended several miles from the stream on both sides of the valley. A few places offered a way through the breaks combined with a useable ford, and the Nez Perces knew these places well. Once across the Missouri, they would still face a few mountain ranges before reaching Canada, but the paths through them were familiar and easy to negotiate.

The Nez Perces were deeply tired and had lost an undetermined number of horses, but the pursuers under Sturgis were worse off. Their cavalry's corn-fed horses, unused to lengthy marches with only pasture for feed, were fading fast and had started to suffer from painful hoof infections. By the end of the first march north of Canyon Creek, the command was spread out over the last ten of the day's thirty-seven miles, and one out of three cavalrymen was on foot and leading his mount. The men felt the kind of tiredness that brought sleep in midsentence, and with the tents left behind they passed the nights shivering with only greatcoats and saddle blankets for cover. They were awfully hungry. The supplies from Fort Ellis had never shown up, which left them to subsist for a second week on half rations or less. The night of the battle, they were down to flour mixed with water and baked in tin plates, and the next night a bit of bacon. Some of the men improvised. "Tonight we are dining off of Pony meat," a private wrote in his diary.[30] The next day, September 15, took them to the Musselshell River, but with the Nez Perce column well ahead and with no sign of the supply train, Sturgis decided it was time to wait for Howard.[31]

His men spent the next few days resting and keeping to their diet of horses, mules, and the few remaining rations. The one abundance was buffalo berries, the fruit of a hardy, tree-sized shrub (*Shepherdia argentea*) that is common from the northern plains to the Arctic. Modern sources note that in early autumn the berries are "tart." A scout was more emphatic; they were so bitter that they "put on a pucker that never comes off." He claimed his mouth remained contracted forty-three years later.[32]

It was nearly another week later, September 21, when Howard and Cushing's supplies caught up with Sturgis.[33] Howard had taken the wounded down the Yellowstone as far as a famous landmark, Pompey's Pillar, and from there had turned north to rendezvous on the Musselshell River. The time had come, once again, to evaluate his prospects.

He had virtually no chance to catch the Nez Perces on his own. "We are still pegging along after the Indians," his chief of staff wrote home: "They are moving 35 and 40 miles a day while we are dragging our worn-out horses and leg-weary men along at a rate of 12 and 15. It looks like a perfect farce."[34] Howard's view was reflected in the size of his command. A substantial portion was sloughed off after Canyon Creek. Fisher and his scouts, their term of service up, threw up their hands and went home, and on September 27 Howard told Major Sanford and the First Cavalry to start back to Idaho via the Union Pacific Railroad connection at Corinne, Utah. He would make do with Sturgis and his companies of the Seventh Cavalry. Meanwhile, he resumed the pursuit, but "in a less hurried manner than heretofore."[35] Later, his slowing down became part of an ongoing unpleasantness with Miles over how to divide the plaudits for ending the war.

The Nez Perces, as anticipated, passed through Judith Gap into Judith Basin. This beautiful pastureland was traditionally fine for bison hunting, but its herds now were much diminished, and the bands' food stores were running dangerously low. Some white settlement was sprinkled through here, and with Howard well behind them the Nez Perce began scouting ahead to spot any trouble or possibilities. Yellow Wolf told of finding four white men who fired on him. Although slightly wounded, he shot two of them, and when the others ran away, he took their horses and some flour. Whites were like "little flies," he told friends back in camp: "Sometimes they light on your hand. You can kill them!"[36] Some warriors fell on a camp of Crows, vented their anger on them, and took away some dried bison meat. Others paid a friendly visit to a trading stockade where they had done business in years past.

Beyond Judith Gap they made excellent time, at one point covering seventy-five miles in a day and a half. On September 23, they reached the Missouri River at Cow Island crossing. As the name implies, an islet part way across, plus an unusual shallowness, made for an ideal ford. From the south, there was a good trail through the Missouri Breaks, and once across the big river, a small tributary, Cow Creek, offered a way out of the basin to the north. The island and the shallows also made this spot the highest upriver point reachable by steamboat once the water level dropped in late summer. Goods on their way to the northern Rockies and southern Canada were unloaded here and carried by wagon to Fort Benton on the upper Missouri. The trade was considerable, measuring in the thousands of tons. Thus Cow Island, a traditional north-and-south crossing of plains hunters, had become in the new order a transition point in lines of supply tying together the northern plains and mountains with the nation to the east.

For the moment, that worked to the Indians' advantage. On the northern bank were great mounds of material recently offloaded from a steamboat, a pile of food as tall as a house, Yellow Wolf said. Guarding it were only a dozen soldiers and a few civilians. To the hungry, this must have seemed like manna from heaven—or at least from St. Louis. First, they moved a little upstream and got their column safely across the Missouri and on its way up Cow Creek. Next, a few men approached the tiny command bermed in behind some breastworks. Sergeant William Moelchert was in charge. Someone, probably Poker Joe, asked politely for some supplies. Moelchert refused. The delegation walked away, returned, and offered money "as they were hungry and [had] nothing to eat," but the sergeant again said no. After a third plea, he gave over a side of bacon and half sack of hardtack, and, he said later, "they thanked me very kindly."[37]

Moelchert was either astonishingly brave or dimwitted. The Nez Perces were asking with civil generosity for what they could take whenever they wished, which is what they did next. Once their people were in camp about two miles up Cow Creek, younger warriors came back and started firing from a hillside. The shooting, mostly potshots for amusement and to keep the soldiers behind their embankment, continued much of the night. Meanwhile, the Nez Perces helped themselves to sacks of flour, rice, and beans, sides of bacon, and quantities of coffee, sugar, hardtack, and other supplies. "Whoever wanted them, took pans, cooking pots, cups, buckets," Yellow Wolf recalled; "Women all helped themselves." Scouts tracked the bands over the next days by the packages of fine cut tobacco, beans, and "coffee berries" tossed aside during their march.[38] Moelchert's stance, potentially disastrous and in any case absurd, was later parodied by one of the civilians in a note to his boss: "Chief Joseph is here, and says he will surrender for two hundred bags of sugar. I told him to surrender without the sugar. He took the sugar and will not surrender. What shall I do?"[39] In the end, there were minor injuries on each side, and a soldier riding unwittingly into the action was killed. After the looting, some young men whom Yellow Wolf called "the bad boys," the same term he had used for those attacking the Yellowstone tourists, torched the rest of the stores in an enormous bacon-fat bonfire.

As the Nez Perces continued northward with their new, most welcome burdens, they caught up with a wagon train that had left with a load of freight just before they had arrived. The fifteen wagons had moved slowly up Cow Creek—the trail required crossing the stream thirty-two times—and its crew had been camped a few miles beyond the creek head during the shooting and looting on the river. The next day, they had gone a few miles more and stopped for nooning when the Nez Perce column appeared and went into camp a mile and a half away. The Nez Perces at first were as cordial as they had been initially at Cow Island. A leader (Poker Joe?) spoke "very kindly" to the white men and warned them of a large Sioux party in the area. Some poked around in the wagons, but the only theft was of a pair of blankets. Mostly they asked for food. After a nervous night, the wagon crew was collecting their oxen when leaders in the Nez Perce camps suddenly began shouting orders, and shortly afterward warriors attacked the train. One man was killed, but the rest escaped down the many coulees that cut through the plain.

Apparently what triggered the abrupt change was word that an armed force was approaching from the south. The freighters had said that they knew of no soldiers in the area, and when some showed up, the Nez Perces probably suspected they had been tricked. After setting the wagons on fire—there were many barrels of whiskey, so the blaze must have been another dandy—a party of warriors rode to meet the new threat.

It was a small group; thirty civilian volunteers and one soldier led by Major Guido Ilges, in charge of the Seventh Infantry's F Company at Fort Benton. Ilges had heard from a trading outpost downstream that the Nez Perces were heading his way, but F Company, which had fought at the Big Hole, was down to barely a dozen troops, so he had raised the volunteers to go with him. They arrived at Cow Island the day after the fight and bonfire and moved up Cow Creek in pursuit. Ilges wisely decided to stay in the covering terrain around the head of the creek and sent out a few men in an attempt to lure the warriors into a trap. Instead of taking the bait, the warriors climbed into the hills above the creek and sent down their usual accurate rifle fire. One man was killed, shot through the forehead as he peeked above a rock, and another was saved only because the bullet struck his belt buckle. After several hours, the Nez Perces broke it off and rode away to the north, and Ilges and his men returned to Cow Island.[40] By then, the bands had broken camp and were several miles up the trail toward Canada.

This day, September 25, would be momentous for the Nez Perces, but not because of their scrape with Ilges. At an evening council, a simmering conflict came to a head. Since the fight at the Big Hole, Poker Joe (Lean Elk) had directed the march. Now, more than six weeks later, a rising discontent pushed him out of that role. The fleeing families were profoundly weary. They had traveled nearly fifteen hundred miles. Besides the physical and emotional drain, there were the psychological costs of the deaths, the awful memories, and the constant vigilance and tension. Even with the infusion of food at Cow Island, supplies were running perilously short.

(Teamsters with the wagon train had noticed that the warriors' cartridge belts, especially those of the younger men, were nearly empty.) Many of the horses were almost spent, with sore hooves and backs, and along that morning's march alone, twenty or so had been left crippled or dead. The bands had never replaced their lodge poles, and at this latitude the nights were already increasingly cold, which sapped their energies still more.

The situation might seem to argue for pushing ahead as fast as possible. Best to get across the line and out of reach before resting and rebuilding reserves. But a psychological dynamic worked to the opposite. As far as the Nez Perces knew, their only serious pursuit was from Howard, and General Day After Tomorrow was far to their rear. The seventy or so miles to Canada could easily be covered before Howard could catch up. Brushing back Ilges likely boosted their sense of control, as did the seizure of supplies.

These late upticks of fortune nudged them toward a final, fatal mistake. Some now argued for slowing down. Give the weakened people a little more rest, the horses a little healing. Do a little hunting. Many Wounds recalled that at the council, Looking Glass, the man Poker Joe had replaced, took up the challenge; he upbraided Poker Joe for "causing old people weariness" and insisted that he now was the leader. "All right, Looking Glass, you can lead," Poker Joe reportedly answered; "I am trying to save the people, doing my best to cross into Canada before the soldiers find us. You can take command, but I think we will be caught and killed."[41] The recollection sounds a little too much like a we-told-you-so retrospective, but whatever was said, Looking Glass now replaced the man who had replaced him.

He returned to a more languid pace, as before the Big Hole, but also, as he had before, he failed to consider that someone else might have entered the game. For the next four days, the bands moved in half-day marches that started late and ended early. They threaded the wide gap between another two small ranges, the Little Rocky Mountains to the east and the Bear's Paw Mountains to the west. On September 28, they ran across some Assiniboins, whom they called the Walk-Around Sioux, and took time for some leisurely visiting. The next day, Looking Glass again called a halt at noon just to the north and east of the Bear's Paw range. Camp would be along Snake Creek, a small tributary of the Milk River, about a dozen miles due north, that flowed west to east. The Milk River, so named by Lewis and Clark because its muddy water reminded them of coffee and milk, was only about twenty-five miles from the Canadian line. Had the bands kept to their earlier vigorous pace, they would now have been over the boundary.

Looking Glass had reasons to stop at Snake Creek. Without lodges, the people suffered increasingly from the biting winds of approaching winter, and the creek had carved out a broad depression that provided some protection. Most inviting, scouts had killed a few buffaloes. The hungry families would spend the afternoon and evening preparing and eating the fresh meat. The kill was especially welcome. The plains north of the Yellowstone River had always been prime hunting grounds where dozens of square miles might be furred over with bison. There was plenty of residual evidence. The Nez Perces called the Snake Creek campground Tsanim Alikos Pah, the Place of the Manure Fires.

Over the past quarter century, however, hunters had found fewer and fewer of the animals, and during this summer's journey they had been alarmingly scarce. The absence likely contributed to the people's chill mood and raised worries about feeding themselves across the border. While the fresh kills at Snake Creek must have been a relief, it was obvious that the once vast numbers of bison were dwindling rapidly.

Where had they gone?

*Bison bison americanus* is the largest land animal in the Western Hemisphere. Some adult males weigh a ton. A much larger relative, *Bison antiquus,* with a horn spread of up to six feet from tip to tip, vanished about ten thousand years ago at the end of the last Ice Age. Its extinction and that of many other large grazers and carnivorous predators opened a large ecological niche for the modern bison, which survived and proliferated after that great die-off. In 1600, bison ranged over two-thirds of the present-day United States—south to the Mexican deserts, north well into Canada, west into the Great Basin, and east nearly to the Atlantic coast. English colonists saw their first bison along the Potomac River.

The bison's true home was the grassland at the continental center. The best estimates today place their peak numbers on the Great Plains at between twenty-five and thirty million. That peak was in the early nineteenth century. Major Stephen H. Long's expedition in 1820 saw herds massing for the summer rut along the Platte River, "blackening the whole surface of the country." When the wind shifted and carried his men's scent into the herd, the animals it touched started and surged against their neighbors. Long's men watched their own smell make its way by wind for eight or ten miles, a current of agitation through the closely packed animals.[42]

A little more than sixty years later, the American bison was nearly extinct. Its near elimination is linked in popular memory with the Great Hunt, the mass slaughter of 1872–84 accomplished by teams of white hunters who killed the animals in the millions, stripped them of their hides, and left the rest as carrion. That episode did indeed push the herds to the edge of annihilation, but by the time the hide hunters began their bloody work, the buffalo population had already shrunk at least by half. The drop in numbers began as early as the 1820s and was well advanced by the 1860s. How that happened is a reminder of the transformations creating the new America, the wider changes that had pulled the Nez Perces into their present predicament.

Indians were partly responsible. The eighteenth and nineteenth centuries saw a dramatic increase in the plains Indian population as the rise of the horse culture made the region far more desirable. Horses not only drew more Indians onto the plains but also ended the bison's advantage against hunters afoot. In effect, man and animal fused into a single hunting creature, the ultimate bison nightmare: a fast, big-brained, grass-eating predator.

The hunting toll increased geometrically. The Indians' well-known custom of consuming every part of the bison had a less-recognized implication. Because they relied on the animal for so much, they had to kill a lot of them, about six bison per person per year, to support themselves.[43] Thus, for every person added to the human population, six bison were subtracted annually. Outlanders like the Nez Perces who had traditionally visited to hunt also picked up the pace and took more animals.

Subsistence hunting alone, however, could not account for the drop in numbers. Mounted hunters were taking more—lots more—bison for an additional reason: trade. In the 1820s, the bison entered the international flow of commerce on a greater scale. They did so in a new form—as lap robes used both for home decor and to keep travelers warm as they rode in wagons, carriages, and sleighs during the winter in the Northeast and in Europe. The robe trade expanded rapidly, especially on the northern plains.[44] Hunters became discriminating bargainers, insisting on Chinese vermillion, cutlery from Sheffield, beads from Venice, and guns from Birmingham. Blackfeet and Crows, the mountain man Edward Denig wrote, "pride themselves on the cut of their coat" and other fine clothing.[45] The more they were caught up in the market, the more trade expanded. About ninety thousand robes a year passed through St. Louis during the decade after 1835. By the late 1840s, the estimate was 110,000 a year.[46]

Indians added to the toll with the way they hunted.[47] Because they much preferred the more pliable hides of females taken in autumn, after the fur had thickened for winter, they killed many pregnant cows, dealing a double hit to the herds. They tossed some hides aside as too shabby or botched in processing, so by some accounts there were as many as three bison killed for every robe shipped to market.[48] By 1872, the strain was really starting to show. Lieutenant Gustavus Doane surveyed Montana's Judith Basin and concluded that "the end of the buffalo is at hand." Overzealous Crows killed cows almost exclusively, fatally wounded two for each one killed on the spot, and turned only one hide out of three killed into a robe. He predicted that bison could supply the Indians for no more than five more years.[49]

Five years later the Nez Perces, heading north through Judith Basin, did indeed find the pickings slim. Here and across the Great Plains, the bison's numbers were dwindling, in part because Indians had eagerly connected themselves to a larger world, first through horses, and then by increasingly vigorous hunting for an international market.[50]

Whites in the great expansion were also part of the problem, and long before the Great Hunt. Although overland travelers killed very few bison, contrary to popular belief, they cut trees along rivers for fuel, destroying the living quarters that bison, Indians, and their horses all needed as sanctuaries from winter storms and cold. The overlanders' millions of oxen and cattle might also have passed along bovine diseases. White settlement on the plains—the number of farms in Kansas increased between 1860 and 1880 from 10,000 to 239,000 and in Nebraska from 3,000 to 63,000—was a massive assault on the bison's environment. Farmers cut more trees from the bottomlands and replaced the bison's food with their own, plowing under native grasses to plant crops.

The bison was in crisis well before white professional hide hunters did their worst, which makes the Great Hunt, from one angle, just one more case of people chasing possibilities sprung loose by changes of the day. From another angle, however, what happened was different indeed. In its scale and in its raw expression of the new order, the slaughter was unique.

Put simply, factories ate the buffaloes. In the 1870s, there was a hungry global demand for leather, not only for boots, belts, furniture, and other consumer goods but also for gaskets and belts needed in factory machines before the era of rubber and other synthetics. The demand pulled heavily on cattle populations in the United States, Argentina, and elsewhere. An alternative would be welcome, and in 1871 a few enterprising plains businessmen asked an obvious question: How about bison? They sent several hundred freshly skinned hides to tanneries in New York City, England, and Germany, where experiments soon showed that bison leather was as serviceable as that of cattle.

Virtually overnight, the bison became an accessible and highly desirable commodity on a world market. Word went out that "green" or "wet" hides would bring an excellent price, typically about $3.50 each. Without the laborious work of turning a hide into a robe, the processing was far faster, and because the bison's hair was no longer pertinent, hunters could work in the summer when the animals massed in huge, vulnerable numbers. An infrastructure of railroad and telegraph was in place for gathering, marketing and delivering the hides. A team of "buffalo runners," shooters and skinners operating on minimal expenses, would go after "shaggies" that gathered in groups ranging from fifty or so to many thousands. Hunters shot from downwind with forty- and fifty-caliber Remington and Sharps rifles that were accurate up to six hundred yards. It was death methodical, shot after shot, hour on hour, with rifles lubricated and cooled with buckets of water. (In a linkage between the modern market's near extinction of two of the world's most prolific larger creatures, a favorite lubricant was whale oil.) Kills of twenty-five or thirty a day were common, forty or fifty not unusual. Skinners then stripped and scraped the hides, which stiffened into "flint" hides that were hauled in wagons to the nearest railway connection. They were shipped to eastern

**Figure 15.3** The "Great Hunt" devoured the plains bison with a factorylike efficiency

tanneries where they were processed, sliced, and shaped into their new uses.

The Great Hunt was wildly wasteful. Hides of poor quality were left on the animal or in camp, and nearly all the meat was left for coyotes and vultures.[51] The obliterative killing moved from western Kansas and eastern Colorado in 1872 to western and central Texas, where it brought on the Red River War that broke the power of the Comanches and Kiowas. Around 1880, the slaughter shifted to the final arena, the northern plains, when the defeat of the Sioux cleared the way for unrestrained hunting. Here the mass killing finally stopped. There were so few targets left that the effort wasn't worth it. Between 1882 and 1884, the number of hides shipped off the northern plains dropped from around two hundred thousand to three hundred.

The slaughter left the plains flecked with tens of thousands of tons of bison bones that were now put to their own uses, ground into fertilizer and cut and stamped into corset staves, dice, and sundry consumables. "Bone pilgrims," many of them cash-starved homesteaders, scoured the country, hauled their loads to rail towns, and stacked them for shipping where hides had recently waited. By 1890, they had picked the country virtually bare.

Seen with a cold eye, the Great Hunt was impressive. It came within a hair of an erasure unique in recent natural history. Had the bison been fully wiped out, and had scientific bone hunters a few thousand years from now set out to gather physical remains to reconstruct life in the mid-continent, they could present a picture with no suggestion of the animals, some the size of two-year-old elephants, that had gathered in herds covering whole counties and had darkened the land as a single tissue that rippled as it registered a predator's scent on the wind.

With an eye to human consequence, however, the killing could not have been worse for the region's Indians. The Great Hunt denied them the wherewithal for trade and took away much of what they used to feed, clothe, and house themselves, as well as to worship, play, comb their hair, and swat flies. Add the corralling of the horse culture, and the plains Indians were left with no choice but submission, at least in the forms of their material life.

Some would suggest that the army orchestrated the Great Hunt to knock the props out from under the Indians' autonomy. The military certainly encouraged and supported the hunt, but it did not plan it and carry it out. If it had, it would have been a case of efficiency unique in the history of government performance. The real force behind the killing was summed up by the hunter Frank Mayer. With a cartridge costing twenty-five cents, he could obtain a hide he could sell for $5. Killing a hundred bison a day netted him $6,000 per month, triple the salary of the president; "Was I not lucky that I discovered this quick and easy way to fortune? I thought I was."[52]

Indians were not up against just the army. They faced a competitive, acquisitive culture with many thousands like Frank Meyer who looked on every western resource as possible income once it was plugged into the economic network. In 1872, the bison was suddenly much more plug-gable. Overnight, there was a limitless demand for hides, no need for Indians in the system, and no reason to stop killing until the bison were gone. The businessmen behind that system did not act out of animus. They wanted profits. When they could get them with the Indians prof-iting, too, that's what they did. When the chance came to make more money faster by eliminating Indians from the equation, they did that. When it was all over, they turned to other business.

The Nez Perces passed through the northern plains on the eve of that final convulsion. Had they come only seven years later, they would have found no bison at all. They shared some responsibility for that calamity. Simply by taking part in the region's trade, they unknowingly embedded their lives and fates in dynamic, enormously complex arrangements that reached over much of the planet. The years between the 1840s and 1877 saw the West become far more firmly enmeshed. The near obliteration of the bison was only one consequence.

That very connectedness saved the bison. By the 1880s, the buffalo was emerging as a totemic figure in a new American identity. Advertisers soon would trot it out to sell everything from whisky to prunes. It soon would appear on state flags and national nickels. In 1886, the government's lead-ing scientific agency, the Smithsonian Institution, sent William Hornaday to locate any surviving bison so posterity could see the real thing. Hornaday found more than fifty on a Montana ranch—and killed them. Assuming their extinction, he wanted to preserve the best remaining specimens. By then, however, efforts had begun to reseed the West with the shaggies. Some were bought from private herds and placed in the new shrine of imagined timelessness, Yellowstone National Park. In 1905, the American Bison Society was formed, with Hornaday as president and Theodore Roosevelt as honorary president, and Congress soon provided the funds to buy and fence preserves in Montana and Oklahoma. With the new America now tied together into one entity, its central govern-ment could find the best candidates for seed herds, however improbable the location, and shuttle them wherever needed. Oklahoma's starters, six bulls and nine cows, arrived in 1907 via rail from the Bronx Zoo.

# PART III

# CHAPTER 16

# Under the Bear's Paw

The Nez Perces were in no hurry to leave Snake Creek on the morning of September 30. During the night, Wot-to-len (Hair Combed Over Eyes) dreamed of being in this very camp, but now gloomed with battle smoke hanging dark and low and with the creek running red with the blood of his people and of soldiers. He awoke and walked among the sleeping families, then returned to dream again of smoke and blood, this time also with fallen leaves and withered flowers followed by springtime grass, sunshine, and peace. In the morning, he went about the camp calling out his dream to the people. Looking Glass scoffed, as he had with Shore Crossing's and Lone Bird's premonitions before the attack at the Big Hole. Build fires and give the children plenty of time for breakfast, he told the women.[1] It was after eight o'clock before some families began to bring pack horses in from their pasture on a grassy plateau a few hundred yards to the west. Guards had been posted as usual to the south, but with any pursuers presumably days behind them, they felt no urgency. Some played cards.[2]

Only a few miles away, nearly four hundred mounted troops advanced toward the camp at a trot. Just two weeks earlier, few would have taken the bet that the army would catch the Nez Perces this side of Canada, but twelve days of aggressive marching, along with some strokes of luck, had brought Nelson Miles to an unlikely rendezvous with the quarry that had eluded Howard for three and a half months.

Miles had gotten the order to chase the Nez Perces on September 17. Within an hour, he had his men preparing to leave the Tongue River cantonment. That night, officers said their goodbyes to their families, with one wife singing "Sweet Bye and Bye" and "On the Other Side of Jordan," and the next day Miles set off with two companies of the Seventh Cavalry.

**Figure 16.1** Site of the final battle, looking south from Snake Creek to the Bear's Paw mountains

He soon added another company of the Seventh, three from the Second Cavalry, five companies—four mounted and one foot—from the Fifth Infantry, and a wagon train and nearly thirty white, Sioux, and Cheyenne scouts.[3] The command totaled about 530 men. Miles moved by gradually lengthening marches to the Missouri River where the Musselshell entered it from the southwest. Here he enjoyed two bits of good fortune. He was able to catch the recently departed steamboat *Fontenelle* for use in ferrying his men and wagons. And a small boat from upstream brought the news of the Nez Perces' clash at Cow Island two days earlier. Miles, assuming that the bands were still south of the Missouri, was about to cross the Mussellshell and proceed up the Missouri's south bank, which would have left him hopelessly behind. Now he knew both that the Nez Perces were already across the Missouri and, given their route up Cow Creek, that they were likely heading toward the Bear's Paw Mountains.[4]

Quickly Miles crossed the river, cut loose from the wagon train, and with rations for eight days, struck northwestward on another series of rapid marches. He guessed correctly that the Nez Perces had threaded the gap between the Bear's Paw Mountains (actually a series of eroded ridges)

and another isolated group to the east, the Little Rocky Mountains. To keep the element of surprise, Miles stayed east of the Little Rockies, using them as a blind, while fanning his scouts ahead of him to look for the prominent trail left by hundreds of people and more than a thousand horses. His luck at the Missouri crossing had improved his odds of making contact, but he still had to feel his way across a wide country and make up time while doing it. The switch in Nez Perce leadership and Looking Glass's take-it-easy approach was yet another break for Miles.

On September 29, his scouts found the bands' trail and their recent camp. Now Miles stood on a delicate balance. There was no way to know how far ahead his quarry was or how fast they were moving. His men had ridden about two hundred miles in ten days, sometimes staying in the saddle until two and three o'clock in the morning, yet they would have to move quickly and fight at their best if the Nez Perces were found. The Canadian border was barely a day away. Catch them now, Miles knew, or they were gone. At dark on September 29, he put his men into camp with orders to build no fires.[5]

He roused them at two o'clock the next morning, and they were feeling their way along the bands' trail when, soon after daybreak, a Cheyenne scout came racing back: the Nez Perce camp was a few miles due north. Miles immediately ordered his troops to mount and set off on a trot. The last couple of days had been rainy, but this one was clear, cool, and still. "My God!" Captain Owen Hale joked; "Have I got to be killed on this beautiful morning?"[6] Later Miles described the men around him as "light-hearted" and "resolute," smiling and cracking wise. An officer hummed a popular hymn, "What Shall the Harvest Be?" in cadence with his horse's gait.[7] When the Nez Perces proved to be farther away than thought, Miles sent the command into a gallop, and when he topped a rise and saw the smoke from fires along Snake Creek about a mile away, he called a brief halt to reform his ranks. The three companies of the Seventh Cavalry were on the right, the three of the Second Cavalry on the left, and the four of the mounted Fifth Infantry in the center but somewhat behind. The cavalrymen put themselves into columns of fours. Then Miles ordered the charge and a full assault—as a correspondent wrote, "neck or nothing."[8]

Meanwhile, two Nez Perces returning from a visit to nearby Assiniboians had seen stampeding bison and reasoned, perhaps correctly, that soldiers had spooked them. Looking Glass again assured the camp that they were safe: "Do not hurry! Go Slow! Plenty, plenty time." A precious hour passed. Then a warrior appeared on a nearby bluff, circling his horse and waving a blanket. It was a traditional long-distance warning: "Enemies right on us! Soon the attack!"[9]

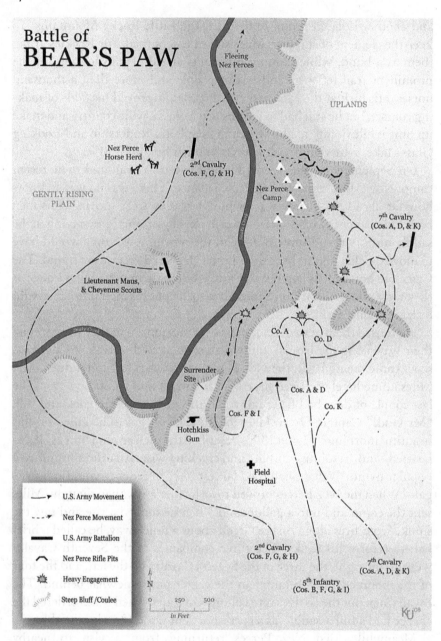

Battle of
# BEAR'S PAW

Immediately the camp was in turmoil, and moments later came a low, gathering rumble and shuddering of the earth. "Horses! Horses!" Joseph called out, "his voice...above all the noise....Save the horses!"[10] With the same impulse that had sent him and No Heart (Teminisiki) to protect the herd at the Big Hole, Joseph and several others crossed Snake Creek and sprinted toward the animals that had been grazing to the west. Other men grabbed their guns and, quickly surveying the situation, ran to find the best spots to meet the assault. Women and children hurried toward whatever protection they could find.

Now terrain worked to the bands' advantage—and ended Miles's run of good luck. The camp was in a kidney-shaped depression about six acres in area, well below the surrounding plain. Looking Glass probably had chosen it for its protection against the cold wind, but it turned out also to be as good a defensive position as the area could offer. It was open only to the north and west, opposite to Mile's approach. To the south, the direction of attack, a bluff thirty to fifty feet in height rose up sharply. It would stop any charge. To the east the ground rose also, but not so steeply, and was cut more or less perpendicularly by a series of coulees, varying in depth and thick with sagebrush; these offered ideal cover for defensive fire.[11] None of that, however, was visible to the hundreds of horsemen thundering down on the camp. They approached across a tableland above, so their view was over the Nez Perces and across the creek to the horse herd, which they saw in agitation as men and women tried desperately to save the animals, their true lifeline for escape, by stampeding them away from the soldiers.

Miles's first plan relied mostly on the Second Cavalry, the most seasoned of his command. One company was to loop around to the west to the far side of the camp. They were to seize the horses and meet any Nez Perces who tried to flee in that direction. The other two companies of the Second were to slam directly into the camp from the south. The three companies of the Seventh Cavalry were to support them on the right, staying somewhat to the rear. The four companies of mounted infantry would follow in further support.

That plan went quickly awry. Riding ahead of the Second Cavalry were Cheyenne scouts. They were supposed to lead the two cavalry companies spearheading the attack directly into the camp, but the scouts' main concern was acquiring horses, and when they saw the herd on the far side being spooked away, they veered off and dashed for them, skirting around the camp to the west. The Second Cavalry, still thinking they were making a frontal assault, followed them. Now they were out of the initial fight.

Miles adjusted by ordering the Seventh Cavalry to lead the attack. Those three companies, however, were dominated by green troops. They called themselves Custer's Avengers, an inadvertent reminder that fifteen months earlier the same units had been literally shot full of holes at the Little Big Horn and afterward filled with men innocent of battle experience. The only reason they were here, in fact, was because they had been too unseasoned to be sent earlier to fight with Sturgis and so were at the Tongue River cantonment, available, when Miles got his orders.[12] Now it was their job to deliver the first crucial punch. Only at about fifty yards did they get a sense of what they faced. Company K under Captain Hale, farthest to the right, saw the ground fall steeply away to the left, which forced him rightward along a ridge, ahead of the others. Suddenly Nez Perces hidden in coulees in front and to the side of their approach delivered a withering fusillade. Slightly behind Hale and to his left, the Seventh's other two companies came directly onto the bluff. Right before them was a drop of forty or so feet. As they pulled hard on their reins to keep from toppling over, fighting to control their mounts, more Nez Perces rose up from just under the lip of the cut bank and fired at close range. A private later stated the obvious: "Those Indians stopped our charge cold."[13]

These two companies pulled back, dismounted, reformed. As they did so, a warrior shot and killed the horse of Captain Edward Godfrey of Company D. The fall left him stunned, with his firing arm temporarily paralyzed, but he was saved when his trumpeter and sergeant came up and drew the warrior's fire. ("Well, Captain I got it," the trumpeter told Godfrey right afterward. "Did you kill him?" the captain asked. "I don't know," the trumpeter answered, "but he shot me here," pointing to his side.) Meanwhile, Hale's Company K was being "severely handled." Green as they were, those soldiers did not bolt in the face of the vigorous fire from the coulees but dismounted and struggled forward, and for a time the fighting was hand to hand. The ground writhed with wounded. A private had his arm crushed by one bullet, his side creased by another, his scalp furrowed by a third. After crawling away, he found nine more bullet holes in his coat.[14] The pressure eased when Miles sent Companies A and D, now afoot, to their aid at double-time.[15] That, however, exposed them to an awful crossfire. Godfrey, remounted to lead the movement, was hit in the side, and Captain Myles Moylan, leading Company D, was struck in the upper thigh soon after reaching Hale, who by now had pulled his men back a couple of hundred yards to regroup. Soon afterward, Hale, who had wondered whether he would be killed on such a beautiful morning, died from a bullet just under his Adam's apple. Hale's lieutenant, Jonathan Biddle, had been left wounded on the contested ground. His was one of several bodies later found riddled with shots from both sides.[16]

The beleaguered Seventh now got help from the four companies of Fifth Infantry, who took the rim of the bluff and from there fired on the warriors to their right who were inflicting such damage from the ravines. Caught in a crossfire from the Fifth and the Seventh, the warriors pulled back a bit, which gave Miles a chance to assess the situation. With his first assault stalled, he decided on a second charge. He sent Lieutenant Henry Romeyn to take command of the Seventh Cavalry and shore it up with his Company G of the Fifth Infantry.[17] He was told to try again from the general direction of the Seventh's first attack, from the southeast. Another twenty-five men were to make a run at the camp through a ravine from the southwest.

This second assault failed more quickly than the first. As Romeyn stood and waved his hat to start the charge, one bullet hit his belt, and others blew away his field glasses, his hunting knife, and part of his ear. Another struck his chest and passed through a lung. As men all around him were being wounded or killed, he turned and began walking to the rear for medical help. The charge stopped before it really began. Meanwhile, the other twenty-five troopers, cheering and yelling, managed to reach the edge of the camp, but, one of them recalled dryly, "for lack of support on the right and left…after getting in we could not stay." With a third of the unit wounded, two fatally, they pulled back and later crawled to safety.[18]

Miles had attacked with almost total surprise and with a mounted command of superior numbers. Yet he not only had failed to take the Nez Perce camp; he had been badly mauled. Only one Seventh Cavalry officer remained alive and unhurt. All three first sergeants were dead, and the other sergeants dead or wounded. Two officers and two sergeants of the Fifth Infantry had been severely wounded. Clearly, the Nez Perces again had singled out those in command, although the sheer intensity and accuracy of rifle fire were also part of it. "The bullets hum all the notes of the gamut, fit music for the dance of death," the resident surgeon wrote later: "Zip, zip, zip, thud thud; the dirt is thrown up here and there, while others go singing overhead. Riderless horses are galloping over the hills, others are stretched lifeless on the field. Men are being struck on every side."[19] Miles's men had fought bravely and well, but in soldierly performance, the Nez Perces were clearly better. With only moments to gauge the situation, they had made the best use of the field, blocked and turned a powerful cavalry charge, and inflicted far more damage than they got.

And yet at the end of the day, in fact after the first hour, the Nez Perces had lost the battle and lost the war. The key engagement was not along the bloody front to the south and east of the camp but to its rear, on the west and north, among the horses. Joseph, Yellow Wolf, and several others had raced for the herd at the first alarm. In camp, a man offered

Bird Alighting (Peopeo Tholekt) one of the few horses there to go gather others: "This is perhaps to be the last day! *You* will die and *I* will die!" Black Eagle had been wearing warm army boots ("soldier shoes"), but now he threw off the clodhoppers, tore up a blanket as a makeshift rope, and made for the herd. From the higher ground, Yellow Wolf looked back: "Hundreds of soldiers charging in two wide, circling wings. They were surrounding our camp."[20] What followed seemed a formless melee. Women already among the horses, meaning to bring them in for packing, tried to mount and save as many as they could, but the rattle of gunfire and sudden commotion ("Then the crack of guns filled the air," Shot-in-Head remembered; "Everybody was outside, running here, there, every-where") sent most animals scattering. Cheyenne scouts, seduced away from the frontal assault on the camp by the sight of horses running away, arrived well ahead of the cavalry. Heyooom Iklakit (Grizzly Bear Lying Down) confronted one at a distance and upbraided him in sign language: "You must be crazy! You are fighting your friends. We are Indians. We are humans. Do not help the whites!" The scout agreed to harm no Nez Perces, but Yellow Wolf soon saw him shoot and kill a woman.[21]

It seemed a mindless swirl, but soon it took a shape. With the herd scattering and the cavalry approaching, the impulse emerged to save some horses and to gather and send women and children off toward Canada and safety. Black Eagle, Bird Alighting, and others gave the horses they had caught to women "skipping for their lives." Joseph's twelve-year-old daughter, Kapkap Ponmi (Noise of Running Feet), had been with the horses at the attack. He gave her a rope and told her to find a mount and save herself. The boy About Asleep (Ealahweemah) was told by his father to do the same. He had ridden half a mile when he realized his younger brother, whom he had saved at the Big Hole, was left behind. He rode back, found the boy, pulled him up behind him on the horse, and galloped off. Two soldiers chased them, shooting a braid off his brother's head, but the pair escaped.[22]

The boys were saved partly through a typically spontaneous maneuver. When the warriors in the pasture realized the scope of the attack—looking back, one saw the bluff on the camp's south edge "black with soldiers"—and as Cheyenne scouts and cavalrymen closed in on them, they wheeled to put themselves between the troops and their fleeing families. "The Nez Perces were very brave and crowded on the soldiers," a Cheyenne scout recalled.[23] This counterattack bought time for women and children to get well away and, for a time, to be safe, but in the process the Nez Perces had to abandon and lose more horses. The cavalry captured probably about five hundred, although Miles would claim considerably more. Many animals ran off. The escaping Nez Perces managed to catch maybe two or three hundred and began moving with them north toward Canada.

Now the fight on the pastureland was winding down, and the warriors in it faced a hard choice. Some joined those escaping. Others returned to help defend the camp—a camp now without horses and pinned under the rifles of Miles's men.

The Nez Perces had held their own. They had fought as bravely and effectively as at White Bird Canyon. (The overall casualty rate for the Seventh Cavalry was well above that of Perry's command.) Their impromptu positioning equaled the maneuvering at the Clearwater, and their defense was as furious as at the Big Hole. But it was not enough. In the earlier battles they had driven their attackers off, or penned them up, or left them behind, which meant that every battle had ended with their keeping the two requisites for staying free—horses and an avenue of escape. As long as they had mobility and options, in a West that still had some unfettered room, they could keep pursuers guessing and off balance. That, and of course courage, stamina, strokes of tactical brilliance, luck, and their opponents' miscues, so far had offset the numbers, the technology, and the coordinated power of the reconstructed nation.

Horses and space had allowed the Nez Perces to act out their claim as an independent people. Both were lost at the end of the first day under the Bear's Paw. The only choices left were when and how to accept the larger loss—that of a way of life.

The Nez Perces lost as well several of their most gifted warriors. Among the first to die was Joseph's brother Ollokut, shot in the head as he crouched behind a rock while helping turn back the Seventh Cavalry's charge. Toohoolhoolzote, the "cross-grained growler" whose confrontation with Howard many Nez Perces considered the spark of war, took a position with others on a rocky ridge on the north edge of camp. There he was shot and killed. Lone Bird (Peopeo Ipsewahk), who on the eve of the Big Hole had warned his people with a "shaking heart" of impending disaster, was one of three men who were inadvertently killed when they ventured out on a tangent and were mistaken for enemy scouts by the Palouse leader Husishuis Kute (Bald Head). Poker Joe died from friendly fire as well. Four of five band leaders survived—White Bird, Huishuis Kute, Looking Glass, and Joseph, who after sending his daughter toward Canada had galloped through heavy fire to the camp, where his wife had handed him his rifle: "Here's your gun. Fight!"[24] The toll of their losses—the best estimate is twenty-two dead, about as many as on the other side—was awful. At the beginning of the attack, they had had roughly one fighting man for every five against them. Now the imbalance was much greater.

Late in the day, the wind shifted strongly from the north, and soon it was snowing; five inches had fallen by morning. Yellow Wolf was still on the highland where he had fought for the horses, and there he waited, shivering, until he could slip into the camp in the dark. He found a despairing scene: "You have seen hail, sometimes, leveling the grass. Indians were so leveled by the bullet hail.... Children crying with cold. No fire. There could be no light. Everywhere was crying, the death wail."[25] Survivors dug shelters in the cutbank for women, children, and the wounded and shallower scoops as rifle pits high enough on ridges and bluffs for effective fire at the troops. All night, women and men worked steadily with butcher knives, hatchets, camas hooks, and trowel bayonets taken from troops at the Big Hole. They flung the dirt away with pans and skillets. Noncombatants huddled in the pits under bison robes and sheets of canvas that snubbed the worst of the wind. "Misery every where!" a woman remembered: "Cold and dampness all around!"[26]

The next day the firing resumed, with some bravado to shore up morale. A young warrior emerged unharmed from a storm of rifle fire after he stood exposed, stripped to a breech-cloth, and blowing lengthily on a bone whistle.[27] The wind and snow kept at it and left both sides at a miserable par. A makeshift hospital had been set up well behind the tall bluff, and the suffering there mirrored that in the pits along Snake Creek. A private whose arm was crushed from elbow to wrist by a bullet—he would lose it to amputation five days later—crawled there and found several others, "all calling for the Doctor, and begging for water, some cursing, some praying, some crying, and some laughing."[28] As the hours passed and the shock wore off, the wounds stiffened, and the injured suffered terribly from the cold. Because Miles had cut loose from his wagon train, his men were without tents, and now they shivered in the early fall storm.

One possibility of escape remained, much on the minds of both the Nez Perces and the soldiers. The Sioux under Sitting Bull were only about eighty miles north, on Frenchman Creek. As matters now stood the bands, stuck in their camp, could only grow colder and hungrier while Miles waited them out.[29] If the Sioux learned of the situation from the fleeing Nez Perces, however, they might be there in two or three days. Miles's command was also battered and tired and low on ammunition, and if a fresh and well-armed body of warriors came down on them, pressing them against the determined Nez Perce sharpshooters, the result

Figure **16.2** Miles's initial attack at Snake Creek

might be ugly. Custer's Avengers might need some avengers of their own. If the current siege remained a siege, that is, time was on Miles's side. If it turned into something else, time could kill him.[30] All were on edge. At one point, the soldiers heard the rumble of what they thought were attacking Sioux. It turned out to be a running bison herd.[31] The Nez Perces also looked north, in desperate hope of help from King George's Land.[32] There was one significant consequence. While in one of the rifle pits, Looking Glass heard that an Indian was riding toward the scene. He jumped up for a look and was killed instantly, shot through the forehead. A vital player in the story, some would say much to the harm of the Nez Perces, was gone.[33]

Even as each side looked toward the horizon, events moved jerk-ily toward resolution. On the second day a truce was arranged, partly through Cheyenne scouts hoping to spare the children and elderly from more suffering. They simply rode into the camp, which they found "a sad looking place.... The bodies of the Nez Perce were everywhere."[34] Once the firing stopped, soldiers retrieved their dead and brought in a few wounded, some of whom had survived with water brought by Nez Perces.[35]

Conversations began between Miles and Tom Hill, half Nez Perce and half Delaware, who had joined the bands in the Bitterroot valley.

Comfortable in English, Hill later told how in answer to Miles's questions he reported the deaths of several prominent men at the Big Hole and at the Bear's Paw—interesting, if accurate, since it showed Miles's surprising knowledge of Nez Perce leadership. Miles, he said, then announced: "'The War is over. Call Joseph to come.'"[36] Joseph came forward under a white flag with a few others and even handed over a few firearms. When Miles pressed for unconditional surrender, however, Joseph demurred, and the meeting ended. Then, as the Nez Perces started back to the camp, Miles called Joseph back and ordered him held under guard. Invited under a flag of truce, he was made a captive.[37]

This gross breach of rules is puzzling. The best guess is that Miles, frustrated that Joseph would not surrender and fearful that the Sioux might come galloping at any minute, hoped to use him as a hostage to bring a quick end to the siege. If so, he miscalculated badly. Joseph had no authority to surrender the camp. He met with Miles because Miles had called for him and because, now that the fighting was about over, he was once again the obvious negotiator. Beyond that, his only role was to report what Miles offered.[38] By grabbing Joseph under a white flag, Miles was not forcing the Nez Perces' hand, only giving them one more reason to distrust their enemy. It would be four days before they would talk to Miles again.

Whatever leverage Miles thought he had he lost because one of his officers, Lieutenant Lovell Jerome, had entered the camp during the truce and after strolling around a bit was seized when the Nez Perces learned of Joseph's situation. Although some wanted to harm or kill Jerome, he was treated well, fed, given blankets, and sheltered in a pit.[39] How Joseph was treated became a matter of later argument. Joseph himself later said only "I remained with [Miles] all night," but some Nez Perces claimed he was handcuffed, bound, and even rolled in a blanket and laid down with the mules. Those on the army side either say nothing of such treatment or dismiss the charge as—in the words of an officer who was not there at the time—"absolute rot." The same sources, it's worth noting, almost completely gloss over Joseph's improper arrest.[40] The next day, October 2, Miles exchanged Joseph for Jerome. The standoff continued.[41]

During the lull, Miles brought up two Hotchkiss guns that opened up on the camp after the hostage swap, but they were no more help than others had been throughout the campaign, this time because they could not train on targets so close and below their usual angle of fire. Finally, their handlers sank the guns' trails so they could fire sharply upward, mortar-like, into the camp. The only casualties were an elderly woman and her granddaughter who were suffocated when a shell collapsed a pit and buried them alive. They were the battle's last fatalities.[42] Other than that, each side sniped at the other, to little effect. As with earlier set-tos, soldiers later were full of tales of Nez Perce sharpshooting—nailing small stones set in view, taking off a lock of hair from someone hazarding a peek.[43]

Meanwhile, some of the Nez Perces who had broken free—estimates vary from as few as 40 to as many as 171—made it to the Sioux camp on Frenchman's Creek, probably on October 3. According to one account, the war might have ended very differently if not for a moment's garbled communication. When the first refugees were asked, by sign language, the location of the battle and siege, they gave the sign for "stream," which was taken to mean not Snake Creek and the Milk River but the Missouri River, much too far to the south to reach in time to help. Another day or two passed before others, like Peopeo Tholekt, arrived and corrected the error. Some say a large party then set out, but on the way they met the last escapees and heard of the surrender. Had the first answer been clearer, the Sioux at the least might have shaken things up at Snake Creek. It was easily within striking distance, they said, "just as from head to pillow!"[44]

Help did come to Miles, with more on the way. Late on October 1, his support wagons caught up with him. Now his men had tents, more blankets, and ample food and ammunition. Three days later, Howard arrived. At Carroll on the Missouri River, he had cut loose from Sturgis and taken a small infantry force upriver via steamboat to Cow Island, and then had set off with twenty or so men to find Miles. A dozen miles from Snake Creek, he met two couriers who told him what had happened. He hurried ahead. Approaching Snake Creek in the dark, he heard shots and saw gun flashes and called out who he was, presuming the firing was at him, but soon Miles himself rode up with the word: "We have the Indians corraled [*sic*] down yonder in the direction of the firing."[45]

With this "grateful news," Howard and Miles went into a long meeting during which Howard, surely to Miles's relief, said he would leave Miles in command to "finish the work he had so well begun."[46] With Sitting Bull still at the edge of their thoughts, Howard sent immediately for Sturgis, who in fact had already gotten word and was leading both cavalry and infantry toward the action. He was at the Little Rocky Mountains, a couple of days away.[47]

Now the end game was close. With Howard were two treaty Nez Perce scouts, Jokais (Worthless or Lazy), known to whites as Captain John, and Meopkowit (Baby or Know Nothing), called Captain George or Old George, who had stayed with Howard because each had a daughter among the nontreaties.[48] On the morning of October 5, they hailed the camp ("All my brothers, I am glad to see you alive this sun!") and approached under a white flag. They met with leaders, assured them that Howard and Miles wished to end the war, and reported that if they surrendered, Miles intended to send them back to Idaho in the spring. There followed several hours of discussion among the Nez Perce leaders, punctuated by negotiation with Miles and Howard.

As so often in the past, neither side understood just who they were talking to. Miles and Howard thought Joseph was in charge, but he wasn't. The Nez Perces in turn thought either Miles or Howard or both together could decide their fate, but they couldn't. As part of a command structure, they would follow orders from others. They could recommend, but only recommend, what should happen to the Indians.

Nez Perce leaders worried about their immediate fates, particularly whether they might be hanged like the resisters of 1858, and about how their injured would fare ("we had never heard of a wounded Indian recovering in the hands of white men," Joseph said later). They wondered whether they would be expected to see to their own needs as captives, and if so, whether they would have some horses and weapons. Pride pulled against giving up. Having fought so long and so well, with so many dead, a humiliating end would be hard to swallow. On the other hand, the children and elderly in camp were suffering terribly, and leaders wanted badly to learn what had happened to those, among them Joseph's older daughter and one of his wives, who had last been seen running away during the early fighting, many barefoot and scarcely clothed.[49] There were assurances. One Cheyenne and one Nez Perce account mention specific promises that none would be hanged.[50]

The most pressing questions were about their fate in the longer run. Would they be allowed to return at least to a generalized homeland, that part of Idaho and Oregon where they had always lived? Or would they be exiled? None had ever seen Indian Territory, but they certainly had heard of it. Howard himself had raised it as a weapon. "You will have to be taken to the Indian Territory," he had told Toohoolhoolzote as he hustled him to the guardhouse; "I will send you there if it takes years and years."[51] Would surrendering send them to that awful place, far from where Coyote had sprung them to life?

Thinking Miles and Howard held their fate, the Nez Perces spent great effort grilling Captain John and Old George to determine which officer was more in command. A crude consensus formed that Miles was "headman," and if he indeed were in charge, that was to the good. They mistrusted him slightly less and hated Howard a lot more. Miles had said the bands would be returned to Idaho, and he seemed marginally more sympathetic, which nudged them toward settling.[52]

Miles and Howard waited and jittered; the Nez Perces hashed through what they had heard; Captain John and Old George shuttled back and forth. Hours passed, and pressures mounted, including the military's tightening pinch. On the night of the fourth, some men had crawled under a protective fire to within fifty yards of the camp and dug themselves in. At dawn, a soldier wrote, "our boys began to poor [*sic*] lead into their pits and by ten in the morning they squealed."[53] Especially as hope faded for help from Canada, giving in seemed increasingly inevitable.

In the end, according to Yellow Wolf, honor tipped the decision. Some Nez Perces had chafed at their impression that when Joseph had met with Miles, Joseph had asked to end the fight. On one of Captain John's and Old George's visits, they brought this message:

> "Those generals said to tell you: 'We will have no more fighting. Your chiefs and some of your warriors are not seeing the truth. We sent our officer [Jerome] to appear before your Indians—sent all our messengers to say to them, "We will have no more war!'
> Then our man, Chief Joseph spoke, "You see, it is true. I did not say 'Let's quit!'
> "General Miles said, 'Let's quit.'
> "And now General Howard says, 'Let's quit!' "
> When the warriors heard those words from Chief Joseph, they answered, "Yes, we believe you now."
> So when General Miles's messengers reported back to him, the answer was, "Yes."[54]

That yes was not a collective yes, just one man's assent, albeit it a man many would choose to follow. A sizeable minority in the camp, most of them from the bands of White Bird and the late Looking Glass and Toohoolhoolzote, chose to make a try for Canada. White Bird deeply distrusted white leaders, apparently never considered surrendering, and as one who had always pushed for Canada instead of Crow country, would not miss his chance now. After dark, he and others so inclined slipped through the cordon of soldiers, who apparently played it loose, caught up in the mood of release and assuming it was finished.[55] These escapees joined others who had broken away during the first fighting but had stayed, watching from the fringes, to see how things turned out. The refugees felt their way in strings and clusters across the blustery flatlands toward the international boundary. While Miles and Howard left the impression that only a handful had slipped through their hands, the Nez Perce Black Eagle compiled a list of 233 or 234 who broke free between the attack on September 30 and October 6.[56] If he was close to accurate, more than a third of those who were at Snake Creek when Miles ordered the first charge eventually got away.

Soon after Joseph's message, a final parlay was held at a grassy spot between the two lines. Apparently, it deepened Joseph's impression that Miles was in charge and would send them home to Idaho.[57] Yellow Wolf has Miles brimming with goodwill: "No more battles and blood! From this sun, we will have good time on both sides...plenty time for sleep, for good rest." Howard, he said, was the same: "It is plenty of food we have left from this war....All is yours."[58] The understanding sealed, the two groups returned to their camps, and a couple of hours later, between two and three o'clock in the afternoon on October 5, came the formal surrender. Joseph rode slowly up a steep rise at the west end of the bluff. Walking beside him were five other men, their hands on his horse's flanks or on his leg. The six spoke softly among themselves. Joseph's chin was on his chest and his hands crossed across the saddle's pommel. His Winchester carbine lay across his lap. A gray shawl was around his shoulders, and his hair was in two braids and tied up with otter skin. It was obvious that, if not the bands' war leader, he had put his life repeatedly on the line. He had grazing wounds on his forehead, his wrist, and the small of his back, and the sleeves and body of his shirt were peppered with bullet holes. Miles later "begged the shirt as a curiosity."[59]

Standing and waiting for Joseph were Howard, Miles, Lieutenant Wood, and two other officers. Ad Chapman, the civilian who had been present since the fighting at White Bird, was there as interpreter. As Joseph dismounted and approached, his companions stepped back. Facing Howard, Joseph offered his rifle, but Howard, following his promise to let Miles finish the business, stepped away and gestured toward Miles. He took the carbine. All shook hands. Joseph, with Chapman translating, seems to have said something like "From where the sun now stands, I will fight no more." With that, it was over.

# CHAPTER 17

# Going to Hell

On November 19 the Nez Perce prisoners, headed by Miles and Joseph on horseback, entered Bismarck, Dakota Territory. They were exhausted from the war and more than six weeks of on-and-off travel since the surrender. Much of the town had gathered along the route, and in case of trouble the troops formed a protective line around the refugees. At Fourth and Main Streets, the townsfolk made their move: they launched a major food assault. Men and women surged forward and broke through the perimeter with armloads of eatables. "I seen our restaurant waitress beating her way through the hollow square with one half of a boiled ham," a witness remembered. Its defenses overwhelmed, the procession stopped until each prisoner and most soldiers had received something.[1]

The captives could not have known it, but they were headed for an eight-year exile. They would call it a living hell. It was a time of humiliation and suffering that claimed nearly half of their number and nearly all of their youngest children. Physically and psychologically, it was a horror. And yet, as the reception in Bismarck suggested, this lowest point in their history came as Joseph and the Nez Perces were being widely embraced as models of Native American character and behavior. This disjunction was more than an oddity. It said something about a transition in how Americans thought about their nation and what it meant to be part of it.

A clue to that larger meaning is in a short article that had appeared in Bismarck's newspaper, the *Tri-Weekly Tribune,* three weeks before the prisoners arrived. The paper reported the message of surrender sent by Joseph to Howard at Snake Creek—furnished, the editor said, by an officer recently arrived by steamer:

Tell General Howard I know his heart. What he told me before, I have in my heart. I am tired of fighting. Our chiefs are killed.

283

Looking Glass is dead. Toohoolhoolzote is dead. The old men are all dead. It is the young men who say yes and no. He who led on the young men is dead. It is cold and we have no blankets. The little children are freezing to death. My people, some of them, have run away to the hills and have no blankets, no food; no one knows where they are—perhaps freezing to death. I want to have time to look for my children and see how many I can find. Maybe I shall find them among the dead. Hear me my chiefs. I am tired; my heart is sick and sad. From where the sun now stands I will fight no more forever.[2]

Over the next month, the speech received far wider play in the *New York Times,* Chicago's *Daily Inter-Ocean,* and *Harper's Weekly*.[3] From there, it was reprinted extensively in the press and appeared in the official record in Howard's report to the secretary of war for 1877–78.

Joseph's words would become the most enduring artifact of the Nez Perces' long ordeal. They are probably the most quoted of all native figures in all the nation's Indian wars, arguably second only to the Gettysburg Address as the most familiar short speech of that era. Whether this was Joseph's message, however, is highly questionable. The question is more than one of those spats historians relish just for spat's sake. It suggests something important about how the Nez Perces, and all Indians, were being tied into the new nation, not just physically, politically, and economically but also mythically.

There is no doubt that on October 5, 1877, Joseph sent word that he was ready to give up the fight. It is highly likely that later, as he handed over his rifle, he said something translated as something like "From where the sun now stands, I will fight no more."[4] The question is whether his message, as reported, jibed with the 150 words of the speech that was soon peppered throughout the nation's press.

Two points cloud the matter. The first concerns how the words got from Joseph to Howard and Miles. Joseph could not have said the words as recorded. He didn't speak English. Whatever he said, he said it in Nez Perce to the two emissaries from Miles and Howard, Captain John and Old George, who relayed the message to the army's interpreter, Arthur Chapman, who translated for the officers. Thus the message, whatever it was, had passed from Joseph through two or three persons and one translation by the time it was received. As in the child's game of Telephone, there was plenty of room for muffing the transmission along the way, so whatever Joseph said might have changed considerably by the time it came out the other end. This assumes, of course, that the words Chapman spoke, true or not to what Joseph had originally said, were *those* words—

that Chapman said something like "These men say that Joseph said, "Tell General Howard I know his heart...."

But how do we know that? How do we know that what ended up in the newspapers and the history books was Chapman's translation? There are several accounts of the day's events, including one from Joseph, and we might expect that at least some would include something of the famous speech. In fact, only one person reported it as the well-known version. That man said he wrote down the words at the time, but he later said the document had been lost.[5] No one else, then or later, ever claimed to have seen it. Questions about this famous speech thus narrow down to the one and only person who said he heard and recorded it: Charles Erskine Scott Wood, Howard's aide-de-camp. He was standing there with Howard, Miles, Chapman, and the others when Captain John and Old George brought Joseph's concession and Chapman translated it. Wood supplied the speech to the Bismarck editor and to *Harper's Weekly*. The question is whether the speech Wood supplied was faithful to what Chapman said or was, fully or in part, Wood's invention.

Wood had already shown a gift and fondness for getting into print. He was a talented artist, ranking close to the top of the West Point class of 1874 in drawing (and just as high in number of disciplinary demerits). During the campaign, he had supplied sketches and information, and probably copy, to *Harper's* and the Chicago's *Daily Graphic,* and the day before the surrender speech first appeared in print, the *Chicago Tribune* published Wood's account of the final battle. Clearly, he had a sense of what appealed to the public. Just as clearly, he was drawn personally to Indians and native life. He had joined the campaign after an extended trip in Alaska during which he had been living part of the time with Indians, hearing their stories, studying their customs, attending their feasts, and on at least one occasion accepting sexual favors.[6] Early in the campaign, right after helping to bury the rotting corpses at White Bird, he wrote in his journal of feeling "no disposition to show any quarter," but soon afterward, after spending time with Red Heart's captives, he mused on those "unhappy people and the fate before them" and was having "thoughts on the Indian as a human being, a man and a brother."[7] A week later he stopped journaling, but one of his last entries is intriguing: "Reminded...of De Quincey's *Flight of a Tartar Tribe*"—a reference to Thomas De Quincey's heroic and highly romanticized account of an episode in 1771 when Tartar warriors, their families, and their herds fled czarist troops for thousands of miles.[8]

The surrender was the first time Wood saw Joseph. He seems to have been immediately drawn to him, and after the two men visited extensively,

**Figure 17.1** Charles Erskine Scott Wood soon after graduation from West Point

they engaged in a gesture of friendship fitting for two horseback war-riors—they traded saddles. Their relationship would deepen after Joseph was finally allowed to return to the Pacific Northwest. Wood entertained him in his home, arranged for the casting of a bronze medallion portrait of him by the prominent sculptor Olin Warner, and for two years running sent his son, Erskine, beginning when he was twelve, to live with Joseph for months at a time.

By then, Wood's early sympathy for Indians and admiration for Joseph was evolving into an increasingly radical critique of the government's role in the war, of the government's general treatment of Indians, and of government, period. After leaving the army, he became what is argu-ably the ultimate oxymoron—an anarchist lawyer. He wrote articles for the *Masses,* helped defend Emma Goldman, and became a close friend of Clarence Darrow and Lincoln Steffens. What happened to the Nez Perces, he would write, was just one instance of "the uniformly bad faith with which the colossal machinery of our Government treats the insig-nificant Indian."[9] Of his years in uniform, Wood would write that "in my youth, I, stupid, fought / Wearing the livery of the State / Whose might is by the richest bought—/ A bully which protects the great."[10]

By then he was emerging as a notable western literary figure best known for his iconoclastic bestseller, *Heavenly Discourses* (1927) and a collection of poems, *The Poet in the Desert* (1915, revised 1918). In the latter and in many unpublished verses, he returned over and over to the war and the injustices behind it. Of the horrifying scene of the White Bird corpses, he wrote: "Nature will make excellent manure / Of musicians, artists, arti-sans, artificers…, / Sacred receptacles of unspoken dreams." Against his government's bullying and corruption, Wood offered the Indian's supe-rior spirit, as epitomized by one man: "They instructed my civilization. / Stately and full of wisdom / Was Hin-mah-too-yah-Laht-Kt; / Thunder rolling in the mountains; / Joseph, Chief of the Nez Perces."

Wood wrote this decades after the surrender at the Bear's Paw, but as part of a trajectory, it says something about him as he was in 1877. The words he said he faithfully recorded are writerly, so much so that one scholar suggests that Wood initially meant them to be a sonnet.[11] The man they gave the public, one with fatherly virtues sound enough to entrust a son to, spoke in the native cadences expected in literature of the time and fit a Romantic ideal of the day, the honorable savage accepting his fate. Wood composing a speech for his new saddle-swapping friend seems at least as likely as his taking honest dictation.

Much later, Wood muddied the issue still more. "I took [the speech] for my own benefit as a literary item," he explained in a letter in 1936, the same year he wrote his son that "Joseph's speech and David's lament for Absalom [are] perfect examples of what eloquence may lie in simple prose statement."[12] This last he wrote on the flyleaf of Chester Anders Fee's newly published *Chief Joseph: The Biography of a Great Indian,* which opened with a foreword by Wood. In the foreword he changed the story he had told for nearly sixty years into one more directly dramatic. No middlemen now. Joseph gave the speech himself, not via Captain John and Old George, and he gave it presumably in English as he handed his rifle to Miles. Some have suggested that in old age Wood had come to believe a cleaner version that had morphed in his mind over the years. Not so, however. Scarcely a month after the surrender, a report with Wood's literary fingerprints all over it described the scene almost exactly as he described it nearly sixty years later, with Joseph saying those famous words directly to Miles.[13] Apparently, that is, Wood composed the two different versions at the start, weighed them, chose one, and then much later pulled out the other.

We'll never know just how authentic the speech is. The best guess is that Wood started with something of what Joseph sent to Howard and Miles. Over the next days, as he came to know the man, he fashioned and embellished it into a statement that presented Joseph, and through him the people Woods had come to admire, as ennobled and dignified, deserving sympathy and a victor's compassion.

The question of the speech's authorship, however, finally is less interesting than two others. Why did the public respond as it did? And what did that response say about the mythic role Indians would play in the new America?

As Americans settled into a new identity, they seemed to feel a need to settle up with Indians. Native peoples, specifically those fighting and losing, were thoroughly tangled into the story of the earlier America and how it had come to be. Now it was time to fit them into the vision of what America was becoming.

An older impression was of Indians as hot-eyed and hateful, wily and merciless, incapable of turning this land to God's true intentions. That view had always been most common where contact had been closest between Indians and whites, and so now it persisted in most in the West. The day after the surrender at the Bear's Paw, an editorial in the *San Francisco Chronicle* described the typical Indian as "a filthy, lazy, treacherous and revengeful fellow, not fit generally to be ranked with humanity," going on to deplore the "pernicious sentimentality" of easterners who "regard the savage through Hiawatha spectacles."[14] The reference was to another, far more positive perspective that had also existed since Europe's earliest contact. As Indians' actual threat to national interests diminished, now almost to the vanishing point, this point of view took on new shadings. Most obvious was guilt—admissions of mistreatment, fraud, bullying, unwarranted assaults, and solemn promises violated or unmet. The usual response, however, was not to call for returning any land. but to declare a kind of ethical bankruptcy. The debt was so huge, the ill treatment so great, and the results so irreversible, that repayment had to be devalued into the emotional and mythic.

There were several variations. In one, guilt was mixed with nostalgia. In an impulse similar to the one that helped create Yellowstone National Park, Americans idealized Indians as part of the endangered wild. Responses ranged from "playing Indian" in various public displays to putting native images on official seals, flags, and eventually coins.[15] The early hostile images persisted—individuals like Sitting Bull could still be excoriated—but as the last western wars wound down in the 1870s, the positive impression of Indians increasingly prevailed, with certain virtues rising to the top: honorable behavior, eloquence and dignity, courage against opponents, and mercy toward innocents. Being handsome didn't hurt. These Victorian ideals were common throughout the Atlantic world, yet by attributing them to Indians and by identifying themselves with Indians, white Americans could make those virtues feel home-grown and distinctively their own. The best traits of the imagined native character were called the natural products of the American wild, and because wilderness was said to have shaped the national soul as well, those traits now were granted to all Americans, Indian and white. That made those qualities, like Yellowstone's grizzlies, something to be preserved.

Preserving "wild Indians" themselves was not part of the plan.[16] When it came to people, not waterfalls and trees, the passing of the wild was called inevitable. One reason was practical. Landscapes could be groomed and managed according to what the public expected, while people, as the Nez Perces made clear, acted on their own. The new America, besides, was to be a superior human community, and a true community cannot abide stark divisions like those making a wilderness park, deep lines separating the civilized and the wild. Everyone in the new America would have to meet on common cultural ground—aliens immigrating to it, slaves emancipated inside it, Indians having their lands forcibly taken into it.

The result was a paradox. When associated with the wilderness and the past, living Indians might be admired and sometimes venerated. Their essential qualities, it was said, must somehow survive and be cultivated.

But letting the same persons continue to live the lives that had supposedly produced those qualities—that was forbidden. As part of the emerging America, Indians were told either to change or to die.

A traveler in the postwar nation would have seen plenty of these garbled messages. Indians as "vanishing Americans" appeared prolifically in high and low art, as brave warriors defeated and elders gazing sadly at bison skulls, yet the same Indians, now called "first Americans," were held up to Russian and Polish immigrants as models of national virtues vital to modern life. Indians who made the transition into contemporary America were cause for special pride, as at the opening in 1883 of the nation's crowning modern achievement, the Brooklyn Bridge. Leading the parade was the band from the Carlisle Indian School—Lakota and Apache boys playing patriotic airs and wearing trim uniforms and respectable haircuts. Not many years later, the Boy Scouts of America and the Woodcraft Indians were organized, dedicated to pushing white youths in the other direction, making them more like Indians, so native values might persist in modern life. The goal, according to the first *Boy Scout Handbook,* was "incorporating the principles of the Indians with other ethical features bearing on savings banks, fire drills, etc."

Then there were names. As the West beyond the Mississippi was organized into a new political order that obliterated Indian sovereignty, several of new states took names derived from Indian ones. So did thousands of counties, towns, rivers, creeks, and mountains. Millions of white Americans would move through life anchored in a mythic past that idealized peoples who were being finally and fully dispossessed and culturally assaulted during the same years. There were notable ironies. The architect of the army's hard-line policy toward resistant Indians—run them down and hit them until they submit or die—and the man most responsible for sending the Nez Perces into exile was William T. Sherman, whose middle initial stood for "Tecumseh."

This was the context in which first Joseph and then his supposed speech entered the public sphere. The timing was perfect on two counts. Because the Nez Perce War immediately followed the Sioux conflict, it positioned Joseph as an ideal contrast to the freshly minted villains Sitting Bull and Crazy Horse. And Joseph's surrender, ending a war that had begun only weeks after the defeat of the Sioux, could plausibly be seen as the end of all Indian wars. At some level, "I will fight no more forever" could be heard as the valedictory of eight generations of warriors.

Joseph fit beautifully what the public seemed to need, beginning with how he looked. Among Nez Perces—described as fine specimens with features including that dime novel favorite the Roman nose, "the infallible indicator of courage, resolution and tribular intelligence"—Joseph still stood out.[17] A sketch of him published during the campaign was said to show special "intelligence and strength of character," and reports about the surrender noted eyes as piercing as an eagle's and a gentle face that had nearly feminine beauty yet was "intensely strong." Another description made the racial implication explicit. Except for its absence of beard and a stolid, melancholy air, the face of this "light colored Indian…might be that of a European." His cheekbones were no higher than a white man's, and his "brain cavity [was] ample."[18]

As for how he used that brain, because Joseph was wrongly thought to have directed the war, he won full credit for the strategic talents of other leaders, all now dead or fled. By the war's end, the press was calling Joseph the Red Napoleon. Following the battle at the Big Hole, the *New York Times* wrote that under Joseph, the Nez Perces had fought with skills as excellent "as if they had been acquired at West Point," while the *New York Tribune* ranked the Nez Perces above the "cavalry men of the Don and Volga." Even some of the typically hostile western press praised the warriors, in a Montana editor's words, as "a match for an equal number of the best troops in the world."[19] They were praised as well for what they did not do. They had "turned a new leaf in Indian warfare by scalping no dead, killing no wounded, treating captives with kindness, generally sparing women and children, [and] invariably respecting the flag of truce." Joseph's wartime behavior, an Arizona editor wrote, was "almost too humane for belief."[20] The war itself was explained by *Harper's Weekly,* the *Nation,* and *Frank Leslie's Illustrated Weekly,* among others, as a manifestation of "frauds and downright robbery" and the machinations of the government's "rascally representatives."[21] Only five days after the news came that the war was over, a *New York Times* editorial declared that "in its origin and motive [it was] nothing short of a gigantic blunder and a crime."[22]

By the time Joseph reached Bismarck, he was emerging as a media darling. Articles ranged in tone from curiosity to appreciation to outright idolizing. A reporter in Bismarck from the *St. Louis Globe-Democrat* wrote that this "ideal Indian" was "just the character to live in romance and poetry. Oceola, Tecumseh and Metamora [Metacom, or King Philip] will now step back for a new star has arisen to eclipse them." All acknowledged the intelligent features and "taking air" of this "prince in misfortune," sad and silent: "A more noble captive has never graced our land.[23]

This Joseph, the melancholy prince, a reluctant warrior resigned and stoic in defeat, was right out of classical tradition, but he was tied also to the present at an American turning point. Here was another, much more revealing bit of timing. When Joseph said he would "fight no more," speaking by implication for all Indians and seeming to end two and a half centuries of native resistance, the promise was to bring the West fully into the union—a promise that came just a few months after that other resistant region, the South, seemed to have been finally drawn back in, with the end of federal occupation.

Given the timing, it is hard to miss a resonance between Joseph's surrender and another one in April 1865. The Bear's Paw was the West's Appomattox. Chronologically, the two were bookends to reconstruction as usually defined, and they confirmed two of the Greater Reconstruction's prime accomplishments—keeping a rebellious South in the union and pulling into the nation a vast and varied West.

The play between the two surrenders went well beyond that. At both, at least as the public perceived them, a greatly gifted commander accepted defeat after brilliant victories against outrageous odds. Both Joseph and Robert E. Lee were abandoning a lost cause, heroically fought, to spare their peoples further suffering. Appomattox and the Bear's Paw played their mythic parts in knitting together the nation—drawing everyone toward the cultural high ground, leaving the defeated some pride, and offering the winners feelings of magnanimity. It is no surprise, then, that both became such poignant favorites, and no wonder that Robert E. Lee and Chief Joseph became the new America's most beloved losers.

After Joseph's surrender on October 5, knots of Nez Perces had crossed over to give up their arms while curious soldiers had walked around the Nez Perce camp along Snake Creek. Hot meals were served, blankets distributed, and the wounded treated. On October 7, the victors and the defeated began a slow march to the Tongue River cantonment on the Yellowstone River. After months of war, the trip had an oddly domestic flavor. The Nez Perces rode easily, "clad in lively colors and strung out in a long line." Young boys flung mudballs at each other in mock warfare.[24] At the Missouri, Howard's men started back to the Pacific Northwest via rail and steamboat. By the time they reached home, many had traveled more than seven thousand miles.[25] Miles continued to Tongue River. When the column arrived and Miles and Joseph were ferried first across the river, the post band struck up "Hail to the Chief." To make it clear which chief they were hailing, it paused in the middle for a popular music hall tune "Not for Joe, Oh No, No, Not for Joseph!"[26]

Miles had told the bands they would stay the winter at Tongue River before heading to Idaho in the spring. Only six days after their arrival there, however, they were ordered to Fort Abraham Lincoln near Bismarck. More than two hundred women, children, elderly, and wounded were floated down the Yellowstone and Missouri rivers in mackinaw boats, while the rest moved overland in frigid weather that left Miles sleepless with worry over the prisoners' condition.[27] How this group traveled told a tale. They were loaded into wagons driven by army teamsters. The formal surrender might have taken place back at the Bear's Paw, but this was their true submission. For the first time in a century and a half, the Nez Perces were unhorsed.

The reason given for the move was that the Tongue River cantonment could not support prisoners. In fact, the decision had been made to send them into exile. Understandably, the Nez Perces would always see this as the foulest betrayal. "I thought we could start again," Joseph said later, and he said that without that assurance, he would never have given up.[28] Howard and Miles had indeed said that the bands would be taken home, and both men had firmly believed it. That had been their most recent word from their superiors. Neither man spoke for those above them, however, any more than Joseph spoke for the people in his camp, and if the orders had changed in the meantime, as they had, the more recent decision would hold. Both Howard and Miles would object. "Every assurance and promise made them by you or me has been disregarded," Miles wrote Howard; "such is the justice of our government." Howard soon waffled and eventually supported the decision. Miles never did. For years, he persistently pressed for the return of the prisoners to their home, even petitioning President Hayes.[29]

Sherman had been pushing for weeks for the exile of the Nez Perces. At the end of August, he had written that the bands should be treated with "extreme severity," with all property seized, leading men executed, and the rest "sent to some other country." When word came of the surrender, he immediately wired that "all these captured Indians must never be allowed to return to Oregon" but sent forever to Indian Territory where, as happy farmers, they would "soon be self-supporting."[30] Besides, he argued, if Washington wasn't properly punitive, others on the Plateau would follow the Nez Perces' example.[31] Meanwhile, some Idaho whites warned that returning warriors would do again everything they had done, while others worried that relatives of white victims would take vigilante revenge on any Nez Perces who returned. The Nez Perces themselves were so bitterly divided that settling nontreaties and treaties together would cause obvious problems. "Humanity prompts us to send them back," the commissioner of Indian affairs would write, but

Figure **17.2** William Sherman pressed to send the Nez Perces into a punishing exile

memories of the killings that had started the war posed "an insuperable difficulty."[32]

The final decision would have to be shared by military and civilian authorities, since at some point the prisoners would be shifted from the army to the Department of the Interior. In mid-November, as the prisoners approached Bismarck, Lieutenant Wood reported from Washington that interior secretary Carl Schurz had agreed to send them to Indian Territory.[33] The defeated Nez Perces, Sherman wrote Howard, "now...are lost to their tribe."[34]

The bands stayed only four days at Bismarck before being moved again, this time to Fort Leavenworth in Kansas. When Joseph got the word, a reporter wrote, he "murmured in his mother tongue, 'When will those white chiefs begin to tell the truth?'"[35] The prisoners were loaded on eleven rail coaches—before leaving, Joseph sold his horse, the last of the herd, for $35—and four days later arrived at what would be their home for nearly eight months. Nothing but tents were available, and Leavenworth's commander, General John Pope, the commander of the Department of Missouri known to being sympathetic to Indians, suggested sending them to Fort Riley, also in Kansas, which had empty barracks and warmer weather. Sherman quickly slapped that down, and Pope settled the families in 108 tents on an abandoned horse-racing track beside the Missouri River.[36] They suffered miserably, first from cold, and a few months later from deadening heat and humidity. Located in a bottom between the river and a lagoon, the camp swarmed with malarial mosquitoes. An official admitted that the site was "the worst place that could have been selected." Another found it "simply horrible."[37]

Here the survivors spent the first anniversary of the start of the war. It must have seemed a long way from the meadows at Split Rocks. Back home it was *hillal,* the season of snow melt and summer rampant, when men pulled coho salmon from the risen streams and women dug up cous in canyons and on the plateaus. At Leavenworth, twenty-one had died during the six and half months since they had arrived.[38] The physician in charge reported that all survivors suffered to some degree from the "poisonous malaria" infesting the bottoms. A visitor wrote the camp's "miserable, helpless, emaciated specimens of humanity" lived in conditions he could compare only to those at the Confederate prison at Andersonville.[39]

Only in May did Congress finally provide $20,000 for moving the Nez Perces to Indian Territory and setting up their new life. The money did not come without a fight, a two-day Senate debate a journalist compared to "a rat terrier's personal encounter."[40] The give-and-take included some of the strangest of the story's many strange moments. Some senators spoke of the Nez Perces with great sympathy, extolled their virtues, and condemned their mistreatment—then said they should be sent into exile. In the classic terms of confessional conquest, they argued that the Nez Perces deserved better than being allowed to go home, where they were sure to be assaulted by vengeful whites and punished for a war that was "our fault, not theirs."[41] Giving the abused Nez Perces what they wanted would be "a horrid cruelty."⁴² There remained one last chance for justice. Indian Territory, set aside for hard-pressed tribes, was "just the place" for the bands. In that safe harbor, under civilizing influences and in a mild climate, they would quickly become good and reliable citizens.

Opponents of sending the bands to Indian Territory argued that such "wild tribes" would slow the steady march toward progress of the Cherokees, Choctaws, and other "civilized tribes" already there. The Nez Perces were also sure to turn their blood lust against citizens in neighboring Texas, Arkansas, and Kansas. Indian Territory, Senator Samuel B. Maxey of Texas warned, must not become "a Botany Bay," a dumping ground for savage killers.⁴³ Ship the Nez Perces back to Idaho and to whatever fate awaited them.

Only in the final moments of debate did one senator, George F. Edmunds, liberal Republican from Vermont, raise an obvious parallel and an obvious question. To remove the Nez Perces was to treat them as permanent prisoners of war. It was tantamount to enslavement, not as bond labor but certainly as confinement and loss of liberty.⁴⁴ How, he implied, could this jibe with America's recent dedication to human liberation? Four million slaves had been freed twelve years before. Would the government now deny these four hundred Indians the basic freedom to live where they wanted?

During their hours of argument, the senators gave only a few minutes to the question whether the Nez Perces themselves should have a voice in where they would go. This made the final vote ironic. It came on an amendment, proposed by Colorado's Senator Henry Teller, providing that the government would pay to resettle the Nez Perces only if "the consent of such band...first be obtained." The amendment failed. Twenty-one voted to let the Nez Perces choose their own fate. These included all who had condemned them as murderous savages. Twenty-seven voted against giving them the choice—voted, that is, to send them into exile. They included all who had praised the Nez Perces' virtues, condemned the government's injustices, and called for fairness and compassion.

As more than four hundred Nez Perces were readied to be sent south to Indian Territory, more than two hundred others had been living for months in another exile, this one to the north. They had escaped the Bear's Paw, either fleeing during the battle's first hours or slipping away after the surrender, and had made their way to sanctuary with Sitting Bull and his Lakota Sioux. Their passage into Canada had been for all a trial and for some a horror. It was bitterly cold. Many were thinly clothed, and some were barefoot. "We had no blankets when we escaped," the wife of Shot-in-Head remembered: "Stormy and snowing. The sun shut from sight and no stars at night, we could not know which way to go. Hungry, half naked and freezing, without matches, we had no fire at night."[45] There were some horses but not nearly enough.

Friendly Crees and a Roman Catholic missionary among the mixed-bloods along the Milk River gave some help, but Gros Ventres and Assiniboins, historically unfriendly and currying favor with the military, killed as many as three dozen of the refugees.[46] Between twelve and fifty others were caught and eventually sent to Leavenworth. Lieutenant Hugh Scott, a young officer seeing some of his first action, got a glimpse of war's realities: starving and ill-clad families, the children especially pitiable, crying constantly until soldiers shot and skinned some bison and wrapped the young in the bloody green hides.[47]

The Nez Perces and the Sioux had been enemies since the rise of horse cultures, and the army had tried to enlist help from reservation Sioux in catching the fleeing bands—a move that had indirectly led to the killing of Crazy Horse in early September.[48] Yet the two groups, as the last in the region resisting the new arrangement, were suddenly natural allies. Now that union was made, and made beyond the nation's reach. Washington's next move was to coax both groups back over the line. Sitting Bull's Sioux—more than four thousand persons, including hundreds of unrepentant warriors—were much the greater concern. Only a week after the first Nez Perces arrived in the Sioux camp, Sitting Bull met with a delegation, led by General Alfred Terry, that tried to lure him across the medicine line. He declined. A dubious document has him baffled at the meeting. Americans had just driven their longtime friends the Nez Perces out of their homes and into exile, he supposedly said, yet here they were offering him, someone they called a "wild man, a hostile...a hater of Americans," a comfortable home if he came back. It made no sense.[49]

What finally pulled both peoples south of the border was not diplomacy but the environmental consequences of the new economy. Canada's bison herds were under even more stress than those in the United States. Since 1862, the native population had soared by as much as two-thirds, with the immigration of metis, Minnesota Sioux, and finally the Lakotas. Results were predictable. "No Buffalo," a Hudson's Bay agent wrote in his journal in 1879: "the Half Breeds living on dogs."[50] As Lakotas crossed more often into Montana to hunt and take cattle from ranches, Nelson Miles was sent with seven hundred troops to secure the area. Facing hunger on one side of the line and the army on the other, the Sioux began defecting. In July 1881, Sitting Bull led the last two hundred, starving and with clothes literally rotting on their bodies, to hand over their horses and weapons at Fort Buford in North Dakota. With them was only one person who had gone north after the Bear's Paw: No Feet (Eskoomskee) or Steps, the adopted slave who had ridden to warn the sleeping camp in White Bird Canyon of Perry's approach. At the Big Hole he had crawled and rolled to safety, and from Snake Creek he had ridden to Canada. There he married among the Sioux, and he remained with them for the rest of his life.

The Nez Perces in Canada looked to White Bird as their leader. In the summer of 1878, a delegation under Lieutenant George W. Baird, who had been at the Bear's Paw, tried to persuade him to return. White Bird said he did not care for the Sioux ("I just camp [here] to pass the time") and said he might surrender if Washington let the Nez Perces at Leavenworth go home, too. Surrender first, Baird countered, and "there is a very good prospect that [all of you] will go back." This was at best disingenuous. Baird must have known that nearly two months earlier, the Senate had voted to send the captives to Indian Territory. White Bird didn't bite, and when each man stuck to his you-go-first position, the council broke up.[51] Several years later, White Bird was murdered. His killer—identified variously as Hasenahmahkikt, Ilamnieenimhoosoos, and Nez Perce Sam—held him, as a powerful *tewat,* responsible for his sons' illness, and following the same tradition that had encouraged the murder of Marcus and Narcissa Whitman, hacked White Bird to death with an ax.[52]

By then, fewer than a hundred Nez Perces remained in Canada. The others had slipped back over the border and made their way home. The largest party, twenty-nine persons under Wottolen, had caused a stir on the way by stealing stock and killing at least one man who refused to give them food. Some were taken in by neighboring peoples or by sympathetic families around Lapwai. Often, however, their reception was hostile. "When I came back to my home country, to Kamiah," one man recalled, "my people there would not look at me. That was because of my being in the war." He and others were ridiculed ruthlessly. He kept his peace "and just let them go," but the animosity added to a deep and lasting division; "I would not forget the awful hardships we had gone through."[53]

There was little overt hostility from whites, probably because the returnees were few and scattered and because the army protected the more obvious targets. Yellow Wolf was one. Soon after returning from Canada, he surrendered. When he saw again the land along the Salmon, "it drew memories of old times, of my friends...my brothers, my sisters! All were gone!...I was alone. No difference if I was hanged."[54] About eighty of those who returned were deported to Indian Territory, but a few were allowed to stay, including Kapkap Ponmi (Noise of Running Feet),

Joseph's twelve-year-old daughter, who had fled the Bear's Paw. She had made it to Canada and returned to Idaho with Wottolen. "I want time to look for my children," Joseph supposedly had said when he capitulated: "Maybe I shall find them among the dead." She died before her father could return.[55]

The Nez Perces had first left home thinking in the old terms, expecting to find refuge by crossing the Bitterroots. Then they had found that whether they were in Idaho or Montana they were in the same place, a nation newly tied together. Their next move was toward Canada, looking for refuge in the new world of nations and national borders. Being caught just short of the Canadian line was a crushing disappointment. The widow of Ollokut remembered:

> Husband dead, friends buried or held prisoners. I felt that I was leaving all that I had but I did not cry. You know how you feel when you lose kindred and friends through sickness-death. You do not care if you die. With us it was worse. Strong men, well women, and little children killed and buried. They had not done wrong to be so killed. We had only asked to be left in our own homes, the homes of our ancestors. Our going [from Snake Creek to Canada] was with heavy hearts, broken spirits.

There was one consolation, however: "We would be free. Escaping the bondage sure [to follow] with the surrendering. All lost, we walked silently on into the wintry night."[56]

But life in Canada was no freer. Canada was just another state with the same goal, bringing its West under centralized command. The Nez Perces could stay on the north side of the line, nibbling the edge of what Canada would spare, or they could cross back over and live on whatever terms a consolidated United States would offer. One nation or the other would play them as it chose. In that, the Nez Perces stood for all Indians in 1878. They were not a power to be reckoned with. They were a nagging problem to be cleared up.

On July 9, 1878, the army at Fort Leavenworth officially handed the Nez Perces over to the Indian Bureau. Ten days later, the prisoners were taken from their camp to the rail depot, where they waited for a day in a hammering heat that left one child dead and many prostrate, including Joseph's wife and their interpreter, Arthur Chapman. Before dawn on July 21, they boarded cars and headed south. At Fort Scott, a large crowd waited for hours at the station to see the now famous prisoners.

The whites thronged around the fourth of eight cars for a peep at Joseph, who, "in ill humor on account of the sickness of his wife and the death of three papooses," slammed the door and ordered the blinds drawn. A handful of prisoners from other cars stepped out to sell bows, arrows, and beads as souvenirs and to fill buckets with cool water.[57] The prisoners arrived at Baxter Springs, Kansas, early the same evening. Two more children died during the ride.

The next day, the Nez Perces were taken by wagon the last seven miles to the seven thousand acres set aside for them in the northeastern corner of Indian Territory, near the Peorias, the Miamis, and the recently removed Modocs. They would come to call it Eeikish Pah—The Hot Place or, more simply, The Heat. While they had no theological tradition equivalent to the Christian hell, they had more than forty years' acquaintance with the concept and the image of what it might be like. This was a worldly facsimile.

# CHAPTER 18

# Eeikish Pah and Return

Indian Territory wasn't so bad, commissioner of Indian affairs E. A. Hayt wrote. The temperature there differed only slightly from that in Idaho.[1] While maybe true according to an annual mean, on the basis of human experience the claim was astounding. The summer heat in what is today eastern Oklahoma is relentless, and the low altitude, about eight hundred feet, and high humidity keep the nights close and uncomfortable. For people acclimated to the high, dry air of the Wallowa valley and the Salmon River country, it must have seemed like living compressed in a warm, wet sponge. Winters, too, can be brutal there. Arctic fronts barrel down with snow, sleet, and freezing rain, and as on all the Great Plains, there is little to slow down the punch, certainly nothing like the mountain walls and protective canyons of the Nez Perces' homeland.

The neighboring Modocs, Peorias, and Miamis greeted the new arrivals with corn and fresh vegetables, but otherwise the refugees were in a terrible condition when they arrived in July 1878. Lodge poles had been left at the depot, and for days they lived without shelter in a squally rain. All medicine—quinine being the most important—had been used up, and soon 260 persons, nearly two out of three who had made the trip, were reported sick. Forty-seven died in the first two months. With the twenty-one dead at Leavenworth, the mortality during captivity already was more than half that during the war.[2]

Soon it was clear that the land provided was far too small and its conditions especially wretched, and in June 1879 the Nez Perces traveled in wagons for nine days to a new site next to the Ponca reservation near present-day Tonkawa, Oklahoma. Their new agent, William Whiteman, had not been told when to expect them and so had no supplies or medicines ready. Here the suffering continued. The climate was only marginally better, and Washington proved as slow as ever in meeting its obligations.

Seventy-five houses were ordered built, but two and a half years later, only eighteen persons lived in any. The rest got by in worn-out tipis with canvas rotting off the poles. All depended on rations of dressed beef, beans, flour, and a little hominy and coffee.[3]

Mortality stayed high. In 1880, Joseph wrote through an interpreter that since the end of the war 153 of his people had died, more than a third of the number that had surrendered at the Bear's Paw, and in 1883 the head count of 282 represented a decline of about a quarter since leaving Kansas. "For the first year...many got shaking sickness, chills, hot fever," Yellow Wolf remembered, referring to malaria carried from Leavenworth, and an agent added that seven out of ten suffered also from serious lung diseases. Raven Spy (Kul-Kul Si-Yakth) remembered "that bad smelling water we had to drink, in contrast to our home mountain streams fed by the snows." Most babies born here, and many who came as young children, died.[4] Among them was Joseph's young daughter born back at Tepahlewam on the day of the first killings. The elderly also died at an appalling rate, including William Clark's son Daytime Smoke (Halahtookit). In that one life was incarnate the nation's relation with the Nez Perces, from a birth out of hopeful alliance, through shifting power and mutual maneuvering, to crisis, to war, to banishment. "Unless something is done for them, they will soon become extinct," an agent wrote of the exiles in 1881.[5] Under the depressive pall, doctors wrote that besides the various maladies, despair and homesickness wore away at the people's health.[6]

The news was not all grim. While some men shunned the new life ("Hard work...has nothing to fear from them," agent Whiteman sniffed), others broke sod to grow wheat and prepared gardens for pumpkins, corn, squash, potatoes, tomatoes, and melons. Three years later, their agent boasted of eight hundred bushels of wheat and melons "as fine as I ever saw, and in great abundance."[7] Raising cattle, a passion back on the Plateau, drew more interest. In the summer of 1880, the agent issued the Nez Perces ninety-six heifers and four bulls as a seed herd, and soon he judged their management superior to that of any Indians he had ever known. They "appear to be natural herders," he wrote, apparently unaware of their history of stock raising.[8] Plains farming proved as chancy as ever, however—drought parched the crops in 1884—while neighboring ranchers put some of their cattle in Nez Perce pastures and took some of the exiles' animals into their own herds. In 1884, tribal leaders moved from being ranchers to rentiers, leasing more than 80 percent of their land to a cattleman for $2,000 annually.[9] By then, families were also trafficking in myth and cliché. Their agent reported a healthy income from selling "Indian curiosities and trinkets," moccasins, gloves, and bows and arrows made "in a tasteful manner."[10]

One connection was made to home with the arrival in 1879 of three men, Archie Lawyer, Mark Williams and James Reuben, who were all well connected within the reservation establishment. Archie Lawyer was the son of the man who had played so prominently in securing the treaties of 1855 and 1863, and Reuben had been an interpreter and a scout for Howard early in the war. Devout Presbyterians, they quickly established a church, and the next year the agent reported rigorous Sabbath observance and full meetings in brush arbors and tents.[11] Reuben opened a school, and although the government was slow to provide money for a schoolhouse, the response was good. There were a couple of dozen students in 1880, more than fifty in 1883. Nez Perce parents sent students to boarding schools, including Carlisle Indian School.

These developments—the classes, the sermons, the squash—had a weight beyond whatever material improvement they brought. The Nez Perces were playing out the scheme the government had devised for them and for all Indians, one that missionaries had first introduced more than forty years before and that had been pressed on them and all Indians, and on freed slaves, with special vigor since the Civil War. The nontreaties had resisted. Resistance had led to war and defeat. Then, once in Indian

**Figure 18.1** John Monteith stands above Archie Lawyer (far left), James Reuben (far right), and Mark Williams who joined the exiles

Territory, at least some abruptly began accepting what they had refused for decades. They took up the plow and the cross and sent sons and daughters to school. At least outwardly, they began to don a national identity. As whites were naming counties, creeks, and children after Indians, some Nez Perces reciprocated. A Canadian exile became Samuel Tilden; one in Indian Territory became Jay Gould.[12]

Whatever the motives, doing what the government insisted on was an essential step toward any hope of returning to the Plateau. It was only a step, however. Any real chance depended on Washington radically shifting its position, and for that, significant pressures had to be in play. The key here was Joseph. The man wrongly assigned the role of the war's instigator and prime strategist now found himself in a position to use the power that in fact he never had had before to lead his people in the face of their greatest challenge.

Joseph seems to have begun almost immediately to use his burnished reputation to work toward a return to Idaho. He met the white public in Bismarck and in Kansas, and soon after arriving in Indian Territory he spoke lengthily with a delegation of Commissioner Hayt, three members of the Board of Indian Commissioners and a special congressional committee considering oversight of Indian affairs. In January, 1879 he was allowed a trip to Washington, D.C. with Yellow Bull, considered his second in command, and his interpreter Arthur Chapman. They consulted with President Hayes, Commissioner Hayt, Secretary of Interior Carl Schurz and other officials.

From his first contact with the white public, Joseph made the most of his impressive personal presence. Penned up at Leavenworth, where on a single Sunday five thousand curious locals crowded the camp, he granted interviews and allowed the throng to observe him in his army tent, and on his way to Washington in 1879, dressed in blankets and beaded deerskin, he entertained reporters in a St. Louis restaurant.[13] After greeting President Hayes at a White House reception and bowing low over the first lady's hand, he and Yellow Bull, "models of courtly grace" in blankets and shell earrings, chatted with William Sherman as "great men and richly dressed ladies pressed up to shake the savage hand." At another soiree, a reporter thought Joseph "seemed to have an inward certainty that he was giving elan to the affair" as he stood solemnly in "royal array... wearing that same lofty and melancholy air that makes him so interesting to the people who have abused him so."[14]

There is no record of Joseph's conversations with the president and high officials, but twice he presented his case to the public. On January 17, he spoke for an hour in Lincoln Hall to a large audience of congressmen, cabinet members, and part of the diplomatic corps. As his words were translated, they were interrupted several times with shouts of "Shame!" and at the end the audience gave a thunderous ovation.[15] Not long afterward, Joseph gave his version of events to an editor of the *North American Review,* one of the nation's more widely circulated periodicals; it appeared in April 1879. He laid out the case against Washington, moving through what he considered the misunderstandings, abuses, and betrayals behind the war, always speaking of the broken promise at its end. He described the Nez Perces' pitiable life in exile and their bleak new home—"like a poor man; it amounts to nothing." The performances, always affecting, took him to the moral high ground.

What raised him toward rhetorical brilliance was the way he maneuvered there. He never carped. He not only accepted defeat; he spoke eloquently of the loftiest values of the new America. That last was especially remarkable because it was a full reversal from the last time he had made the case for his people. On the eve of war, Joseph, with Toohoolhoolzote, Ollokut, and others, had insisted that their bands were part of nothing larger than themselves—not a tribe, as Washington claimed, and certainly not part of some vague entity, a nation. A year after the Bear's Paw, when he met the visiting delegation to Indian Territory, his position was radically different. When asked whether Indian affairs should be shifted from the Department of the Interior to the military, he turned that essentially bureaucratic question back to basics. "We should have one law to govern us all," he told them; "All should be citizens of the United States." His answer might have come out of Howard's mouth back at the Lapwai showdown. And if all were Americans, he went on, all should have the same rights. Specifically, all should be able "to come and go when [we] please and be governed all alike."[16] If you see a place where you can find a better life, he went on, then you "better go there." It was the American credo. Why, then, had his people before the war been told that as Americans, they must live in one place and not another? And now, why did a government that preached freedom to all Americans hold his people "as you keep prisoners, in a corral"?

Visiting the national capital and dictating to the *North American Review,* Joseph invoked more widely the values of postwar America— equal justice, free labor, and a continental union of many peoples. Did the white man want peace with the Indian? He could have it:

> There need be no trouble. Treat all men alike. Give them the same law.... I know that my race must change. We cannot hold our own with the white men as we are. We only ask an even chance to live as

other men live. We ask to be recognized as men....Let me be a free man—free to travel, free to stop, free to work, free to trade, where I choose, free to choose my own teachers, free to follow the religion of my fathers, free to think and talk and act for myself—and I will obey every law, or submit to the penalty.[17]

As with his surrender speech, his words might have been changed under the pen of an editor who knew his readers were half in love with their stoical, Roman-nosed chief, although what appeared in print was much in line with what had been taken down verbatim when he had talked to congressmen a few months earlier.

No one can say whether Joseph understood how artfully he was playing to white America. There is one fascinating hint. In November 1877, two days after he arrived as a prisoner in Bismarck, prominent locals honored him and his people's "bravery and humanity" with a public luncheon at the town's leading hotel, the Sheridan House. After dining on beef, potatoes, vegetables, and salmon, Joseph was asked for a few words. Through an interpreter, he talked briefly of "good sentiments in my heart," and then ended: "I expect what I speak will be said throughout the land, and I only want to speak good."[18] By then, in fact, his surrender speech was spreading through the nation's press. Maybe Joseph sensed from reporters and the occasionally adoring crowds something of what he was coming to stand for and how he might put it to use. Wood or Miles might have told him something of what they knew so well—how to reach and work the public in a newly wired-together America.

Whenever and however he got the gift, and whether he used it purposefully or through intuitive genius, within months Joseph was showing his savvy and offering America a deal. Coming fully around from resistant independence, he admitted defeat and embraced the nation. He saw the need to step onto paths of progress, he said, and nodded to the victors as the ones to show him the way. To white America he offered to feed three emotions especially favored at the end of thirty years of violent western conquest—a sense of superiority, the pleasure of painless reconciliation, and the catharsis of cost-free guilt. The appeal was caught in a poem meant to be a verse rendering of Joseph's words in the *Review*. The first public reading was in 1881 in Ralph Waldo Emerson's parlor: "I know my race must soon decay: / I know that we shall fade away, / Unless we march the road you take, / And drink the knowledge which your thirst doth slake. / So be it, then; we ask, we ask, / that you shall set us to your task." All that was asked in return were the promised rights of nationhood. The poem ended: "We will accept it at your hands, / But give us back our lands!"[19]

There was one hitch. Joseph asked in the *Review* to be "free to follow the religion of my fathers." The First Amendment notwithstanding,
however, Christian conversion was part of the price for equal standing for
Indians. In the summer of 1880, Joseph wrote Howard a letter dictated
and translated through James Reuben: "I want you to know now I am
going to be a Christian man, so I want you to make known my wishes to
all ministers in the West....I wish you all remember me in your prayers."
He went on to recount his people's suffering and many deaths while in
exile, then to profess his affection for Howard ("Today I take you as my
true and best friend") and to affirm their brotherhood under God ("our
Great Father of all nations"). The letter's hook was toward the end. You
know you told us we could go back to our country, Joseph said, and "I
know you think of the promises made to me by you." He would walk
in the way of right, and be happy doing it. In return, it would be a "satisfaction" if Howard could now follow through on his promises and do
something for him.[20]

In reply, Howard offered nothing. He was "really glad that you are
trying to become a real Christian," but he had never promised a return
to Idaho, he wrote, and had only given that order to Miles because he
thought those were *his* orders. If left up to him, in fact, he would never
send the bands home, given the hostility of whites there; "I should have
tried to have put you all at some place far removed." He knew the exiles,
"like children," longed to see the mountains of their birth, but Joseph
should persuade his people to stay where they were and build new lives.
Make a garden of the land, he advised, and tell the children to go to school
and grow up happy and industrious, "and you will show yourself a truly
great man."[21]

Nothing before or after even hints that Joseph ever considered becoming a Christian. Sincerity, however, is less the point here than presentation.
Before the war, Joseph had presented, as shrewdly as anyone could have,
who the independent Nez Perces were and, given that, the treatment that
was due them. The showdown and war were the harshest proof that independence was not an option; then exile showed what he could expect if his
people continued to resist the new America. It was on the basis of those
lessons that Joseph played his greatest, and largely unrecognized, role.
He somehow grasped two key facts of the situation. The Nez Perces had
lost power in its usual sense, as control over the basics of their lives, yet
they also had acquired power of another, subtler sort. While the America
reborn from expansion and Civil War demanded that all Indians come
onto a cultural common ground, it was also ready to reward some who
would act the part of honest victims and, even odder, who would speak

out of their victimhood to call the nation to its highest values. History and timing made the Nez Perces ideal to play that part. Joseph saw the opportunity and used it masterfully.

Meanwhile, others down in The Heat followed Joseph's lead. The exiles had many visitors, politicians and religious agents especially. All came away impressed. A journalist arriving at a church service just as worshipers were taking the sacraments found their "transformation truly wonderful" and their progress toward civilization unparalleled among native peoples. James Reuben, an army scout turned minister, was called "the Moses of his tribe, leading them from the burdens of their superstitious beliefs into the light of true religion." Visitors made much of the well-attended schools and flourishing gardens.[22] When white delegations were invited in 1882 to join the bands for the nation's two highest celebratory days, Christmas and July 4, the message was all about submission and reconciliation. At Christmas, a spokesman welcomed guests to a feast he promised was "no heathenish rite, no relic of barbarism," and after lamenting that war and disease had brought his people to a sad pass, he invited all to sit and eat as brothers and sisters. On Independence Day, visitors entered a bower hung with war bonnets and ornamented shirts next to American flags and patriotic bunting. The celebration began with a welcoming prayer and singing of "Blest Be the Ties That Bind"; then each Nez Perce approached and greeted each guest. Mothers held out babies' hands to shake.[23] The next year at a schoolhouse meeting, leading New Perce men rose one after another and "expressed their sorrow for the past, their love for the Government, and their submission to Christian principles and to civil law."[24]

These concessions always were married to the firm assertion of wrongs suffered and of the awful present results. "It is only necessary to see these Nez Perces and talk with them to be fully impressed with their claims against the government," a visitor wrote for the *New York Times* in 1883. Their betrayal, "a fact of history," had sent them to a death trap, a malarial sink where "they are doomed" if they stay, the agency doctor said. At the cemetery, the visitor counted about a hundred graves, and just as his guide, Archie Lawyer, indicated two that held his own children, a horseman appeared: Joseph, wearing white men's clothes (something he never did after his return to the Plateau) and a sorrowful expression. Gesturing to the graves, he said through Lawyer that he hoped the Great Father in Washington "'will take pity upon this suffering people.'"[25]

These scenes often feel like theater. A visitor is ushered into church at the moment of communion. Mothers raise up babies to be touched. A respectably dressed Joseph rides up just as Archie Lawyer, with "a deep sob," points to his dead children. If staged, they showed a grasp of Victorian sentiment, but choreographed or not, they made their points. As for how deep the changes truly ran, that is not so clear. After praising how far the Nez Perces had come, the agent provided a table of specifics for 1883. Of the 282 Nez Perces at his agency, forty regularly wore "citizens' dress," and one family in six supported itself by "civilized pursuits." Seven persons, roughly one in forty, spoke reasonable English.[26]

In one particular, the exiles stayed openly outside dominant values, and in that, as in so much else, they differed from the other civic newcomers, the former slaves. "The Negroes are literally crazy about traveling," an observer wrote in 1877. Often the first emancipated act of freedpeople was to take to the road, partly just because they could, but also as an act of self-discovery. To learn who you are, a preacher told his Florida flock, "You mus' move clar away from de ole places what you knows, ter de new places what you don't know."[27] Moving freely as a way to "find yourself" was (and remains) a cherished part of the American mythos. To the Nez Perces and to Indians generally, the idea of striking out in this way was more a nightmare. Identity was rooted in the old places. *Who* one was was inseparable from *where* one's people had been for as long as their collective memory went back in time. This made the Nez Perces' extraordinary flight the more deeply poignant, and made their performance in exile the more revealing. These "brave, good, and generous people," their agent wrote, "long for the mountains, the valleys, the springs, and the clear springs of water of their old home."[28] All their conformity, genuine or not, was in service of returning to where they had begun.

In 1883, after the agent had been recommending it for two years, the government allowed James Reuben to take twenty-nine persons home to Lapwai. Except for two elderly men, all were widows and children.[29] They paid their own way. Whether or not this broke a bottleneck, calls to end the exile for all Nez Perces gained strength and crested two years later. In the spring of 1884, Congress received more than a dozen petitions calling for their return. A memorial from Cleveland was signed by more than five hundred persons, including President James Garfield's widow.[30] Senator Henry L. Dawes of Massachusetts, the author two years later of the General Allotment Act, which systematized the breaking up of tribal lands into individual farms, introduced an amendment to the 1885 Indian appropriation bill to pay for returning the Nez Perces to the Northwest— if the secretary of the interior agreed that it was a worthy idea.

There were mixed opinions about it. Of great concern was the antipathy toward the exiles returning among both Idaho whites and treaty

Nez Perces, many of whom had actively opposed the war. Indictments remained in force against some exiled leaders, although it is unclear who these were, other than Joseph and Yellow Bull, and questionable whether any prosecutions would have been pressed.[31] The compromise, apparently worked out in Indian Territory, was that all would return to the Plateau—some to Lapwai and some into mitigated exile on a reservation at Colville, Washington, nearly two hundred miles to the northwest.

Joseph would not be allowed to go to Idaho. As for those who were allowed to return to Idaho or Colville, they were separated into what the Lapwai agent called "the subdued and the unsubdued." There is debate about what that meant. Certainly, government agents considered what grudges this or that returning warrior might take home and what antagonism he might face in Idaho. The commissioner of Indian affairs wrote that the exiles themselves had a say. Some reasoned that choosing Lapwai would imply accepting that they could never return to their true homes, in the Wallowa or elsewhere off the reservation.

Religion was part of the judging, although to what extent is unclear. A later agent at Lapwai claimed that returnees were given twenty-four hours to pick—Christianity or not—and those who said "not" were sent with their "haughty disposition" to Colville. Yellow Wolf said: "The interpreter asked us, 'Where you want to go? Lapwai and be Christian, or Colville and just be yourself?'" Others said that Christianity was only one of several signs of being more "progressive," meaning less troublesome. Whatever the standards, some Dreamers went to Lapwai, and according to one who was there, as many as half at Colville were Christians.[32] Religious identity, after all, had always been fluid. James Reuben, who had been compared to Moses doing his work in the wilderness with the exiles—Reuben, who had written Joseph's conversion letter to Howard and more than any man had fashioned the image of the Nez Perces in Christian repentance—turned away from the church after his return. His experience in Indian Territory apparently had soured him on assimilation. According to one account, his final reversion from Christianity came when Lapwai's female missionary refused to discuss the biblical significance of foreskins.[33]

Approval for the return finally came eleven months after Congress recommended it. The Nez Perces left behind evidence that they had been there—a tin time capsule sealed in the foundation of the Ponca Indian Industrial School. In it were personal and sacred items—elks' teeth and beadwork, necklaces, earrings, and bracelets. Joseph gave finger rings, Jay Gould horns from a war bonnet. When the capsule was opened in 1934, it was found that most of what had been put inside had been stolen.[34]

On May 22, 1885, the 268 surviving exiles boarded a train in Arkansas City, Kansas, and when they disembarked at Wallula, Idaho, 118 proceeded to Lapwai, while the remaining 150, Joseph and Yellow Bull among them, moved north to the Colville reservation. Their reception in both cases was mixed. There was lingering anger on all sides in Idaho, and at Colville there was already tension between groups native to the place—the Nespelems and Sal Poils—and others removed from nearby, notably the Columbias. Putting still more displaced people onto the reservation naturally brought more hostility. A resentful agent, who complained that "sickly sentiment expressed in the East" had brought the Nez Perces where none wanted them, gave them little help in settling in, and after several months of living in near squalor close to the agency, Joseph and the others moved well away to Nespelem Creek.[35] There they lived by government welfare, limited farming, and traditional means. There was "wild game aplenty," Yellow Wolf remembered, fish, bountiful roots and berries, and lots of deer, "better than Idaho, where all Christian Nez Perces and whites were against us."[36]

That sentiment helps explain the otherwise curious choice made by most exiles several years later. In 1890, the Colville agent argued successfully that it was safe and practical for those at Nespelem to move to Lapwai. Only a few, including Yellow Bull, took up the offer. The rest probably thought in part that their present place was preferable to the perceived hostility at Lapwai. At least as telling, many also clung to the hope of returning to their true homes, most of them to Wallowa. Taking up reservation allotments would close that door forever.

It turned out to be closed anyway. From Nespelem, Joseph again tried to put his public image to use. In 1897, he returned east to make another plea for the Wallowa. Purposefully or not, his visit coincided with the dedication of Grant's tomb and the hoopla surrounding it. He visited New York City's mayor and strolled down Broadway. At Madison Square Garden, he attended the Wild West show of William F. "Buffalo Bill" Cody, who called him "the Napoleon of them all," and during the show Joseph greeted both Nelson Miles and Oliver Howard. Formally commissioned an aide to General Granville Dodge in the dedication parade, dressed in a gray and blue beaded blanket and other "prairie trappings," Joseph rode a sorrel mustang near Cody as a vast column of sixty thousand men marched up Madison Avenue onto a route lined with more than a million onlookers.[37] Joseph also met with Miles and other officials to petition again for a return to his home valley. The plea was well received. The *New York Times* called his request "modest and reasonable."[38]

Figure **18.2** An older Chief Joseph learned to read shrewdly the public and
its needs at the end of the Indian wars

The upshot was that Joseph was allowed brief visits to his home country in 1899 and 1900. On the second visit, he was accompanied by James
McLaughlin, the inspector general of the Office of Indian Affairs, whose
errand it was to feel out local opinion. A few small towns had grown up
in the Wallowas, as well as some orchards and ranches, and although the

population was still thin, the families there were well rooted. On both occasions, Joseph met with residents to ask if room might be made for his people. They were generally polite, although by one report his audience "made considerable sport of the old man" when he said that the valley had never been legally sold.[39] Both times, however, they turned him down, and on the second occasion, at a gathering at Wallowa Lake near where his father was buried, the refusal was emphatic and absolute.

On the way to that meeting, Joseph visited his father's grave, which a local rancher had maintained respectfully. McLaughlin later wrote that Joseph wept.[40] McLaughlin thought he was moved by the rancher's kindness. Perhaps, but he might have remembered his father's last admonition: "When I am gone, think of your country.... This country holds your father's body. Never sell the bones of your father and your mother." He had kept the promise but not the land; that was enough to bring tears out of the thick of grief.

Joseph had been assigned land at Nespelem but had not been on it in seven years, and although he was given a house, he "prefers the traditional teepee," the agent reported, adding that most of the others persisted in "ancient traditions and ... primitive customs." Among the 127 persons in Joseph's band in 1900, there were seventeen farms, only half of which were being worked.[41] It was here that C. E. S. Wood's son, Erskine, lived with Joseph in the summers of 1892 and 1893. Twelve when he arrived, he slept in Joseph's tipi and sat next to him at meals, swam and practiced archery, fished and herded ponies, learned hoop games, and grew so fat in the face from meals that Joseph nicknamed him Red Moon. When his mother wrote to ask about his appearance, he versified: "My hair is long and wavy / And soft as Southdown fleece / Oh it shines and smells like Eden / When I slick her down with grease." Like his father, Erskine went on to be a prosperous attorney. When he died at the age of one hundred in 1980, he was probably the last living person to have known Joseph.[42]

Joseph returned to the East a couple of times. In early 1903, he met with Miles and President Theodore Roosevelt, reportedly dining on bison steaks. (In his first run for national office, Roosevelt had found Joseph useful, defending the war against Filipino independence by arguing that we had done worse against the Nez Perces, and yet the Filipino leader, Emilio Aguinaldo, "in intelligence and integrity 'stands infinitely below' Chief Joseph of the Nez Perces.")[43] That fall, Joseph joined the Indian Congress and *Life on the Plains,* a Wild West show that played Madison Square Garden, and the following spring he attended the commencement of students at the Carlisle Indian School.[44] This was his last public appearance with a white audience, and he shared the stage with, of all people, Oliver Howard. "I used to be anxious to meet him," he said of Howard at a banquet; "I wanted to kill him in war." But now he was pleased to sit by him as a friend: "We are both old men, still we live and I am glad."[45]

Back at Nespelem, at around 5:45 in the afternoon on September 21, 1904, Joseph slumped over in a quick death while sitting by the fire in his tipi. Presumably it was a heart attack or stroke, although the reservation doctor, noting Joseph's deepening despair in recent years, thought sorrow had killed him.[46] He died ninety-nine years and one day after the Nez Perces met their first whites, Lewis and Clark, at Weippe Prairie. One last time, the press praised him as a giant whose reputation had "cast a shadow into every cranny and corner of the country." As always, the praise was on whites' terms. Miles compared him again to Napoleon and to Shakespeare's Caesar, calling him "the noblest Indian of them all."[47] Most of his people were off gathering hops at the time and so were not present when Joseph was buried at noon the next day. The following June, his body was dug up and reburied under a large white monument provided by the state historical society.

Afterward, in a large council lodge a grand feast was held, with several orations. Then Joseph's nephews and the younger of his two wives gave away all of his goods—war bonnets, leggings, guns, blankets, bison robes, sacks of flour, bottles of syrup, dishes, utensils, a large bass drum, and at least ten watches. The giving lasted two days. Interpreters for ten native languages were needed to translate to the crowded lodge.[48]

Over the years, there were suggestions that Joseph's body be moved yet again. The most bizarre came when the *Seattle Post-Intelligencer* endorsed a plan to disinter his remains and pour them into the concrete of the enormous Chief Joseph Dam, which was built in 1956 on the Columbia River on the southwest corner of the Colville reservation. Resisting that dubious honor, authorities instead installed on the wall of the dam's powerhouse one of the brass medallions commissioned by C. E. S. Wood. A more serious proposal to move the body back to Oregon close to his father finally was rejected when leaders at Nespelem opposed the change.[49] Joseph remains there, far from the Wallowa and seventy yards from a Christian church.

# EPILOGUE

The last survivor of the war was Josiah Red Wolf. Four when he left Idaho, he had seen his mother and sister killed at the Big Hole and after the Bear's Paw had been taken to Canada. He returned to Lapwai, where he became a cobbler and accomplished country-and-western musician. His death in 1971, at ninety-eight, was noted in *Time* magazine's "Milestones" column.[1] Four years earlier, he had turned the first shovel of dirt for a new visitors' center at the Big Hole National Battlefield, a few hundred yards from where his sister and mother had been shot nine decades earlier. It is one of thirty-eight sites in the Nez Perce National Historical Park. The Nez Perce National Historical Trail, established in 1968, was another federal recognition that the war was an American story worth remembering.

There have been efforts to put the past to rest. At the fight at the Big Hole, Five Wounds was killed charging Gibbon's trenches to fulfill his promise to die on the same day as Rainbow. He died so close to the enemy that his friends could not retrieve his body, and after the Nez Perces withdrew, he was decapitated and his head sent to the Army Medical Museum in Washington, D.C., one of more than two thousand Indian skulls taken from across the West. In 2005, the great-grandson of Five Wounds, the Nez Perce historian Otis Halfmoon, Jr., brought the skull and two others from the war home for burial.[2] One of the two others was laid to rest at the Bear's Paw battlefield. Thirty years earlier, Gros Ventre and Assiniboin residents of the nearby Fort Belknap reservation had told of hearing gunshots from the camp along Snake Creek, as well as crying children and the screams of horses. They contacted the Nez Perces, many of whom gathered there on the centennial of the battle to give the spirits peace. No more anguished sounds were reported.

Today, Nez Perces hold annual observances, including a powwow at the White Bird battlefield, to commemorate the war and to honor those who died in it—somewhere between 95 and 145 persons. There have been special ceremonies at other battle sites and at the Leavenworth confinement, and in 2003 a granite monument was erected at St. Louis's Calvary cemetery to mark the final resting place of Man of the Morning and Black Eagle, two of the four men who came from the Plateau in 1831, courting advantage from white America.

Divisions among the Nez Perces continued on the reservations, as always centering often on religion. At the Presbyterians' Fourth of July gatherings, "the ancient rites celebrating the coming of summer came together with the mysterious God of the white man." Especially irritating to missionaries was the extensive praying before horse races.[3] Roman Catholic fathers, while insisting on basic doctrines and religious duties, were more tolerant of hair style, drinking, and even beliefs in tutelary spirits. Two traits among converts especially pleased them—their determined fasting and their confessing of sins in extreme detail.[4]

The reservations in Idaho and Washington remain today, although under the Dawes Allotment Act (1887) all land was surveyed, and what had been the common possession of them all was issued to tribal members as discrete holdings. The land left over, the great majority of reservation acreage, was opened to white settlement. In Idaho, Nez Perce families and individuals received 175,026 acres, less than a quarter of the 1863 reservation that itself was a massive reduction of promised lands. The rest, nearly six hundred thousand acres, was put up for sale in 1895. At long last, a local booster wrote, this country "dowered with...nature's richest gifts," and "wealth undreamed of" would pass from Indians to "the domination of Caucasian energy."[5] Left with roughly 2 percent of the land that was supposedly secured under Isaac Stevens's 1855 treaty, on parcels scattered among white landholders, the Nez Perces lived by government support, by leasing land to whites, and by a little ranching, gardening, fishing, gathering, and selling moccasins and other artifacts. The annual per capita income in Lapwai in 2000 was $10,159, well under a third of the national average.

In Joseph's home country, the trigger of war, settlement never took off. Not easily visited even now, Oregon's huge Wallowa County, two-thirds the size of Connecticut, grew in population from 5,538 in 1900 to 7,226 in 2000, an average of seventeen persons a year. Its population density of two persons per square mile still qualifies the Wallowa country as a frontier under the famous standard of the 1890 census.

The war cost the military 257 casualties, 115 killed and the rest seriously injured, and its monetary cost was set at just under $1.9 million. Then there was the loss of pride. In every engagement but the last, the army was fought to a draw or badly beaten. Surviving officers were polled on why it had taken so many months, so much money, and so many lives to contain outnumbered opponents who labored under huge disadvantages. Answers stressed the soldiers' lack of drills and target practice beforehand, the shortcomings of cavalry mounts, and the need for higher pay and better equipment. John FitzGerald, Howard's surgeon on the campaign, suggested another reason: "superiority of enemy."[6]

Howard caught a lot of heat. Prickly and prone to playing the martyr—stitched into his piano cover at home was a verse from Matthew: "Blessed are ye when men shall revile you, and persecute you, and say all manner of evil against you falsely, for my sake"—he defended himself over and over in the years ahead.[7] He owned up to few errors, found many extenuations, and explained his own shortfalls by touting Joseph's exceeding brilliance as a commander.[8] At no point did Howard hint of recognizing any contradiction between risking his own life to free southern slaves to live as they wished and forcing western Indians to live and work in a place and by customs of their new masters' choosing. Howard fared well professionally. After putting down a brief outbreak among the Bannocks and some Paiutes in 1878, he was made superintendent of West Point, and then commander of the Department of the Platte, Division of the Pacific, and Division of the East. He died in Burlington, Vermont, in 1909, just shy of his seventy-ninth birthday.

John Gibbon was given several higher commands and promoted to brigadier general in 1885. He retired to Maryland in 1891 but returned several times to the Northwest for pleasure trips, once to fish near Joseph's camp at Nespelem. Like Howard, he wrote extensively, articles advocating reforms of the army and women's suffrage and, the year before his death from pneumonia in 1896, a vivid account of the fight at the Big Hole. Unlike Howard, Gibbon could look back with a disarming humor. Describing the Nez Perces' counterattack at the Big Hole, he wrote: "our front appeared to be in the form of a circle."[9] During a speech in 1881, he read from a poem purportedly relating the Montana governor's reply when Gibbon asked him for advice after the battle:

> Your dispatch, trusty soul,
> I answer this minute.
> If you're near a Big Hole,
> You better crawl in it![10]

Nelson Miles rose well above Gibbon and Howard. After pushing Sitting Bull toward surrender by harrying him along the Canadian border, he turned to the West's other new boundary, the one with Mexico, and secured Geronimo's surrender in 1886. He was commander of the Division of the Missouri at the time of the Wounded Knee massacre in late 1890. Ten years later, he was made lieutenant general, the army's highest rank. He kept making enemies, now at the highest levels. President William McKinley thought him insubordinate and denied him any meaningful role in the Spanish-American War. Theodore Roosevelt scorned him as a "brave peacock," a critter Roosevelt knew well from his own mirror. A preening chest-puffer, relentlessly and insufferably self-serving, Miles nonetheless always pressed the government to honor what he had told Joseph at the Bear's Paw and to return all Nez Perces to Idaho, something he surely knew would blunt his ambitions.

In 1925, attending a circus in New York City with his grandchildren, he dropped dead of a heart attack while standing during the national anthem. He thus died appropriately, in performance, the public patriot on display, part of the show and in honest commitment. He is interred in one of the two mausoleums at Arlington National Cemetery.

Six years before Miles's death, two Nez Perces, Howowenew and David Scott, called on Erskine Wood at his Portland home. Full citizenship was finally to be conferred on the Nez Perces, and Howowenew had questions. Wood recorded them on the last page of the diary he had kept as a boy during his second summer with Joseph twenty-six years earlier. "We are the old Indians. Our skin is red," Howowenew said: "So how are you going to make us citizens?" And why should they be, he went on, "when our fathers had this land always?" He did not know what would happen to his people, but he did know who they were: "We are the Indians, full blood Indians. And we are different from the white people. We do not want to be citizens. I guess that is all Mr. Erskine."[11]

The Nez Perces, of course, did receive citizenship, and many thousands of them would fulfill its roles honorably, including fighting in the nation's later wars. They filled those roles even as they worked to keep alive the language, customs, beliefs, traditions, and all that made up what it meant to be the Nimiipuu, the Real People, which meant that the questions from Howowenew and the "old Indians" stayed alive as well. Their questions are part of broader ones about America during one of its greatest times of change.

Between 1845 and 1877, two events reconstructed the nation—its expansion to the Pacific and the Civil War that held the expanded America together. Each event set loose it own consequences and helped carry the nation onto its present course, and yet each also raised and pressed questions that, at the bottom, were much the same. The most vexing regarded the nation's human composition. Who would be the Americans, and what obligations would bind them together?

The questions had been there from the start. The nation was born audaciously, as Alan Trachtenberg writes, as "a civil realm of laws, rights, and citizenship," a people united not by blood and tradition but only by a collective commitment to institutions and ideals.[12] The nobility of such an idea lies in its expansiveness. Everyone is potentially welcome. But because there were none of the usual adhesions other nations had, no unifying history and mythic blood bond, national identity in practice came to rely on everyone committing as well to a few cultural underpinnings—language, broad religious categories, and notions of property and family. The more varied the American people, the more the reliance on that common ground. This is the paradox of the American experiment. Widening the United States' political community has meant constricting its cultural boundaries, and the greater the political *in*clusion, the greater the apparent need for cultural *ex*clusion—and the greater the need to tighten what it has meant to be American.[13]

Westward expansion and the Civil War brought this paradox sharply into focus. Never had such a diversity of peoples been brought within the nation's borders. Never had there been such tortuous dissent over civic membership among those long within the national household. One result was the nation's moral high point, emancipating and granting citizenship to southern slaves. Another was the violent and coercive assault on other people's most essential possessions—their foundational beliefs and their understanding of who they were. Both, the ending of bondage and the cultural aggression, were seen as part of the same process, the fulfillment of lofty purpose and national destiny. "E pluribus unum" has always been both an invitation and a threat.

The Greater Reconstruction began in conquest and expanded promise. It unfolded through appalling bloodshed, liberation, consolidation, and cultural assault. It ended with the nation fighting its last Indian war against its most persistently loyal native ally. As a pivotal moment, that war offers the chance to look back on the muddy lessons of nation-making and ahead with questions about an America that continues to enrich its human mix—whether its room for toleration might grow to match the expanse of the land itself. These questions might begin in conversation with the Nez Perce story and those who lived it.

Yellow Wolf (Hemene Moxmox) fought in every significant battle of the war. He played prominent roles in stopping the attack at the

**Figure E.1**  Yellow Wolf two years after he began his friendship with Lucullus
McWhorter

Clearwater, capturing the howitzer at the Big Hole, and stealing Howard's mules at Camas Meadows. He tried to save the horses at the Bear's Paw, and then returned to the camp to fight. He was wounded five times in four months. After the surrender, he slipped away to Canada, crossed back over to Idaho, was arrested and taken to Indian Territory, and finally settled near Joseph, his uncle, at the Colville reservation. He was good at surviving.

Thirty years after the war, while Yellow Wolf was traveling near the Yakima River, one of his saddle horses cut its leg badly on a wire fence. He approached a rancher he had never met, a transplanted Virginian named Lucullus McWhorter, and asked him to watch after the horse, which McWhorter did, for ten months and without charge, as was fitting by Nez Perce etiquette. Yellow Wolf and McWhorter became friends.

Over the next eighteen years, Yellow Wolf gave his memories to McWhorter. He spent many summers on McWhorter's ranch and, with other veterans of 1877, traveled with him to battle sites, narrating the events of the summer war, pointing out where this and that had happened, correcting what he thought others had misstated. McWhorter took it down, and in 1940 it was published as *Yellow Wolf, His Own Story*.

More than fifty years after the war, Yellow Wolf told his friend: "I am aging....I would like finishing it as truth, not as lie." And having survived this long, he would tell his truth to those who came after him: "It is for them! I want the next generation of whites to know and treat the Indians as themselves." War, he wanted to tell them, "is made to take something not your own."

Living that long, he also spoke for those who had gone before him, men and women who had lived out that summer of 1877, from Split Rocks to the Bear's Paw. On August 20, 1935, shrunken and feeble at seventy-nine, Yellow Wolf told his family he would die the next morning at dawn, "as the sun rested on the edge of the horizon." He did, saying, "My old friends have come for me! There they are! Do you not see them!"[14]

# ACKNOWLEDGMENTS

My thanks begin with the University of Arkansas, which has given generous financial support over the years, and to the Henry E. Huntington Library, where a fellowship for 2002–3 allowed access to the library's superb collections, time to write, and the invaluable chance to learn from the library's fine staff and fellow researchers. Like so many others, I have benefited as well from the staffs of the Newberry Library, Yale University's Beinecke Library, the Western History Collection of the Denver Public Library, the Brigham Young University Library, the Washington State University Library, the Montana Historical Society and the Idaho State Historical Society. I owe special thanks to four persons—Robert Applegate, archivist of the library of the Nez Perce National Historical Park in Spalding, Idaho; Kim Scott of the special collections of the Montana State University Library; and Doug Erickson and Paul Merchant of the Special Collections of the Watzek Library at Lewis and Clark College.

Three historians of the war, Jerry Greene, Jack McDermott, and Bill Lang, generously shared their research and counsel. I learned much as well from two great scholars now no longer among us—Alvin M. Josephy, Jr., and Merle Wells. Sherry Smith gave an exceptionally close and most helpful reading of part of the manuscript. Of the many others who helped with advice, information, and encouragement, I owe special thanks to Richard White, Bob Utley, Pat Bauerle, Barney Old Coyote, Judy Austin, George Venn, Otis Halfmoon, Jr., Roberta "Bobbie" Conner, and Tom Green. Several friends in the Department of History at the University of Arkansas, served as sounding boards for ideas and boosted morale: Jeannie Whayne, Patrick Williams, Lynda Coon, Mike Pierce, Charles Robinson, Beth Schweiger, Randall Woods, and David Chappell. Research assistants helped me in the trenches: Julie Courtwright, Joe Key, Brian Hurley, Derek Everett, Matt Stith, and Rob Bauer. Two editors at

Oxford, Peter Ginna and Tim Bent, have been saints of patience, editorial direction, and good-humored advice.

To my extended, and ever more extensive, family I give my loving thanks for sustaining affections and for indulging my preoccupations: Elizabeth and Randy; Bill and Laura; Richard, Garth, and Anne; Sherrie, Destini, and London; Jacob and Noah; Jodie, Christin, and William; Richard and Dena; George and Lynn; Bob and Marcie; Jackie, Gary, Brian, and Pietro; and the best of nephewdom, George, William, John, and Charles. I save my profoundest gratitude for my wife, Suzanne Stoner, whose integrity and courage ground my world and whose laugh illuminates it.

I dedicate this book to my students. I figure there have been nearly ten thousand of them. The best have made life a joy, and even the worst have helped make it possible to work the best gig in the world.

# A NOTE ON SOURCES

Browsing through the notes in each chapter should make clear the remarkable range of primary and secondary sources available on the Nez Perces. The following items will be especially useful to anyone interested in pressing farther into the story.

An essential work on the history of the Nez Perces is Alvin M. Josephy, Jr., *The Nez Perce Indians and the Opening of the Northwest* (Boston: Houghton Mifflin, 1997). His coverage of the Nimiipuu's early contact with whites, their intricate relations with neighboring groups, and the events prior to the war is especially valuable. Francis Haines, *The Nez Perces: Tribesmen of the Columbia Plateau* (Norman: University of Oklahoma Press, 1955), is briefer but still worthwhile. As a military history of the war itself, Jerome A. Greene's, meticulously researched *Nez Perce Summer, 1877: The U.S. Army and the Nee-Me-Poo Crisis* (Helena: Montana Historical Society Press, 2000), will likely remain the standard source. Other historians, each with his or her own slant, have been drawn to the war: Merrill D. Beal, *"I Will Fight No More Forever": Chief Joseph and the Nez Perce War* (Seattle: University of Washington Press, 1963); Mark H. Brown, *The Flight of the Nez Perce* (New York: Putnam, 1967); Bruce Hampton, *Children of Grace: The Nez Perce War of 1877* (New York: Holt, 1994); David Lavender, *Let Me Be Free: The Nez Perce Tragedy* (Norman: University of Oklahoma Press, 1992); Candy Moulton, *Chief Joseph: Guardian of the People* (New York: Tom Doherty, 2005); Martin Stadius, *Dreamers: On the Trail of the Nez Perce* (Caldwell, Idaho: Caxton Press, 1999); and Brian Schofield, *Selling Your Father's Bones* (London: HarperPress, 2008). Two extensively researched books consider two of the war's most important battles: John D. McDermott, *Forlorn Hope: The Battle of White Bird Canyon and the Beginning of the Nez Perce War* (Boise: Idaho State Historical Society, 1978), and Aubrey L. Haines, *An Elusive*

*Victory: The Battle of the Big Hole* (West Glacier, Mont.: Glacier Natural History Association, 1991). A recent book thoroughly covers the Nez Perce exile in Indian Territory: J. Diane Pearson, *The Nez Perces in the Indian Territory: Nimiipuu Survival* (Norman: University of Oklahoma Press, 2008).

Nez Perce voices on the war, its background, and its aftermath have been preserved in several archives. The most valuable by far is the L. V. McWhorter Collection in the special collections of the Washington State University Library, which houses the results of McWhorter's decades of devoted work at interviewing and corresponding with dozens of participants, Nez Perce and white. The collection also includes scores of invaluable photographs and artifacts. McWhorter's history of the war, *Hear Me My Chiefs! Nez Perce History and Legend* (Caldwell, Idaho: Caxton Press, 2001), includes some of the most valuable testimony he gathered, as does his account based on his chief informant, *Yellow Wolf: His Own Story* (Caldwell, Idaho: Caxton Printers, 1995). Another historian and collector, Walter M. Camp, also interviewed and corresponded with many of those in the war and in other western conflicts. His papers are in three archives: the Harold B. Lee Library at Brigham Young University, the Western History Collections at the Denver Public Library, and the White Swan Library at the Little Big Horn National Battlefield. The libraries at the Nez Perce National Historical Park in Spalding, Idaho, and at the Big Hole National Battlefield in Wisdom, Montana, also contain Nez Perce accounts. On the latter part of Joseph's life, see M. Gidley, *Kopet: A Documentary Narrative of Chief Joseph's Last Years* (Seattle: University of Washington Press, 1981). A recent intriguing work considers how the telling of the Nez Perce story has evolved and how the voices of the Nez Perces themselves have persisted: Robert R. McCoy, *Chief Joseph, Yellow Wolf, and the Creation of Nez Perce History in the Pacific Northwest* (London: Routledge, 2004).

On the military side, essential collections of unpublished primary sources are the Oliver O. Howard Papers at Bowdoin College, the papers of C. E. S. Wood and the Fort Dalles Collection at the Henry E. Huntington Library, the Albert Sully Papers and George W. Baird Papers at the Beinecke Library, the Gustavus Doane Papers at the special collections of the Montana State University Library, and the Wood Family Papers at the special collections of Lewis and Clark College. The Montana State Historical Society in Helena and the Idaho State Historical Society in Boise house several collections touching on the war, including some of the military participants. Research files compiled by Jerome A. Greene while preparing his military history, including materials copied from many other archives, are available in the library of the Nez Perce National Historical Park in Spalding, Idaho. Several contemporary accounts by participants are gathered in Peter Cozzens, ed., *Eyewitnesses to the Indian Wars, 1865–1900: The Wars for the Pacific Northwest* (Mechanicsburg, Pa.: Stackpole Books, 2002). On a crucial figure in the war and the shaping of the popular image of Joseph, see George Venn's excellent *Soldier to Advocate: C. E. S. Wood's 1877 Legacy: A Soldier's Unpublished Diary, Drawings, Poetry, and Letters of Alaska and the Nez Perce Conflict* (La Grande, Ore.: Woodcraft of Oregon, 2006).

On Nez Perce culture, society, religion, and economy, two essential works are Allen P. Slickpoo, Sr., and Deward E. Walker, Jr., *Noon Nee-Me-Poo (We, the Nez Perces): Culture and History of the Nez Perces* (Lapwai, Idaho: Nez Perce Tribe of Idaho, 1973), and Deward E. Walker, Jr., *Conflict and Schism in Nez Perce Acculturation: A Study in Religion and Politics* (Moscow: University of Idaho Press, 1985), as well as an excellent doctoral dissertation completed at Washington State University in 1977: Alan Gould Marshall, "Nez Perce Social Groups: An Ecological Interpretation."

On a crucial part of the story, the spiritual exchanges and conflict, and the rise of indigenous prophets, see especially Larry Cebula, *Plateau Indians and the Quest for Spiritual Power, 1700–1850* (Lincoln: University of Nebraska Press, 2003); Robert H. Ruby and John A. Brown, *Dreamer-prophets of the Columbia Plateau: Smohalla and Skolaskin* (Norman: University of Oklahoma Press, 1989); Click Relander, *Drummers and Dreamers* (Seattle: Caxton Printers, 1986); James Mooney, *The Ghost-Religion and the Sioux Outbreak of 1890, Fourteenth Annual Report of the Bureau of Ethnology to the Secretary of the Smithsonian Institution, 1892–93,* pt 2. (Washington, D.C.: Government Printing Office, 1896), and two works by Clifford Merrill Drury, *Henry Harmon Spalding: Pioneer of Old Oregon* (Caldwell, Idaho: Caxton Printers, 1936), and *The Diaries and Letters of Henry H. Spalding and Asa Bowen Smith Relating to the Nez Perce Mission, 1838–1842* (Glendale, Calif. Arthur H. Clark, 1958). Two works document the causes and grim consequences of epidemics on the Plateau: Robert Boyd, *The Coming of the Spirit of Pestilence: Introduced Infectious Diseases and Population Decline among Northwest Coast Indians, 1774–1874* (Seattle: University of Washington Press, 1999), and Elizabeth A. Fenn, *Pox Americana: The Great Smallpox Epidemic of 1775–82* (New York: Hill and Wang, 2001).

Two treaties, in 1855 and 1863, structured the government's position on the Nez Perces and framed its case that led to the crisis of 1877. The official record on the first has been republished: *A True Copy of the Record of the Official Proceedings at the Council in the Walla Walla Valley, 1855,* ed. Darrell Scott (Fairfield, Wash.: Ye Galleon Press, 1985). On the second treaty, a remarkable collection of published and unpublished government records and contemporary newspaper and periodical writings are gathered in Dennis Baird, Diane Mallickan, and W. R. Swagerty, eds., *The Nez Perce Nation Divided: Firsthand Accounts of Events Leading to the 1863 Treaty* (Moscow: University of Idaho Press, 2002). Published government documents richly document the federal side of the story. Especially valuable are agency reports included in annual reports of the secretary of the interior and, for the war, its immediate background, and aftermath, the report of the secretary of war for 1877. The letterbooks and some correspondence of a vital player, agent John Monteith, are in the library of the Nez Perce National Historical Park in Spalding, Idaho.

Finally, a fascinating collection of early Nez Perce drawings of the war have been published: Scott M. Thompson, *I Will Tell of My War Story: A Pictorial Account of the Nez Perce War.* And if some readers might be drawn to follow the course of the war by tracing the route of the bands in their extraordinary bid for freedom, they can consult Cheryl Wilfong, *Following the Nez Perce Trail: A Guide to the Nee-Me-Poo National Historic Trail with Eyewitness Accounts* (Corvallis: Oregon State University Press, 1990).

# NOTES

## Abbreviations

BL:  Beinecke Rare Book and Manuscript Library, Yale University, New Haven, Connecticut.

HL:  Huntington Library, San Marino, California.

*HM:*  Lucullus V. McWhorter, *Hear Me, My Chiefs! Nez Perce History and Legend*. Caldwell, Idaho: Caxton Press, 2001.

McW:  Lucullus V. McWhorter Papers, Special Collections, Washington State University Library, Pullman.

MHS:  Montana Historical Society, Helena.

NA:  National Archives and Records Administration, Washington, D.C.

NL:  Newberry Library, Chicago.

NPHP:  Library and Archives, Nez Perce National Historical Park, Spalding, Idaho.

*NPI:*  Alvin M. Josephy, Jr., *The Nez Perce Indians and the Opening of the Northwest*. Boston: Houghton Mifflin, 1997.

*NPJ:*  O. O. Howard, *Nez Perce Joseph: An Account of His Ancestors, His Lands, His Confederates, His Enemies, His Murders, His War, His Pursuit and Capture*. Boston: Lee and Shepard, 1881.

OOH:  Oliver O. Howard Papers, Special Collections, Bowdoin College, Brunswick, Maine.

*SW:*  *Report of the Secretary of War, 1877*. H.Exec.Doc.1, pt 2, 45th Cong., 2nd sess.

WCP:  Walter C. Camp Papers, Harold B. Lee Library, Brigham Young University, Provo, Utah.

YJIV:  Young Joseph, "An Indian's View of Indian Affairs," *North American Review* 128:269 (April 1879): 412–33.

*YW:*  Lucullus Virgil McWhorter, *Yellow Wolf: His Own Story*. Caldwell, Idaho: Caxton Printers, 1995.

## Preface

1. *Chicago Tribune,* October 11, 1877.

## Chapter 1

1. *YW,* 205–12.

2. Deward E. Walker, Jr., *Blood of the Monster: The Nez Perce Coyote Cycle* (Worland, Wyo.: High Plains, 1994), 9–11.

3. As is often the case with Indian peoples, the origin of the name Nez Perces is muddy. It first was used by Lewis and Clark, who wrote that the Shoshonis to the east had used it. Once they had made contact, the captains referred to the Nez Perces as both the pierced nose people and the Chopunnish, which may have been a reference to nose-piercing; a mishearing of yet another term used for the Nez Perces, the Sahaptin; or an evolved borrowing of a self-designating term from someone else. Gary E. Moulton, ed., *The Definitive Journals of Lewis and Clark: Through the Rockies to the Cascades* (Lincoln: University of Nebraska Press, 1988), 5:89, 222; *NPI,* 645–46; Haruko Aoki, " 'Chopunnish' and 'Greenwood Indians': A Note on Nez Perce Tribal Synonymy," *American Anthropologist* 69:5 (October 1967): 505–6; Haruko Aoki, *Nez Perce Grammar,* University of California Publications in Linguistics, vol. 62 (Berkeley: University of California Press, 1970), 1, 2–3.

4. The following summary is based largely on these sources: Alan Gould Marshall, "Nez Perce Social Groups: An Ecological Interpretation," Ph.D. diss. (Washington State University, 1977), 12–36; D. W. Meinig, *The Great Columbia Plain: A Historical Geography* (Seattle: University of Washington Press, 1968), 3–25; Deward E. Walker, Jr., "Nez Perce," in *Plateau: Handbook of North American Indians,* vol. 12, ed. William C. Sturtevant (Washington, D.C.: Smithsonian Institution, 1998), 420–29; Rexford F. Daubenmire, "An Ecological Study of the Vegetation of Southeastern Washington and Adjacent Idaho," *Ecological Monographs* 12:1 (January 1942): 53–79; Anne E. Black et al., "Biodiversity and Land-use History of the Palouse Bioregion: Pre-European to Present," in T. D. Sisk, ed., *Perspectives on the Land Use History of North America: A Context for Understanding Our Changing Environment* (Washington, D.C.: United States Geological Survey, 1998); Allen P. Slickpoo, Sr., and Deward E. Walker, Jr., *Noon Nee-Me-Poo (We, the Nez Perces): Culture and History of the Nez Perces* (Lapwai, Idaho: Nez Perce Tribe of Idaho, 1973), 29–65; Deward E. Walker, Jr., *Conflict and Schism in Nez Perce Acculturation: A Study in Religion and Politics* (Moscow: University of Idaho Press, 1985), 9–30; Francis Haines, *The Nez Perces: Tribesmen of the Columbia Plateau* (Norman: University of Oklahoma Press, 1955), 3–27; Robert R. McCoy, *Chief Joseph, Yellow Wolf, and the Creation of Nez Perce History in the Pacific Northwest* (London: Routledge, 2004), 18–38; Alvin M. Josephy, Jr., "Origins of the Nez Perce Indians," *Idaho Yesterdays* 6 (spring 1962): 2–13.

5. For an excellent summary of Nez Perce subsistence resources, see Marshall, "Nez Perce Social Groups," 36–76.

6. Ibid., 62.

7. Ibid. This point is central to Marshall's thesis. For a summary, see 150–53.

8. Ibid., 134–38.

9. Ibid., 49.

10. Madge L. Schwede, "An Ecological Study of Nez Perce Settlement Patterns," M.A. thesis (Washington State University, 1966); Walker, *Conflict and Schism,* 11–13.

11. See Walker, *Conflict and Schism,* 16–18, and Marshall, "Nez Perce Social Groups," 139–42, for concise summaries of Nez Perce leadership structures.

12. Ibid., 140.

13. Slickpoo and Walker, *Noon Nee-Me-Poo,* 52–54.

14. Marshall, "Nez Perce Social Groups," 120–42; Walker, *Conflict and Schism,* 9–10.

15. Deward Walker identifies the characteristics of Plateau native society, the essentials described here for the Nez Perces: linear riverine settlement, diverse subsistence base, a complex fishing technology, material crossutilization, extensive intermarriage and with that extensive links among groups, limited political integration, and relatively uniform systems of mythology and art. Deward E. Walker, Jr., introduction to Sturtevant, *Plateau,* 12:3.

16. Marshall, "Nez Perce Social Groups," 149–50.

17. Anthropologists have described Nez Perce society as "marked by a poverty of political institutions," "devoid of superordinate devices of social control," and having "a low level of socio-cultural integration." Walker, *Conflict and Schism,* 15, 18.

18. Haines, *Nez Perces,* 17–25; Francis Haines, "The Northward Spread of Horses to the Plains Indians," *American Anthropologist* 40:3 (July 1938): 429–37; Herbert J. Spinden, "Nez Perce Tales," pt. 2, *Journal of American Folk-Lore* 21:81 (1908): 158. Spinden points out how the story of the white mare "shows how readily history becomes distorted." By the traditional story, the Nez Perces acquired horses from the Shoshonis with beads given them by Lewis and Clark; in fact, Lewis and Clark arrived to find the Nez Perces rich in horses, bred from ones acquired at least seventy years earlier.

19. Slickpoo and Walker, *Noon Nee-Me-Poo,* iii.

20. Moulton, *Definitive Journals,* 5:256; Alexander Ross, *The Fur Hunters of the Far West,* edited by Milo Milton Quaife (Chicago: R. R. Donnelly, 1924), 7.

21. Henry Miller, "Letters from the Upper Columbia," *Idaho Yesterdays* 4 (1960–61): 21.

22. Walker, *Conflict and Schism,* 14.

23. Elizabeth A. Fenn, *Pox Americana: The Great Smallpox Epidemic of 1775–1782* (New York: Hill and Wang, 2001), 273.

24. *NPI,* 38.

## Chapter 2

1. A few Nez Perces previously had been captured by Blackfeet or Atsinas and taken East, where they had met whites. One of these former captives would soon play a critical role in the story. Allen P. Slickpoo, Sr., and Deward E. Walker, Jr., *Noon Nee-Me-Poo (We, the Nez Perces), Culture and History of the Nez Perces* (Lapwai, Idaho: Nez Perce Tribe of Idaho, 1973), 1:67.

2. Gary E. Moulton, ed., *The Definitive Journals of Lewis and Clark: Through the Rockies to the Cascades* (Lincoln: University of Nebraska Press, 1988), 5:222.

3. For a fine discussion of the unsettling effects of the protohistoric period and the resulting prophecies, see Larry Cebula, *Plateau Indians and the Quest for Spiritual Power, 1700–1850* (Lincoln: University of Nebraska Press, 2003), chap. 2.

4. Allen V. Pinkham, Sr., "We Ya Oo Yet Soyapo," in *Lewis and Clark through Indian Eyes,* ed. Alvin M. Josephy, Jr., with Marc Jaffe (New York: Knopf, 2006), 155.

5. Untitled statement (in handwriting of Camille Williams, or War Singer), box 7, folder 14, McW; *HM,* 17–18.

6. Gary E. Moulton, ed., *The Journals of the Lewis and Clark Expedition: The Journals of Joseph Whitehouse, May 14, 1804–April 2, 1806* (Lincoln: University of Nebraska Press, 1997), 329.

7. Gary E. Moulton, ed., *The Definitive Journals of Lewis and Clark: From the Pacific to the Rockies* (Lincoln: University of Nebraska Press, 1991), 7:237–49. For accounts of this crucial council, see James P. Ronda, *Lewis and Clark among the Indians* (Lincoln: University of Nebraska Press, 1998), 222–27, and *NPI,* 10–15.

8. Moulton, *Definitive Journals of Lewis and Clark,* 7:242, 248, 258.

9. *NPI,* 46–51.

10. A face-off in 1814 had a revealing ending. A young Wallawalla stood up against angry warriors wanting to kill a British party and pointed out that the only way they could stand against their true enemies, the Shoshonis, was with guns and ammunition that only the whites could supply. To get new power, he was saying, we have to accept that they have some power over us. The confrontation, which ended peacefully, was the last between the British and the area's natives. Ross Cox, *The Columbia River,* ed. Edgar I. Stewart and Jane R. Stewart (Norman: University of Oklahoma Press, 1957), 202–4.

11. Washington Irving, *The Works of Washington Irving: The Adventures of Captain Bonneville* (New York: Cooperative Publication Society, n.d.), 231, 233.

12. *NPI,* 69–70.

13. Ibid., 125–26.

14. Charles L. Camp, ed., *James Clyman, Frontiersman: The Adventures of a Trapper and Covered-Wagon Emigrant as Told in His Own Reminiscences and Diaries* (Portland, Ore.: Champoeg Press, 1960), 150, 159–60.

15. Daniel J. Boorstin, *The Americans: The National Experience* (New York: Random House, 1965), 13–14.

16. Hiram Martin Chittenden, *The American Fur Trade of the Far West* (New York: Press of the Pioneers, 1935), I, 397.

17. Hubert Howe Bancroft, *History of Oregon, vol. 1, 1834–1848,* in *The Works of Hubert Howe Bancroft* (San Francisco: History, 1886), 24:155.

18. W. H. Gray, *A History of Oregon, 1792–1849, Drawn from Personal Observation and Authentic Information* (Portland: Harris and Holman; San Francisco: H. H. Bancroft, 1870), 214–15.

19. A. J. Allen, *Ten Years in Oregon: Travels and Adventures of Dr. E. White and Lady West of the Rocky Mountains* (Ithaca, N.Y.: Mack, Andrus, 1848), 182. White's account of this crucial meeting is also in his annual report appearing in *Message from the President of the United States, 1843,* S.Doc. 1, 28th Cong., 1st sess., Serial Set 431, 1:423–55.

20. *HM,* 64.

21. Allen, *Ten Years in Oregon,* 189–90.

22. Ibid., 186–87; Bancroft, *History of Oregon,* 1:269–72.

23. The missionary quoted was Narcissa Whitman. Robert Boyd, *People of the Dalles: The Indians of Wascopam Mission* (Lincoln: University of Nebraska Press, 1996), 164. The other was William H. Gray, who served with Spalding. Gray, *History of Oregon,* 214.

24. Allen, *Ten Years in Oregon,* 183–84.

25. *Message from the President, 1843,* 449.

26. White's actions over the previous several years before the 1842 meeting all point toward his having such a presumption—and doing what he could to follow its implications. He had ushered in the first party of overland settlers and anticipated hundreds more. He was one of thirty-six settlers who had petitioned Congress three years earlier to extend American sovereignty over Oregon, "the germ of a great State," and to establish laws regulating relations between whites and Indians as a means of stimulating immigration. He wrote with strong encouragement to an army officer looking into establishing a military post of a thousand men at the mouth of the Columbia. The year after his meeting with the Nez Perces, he used his report to tout the healhfulness and fertility of Oregon and to give advice for immigrants. The head of the Hudson's Bay Company knew him for what he was, "an instrument in the hands of that party" urging the U.S. government "to take military possession of the Oregon Territory." Clifford M. Drury, *Marcus and Narcissa Whitman and the Opening of Old Oregon* (Glendale, Calif.: Arthur H. Clark, 1973), 2:91; "Memorial of a Number of Citizens of the Oregon Territory, Praying Congress to Take Possession of, and Extend Their Juristiction over, the Said Territory," S.Doc. 154, 25th Cong., 3rd sess.; "Military Posts: Council Bluffs to the Pacific Ocean," H.Rpt. 830, 27th Cong., 2nd sess., 54; Elijah White to J. M. Porter, November 15, 1843, in *Report of Commissioner of Indian Affairs, 1843,* H.Doc. 2, 28th Cong., 2nd sess., Serial Set 463, 1:493–94.

27. *Message from the President, 1843,* 428–29.

## Chapter 3

1. Hiram Martin Chittenden, *The American Fur Trade of the Far West* (New York: Press of the Pioneers, 1935), 2:638, 896–99.

2. On *wey-ya-kin* powers (alternate spellings include especially "Wyakin" and "Weyekin"), see *YW,* 295–300; Alvin M. Josephy, Jr., "Origins of the Nez Perce Indians," *Idaho Yesterdays* 6 (spring 1962): 11–13; Deward E. Walker, Jr., *Conflict and Schism in New Perce Acculturation* (Moscow: University of Idaho Press, 1985), 18–27; J. M. Cornelison, *Weyekin Stories: Titwatit Weyekishnim* (San Francisco: E. L. Mackey, 1911). Cornelison was missionary to the Umatillas.

3. Larry Cebula, *Plateau Indians and the Quest for Spiritual Power, 1700–1850* (Lincoln: University of Nebraska Press, 2003), 177.

4. J. Orin Oliphant, "A Project for a Christian Mission on the Northwest Coast of America, 1798," *Pacific Northwest Quarterly* 36:2 (April 1945): 99–214.

5. *NPI,* 87.

6. To complicate the question further, when Samuel Parker was sent by Methodist leaders to the Northwest in 1835, he wrote in his journal that it was his impression that the four men had not been sent to seek out the Bible but rather had gone simply out of curiosity. Interestingly, this opinion was omitted when the journal was published. Archer B. Hulbert, "Undeveloped Factors in the Life of Marcus Whitman," in James F. Willard and Colin B. Goodykloontz, eds., *The Trans-Mississippi West: Papers Read at a Conference Held at the University of Colorado, June 18–June 21, 1929* (Boulder: University of Colorado, 1930), 90–91.

7. Quoted in *NPI,* 87 and 91.

8. Robert Boyd, *The People of the Dalles: The Indians of Wascopam Mission: A Historical Ethnography Based on the Papers of the Methodist Missionaries* (Lincoln: University of Nebraska Press, 1996), 186–88.

9. Hulbert, "Undeveloped Factors," 92.

10. Clifford Merrill Drury, *Henry Harmon Spalding: Pioneer of Old Oregon* (Caldwell, Idaho: Caxton Printers, 1936), 115–17.

11. Henry Spalding to "Ever dear parents, brothers and sisters," February 16, 1837, copy in correspondence file, Henry Harmon Spalding Papers, NPHP (original in Presbyterian Historical Society, Philadelphia).

12. The man who devised this system was the remarkable John Pickering, son of Timothy Pickering, prominent revolutionary figure and secretary of state. His mastery ranged from Greek and Hebrew to Oriental languages, and he produced one of the earliest compilations of Americanisms. To facilitate the translation of English and other languages into various Indian languages, in 1820 he wrote *On the Adoption of a Uniform Orthography of Indian Languages of North America.*

13. Howard Malcolm Ballou, "The History of the Oregon Mission Press," *Oregon Historical Quarterly* 23:1 (March 1922): 39–48; 23:2

(June 1922): 101–9. A later version of the Gospel of Matthew is *Matthewyim Taaiskt: The Gospel According to Matthew Translated Into the Nez Perce Language, by Rev. H. H. Spalding* (New York: American Bible Society, 1871), copy in BL.

14. "Wilupupki 1842," pamphlet, Ayer 3A 612, NL.

15. The most thoughtful summary of these events is in *NPI,* 165–70, 180–82. The two episodes also offer an instance of the emotional crosscurrents in later accounts by participants. A Jesuit priest, J. B. A. Brouillet, wrote a version putting William Gray and Spalding in the worst light and telling of harsh policies and their humiliation at the hands of the Nez Perces. Gray later wrote a history of Oregon that included a refutation of Brouillet and a spirited defense of his actions. See J. B. A. Brouillet, *Protestantism in Oregon: Account of the Murder of Dr. Whitman and the Ungrateful Calumnies of H. H. Spalding, Protestant Missionary* (New York: M. T. Cozens, 1853), especially pp. 18–19, and William Henry Gray, *A History of Oregon, 1792–1849, Drawn from Personal Observation and Authentic Information* (Portland, Ore.: Harris and Holman, 1870), 510–11.

16. Clifford Merrill Drury, *The Diaries and Letters of Henry H. Spalding and Asa Bowen Smith Relating to the Nez Perce Mission, 1838–1842* (Glendale, Calif.: Arthur H. Clark, 1958), 109, 122, 133–34.

17. Ibid., 108.

18. Francis Paul Prucha, "Two Roads to Conversion: Protestant and Catholic Missionaries in the Pacific Northwest," *Pacific Northwest Quarterly* 79:4 (October 1988): 130–32.

19. Drury, *Henry Harmon Spalding,* 182.

20. There was, it is true, debate among some Protestants on whether missionaries should pursue conversion first, before what they usually called "civilizing." Asa Smith sometimes seems to take a position close to that, and Methodists especially addressed the question regarding their Oregon missions under Jason and Daniel Lee. In practical terms, however, the distinction between religious and cultural conversion mostly dissolved. The Methodist Missionary Society's annual report for 1841, for instance, emphasized that preaching the gospel was the top priority in Oregon, then quickly went on to tell of schools operating, boys and men farming, girls and women sewing, knitting, and learning household chores and generally practicing the basics of civilized life. "We may look," it concluded, "with the divine blessing, for a nation to be raised up in the Oregon country from the wretchedness of barbarism to the blessedness of a civilized and Christian people." See Robert J. Loewenberg, *Equality on the Oregon Frontier: Jason Lee and the Methodist Mission, 1834–43* (Seattle: University of Washington Press, 1976), especially chaps. 4 and 5, for a discussion of the issue. The quotation is from p. 101.

21. Henry Spalding to "Ever dear parents, brothers and sisters," February 16, 1837.

22. Drury, *Spalding and Smith,* 124–44, 202–3.

23. In the dramatic story of Whitman's hazardous journey, his appeal to the board, and their choosing to reverse their decision, a neglected factor

is that of money. One historian has pointed out that the board's decision to abandon the missions came in a year when the society ran a deficit, whereas when they affirmed the missions and sent out William Craig with the three new pairs of missionaries, they were nicely in the black. Hulbert, "Undeveloped Factors," 92–93.

24. Greeley quoted in David Lavender, *Westward Vision: The Story of the Oregon Trail* (New York: McGraw-Hill, 1963), 368.

25. John D. Unruh, Jr., *The Plains Across: The Overland Emigrants and the Trans-Mississippi West, 1840–60* (Urbana: University of Illinois Press, 1982), 84.

26. For an excellent analysis of the Whitmans as agents of national intrusion into the Northwest, see Cameron Addis, "The Whitman Massacre: Religion and Manifest Destiny on the Columbia Plateau, 1809–1858," *Journal of the Early Republic* 25:2 (summer 2005): 221–58.

27. *NPI*, 224; Lavender, *Westward Vision*, 381; Archer Butler Hulbert and Dorothy Printuip Hulbert, eds., *Marcus Whitman, Crusader*, pt. 3, *1843–1847* (Colorado Springs: Stewart Commission of Colorado College, 1941), 102.

28. Drury, *Henry Harmon Spalding*, 234, 325.

29. *Message from the President of the United States to the Two Houses of Congress*, Sen. Doc.1, 28th Cong., 1st sess., Serial Set 431, 1:460.

30. Clifford M. Drury, *Marcus and Narcissa Whitman and the Opening of Old Oregon* (Glendale, Calif.: Arthur H. Clark, 1973), 2:153.

31. Drury, *Henry Harmon Spalding*, 323.

32. Quoted in Robert Boyd, *The Coming of the Spirit of Pestilence: Introduced Infectious Diseases and Population Decline among Northwest Coast Indians, 1774–1874* (Seattle: University of Washington Press, 1999), 147.

33. Drury, *Henry Harmon Spalding*, 332.

34. Drury, *Marcus and Narcissa Whitman*, 2:209; "Indian war in Oregon and Washington Territories. Letter from the Secretary of the Interior, transmitting, in compliance with the resolution of the House of the 15th instant, the report of J. Ross Browne, on the subject of the Indian war in Oregon and Washington Territories. January 25, 1858," H.Ex.Doc. 38, 35th Cong., 1st sess., Serial Set 955, 9: 27.

35. "Indian war in Oregon and Washington Territories." 26.

36. Drury, *Marcus and Narcissa Whitman*, 2:239.

37. Drury, *Henry Harmon Spalding*, 343–44.

38. Ibid., 345.

39. Ibid., 371.

40. On Lawyer, see Clifford Drury, "Lawyer, Head Chief of the Nez Perce 1848–1875," *Idaho Yesterdays* 22:4 (winter 1979): 2–24.

41. Drury, *Henry Harmon Spalding*, 213.

42. *NPI*, 191.


# Chapter 4

1. During the past quarter century, an enormous literature has grown around the role of diseases in the European conquest. A few of the more

recent works that synthesize and critique that scholarship are Michael R. Haines and Richard H. Steckel, eds., *A Population History of North America* (Cambridge: Cambridge University Press, 2000); Noble David Cook, *Born to Die: Disease and New World Conquest, 1492–1650* (Cambridge: Cambridge University Press, 1998); David P. Henique, *Numbers from Nowhere: The American Indian Contact Population Debate* (Norman: University of Oklahoma Press, 1998); Ann F. Ramenofsky, Alicia K. Wilbur, and Anne C. Stone, "Native American Disease History: Past, Present, and Future," *World Archaeology* 35:2 (October 2003): 258–75.

2. For a thorough discussion of different possibilities of how, when, and where smallpox first arrived, see Robert Boyd, "Smallpox in the Pacific Northwest: The First Epidemics," *BC Studies* 101:1 (spring 1994): 5–40.

3. Clifford Merrill Drury, *The Diaries and Letters of Henry H. Spalding and Asa Bowen Smith Relating to the Nez Perce Mission, 1838–1842* (Glendale, Calif.: Arthur H. Clark, 1958), 136–37.

4. Boyd, "Smallpox in the Pacific Northwest"; Robert Boyd, *The Coming of the Spirit of Pestilence: Introduced Infectious Diseases and Population Decline among Northwest Coast Indians, 1774–1874* (Seattle: University of Washington Press, 1999), 21–49.

5. Howard Stansbury, *An Expedition to the Valley of the Great Salt Lake of Utah Including a Description of Its Geography, Natural History and Its Minerals, and an Analysis of Its Waters; With an Authentic Account of the Mormon Settlement* (Philadelphia: Lippincott, Grambo, 1855), 43–44.

6. Gary E. Moulton, ed., *The Definitive Journals of Lewis and Clark: Up the Missouri to Fort Mandan* (Lincoln: University of Nebraska Press, 1987), 3:191.

7. For a discussion see Larry Cebula, *Plateau Indians and the Quest for Spiritual Power, 1700–1850* (Lincoln: University of Nebraska Press, 2003), 45–51. To the impact of disease and trade Cebula adds an "information revolution" as Plateau peoples' awareness of a wider world increased.

8. Plateau people were later emphatic that the prediction of the whites' arrival came entirely from visions, although certainly by 1800 there was plenty of indirect knowledge of whites and their push toward the West. On the Prophet Dance see Leslie Spier, *The Prophet Dance of the Northwest and Its Derivitives: The Source of the Ghost Dance,* General Series in Anthropology, no. 1 (Menasha, Wisc.: George Banta, 1935); David F. Aberle, "The Prophet Dance and Reactions to White Contact," *Southwestern Journal of Anthropology* 15:1 (spring 1959): 74–83.

9. Washington Irving, *Astoria, or Anecdotes of an Enterprise beyond the Rocky Mountains,* ed. Edgeley Todd (Norman: University of Oklahoma Press, 1964), 117–18; Boyd, *Coming of the Spirit of Pestilence,* 113.

10. Elizabeth A. Fenn, "Biological Warfare in Eighteenth-century North America: Beyond Jeffery Amherst," *Journal of American History* 86:4 (March 2000): 1552–80. Whether or not Amherst's suggestion was followed, a subordinate had already sent two blankets and a handkerchief from a smallpox ward to nearby Indians.

11. Clifford M. Drury, *Marcus and Narcissa Whitman and the Opening of Old Oregon* (Glendale, Calif.: Arthur H. Clark, 1973), 2:92.

12. Hazard Stevens, *The Life of Isaac Ingalls Stevens* (Boston: Houghton, Mifflin, 1900), 2:19.

13. *Johnson v. McIntosh*, 21 U.S. 590 (1823).

14. In 1758, the international law philosopher Emer de Vattel had written that because all the earth had to be cultivated to feed its peoples, those who refused the plow, even if otherwise peaceful, had "no reason to complain, if other nations, more industrious," took their lands. Any who both refused to farm and preyed on their neighbors for their needs, he added, "deserve to be extirpated as savage and pernicious beasts." Emer de Vattel, *The Law of Nations; or, Principles of the Law of Nature, Applied to the Conduct and Affairs of Nations and Sovereigns. From the French of Monsieur de Vattel* (Philadelphia: T. and J. W. Johnson, 1883).

15. Isaac Stevens to George Manypenny, December 26, 1853, RG 75, Indian Affairs, M234, Letters Received by Office of Indian Affairs, 1824–81, roll 907: Washington Superintendency, 1853–80, frames 107–13; Stevens to Manypenny, December 29, 1853, frames 119–21, NA.

16. An entire issue of the journal of the Oregon Historical Society is devoted to various aspects of this important series of treaties: *Oregon Historical Quarterly* 106:3 (January 2005).

17. Stevens, either putting a bright face on this or woefully misinterpreting the signals, saw this aloofness as an impressive "haught carriage" straight out of James Fenimore Cooper. Stevens, *Life of Isaac Ingalls Stevens,* 2:38.

18. Ibid., 34–35.

19. Kip Lawrence, *Indian Council in the Valley of the Walla-Walla* (San Francisco: Whitton, Towne, 1855), 17–18.

20. *A True Copy of the Record of the Official Proceedings at the Ccouncil in the Walla Walla Valley, 1855,* ed. Darrell Scott (Fairfield, Wash.: Ye Galleon Press, 1985), 37–43.

21. Ibid., 42.

22. Ibid., 55, 57.

23. Ibid., 72.

24. Ibid., 57, 60.

25. Ibid., 63–64.

26. Ibid., 80, 82.

27. Clifford Drury, "Lawyer, Head Chief of the Nez Perce, 1848–1875," *Idaho Yesterdays* 22:4 (winter 1979): 2–12.

28. YJIV, 417.

29. *True Copy of the Record of the Official Proceedings,* 82–83.

30. Ibid., 89–91.

31. Lawrence, *Indian Council,* 26.

32. The description "short and very violent" is in ibid., 27.

33. *True Copy of the Record of the Official Proceedings,* 98–104.

34. Ibid., 110.

35. Even genuinely heartfelt testimonies of their unbreakable bond with the land occasionally hinted of trying to strike a better deal. In a speech on their intimacy and union with the earth, Young Chief of the Cayuses began "I do not see the offer you have made us yet. If I had the money in my hand then I would see" and ended by imagining God telling Indians not to give up their land "unless you get a fair price." Ibid., 77. It is possible, of course, that Young Chief was speaking sarcastically. Alvin Josephy, however, takes the remarks seriously as an example of "the Indians' sacred belief in their Earth Mother...already twisted by some of the leaders who were trying to adjust to white culture." *NPI*, 325.

36. Palmer had his own simile for the same point: settlers, he said, would come "like grasshoppers on the plains." *True Copy of the Record of the Official Proceedings*, 57, 52.

37. Ibid., 77–87.

38. Lawrence, *Indian Council*, 25.

39. Stevens seems to have applied this common misperception even more to the Plateau. Soon after arriving in Oregon, Stevens had written the commissioner of Indian affairs that Indians east of the Cascades "have much better organization" than those close to the coast and that several of their chiefs "have great authority, not only with their own people, but with the surrounding tribes." Isaac Stevens to George Manypenny, December 29, 1853, frame 115.

40. Stevens, *Life of Isaac Ingalls Stevens*, 2:42. The comparison with the crier is made by Allen P. Slickpoo, Sr., *Noon Nee-Me-Poo (We, the Nez Perces), Culture and History of the Nez Perces* (Lapwai, Idaho: Nez Perce Tribe of Idaho, 1973), 78.

41. Theodore Winthrop, *The Canoe and the Saddle: Adventures Among the Northwestern Rivers and Forests* (Boston: Ticknor and Fields, 1863), 234.

42. *True Copy of the Record of the Official Proceedings*, 80, 82

43. The dramatic account is in Andrew Dominique Pambrun, *Sixty Years on the Frontier in the Pacific Northwest* (Fairfield, Wash.: Ye Galleon Press, 1978), 95. Some serious scholarship has cited Pambrun at face value. See for instance N. Bruce Duthu, *American Indians and the Law* (New York: Viking Press, 2008), xix, and Clifford E. Trafzer and Richard D. Scheuerman, *Renegade Tribe: The Palouse Indians and the Invasion of the Inland Pacific Northwest* (Pullman: Washington State University Press, 1986), 57. Nothing remotely resembling Stevens's public threat is in any other source, however, and the particulars of Pambrun's brief account are at odds with the facts. He refers to one treaty, while there were three. He has all chiefs signing in open council, while only the Nez Perces did so; the Cayuses/Umatillas and the Yakimas had signed their treaties two days earlier after the council had adjourned for the day. Pambrun places Looking Glass's dramatic arrival just after the public treaty signing, but the incident was a few days prior. But Pambrun was at the council (he is listed on the official treaty as interpreter for the Yakimas), and his account may say something about the tone of the gathering and of Kamiakin's mood at its end. The original manuscript is at Whitman College in Walla Walla, Washington.

44. *NPI,* 337–38.

45. For reported particulars of abuses of Indians in this modest gold rush, see John Beeson, A *Plea for the Indians; With Facts and Features of the Late War in Oregon* (New York: J. Beeson, 1857).

46. Ibid., 357.

47. Hubert Howe Bancroft, *The Works of Hubert Howe Bancroft, vol. 31, History of Washington, Idaho, and Montana, 1845–1889* (San Francisco: History Company, 1890), 141 n.

48. "Joint Resolutions, Relative to Citizens and Settlers in Walla-Walla County Being Driven from Their Homes and Claims by the Military Authority of Washington Territory," in *Message of the President of the United States to the Two Houses of Congress at the Commencement of the Second Session of the Thirty-fifth Congress: December 6, 1858,* S.Exec.Doc. 1, pt. 2, 35th Cong., 2nd sess., Serial Set 975, 2:341–42.

49. On this stage of the conflict, see Jack Dozier, "The Coeur d'Alene Indians in the War of 1858," *Idaho Yesterdays* 5 (fall 1961): 22–32.

50. *Message of the President of the United States, December 6, 1858,* S.Exec. Doc. 1, pt. 2, 35th Cong., 2nd sess., Serial Set 975, 2:346–48.

51. Ibid., 386–94.

52. Ibid., 400.

53. Ibid., 403–4.

54. D. W. Meinig, *The Great Columbia Plain: A Historical Geography* (Seattle: University of Washington Press, 1968), 156–57; Robert Selden Garnett to R. M. T. Hunter, April 20, 1856, in Charles Henry Ambler, ed., *Correspondence of Robert M. T. Hunter, 1826–1876. Annual Report of the American Historical Association, 1916,* 2:188–89.

## Chapter 5

1. Dr. Ralph Burcham, ed., "Orofino Gold!" *Idaho Yesterdays* 4 (fall 1960): 8.

2. News accounts are reprinted in "Gold in 1860: Newspaper Reports of the Pierce Gold Strike," *Idaho Yesterdays* 3 (fall 1959): 14–15, 18–19.

3. Ibid., 15.

4. "News from the Nez Perce Mines," *Idaho Yesterdays* 3 (winter 1959–60): 19–22.

5. Ibid., 23, 25.

6. "Clearwater Gold Rush," *Idaho Yesterdays* 4 (spring 1960): 12, 14.

7. Miller, "Letters from the Upper Columbia," 14–20.

8. Hubert Howe Bancroft, *The Works of Hubert Howe Bancroft, vol. 31, History of Washington, Idaho, and Montana, 1845–1889* (San Francisco: History Company, 1890), 239.

9. "The Salmon River Mines," *Idaho Yesterdays* 6 (spring 1962): 40–48; "Fabulous Florence!" *Idaho Yesterdays* 6 (summer 1962): 22–31; William S. Greever, *The Bonanza West: The Story of the Western Mining Rushes, 1848–1900* (Norman: University of Oklahoma Press, 1963), 259–61; Bancroft, *Works,* 31: 240–41.

10. Miller, "Letters from the Upper Columbia," 15–16.

11. "Gold in 1860," 19.

12. Dennis Baird, Diane Mallickan, and W. R. Swagerty, eds., *The Nez Perce Nation Divided: Firsthand Accounts of Events Leading to the 1863 Treaty* (Moscow: University of Idaho Press, 2002), 38–39, 43–44. This superb gathering of material from official records and contemporary newspapers and other material is an invaluable resource on the critical period between the treaties of 1855 and 1863 and on the making of the second treaty. Much of the material cited here is in this collection. Where I have had access to the original sources I have cited them.

13. Burcham, "Orofino Gold," 9.

14. Baird et al., *Nez Perce Nation Divided*, 49–51.

15. Ibid., 52–53, 55–58, 70.

16. Ibid., 72; Miller, "Letters from the Upper Columbia," 19.

17. Baird et al., *Nez Perce Nation Divided*, 108, 110, 115, 124–25, 128, 136.

18. Ibid., 86, 107.

19. A. J. Cain to Edward R. Geary, December 29, 1860, RG 75, Indian Affairs, M234, Letters Received by Office of Indian Affairs, Oregon Superintendency, 1842–80, microfilm, roll 612, frame 854, NA.

20. Baird et al., *Nez Perce Nation Divided*, 72; Miller, "Letters from the Upper Columbia," 19.

21. Baird et al., *Nez Perce Nation Divided*, 143–44.

22. Ibid., 141–43.

23. Ibid., 56.

24. On Smohalla and his religion, see Robert H. Ruby and John A. Brown, *Dreamer-prophets of the Columbia Plateau: Smohalla and Skolaskin* (Norman: University of Oklahoma Press, 1989); Click Relander, *Drummers and Dreamers* (Seattle: Northwest Interpretive Center, 1986); James Mooney, *The Ghost-Religion and the Sioux Outbreak of 1890, Fourteenth Annual Report of the Bureau of Ethnology to the Secretary of the Smithsonian Institution, 1892–93*, pt. 2 (Washington, D.C.: Government Printing Office, 1896), 708–45; Deward E. Walker, Jr., and Helen H. Schuster, "Religious Movement," in *Plateau: Handbook of North American Indians,* ed. William C. Sturtevant (Washington, D.C.: Smithsonian Institution, 1998), 501–7. Smohalla was sometimes also called Yuyunipitqana (the Shouting Mountain) by his followers, and by whites Big Talk on Four Mountains. Ruby and Brown, *Dreamer-Prophets,* 19.

25. Ruby and Brown, *Dreamer-Prophets,* 213.

26. Ibid., 31–32.

27. E. L. Huggins, "Smohalla, the Prophet of Priest Rapids," *Overland Monthly and Out West Magazine* 17:98 (February 1891): 213.

28. Ibid., 209.

29. R. David Edmunds, *The Shawnee Prophet* (Lincoln: University of Nebraska Press, 1983), 38.

30. Vittorio Lanternari, *The Religions of the Oppressed: A Study of Modern Messianic Cults* (New York: Knopf, 1963), 238–42, 288–91.

31. Deward E. Walker, Jr., *Conflict and Schism in Nez Perce Acculturation: A Study of Religion and Politics* (Pullman: Washington State University Press, 1968), 34–35.

32. The two prophets, according to later informants, were tuhulkulcut and wiskaynatonmay. The latter was especially influential, and the rituals described were attributed to her. Walker, *Conflict and Schism,* 49–51.

33. Huggins, "Smohalla, the Prophet of Priest Rapids," 212.

34. "Fallacies of History: No Messiah for the Nez Perces," box 8, folder 40, McW.

35. *HM,* 86.

36. E. Giddings, "Report of Surveyor General," *Message of the President of the United States to the Two Houses of Congress at the Commencement of the Third Session of the Thirty Seventh Congress. December 1, 1862,* H.Exec.Doc. 1, pt. 2, 37th Cong., 3rd sess., Serial Set 1158, 3, 167. The numbers are from the vaguely defined Nez Perce and Idaho counties, covering the upper and lower Nez Perce areas, respectively. The census of 1860 set the population of Washington Territory at twelve thousand.

37. Ibid., 163–66, 432.

38. Baird et al., *Nez Perce Nation Divided,* 194.

39. Ibid., 221, 222, 284.

40. Ibid., 154; Giddings, "Report of Surveyor General," 164.

41. Baird et al., *Nez Perce Nation Divided,* 193, 220, 255, 284.

42. Ibid., 159.

43. Ibid., 189; Charles Hutchins, Report, Nez Perce Indian Agency, June 30, 1862, in Report of the Secretary of the Interior, in *Message of the President of the United States, December 1, 1862,* 2:567.

44. Ibid.; Baird et al., *Nez Perce Nation Divided,* 163.

45. "Report of the Commissioner of Indian Affairs," in *Message of the President of the United States, December 1, 1862,* 2:447.

46. Ibid., 132, 142.

47. *The War of the Rebellion: A Compilation of the Official Records of the Union and Confederate Armies,* ser. 1, vol. 50, pt. 2 (Washington, D.C.: Government Printing Office, 1897), 206–8.

48. Baird et al., *Nez Perce Nation Divided,* 213.

49. Richard White, "Frederick Jackson Turner and Buffalo Bill," in James R. Grossman, ed., *The Frontier in American Culture: Essays By Richard White and Patricia Nelson Limerick* (Chicago: Newberry Library, 1994), 27.

50. The statements and quotations that follow are from Nesmith's remarks, *Congressional Globe,* 37th Cong., 2nd sess., 2095–96.

51. C. H. Hale to Wm. P. Dole, May 22, 1863, RG 75, Indian Affairs, M234, Letters Received by Office of Indian Affairs, Washington Superintendency, 1863–64, microfilm, roll 908, frame 320, NA.

52. C. H. Hale to Wm. P. Dole, May 11, May 22, 1863, roll 908.

53. "Documents Relating to the Negotiation of the Treaty of June 9, 1863, with the Nez Perce Indians," Documents Relating to the Negotiations of Ratified and Non-ratified Treaties with Various Indian Tribes, 1801–69,

RG 75, T494, roll 6, frame 663, NA. There is at least one strong suggestion that those favoring a new treaty, even those who knew better, recognized the need to insist on tribal coherence and to deny the autonomy of bands. During the discussion in the Senate, after Nesmith called for funds for a new treaty, he was questioned by his colleague from Iowa, James W. Grimes:

**Mr. Grimes:**   Is there more than one band of these Indians?
**Mr. Nesmith:**  There is but one tribe.
**Mr. Grimes:**   Will it be necessary to hold more than one treaty [council] to accomplish this purpose?
**Mr. Nesmith:**  They would have to be assembled at some point on the reservation, and be subsisted during the time the council was held. There is but one tribe proper of them, but they are separated in different localities.

Nesmith was sliding past Grimes's question. He had lived in Oregon for twenty years and for two years had served as Indian superintendent of Oregon and Washington. It is inconceivable that he was ignorant of the bands' autonomy and their factional divisions. *Congressional Globe,* May 13, 1862, vol. 32, part 3, 27th Cong., 2nd sess., 2096.

54. "Documents Relating to the Negotiations," frames 671–702. While Lawyer took the lead in these positions, he was not the only one making the points. Ute-si-mil-e-kum said the same: "The boundary [of 1855] was fixed, the law was fixed....We cannot give up our country. You but trifle with us" (frame 694).

55. Baird et al., *Nez Perce Nation Divided,* 342; "Documents Relating to the Negotiation," frames 681, 696–98.

56. "Documents Relating to the Negotiation," frames 708–10.

57. C. H. Hale to [William P. Dole], June 30, 1863, ibid., frames 749–51.

58. Ibid., frame 751.

59. Baird et al., *Nez Perce Nation Divided,* 382–84.

60. "Documents Relating to the Negotiation," frames 714–15.

61. Ibid., frames 717–18.

62. Ibid., frames 720–22.

63. Baird et al., *Nez Perce Nation Divided,* 375.

64. Ibid., 383.

65. Bruce Hampton, *Children of Grace: The Nez Perce War of 1877* (New York: Avon Books, 1994), 32.

## Chapter 6

1. *Condition of the Indian Tribes. Report of the Joint Special Committee, Appointed Under Joint Resolution of March 3, 1865, With an Appendix March 3, 1865,* S.Rpt. 156, 39th Cong., 2nd sess., Serial Set 1279, 1:10, 12.

2. "Grievances of the Nez Perces. Speeches of Shadow of the Mountain, or Lawyer (Head Chief), and Gov. Lyon, at Lewiston, Idaho Territory, August 23rd, 1864," broadside, BL.

3. John Monteith to Commissioner of Indian Affairs, February 14, 1874, John B. Monteith Letterbook, NPHP.

4. Annual Report of the Nez Perce Agency," in *Annual Report of the Commissioner of Indian Affairs to the Secretary of the Interior, for the Year 1875* (Washington, D.C.: Government Printing Office, 1875), 260–61; "Report of the Commissioner of Indian Affairs," in *Annual Report of the Commissioner of Indian Affairs to the Secretary of the Interior, for the year 1874 (Washington, D. C.:* Government Printing Office, 1874), 54–55; "Annual Report of the Nez Perce Agency," in *Annual Report of the Commissioner of Indian Affairs, for the year 1875,* 245–46.

5. Deward E. Walker, Jr., *Conflict and Schism in Nez Perce Acculturation: A Study of Religion and Politics* (Moscow: University of Idaho Press, 1985), 52–53; Robert R. McCoy, *Chief Joseph, Yellow Wolf, and the Creation of Nez Perce History in the Pacific Northwest* (London: Routledge, 2004), 165–66.

6. The scholar who has most closely studied this period of conversions points out that it was probably no coincidence that the sharpest spikes in Roman Catholic conversions came in the two years of greatest stress and turbulence, 1872 and 1877. Walker, *Conflict and Schism,* 49, 53.

7. Francis Paul Prucha, *The Great Father: The United States Government and American Indians* (Lincoln: University of Nebraska Press, 1984), 1:485–89.

8. *Report of the Indian Peace Commissioners. Message From the President of the United States, Transmitting Report of the Indian Peace Commissioners, January 14, 1868,* H.Exec.Doc. 97, 40th Cong., 2nd sess., Serial Set 1337, 11:16.

9. Ibid., 4.

10. *Report of the Secretary of the Interior,* November 15, 1869, H.Exec. Doc. 1, pt. 3, 41st Cong., 2nd sess., Serial Set 1414, 3:vii; "Report of the Commissioner of Indian Affairs," in *Message from the President of the United States to the Two Houses of Congress, At the Commencement of the Third Session of the thirty-Fourth Congress. December 18, 1856,* H.Exec.Doc. 1, pt. 1, 34th Cong., 3rd sess., Serial Set 893, 1:574.

11. "Report of the Commissioner of Indian Affairs," in *Message of the President of the United States, to the Two Houses of Congress, at the Commencement of the Second Session of the Thirty-first Congress. December 2, 1850,* H.Exec.Doc. 1, 31st Cong., 2nd sess., Serial Set 587, 1:35–36.

12. *Report of the Secretary of the Interior, 1869,* H.Exec.Doc. 1, pt. 3, 41st Cong., 2nd sess., Serial Set 1414, 3:viii.

13. Prucha, *Great Father,* 1:492.

14. Ibid., 485–86.

15. Quoted in Francis Paul Prucha, *American Indian Policy in the Formative Years: The Indian Trade and Intercourse Acts, 1790–1834* (Lincoln: University of Nebraska Press, 1962), 220–21.

16. Robert F. Berkhofer, Jr., *Salvation and the Savage: An Analysis of Protestant Missions and American Indian Response, 1787–1862* (New York: Atheneum, 1972), 9; Robert H. Keller, *American Protestantism and United States Indian Policy, 1869–82* (Lincoln: University of Nebraska Press, 1983), 156, 159.

17. Linda K. Kerber, "The Abolitionist Perception of the Indian," *Journal of American History* 62:2 (September 1975): 277–78.

18. Ibid., 286.

19. "Report of Board of Indian Commissioners," in *Report of Secretary of the Interior, 1869,* 3:429.

20. For the distribution of agencies by denomination, see *Report of the Secretary of the Interior, 1872,* H.Exec.Doc. 1, pt. 1, vol. 1, 42nd Cong., 3rd sess., Serial Set 1560, 3:462–63.

21. *Red Man* 10:6 (July–August 1890).

22. The quotation is from Charles Robinson, head of a leading Indian boarding school, Haskell Institute. *Report of Secretary of the Interior, 1889,* H.Exec. Doc. 1, pt. 5, vol. 2, 50th Cong., 2nd sess., Serial Set 2637, 11:262.

23. *Report of the Secretary of the Interior, 1890,* H.Exec.Doc. 1, pt. 5, vol. 2, 51st Cong., 1st sess., Serial Set 2725, 12:96.

24. "Report of Lieutenant General W. T. Sherman," in *Message of the President of the United States and Accompanying Documents, to the Two Houses of Congress at the Commencement of the Third Session of the Fortieth Congress,* H.Exec.Doc. 1, pt. 3, 40th Cong., 3rd sess., Serial Set 1367, 3:8.

25. See *HM,* 177–87, for summaries of these bands at the time of the outbreak of war.

26. Camille Williams questionnaire, box 7, folder 34, McW.

27. *Message from the President of the United States to the Two Houses of Congress, at the Commencement of the First Session of the Twenty-eighth Congress. December 5, 1848,* Sen. Doc.1, 28th Cong., 1st sess., Serial Set 431, 1:461.

28. YJIV, 418.

29. Quoted in *NPI,* 447.

30. For firsthand accounts of these first settlers, see John Harland Horner, "The Horner Papers," unpublished manuscript, 49–59, Enterprise City Library, Enterprise, Oregon.

31. YJIV, 419.

32. Ibid.

33. *Report of Governor Grover to General Schofield on the Modoc War, and Reports of Maj. Gen. John F. Miller and General John E. Ross, to the Governor. Also Letter of the Governor to the Secretary of the Interior on the Wallowa Valley Indian Question* (Salem, Ore.: Marat V. Brown, State Printer, 1874), 66 (italics in original).

34. Ibid., 66.

35. Ibid., 63, 65.

36. On Howard, see William S. McFeely, *Yankee Stepfather: General O. O. Howard and the Freedmen* (New Haven, Conn.: Yale University Press, 1868), and John A. Carpenter, *Sword and Olive Branch: Oliver Otis Howard* (Pittsburgh: University of Pittsburgh Press, 1964).

37. *Report of the Secretary of War, 1875,* H.Exec.Doc. 1, pt. 2, vol. 1, 44th Cong., 1st sess., Serial Set 1674, 2:126, 128–29.

38. *The Status of Young Joseph and His Band of Nez-Perce Indians under the Treaties of the United States and the Nez Perce Tribe of Indians and the*

*Indian Title to Land* (Portland, Ore.: Assistant Adjutant General's Office, Department of the Columbia, 1876).

39. Ibid., 23–29.

40. Ibid., 40–41.

41. Ibid., 61–63.

42. Ibid., 45–46.

43. H. R. Findley to Lucullus McWhorter, February 18, 1935, box 6, folder 32, item 95, McW.

44. *NPI;* Horner, "Horner Papers," 69–72. Wood's report is reprinted in part in *HM,* 127–29.

45. Interview with Yellow Bull, February 13, 1915, WCP.

46. YJIV, 420.

47. The account of Findley hosting the widow is from his son-in-law. *HM,* 130–31.

48. John Monteith to Commissioner of Indian Affairs, November 19, 1872, John Monteith letterbook, NPHP.

49. George Crook, *General George Crook: His Autobiography,* ed. Martin F. Schmitt (Norman: University of Oklahoma Press, 1960), 169.

50. Letter of Frances Monteith to McWhorter, in *HM,* 146–47.

51. For the official account of this important meeting, see "Report of Civil and Military Commission to Nez Perce Indians," in *Report of the Secretary of the Interior, 1876,* H.Exec.Doc. 1, pt. 5, vol. 1, 45th Cong., 2nd sess., Serial Set 1800, 8:607–13.

52. Ibid., 607.

53. Ibid., 608–9.

54. Ibid., 609.

55. War Singer (Camille Williams) remembered that the commissioners "seemed to go against Chief Joseph and his following because of their religion." *HM,* 147.

56. *SW,* 116 (italics in original).

57. Jno. B. Monteith to J. O. Smith [Commissioner of Indian Affairs], copy, March 19, 1877, ser. M91, OOH.

58. Jno. B. Monteith to Oliver Howard, March 19, 1877, ser. M91, OOH; *SW,* 590.

59. Ibid., 115.

60. *NPJ,* 52–53.

61. Ibid., 58–59; *SW,* 593.

62. Linwood Laughy, comp., *In Pursuit of the Nez Perces: The Nez Perce War of 1877* (Wrangell, Alaska: Mountain Meadows Press, 1993), 231–32.

63. YJIV, 419–20.

64. *NPJ,* 59. Howard has a less specific answer to the same effect in *SW,* 594. Joseph similarly had rejected the old rhetorical trope of the Great Father and his Indian children. When the commissioners had said they had come "by the Great Father's orders," he answered that he "asked nothing of the President. He could take care of himself." "Report of Civil and Military Commission to Nez Perce Indians," 608.

65. Laughy, *In Pursuit of the Nez Perces,* 232.

66. "Report of Civil and Military Commission to the Nez Perce Indians," 608 (italics in original).

67. *SW,* 594–95.

68. S. L. Many Wounds to L. V. McWhorter, November 3, 1934, box 12, folder 84, McW. In his account of the war, Yellow Wolf recalled Toohoolhoolzote's words as "I hear you! I have *simiakia* [penis], that which belongs to a man! I am a man, and will not go!" *YW,* 40.

69. John Monteith to Jerome, November 13, 1876, John Monteith letterbook, NPHP.

70. O. O. Howard to "Dear Brother," May 22, 1877, ser. M91, OOH; *SW,* 595.

71. *YW,* 41. Duncan McDonald wrote: "if I have been rightly informed," the fighting came close to beginning there, and "Howard...came near to being a victim at the hands of the Nez Perce warriors." Other Nez Perce testimony agrees that the threat of force was in effect the beginning of the conflict. First Red Feather of the Wing said that when Howard threatened to compel the bands to come in by force, "there was where the war commenced—was declared by General Howard!" Laughly, *In Pursuit of the Nez Perces,* 232; First Red Feather of the Wing narrative, box 6, folder 32, McW.

72. Laughy, *In Pursuit of the Nez Perces,* 233–34.

73. *NPI,* 499.

## Chapter 7

1. *HM,* 177–87.

2. My thanks to Jerome Greene for his help in estimating these numbers; personal correspondence, July 27, 2004. Yellow Bull, who was one of White Bird's band, much later estimated the number of fighting men, including Looking Glass's band, at 270, including 42 experienced warriors. Interview, Yellow Bull, February 13, 1915, WCP.

3. The first dispatch of alarm to Fort Lapwai from Mount Idaho reported the parade and added that about a hundred well-armed men "went through the manoeuvres of a fight." There is no evidence otherwise of maneuvers. John D. McDermott, *Forlorn Hope: The Battle of White Bird Canyon and the Beginning of the Nez Perce War* (Boise: Idaho State Historical Society, 1978), 49.

4. *HM,* 189–91; First Red Feather of the Wing Narrative, box 6, folder 32, McW.

5. The most thorough account of the raids of June 14 and 15 is McDermott, *Forlorn Hope,* 188–230.

6. *HM,* 209–10.

7. Ibid., 202.

8. Ibid., 209–13; McDermott, *Forlorn Hope,* 17–19.

9. Ibid., 15–19.

10. *HM,* 213–15; Interview with Mrs. W. W. Bowman (Margaret Manuel), February 12, 1915, WMC.

11. On the Norton-Chamberlain incident, see McDermott, *Forlorn Hope,* 27–34; *HM,* 218–26; "Hill Beachey Norton Speaks out of the Past," in Norman B. Atkison, *Nez Perce Indian War and Original Stories* (Grangeville: Idaho County Free Press, 1966), 38–39; Luther Wilmot, "Nez Perce Campaign—1877," Big Hole Battlefield National Monument Library, Wisdom, Montana.

12. Lieutenant Charles E. S. Wood apparently was referring to the soldiers' discovery in his journal entry for June 27: "the man of 14 days gooseberry shit celebrity." Charles E. S. Wood, "Diary on Nez Perce Campaign," folder 1, box 26, Charles Erskine Scott Wood Papers, HL.

13. *HM,* 226.

14. The Nez Perces obtained alcohol from two places: James Benedict's store, late on the afternoon of June 14 and the freight wagon of Lew Wilmot and George Ready, early on June 15. If the men who attacked the Norton party were fueled by Benedict's whiskey, they would have had to ride from the camp at Tepahlewam southward to White Bird Creek, attack first the Manuels and then the Benedicts, drink from the whiskey barrels, then ride back northward to and beyond where they had started, about fifteen miles while drunk in the saddle, before locating and attacking the fleeing party. The scenario is highly unlikely and probably impossible. Instead, those who attacked the Nortons and Chamberlains almost certainly were from another group that had not gone south from Tepahlewam but north onto the Camas Prairie, where they shot Lew Day along the stage road and later found and attacked the Nortons and Chamberlains along the same route. These raiders would likely have been the ones who relieved the freight wagon of its intoxicants, and in fact McWhorter specifies that the perpetrators of the "ghastly outrage" got their liquor there. The attack on Wilmot and Ready and their liquor-laden wagon, however, came on the morning of June 15, hours *after* the assault on the Norton-Chamberlain party.

15. McDermott, *Forlorn Hope,* 40–41; Helen Brown Adkison, "Inside Mount Idaho Fort," in Adkison, *Nez Perce War and Original Stories,* 44, 49.

16. Michael McCarthy diary, June 13–14, 1877, Michael McCarthy Papers, Library of Congress.

17. All three dispatches were from L. P. Brown. McDermott, *Forlorn Hope,* 49.

18. For the battle at White Bird, I have relied mostly on by far the most thoroughly researched account, McDermott, *Forlorn Hope.* Other overviews are Jerome A. Greene, *Nez Perce Summer, 1877: The U.S. Army and the Nee-Me-Poo Crisis* (Helena: Montana Historical Society Press, 2000), 34–44; *HM,* 230–61; W. R. Parnell, "The Battle of White Bird Canon," and David Perry, "The Battle of White Bird Canon, Continued," in Cyrus Townsend Brady, *Northwestern Fights and Fighters* (Williamstown, Mass.: Corner House, 1974), 90–111, 112–22.

19. In August, Howard's aide, Henry Clay Wood, compiled a report on civilian losses. He found a mixed situation, with some places virtually untouched, some houses plundered but otherwise undamaged, some totally

ransacked and burned, with the fences torn down so surviving livestock might ravage the gardens. "Portland, Oregon, August 28, 1877. Report of Indian Depredations in Idaho Territory," copy in Jerome Greene Research Papers, box 5, folder 3, NPHP.

20. Perry, "White Bird Canon," 113.

21. McCarthy diary, June 16, 1877.

22. William Coram interview, item 6, Robert S. Ellison Papers, Western History Collection, Denver Public Library; McDermott, *Forlorn Hope,* 79–80; John P. Schorr, "The White Bird Fight," in Peter Cozzens, ed., *Eyewitnesses to the Indian Wars, 1865–1890: The Wars of the Pacific Northwest* (Mechanicsburg, Pa.: Stackpole Books, 2002), 357–58.

23. War Singer questionnaire, November 13, 1942, box 14, folder 104, McW.

24. *SW,* 120; O. O. Howard, *My Life and Experiences among Our Hostile Indians* (Hartford, Conn.: A. D. Worthington, 1907), 285; *HM,* 251; McDermott, *Forlorn Hope,* 82.

25. *HM,* 243–44.

26. In his court of inquiry afterward, Perry noted that in battle a cavalry command without a trumpet was "like a ship at sea without a helm perfectly unmanageable." McDermott, *Forlorn Hope,* 198. By coincidence, this trumpeter, the first army death of the war, had been in the guardhouse at Lapwai when Howard had arrested Toohoolhoolzote, and the two had become "quite friendly and 'chummy.'" Schorr, "White Bird Fight," 356.

27. T. D. Swarts, "The Battle of White Bird Canyon," item 6, Ellison Papers; F. A. Fenn to W. H. Camp, September 19, 1915, WCP.

28. David B. Ousterhout statement, box 10, folder 66, McW.

29. *HM,* 249.

30. Frank Fenn, "The Fight at White Bird Canyon, 1877," in Jerome A. Greene, ed., *Indian War Veterans: Memories of Army Life and Campaigns in the West, 1864–1898* (New York: Savas Beatie, 2006), 263.

31. Frank L. Powers to Walter Camp, November 24, 1913, letter 49, Ellison Papers.

32. Ibid., 265; McDermott, *Forlorn Hope,* 90–94, 101–4; *YW,* 58–61; McCarthy diary, June 16, 1877.

33. Parnell, "Battle of White Bird Canon," 106.

34. *YW,* 56, 56 n.; McDermott, *Forlorn Hope,* 82.

35. McDermott, *Forlorn Hope,* 109.

36. William Coram interview, item 6, Ellison Papers; *HM,* 240–41.

## Chapter 8

1. *SW,* 120.

2. Stephen Perry Jocelyn, *Mostly Alkali: A Biography* (Caldwell, Idaho: Caxton Printers, 1953), 240.

3. P. S. Bomus to Asher Robbins Eddy, December 20, 1877, Mss. FD 291, Fort Dalles Collection, HL.

4. Roy Morris, Jr., *Ambrose Bierce: Alone in Bad Company* (New York: Crown, 1995), 84.

5. Howard was in correspondence with both William Sherman and the solicitor of the treasury in attempts to resolve the issue: William T. Sherman to O. O. Howard, January 20, 1878, K. Rayner to O. O. Howard, January 23, 1878, ser. M91, OOH.

6. Emily McCorkle FitzGerald, *An Army Doctor's Wife on the Frontier: The Letters of Emily McCorkle FitzGerald from Alaska and the Far West, 1874–1878* (Lincoln: University of Nebraska Press, 1962), 263, 266.

7. Charles E. S. Wood, "Diary on Nez Perce Campaign," June 20, 21, 23, 1877, box 26, folder 1, Charles Erskine Scott Wood Papers, HL.

8. Ibid., June 27, 1877. See also "Nez Perce War Diary—1877 of Private Frederick Mayer," entry for June 29, 1877, in *Seventeenth Biennial Report of the Board of Trustees of the Idaho Historical Society* (Boise: Idaho State Historical Society, 1940), 28. Despite Wood's reference, most who wrote on the scene, including Howard, agreed there was no mutilation of corpses. The decay was so great that when the bodies were moved, the scalps and skins, adhering to the ground, came off, giving the appearance of mutilation, which "caused the circulation of the rumor." Jocelyn, *Mostly Alkali,* 227.

9. Wood, "Diary," June 28, 1877.

10. *HM,* 277.

11. Wood, "Diary," June 28, 1877.

12. *Portland (OR) Daily Standard,* July 16, 1877; W. R. Parnell, "The Salmon River Expedition," in Cyrus Townsend Brady, *Northwestern Fights and Fighters* (Williamstown, Mass.: Corner House, 1974), 128; 'Dead Mule Trail," *Harper's Weekly,* September 29, 1877, 763.

13. *SW,* 120–21.

14. The journalist Thomas Sutherland was with Howard during much of the campaign. His dispatches were published in the *Portland (OR) Daily Standard.* The year after the war, he published his account of events, putting Howard in an extremely, sometimes bizarrely, positive light. Here, for instance, he wrote that Howard "drove the Indians from mountain fastnesses" in a bold campaign that "cannot otherwise than be called wise and successful." Thomas A. Sutherland, *Howard's Campaign against the Nez Perce Indians, 1878* [*sic*] (Portland, Ore.: A. G. Walling, 1878). The fact that the year of the war is incorrect in the title of Sutherland's account is a hint of the reliability of what is inside it.

15. For Howard's claim that forty "bucks" had left Looking Glass's band to join the fight, see *Advance,* September 19, 1878.

16. Linwood Laughy, *In Pursuit of the Nez Perces: The Nez Perce War of 1877* (Wrangell, Alaska: Mountain Meadows Press, 1993), 234.

17. *HM,* 264–67.

18. A private under Whipple estimated the number of horses as much greater: fifteen hundred. "Nez Perce War Diary—1877 of Private Frederick Mayer," entry for July 1, 1877, 28.

19. *HM,* 284–85. *YW,* 73–74.

20. "Nez Perce War Diary—1877 of Private Frederick Mayer," July 3, 1877, 28–29. Frank Fenn, a civilian volunteer prominent in the Idaho fighting, later claimed that Rains was "needlessly sacrificed" because Whipple was in a strong position to come to his aid but failed to do so. F. A. Fenn to W. C. Brown, May 11, 1927, W. C. Brown Papers, Western History Collections, Norlin Library, University of Colorado, Boulder, Colorado.

21. *HM,* 287–93; *Idaho Statesman,* July 12, 1877.

22. The seventeen involved are listed in J. G. Royton to Walter Camp, April 9, 1911, WCP. An account of the fight that followed by one of the participants is Luther P. Wilmot, "Narratives of the Nez Perce War," copy, box 5, folder 1, Jerome Greene Collection, NPHP.

23. A civilian with Randall wrote later that the sergeant did in fact go in support of the seventeen, followed by some of the troops, and that Perry then ordered a party to follow, and then afterward arrested the sergeant, who was never tried. F. A. Fenn to Mr. Parker, March 9, 1927, box 12, folder 2, W. C. Brown Papers, Western History Collections, Norlin Library.

24. George M. Shearer to Maj. E. C. Mason, July 28, 1877, copy, box 5, folder 3, Jerome Greene Collection, NPHP.

25. M. McCarthy to Redington, June 14, 1905, copy, box 6, folder 32, item 118, McW.

26. Luther Wilmot, "Nez Perce Campaign—1877," Big Hole Battlefield National Monument Library, Wisdom, Montana.

27. Robert M. Utley, *Frontier Regulars: The United States Army and the Indian, 1866–1891* (Lincoln: University of Nebraska Press, 1973), 15–16.

28. *The Reorganization of the Army. A Report of the Sub-committee of the Committee on Military Affairs Relating to the Reorganization of the Army. March 21, 1878,* H.Misc.Doc. 56, 45th Cong., 2nd sess., Serial Set 1818, 4, 244–46.

29. Don Rickey, Jr., *Forty Miles a Day on Beans and Hay: The Enlisted Soldier Fighting the Indian Wars* (Norman: University of Oklahoma Press, 1963), 17, 126–27.

30. Calculated from Aubrey L. Haines, *An Elusive Victory: The Battle of the Big Hole* (West Glacier, Mont.: Glacier Natural History Association, 1991), app. C, "Soldiers," 155–58.

31. *Report of the Secretary of War, 1883,* H.Exec.Doc., pt. 2, vol. 1, 42nd Cong., 2nd sess., Serial Set 2091, 2:5; Col. F. F. Flynt, in *Reorganization of the Army,* 122.

32. Albert Sully to Sophie, July 11, 1877, box 1, folder 27, Albert Sully Papers, BL.

33. J. W. Redington, "Scouting in Montana in the 1870s," *Frontier* 13:1 (November 1932): 67.

34. John D. McDermott, "Were They Really Rogues? Desertion in the Nineteenth-Century U.S. Army," *Nebraska History* 78:4 (1997): 170.

35. John D. McDermott, "No Small Potatoes: Problems of Food and Health at Fort Laramie, 1849–1859," *Nebraska History* 79:4 (1998): 167.

36. Ibid., 168.

37. Carla Kelly, "'The Buffalo Carcass on the Company Sink': Sanitation at a Frontier Army Fort," *North Dakota History* 62:2–4 (2002): 50, 55.

38. James N. Leiker, "Voices from a Disease Frontier: Kansans and Cholera," *Kansas History* 17:4 (winter 1994–95): 236–53.

39. James E. Potter, "'He Regretted to Have to Die That Way': Firearms Accidents in the Frontier Army, 1806–1891," *Nebraska History* 78:4 (1997): 177, 182.

40. *A Report of Surgical Cases Treated in the Army of the United States from 1865 to 1871,* War Department, Surgeon General's Office, circular no. 3 (Washington: Government Printing Office, 1871), 216–17.

41. *Reorganization of the Army,* 246; Rickey, *Forty Miles a Day,* 99–103.

42. McDermott, "Were They Really Rogues," 166, 171–72; *SW,* vii.

43. Rickey, *Forty Miles a Day,* 131.

44. Lieutenant James H. Bradley, *The March of the Montana Column: A Prelude to the Custer Disaster,* ed. Edgar I. Stewart (Norman: University of Oklahoma Press, 1961), 121; Michael McCarthy diary, May 6, 1877, Michael McCarthy Papers, Library of Congress.

45. *SW,* 593–94.

46. Maj. C. P. Hancock to Oliver O. Howard, September 2, 1877, Maria Hancock to Oliver O. Howard, September 9, 1877, C. P. Hancock to Oliver O. Howard, October 24, 1877, ser. M91, OOH.

47. Rickey, *Forty Miles a Day,* 186–91.

48. Abram B. Brant to Charles H. Dawsey, January 10, 1877 [1878], copy, folder 285, National Archives Non-accessioned Materials, White Swan Library, Little Big Horn National Monument. For another tribute to another "bunky" killed in the same battle, see S. Roy to W. M. Camp, July 10, 1911, WCP.

## Chapter 9

1. *HM,* 294–97; *YW,* 78–79; Camille Williams questionnaire, box 7, folder 34, McW; Luther Wilmot, "Nez Perce Campaign—1877," Big Hole Battlefield National Monument Library, Wisdom, Montana; Ed McConville to Governor Brayman, August 1877, in Eugene B. Chaffee, "Letters of the Nez Perce War to Governor Mason Brayman," in *Fifteenth Annual Report of the Board of Trustees of the State Historical Society of Idaho* (Boise: State Historical Society of Idaho, 1936), 67–68.

2. Lucullus McWhorter, who had nothing good to say about Chapman, wrote that it was he, "badly muddled," who mistakenly led Howard into this difficult spot. Clearly, however, Howard would have realized that by crossing the Clearwater he was putting himself on the opposite side of it from the bands' last known location. He clearly intended to cross—he had written McConville that he would be "down to help him on the other side of the river." Howard wrote that his plan had been to follow Whipple's route to Looking Glass's village and try to get behind the enemy, although

that would also put him across the Clearwater. He probably anticipated that the bands, now that their position was known, would cross the river and was hoping to head them off. *HM,* 297; Ed McConville to Governor Brayman, August 1877, in Chaffee, "Letters of the Nez Perce War," 155.

3. Charles Erskine Scott Wood, "Diary on Nez Perce Campaign," July 11, 1877, box 26, folder 1, and his "Journal of an Expedition against Hostile Nez Perce Indians from Lewiston I. T. to Henry Lake I. T.," box 26, folder 2, both in Charles Erskine Scott Wood Papers, HL; "Colonel Bailey's Story," *HM,* 299–300; *YW,* 85–86.

4. For an excellent recent reevaluation of this important battle, see Jerome A. Greene, "The Army at the Clearwater: Tactical Victory and Strategic Defeat in the Nez Perce War," *Montana* 50:4 (winter 2000): 18–31. The account that follows is taken also from Jerome A. Greene, *Nez Perce Summer 1877: The U.S. Army and the Nee-Me-Poo Crisis* (Helena: Montana Historical Society Press, 2000), 73–96; *NPJ,* 157–70; *SW,* 603–6; *HM,* 294–325; *YW,* 82–95. There is an account by Howard also in *Idaho Tri-Weekly Statesman,* July 17, 1877.

5. C. E. S. Wood to "Old Pins" [Wright P. Edgerson], July 20, 1877, box 1, item 39a, Wood Family Papers, Special Collections, Lewis and Clark College Library, Portland, Oregon.

6. *Portland (OR) Daily Standard,* September 6, 1877, copy, box 4, folder 10, Jerome Greene Collection, NPHP.

7. Michael McCarthy reminiscence, 24, Michael McCarthy Papers, Library of Congress.

8. *HM,* 309–10.

9. Ibid., 314.

10. Ibid., 314, 317.

11. *YW,* 97.

12. Ibid., 322.

13. *SW,* 606.

14. Ibid., 124; W. R. Parnell, "The Salmon River Expedition," in Cyrus Townsend Brady, *Northwestern Fights and Fighters* (Williamstown, Mass.: Corner House, 1974), 132. Sergeant John Schorr later wrote that no one on his side knew how many Indians were killed and injured. John P. Schorr to Lucullus McWhorter, May 20, 1926, box 9, folder 55, McW.

15. *YW,* 91; Stephen Perry Jocelyn, *Mostly Alkali: A Biography* (Caldwell, Idaho: Caxton Printers, 1953), 235.

16. Michael McCarthy reminiscence, 24; *NPJ,* 161.

17. First Red Feather of the Wing Narrative, box 6, folder 32, item 112, McW.

18. *HM,* 319.

19. Ibid., 308–9; *YW,* 99 and 99 n.

20. Edward S. Curtis, *The North American Indian; Being a Series of Volumes Picturing and Describing the Indians of the United States, and Alaska, Written, Illustrated and Published by Edward S. Curtis* (Seattle: E. S. Curtis, 1907–30), 8:22–23.

21. There are innumerable examples. Soon after the battle at White Bird Canyon, Howard wrote that Joseph's success "gives him extraordinary boldness," and later he wrote that Joseph, that "wily enemy," had led his people across the Salmon and back, while at the Cottonwood "Joseph appeared" before Perry. After the Clearwater, "Joseph [was] in full flight westward," but nonetheless "Joseph seems dogged." The trope continued throughout the conflict. Howard to Assistant Adjutant General, June 26, 1877; Howard to Adjutant General, July 5, 1877; A. D. C. Keeler to McDowell, July 12, 1877; Howard to Adjutant General, July 15, 1877, in *SW,* 21–22, 34, 37, 39.

22. *NPJ,* 110–12.

23. C. E. S. Wood, "Chief Joseph, the Nez Perce," *Century* 28:1 (May 1884): 139–40.

24. Soon after the battle, Wood wrote a friend that his eyes had been "ruined" among Alaska's icebergs, presumably referring to snow blindness. He had suffered badly, he wrote, "and I fear weakness and inflammation [*sic*] have become chronic." C. E. S. Wood to "Old Pins" [Wright P. Edgerson], July 20, 1877.

25. Far from being the crafty, determined belligerent in public accounts, Joseph was so reluctant to fight that some feared he would defect and take his people to the reservation. *NPI,* 516.

26. Curtis, *North American Indian,* 8:28.

27. Grostein and Binnard to O. O. Howard, July 26, 1877, copy, box 4, folder 8, Jerome Greene Collection, NPHP.

28. A. D. C. Keeler to McDowell, July 12, 1877; Howard to Adjutant General, July 15, 1877, in *SW,* 37.

29. Howard to Adjutant General, July 14, July 15, 1877; McDowell to Adjutant General, July 14, 1877, *SW,* 39, 41; H. W. Corbett and O. P. Morton to Gen. McCrary and Joseph N. Dolph to President Hayes, copies of telegrams, box 4, folder 8, Jerome Greene Collection, NPHP; Greene, *Nez Perce Summer,* 96. McDowell, while pleased with Howard's work, was not at all happy that he went out of the chain of command and notified the president directly. Skelton to O. O. Howard, July 21, 1877, copy of telegram, box 4, folder 8, Jerome Greene Collection, NPHP.

30. One of Howard's officers defended the decision, writing that it "approached sunset" before they were ready to move, though he later noted that many in the press thought he could have moved ahead with the cavalry, "and they are not alone in that view." Jocelyn, *Mostly Alkali,* 233, 245.

31. *YW,* 103; "Personal Narrative of Wat-tes Kun-nin: Earth Blanket," box 14, folder 104, item 19, McW; *NPJ,* 168.

32. C. E. S. Wood, "Diary on Nez Perce Campaign," July 16, 1877, HL.

33. Luther P. Wilmot, "Narratives of the Nez Perce War," copy, box 5, folder 1, Jerome Greene Collection, NPHP.

34. Thomas Leforge, *Memoirs of a White Crow Indian: As Told by Thomas B. Marquis* (Lincoln: University of Nebraska Press, 1974), 97–98.

35. On this incident, see Donna Sinclair, "They Did Not Go to War," *Columbia* 24 (fall 1998): 24–33.

36. C. E. S. Wood, "Diary," July 19, 1877; C. E. S. Wood to "Old Pins" [Wright P. Edgerson], July 20, 1877.

37. This group had their advocates among the reservation faction. John Monteith wrote that with one possible exception, none had been involved in the fighting, an opinion seconded by James Reuben, a Christian Nez Perce who scouted for Howard and later ministered to the Nez Perce exiles in Indian Territory, and by other nontreaty Nez Perces. Once convinced of their innocence, officials still worried about the wrath of local whites if the group was returned, but after the war Sherman ordered them to be "engrafted" into the Lapwai reservation. In April 1878, bereaved of a woman and small child who had died during the winter, they were released. Led by Red Heart, they made their way to Lapwai. Sinclair, "They Did Not Go to War," 30–33; John B. Monteith to Oliver Howard, December 5, 1877, William Sherman to Oliver Howard, December 12, 1877, ser. M91, OOH.

38. *NPJ*, 167.

## Chapter 10

1. *SW*, 10.

2. According to one rumor, Joseph supposedly had used recent camas-harvesting gatherings at Weippe to inflame other groups and recruit them into an uprising, while another held that seventeen Blackfeet, longtime bitter enemies of the Nez Perces, were sending warriors into the fight. *Idaho Statesman*, July 12, 14, 1877; *San Francisco Chronicle*, August 6, 1877.

3. Stanley R. Davison, "A Century Ago: The Nez Perce and the Tortuous Pursuit," *Montana* 27:4 (October 1977): 7.

4. Charles Erskine Scott Wood, "Journal of an Expedition against Hostile Nez Perce Indians from Lewiston I. T. to Henry Lake I. T.," August 1–August 6, 1877, box 26, folder 2, Charles Erskine Scott Wood Papers, HL.

5. Stephen Perry Jocelyn, *Mostly Alkali: A Biography* (Caldwell, Idaho: Caxton Printers, 1953), 144.

6. Henry Buck, "The Story of the Nez Perce Indian Campaign of 1877," SC 492, Montana Historical Society, Helena.

7. Gilbert Drake Harlan, ed., "The Diary of Wilson Barber Harlan— Farming in the Bitterroot and the Fiasco at 'Fort Fizzle,'" *Journal of the West* 3:4 (October 1964): 504.

8. Linwood Laughy, comp., *In Pursuit of the Nez Perces: The Nez Perce War of 1877* (Wrangell, Alaska: Mountain Meadow Press, 1993), 250.

9. Charles N. Loynes to Lucullus McWhorter, box 12, folder 85, McW.

10. "The commanding officer [Rawn], reinforced by 200 volunteers, proposed at first to attack the hostiles or a least resist their advance, as requested by Gen Howard, until we should get up. But as usual the volunteers weakened, particularly when the Indians, upon being interviewed, agreed to pass through the valley doing no harm if they were themselves unmolested." Jocelyn, *Mostly Alkali*, 243.

11. A civilian who remained after others had left later wrote that Rawn and another officer were drunk at the time and disbelieving that the Nez Perces were escaping via the other trail. Harlan, "Diary of Wilson Barber Harlan," 505.

12. Bruce Hampton, *Children of Grace: The Nez Perce War of 1877* (New York: Holt, 1994), 143.

13. Buck, "The Story of the Nez Perce Indian Campaign"; Harlan, "Diary of Wilson Barber Harlan," 507.

14. Davison, "Century Ago," 7.

15. *San Francisco Chronicle,* August 27, 1877.

16. A man named Grizzly Bear Youth, who had been scouting for the army against the Sioux and so knew something of military realities, fell in with the bands for a while and told them they were fools if they did not head north for the national boundary, and there are vague references to some leaders predicting that plenty more soldiers might await after they crossed the Bitterroots. In-who-lise, a young woman at the time, remembered for instance that White Bird urged that they head to Canada because if they headed for the Crows, "there will be soldiers and white men to bar the way and fight us nearly every day." Andrew Garcia, *Tough Trip through Paradise, 1878–1879* (San Francisco: Comstock, 1967), 209. On Grizzly Bear Youth and his advice: Laughy, *In Pursuit of the Nez Perces,* 252–53; on Canada as a possible destination: 255; Buck, "The Story of the Nez Perce Campaign," 31.

17. Garcia, *Tough Trip through Paradise,* 208–12.

18. Laughy, *In Pursuit of the Nez Perces,* 249.

19. Ibid., 258.

20. According to one story, locals essentially took command. John Humble, one of the civilian leaders, later said he told Rawn that if Rawn made a stand against the bands, Humble would take his men home. Rawn promised not to fight, Humble claimed, and put him in charge of pickets near the ridge where the bands would make their backdoor move the next day; and when the Nez Perces asked for access to the ridge, Humble agreed and moved his guards away. "They said they did not want to fight the citizens," he wrote, "and would go through the valley and molest nothing." Hampton, *Children of Grace,* 141.

21. Garcia, *Tough Trip through Paradise,* 213.

22. Theodore Goldin, "A Bit of the Nez Perce Campaign," typescript reminiscence, NL, 5–6.

23. I thank Martin Ridge for both the phrase "separating the man from the message" and the insight behind it.

24. Alvin F. Harlow, *Old Wires and New Waves: The History of the Telegraph, Telephone, and Wireless* (New York: Appleton-Century, 1936), 306.

25. "The Electric Telegraph," *Placerville (CA) Mountain Democrat,* October 16, 1858.

26. Oliver Wendell Holmes, "Bread and the Newspaper," *Atlantic Monthly* 8:45 (July 1861): 348.

27. Ibid. *Report of the Secretary of the Interior, 1869,* H.Exec.Doc. 1, pt. 3, 41st Cong., 2nd sess. Serial Set 1414, 3:vii–viii.

29. *Report of the Secretary of War, 1883,* H.Exec.Doc. 1, pt. 2, vol. 1, 48th Cong., 1st sess., Serial Set 2182, 2:45–46.

30. G. O. Shields, *The Battle of the Big Hole: A History of General Gibbon's Engagement with Nez Perces Indians in the Big Hole Valley, Montana, August 9, 1877* (Chicago: Rand, McNally, 1889), 28.

31. Interview with Yellow Bull, February 13, 1915, WCP.

32. Jerome A. Greene, *Nez Perce Summer, 1877: The U.S. Army and the Nee-Me-Poo Crisis* (Helena: Montana Historical Society Press, 2000), 109–10, 119–20; Merrill D. Beal, *"I Will Fight No More Forever": Chief Joseph and the Nez Perce War* (Seattle: University of Washington Press, 1963), 96.

33. *YW,* 108–9.

34. The valley had yet another, earlier name. The stream that drained it, called today the Little Big Hole River, was a part of a tributary of the Jefferson River, so named by Lewis and Clark because it was the largest of the three rivers forming the Missouri. (They named the other two after slightly lesser political gods, Madison and Gallatin.) To further consecrate the land, they named the Jefferson's three tributaries after prime republican virtues they attributed to their president. Two were dubbed the Philanthropy and Philosophy. The third, which later became the Big Hole, they named the Wisdom.

35. *HM,* 369.

36. General John Gibbon, "The Pursuit of 'Joseph,'" *American Catholic Quarterly Review* 4 (April 1879): 321–23; James H. Bradley to "My Dear Wife," August 1, August 3, 1877, folder 1, James H. Bradley Collection, SC1616, MHS.

37. Henry Buck wrote of "a dissenting opinion as to the right of our citizens to take up arms in pursuit and consequently only a few were persuaded to join Catlin's command." Those who joined Gibbon were all Civil War veterans, and thus perhaps had more of a national sensibility and sense of affinity with the regular troops. Buck, "Story of the Nez Perce Campaign," 39.

38. Charles A. Woodruff, "Battle of the Big Hole," 9, SC1236, MHS.

39. Ibid., 10.

40. Gibbon, "Pursuit of 'Joseph,'" 335.

## Chapter 11

1. *San Francisco Chronicle,* August 14, 1877.

2. *SW,* 11; Colonel John Gibbon, "A Vision of the Big Hole," 9, Big Hole Battlefield National Monument Library, Wisdom, Montana; G. O. Shields, *The Battle of the Big Hole A History of General Gibbon's Engagement with the Nez Perces Indians in the Big Hole Valley, Montana, August 9, 1877* (Chicago: Rand, McNally, 1889), 83, 103.

3. Edward E. Hardin diary, August 9, 10, 1877, SC 1006, MHS.

4. All published accounts of the war spend considerable attention on the fight at the Big Hole. What follows is based especially on *SW,* 502–5; John Gibbon, "Adventures of American Army and Navy Officers," pt. 3, "The Battle of the Big Hole," *Harper's Weekly,* December 28, 1895, 1235–36; Aubrey L. Haines, *An Elusive Victory: The Battle of the Big Hole* (West Glacier, Mont.: Glacier Natural History Association, 1991); Jerome A. Greene, *Nez Perce Summer, 1877: The U.S. Army and the Nee-Me-Poo Crisis* (Helena: Montana Historical Society Press, 2000), 127–40; *HM,* 366–403; *YW,* 112–60. I have drawn also on unpublished material, notably Col. J. B. Catlin, "The Battle of the Big Hole," SC 520, Tom Sherill, "The Battle of the Big Hole as I Saw It," and Bunch Sherill reminiscence, in Tom and Bunch Sherill Reminiscences, SC 739, Richard Comba, "Report to Adjutant General, Department of Montana," SC 937, all in MHS; Homer Coon, "The Outbreak of Chief Joseph," typescript, BL.

5. *HM,* 376–77.

6. *YW,* 141–43; *HM,* 375–77.

7. Rowena L. and Gordon Alcorn, "Aged Nez Perce Recalls the 1877 Tragedy," *Montana* 15:4 (October 1965): 63.

8. Charles A. Woodruff, "Battle of the Big Hole," 15, SC 1236, MHS.

9. *YW,* 119, 122–23, 143; *HM,* 377–78; Woodruff, "Battle of the Big Hole," 15.

10. Linwood Laughy, comp., *In Pursuit of the Nez Perces: The Nez Perce War of 1877* (Wrangell, Alaska: Mountain Meadow Press, 1993), 260.

11. "The Story of Ow-yen," box 7, folder 38, McW.

12. Charles N. Loynes to Lucullus McWhorter, June 19, 1926, box 8, folder 43, item 157, and Charles N. Loynes to Lucullus McWhorter, March 19, 1940, box 12, folder 85, item 30, McW.

13. Woodruff, "Battle of the Big Hole," 14.

14. Chalres N. Loynes to Lucullus McWhorter, January 23, 1929, box 8, folder 42, item 2, MW.

15. Charles Woodruff to "My Darling Louise," August 11 [12?], 1877, Charles A. Woodruff file, Big Hole Battlefield National Monument Library, Wisdom, Montana.

16. General John Gibbon, "The Pursuit of 'Joseph,'" *American Catholic Quarterly Review* 4 (April 1879): 317–18; John G. Bourke diaries, copies, 25:12–13, Lansing Bloom Papers, Center for Southwest Research, Zimmerman Library, University of New Mexico. Albuquerque, New Mexico.

17. Charles Woodruff to "My Darling Louise," August 11 [12?], 1877.

18. The quotation is from Andrew Garcia, who married a survivor of the battle, In-who-lise, and returned with her two years later. He wrote of her mourning wail on finding graves at the battlefield desecrated. Andrew Garcia to Lucullus McWhorter, April 22, 1929, box 8, folder 42, McW.

19. *YW,* 126, 138; *HM,* 386–87; Peo-peo Tholekt, "Incidents Big Hole Battle," box 8, folder 43, McW.

20. *HM,* 402; Laughy, *In Pursuit of the Nez Perces,* 262.

21. *YW,* 145.

22. Emily McCorkle FitzGerald, *An Army Doctor's Wife on the Frontier: The Letters of Emily McCorkle FitzGerald from Alaska and the Far West, 1874–1878* (Lincoln: University of Nebraska Press, 1986), 214.

23. *SW,* 619.

24. Stanley R. Davison, "A Century Ago: The Nez Perce and the Tortuous Pursuit," *Montana* 27:4 (October 1977): 7.

25. Charles M. Robinson III, *Bad Hand: A Biography of General Ranald S. Mackenzie* (Austin, Tex.: State House Press, 1993), 179, 219.

## Chapter 12

1. Stanley R. Davison, "A Century Ago: The Nez Perce and the Tortuous Pursuit," *Montana* 27:4 (October 1977): 8.

2. *SW,* 609–10; Charles E. S. Wood, "Diary on Nez Perce Campaign," August 10–12, 1877, box 26, folder 1, Charles Erskine Scott Wood Papers, HL.

3. Quoted in Aubrey L. Haines, *An Elusive Victory: The Battle of the Big Hole* (West Glacier, Mont.: Glacier Natural History Association, 1991), 136.

4. Davison, "Century Ago," 10.

5. Henry Buck, "The Story of the Nez Perce Campaign during the Summer of 1877," 51, SC492, MHS.

6. Andrew Garcia to Lucullus McWhorter, April 22, 1929, box 8, folder 42, item 54, McW.

7. Bruce Hampton, *Children of Grace: The Nez Perce War of 1877* (New York: Holt, 1994), 188–89.

8. J. W. Redington, "Scouting in Montana in the 1870s," *Frontier* 13:1 (November 1932): 56.

9. It may have been at this point that some, maybe many, began to realize that they would be no safer among the Crows in buffalo country and that their best bet was to run for the international boundary to the north. The white informant most acquainted with Nez Perce memories, Lucullus McWhorter, wrote that at this point the bands realized that Canada was "now the only hope of escape." *HM,* 406.

10. Alice E. Barrett Reminiscence, SC400, MHS.

11. Gary E. Moulton, ed., *The Definitive Journals of Lewis and Clark: Through the Rockies to the Cascades* (Lincoln: University of Nebraska Press, 1988), 5:76–84.

12. Alexander Cruikshank, "The Birch Creek Massacre," SC 584, and J. D. Wood reminiscence, SC 987, both in MHS; Philip Rand, "The White Man's Account of the Wagon Train Tragedy at Burch [Birch] Creek, Idaho," box 8, folder 43, McW; *HM,* 409–10.

13. *NPJ,* 214.

14. *Claims of the Nez Perce Indians. Letter From the Secretary of the Interior, Transmitting Communication of the Commissioner of Indian Affairs, Inclosing Report of Agent C. T. Stranahan, of the Nez Perce Agency, Together*

*With the Testimony Taken by Him in Support of the Claims of the Nez Perce Indians for Services Rendered by Them During the War with Joseph's Band of the Nez Perces in 1877. March 29, 1900,* S.Doc.257, 56th Cong., 1st sess., Serial Set 3867, 25:61.

15. *SW,* 128.

16. Charles Erskine Scott Wood, "Journal of an Expedition against Hostile Nez Perce Indians from Lewiston, I. T. to Henry Lake, I. T.," August 16, 1877, box 26, folder 2, Charles Erskine Scott Wood Papers, HL.

17. *NPJ,* 219.

18. Ibid., 221.

19. H. J. Davis, "The Battle of Camas Meadows," in Cyrus Townsend Brady, *Northwestern Fights and Fighters* (Williamstown, Mass.: Corner House, 1974), 193.

20. Davison, "Century Ago," 10.

21. *HM,* 417; Linwood Laughy, comp., *In Pursuit of the Nez Perces: The Nez Perce War of 1877* (Wrangell, Alaska: Mountain Meadow Press, 1993), 266.

22. *HM,* 419 n.

23. "Did the Nez Perces Drill for War?" box 8, folder 40, McW.

24. *YW,* 168.

25. On this episode, see *SW,* 129–30, 572–73; Jerome A. Greene, *Nez Perce Summer, 1877: The U.S. Army and the Nee-Me-Poo Crisis* (Helena: Montana Historical Society Press, 2000), 155–60; *HM,* 422–26.

26. *NPJ,* 228.

27. Davis, "Battle of Camas Meadows," 196.

28. Quoted in Hampton, *Children of Grace,* 213.

29. Buck, "Story of the Nez Perce Campaign," 60–61.

30. The quotation is in ibid., 59.

31. *NPJ,* 234.

32. Ibid.

33. Oliver Otis Howard, *My Life and Experiences among Our Hostile Indians* (Hartford, Conn.: Worthington, 1907), 292.

34. Davison, "Century Ago," 11–12.

35. *NPJ,* 234.

36. Davison, "Century Ago," 12–13; C. E. S. Wood to J. S. Gray, August 24, 1877, Captain James T. Gray Correspondence, SC1217, MHS.

37. Davison, "Century Ago," 12; *SW,* 617.

38. U.S. War Department, *Reports of Inspection Made in the Summer of 1877 by Generals P. H. Sheridan and W. T. Sherman of Country North of the Union Pacific Railroad* (Washington, D.C.: Government Printing Office, 1878), 33.

39. Ibid., 81–82.

40. Davison, "Century Ago," 10.

41. Ibid., 9–10.

42. *SW,* 12–13.

43. *Claims of the Nez Perce Indians, March 29, 1900,* 25:61.

## Chapter 13

1. Of the several good histories of Yellowstone National Park, the foundational one remains Aubrey L. Haines, *The Yellowstone Story: A History of Our First National Park,* 2 vols. (Yellowstone National Park, Wyo.: Yellowstone Library and Museum Association, 1977). See also Richard A. Bartlett, *Nature's Yellowstone* (Albuquerque: University of New Mexico Press, 1974), and Paul Schullery, *Searching for Yellowstone: Ecology and Wonder in the Last Wilderness* (Boston: Houghton Mifflin, 1997).

2. Robert B. Smith and Lee J. Siegel, *Windows into the Earth: The Geologic Story of Yellowstone and Grand Teton National Parks* (New York: Oxford University Press, 2000).

3. Joel C. Janetski, *Indians in Yellowstone National Park* (Salt Lake City: University of Utah Press, 2002); Peter Nabokov and Lawrence Loendorf, *American Indians and Yellowstone National Park: A Documentary Overview* (Yellowstone National Park, Wyo.: National Park Service, 2002).

4. *Preliminary Report of the United States Geological Survey of Wyoming, and Portions of Contiguous Territories. (Being a Second Annual Report of Progress,) Conducted Under the Authority of the Secretary of the Interior, by F. V. Hayden, United States Geologist,* H.Exec.Doc. 325, 42nd Cong., 2nd sess., Serial Set 1520, 15, 6.

5. Haines, *Yellowstone Story,* 1:155.

6. William Ludlow, *Report of a Reconnaissance from Carroll, Montana Territory, on the Upper Missouri, to the Yellowstone National Park, and Return, Made in the Summer of 1875* (Washington: Government Printing Office, 1876), 22, 26, 37.

7. Earl of Dunraven, *The Great Divide: Travels in the Upper Yellowstone in the Summer of 1874* (London: Chatto and Windus, 1876), 225.

8. One scholar argues that early national parks had one thing in common—they were "worthless lands." Alfred Runte, *National Parks: The American Experience* (Lincoln: University of Nebraska Press, 1979), 48–64.

9. Helen Hunt Jackson, *Bits of Travel at Home* (Boston: Roberts, 1887), 107; John Muir, *The Mountains of California* (New York: Penguin Books, 1985), 64.

10. P. C. Norris, "Report on the Yellowstone National Park," in *Report of the Secretary of the Interior,* 1877 H.Exec.Doc. 1, pt. 5, vol. 1, 45th Cong., 2nd sess., Serial Set 1800, 8:842; Philetus C. Norris journals, HL, 90.

11. Stanton Fisher, scouting for Howard, wrote in his journal that a second prospector, William Harmon, was taken as well and later escaped and was found by his scouts. S. G. Fisher, "Journal of S. G. Fisher," *Contributions of the Historical Society of Montana* (Helena: State Publishing, 1896), August 26, 1877, 2:272.

12. For Emily Cowan's account of her extraordinary time in Yellowstone, see Mrs. George F. Cowan, "Reminiscences of Pioneer Life," in *Contributions of the Historical Society of Montana* (Helena, Mont.: Independent Publishing, 1903), 4:157–87. See also a short account by her brother, Frank Carpenter, *St. Louis Globe-Democrat,* September 19, 1877.

362   NOTES TO PAGES 219–226

13. Jerome A. Greene, *Nez Perce Summer 1877: The U. S. Army and the Ne-Me-Poo Crisis* (Helena: Montana Historical Society, 2000), 183.

14. Cowan, "Reminiscences," 171.

15. Ibid., 173.

16. Camille Williams to L. V. McWhorter, April 5, 1938, box 7, folder 34, item 72, McW.

17. Cowan, "Reminiscences," 175–77.

18. J. W. Redington, "Scouting in Montana in the 1870s," *Frontier* 13:1 (November, 1932): 58.

19. For a personal account of this episode, see Andrew J. Weikert, "Journal of the Tour through the Yellowstone National Park," *Contributions of the Historical Society of Montana* (Helena: State Publishing, 1900), 3:153–75.

20. Quoted in Mark H. Brown, *The Flight of the Nez Perce* (New York: Putnam, 1967), 332.

21. Kim Allen Scott, *Yellowstone Denied: The Life of Gustavus Cheyney Doane* (Norman: University of Oklahoma Press, 2007), 160–66.

22. *YW,* 173.

23. Cowan, "Reminiscences," 160–66.

24. Weikert, "Journal of the Tour," 157, 171.

25. Cowan, "Reminiscences," 179.

26. Shively's account in the *Helena Independent* was widely reprinted. See for instance *San Francisco Chronicle,* September 12, 1877.

27. *YW,* 171–72.

28. On the several opinions about the route or routes of the bands and whether or not they were lost, see Lee Whittlesey, "The Nez Perces in Yellowstone in 1877: A Comparison of Attempts to Deduce Their Route," *Montana* 57:1 (spring 2007): 48–55; William L. Lang, "Where Did the Nez Perce Go?" *Montana* 40:1 (winter 1990): 14–29; Nabokov and Loendorf, *American Indians and Yellowstone National Park,* 182–85.

29. Fisher, "Journal of S. G. Fisher," 269–82, covers Fisher's entire time with the command. On these early stages, see 269–70. The number of Bannock scouts with Fisher at one point was about eighty, but some were discouraged and soon left, and eventually the number dwindled to around a dozen.

30. Cowan, "Reminiscences," 172; Fisher, "Journal of S. G. Fisher," September 3, 1877, 275.

31. Some accounts show the Nez Perce in one place; others place them elsewhere. One possibility is that all accounts were accurate and that once dispersed, the bands rested in different locations. William Lang writes that the raids of August 31 probably were two separate forays, one from Joseph's camp on the Yellowstone River firing Henderson's ranch, and the other from Looking Glass's camp on the Lamar River attacking the tourists at Mammoth and killing Dietrich. One bunch, either the one from Joseph's camp or perhaps a third one, partially burned the only bridge across the Yellowstone River to slow the pursuit of troops. Lang, "Where Did the Nez Perces Go," 20, 22, 24–25.

32. Lt. Hugh Scott and ten men from Doane's command had been the first to come to Henderson's Ranch after the attack, and they had chased after the raiders. Scott wrote later that Joseph told him the Nez Perces had hoped to descend the Yellowstone onto the plains near present-day Livingston, Montana, but Scott's impromptu pursuit convinced them that a larger force waited there, and with Howard in pursuit from their rear, they realized their only chance lay to the east, over the mountains. The Nez Perce Tom Hill would say that this was especially important because the sight of Crow scouts with Doane and Scott convinced the Nez Perces that they could expect no help from their allies, and so must head for Canada. Hugh Lenox Scott, *Some Memories of a Soldier* (New York: Century, 1928), 65; Hugh L. Scott to Walter Camp, September 22, 1913, Walter Camp to Hugh Scott, January 11, 1914, Hugh Scott to Walter Camp, January 18, 1914, WCP.

33. Henry Buck, "The Story of the Nez Perce Campaign during the Summer of 1877," SC492, MHS.

34. Fisher, "Journal of S. G. Fisher," September 5, 1877, 275.

35. Buck, "Story of the Nez Perce Campaign," 56, 71–72, 82–83, 87–88.

36. Scott, *Yellowstone Denied,* 171–73. Apparently Gilbert's reasoning (if it can be called that) was that since Howard had last been heard from back at Henry's Lake, he must still be there.

37. A published copy of the field order, dated August 29, 1877, is in Captain John T. Gray Correspondence, SC1217, MHS.

## Chapter 14

1. *Deer Lodge (MO) New Northwest,* quoted in Merrill D. Beal, *"I Will Fight No More Forever": Chief Joseph and the Nez Perce War* (Seattle: University of Washington Press, 1963), 186.

2. Jerome A. Greene, *Nez Perce Summer 1877: The U.S. Army and the Nee-Me-Poo Crisis* (Helena: Montana Historical Society Press, 2000), 204–5.

3. *SW,* 507; G. W. Baird to S. D. Sturgis, August 14, 1877, Samuel Sturgis to Gustavus Doane, August 17, 1877, Samuel Sturgis to Gustavus Doane, August 25, 1877, Gustavus Doane Papers, Special Collections, Montana State University Library, Bozeman.

4. *SW,* 508–9; Samuel Sturgis to Gustavus Doane, September 5, 1877, Gustavus Doane Papers.

5. *SW,* 616, 618, 621.

6. *SW,* 508–10, 621–22; Theodore W. Goldin, "A Bit of the Nez Perce Campaign," typescript reminiscence, NL. Stanton Fisher and his scouts found the bodies of three white men killed and rescued a wounded miner who told of two companions killed. S. G. Fisher, "Journal of S. G. Fisher," *Contributions of the Historical Society of Montana* (Helena: State Publishing, 1896), September 10–11, 1877, 277. J. W. Redington wrote of the mining pick: J. W. Redington, "Scouting in Montana in the 1870s," *Frontier* 13:1 (November 1932): 59.

7. S. D. Sturgis to G. C. Doane, September 2, 1877, Gustavus Doane Papers.

8. Goldin, "Bit of the Nez Perce Campaign," 16.

9. *SW, 1877,* 509.

10. Ibid., 510.

11. W. C. Slater to Lucullus McWhorter, May 26, 1927, box 10, folder 65, item 121, McW.

12. *SW, 1877,* 510.

13. Ibid.; Goldin, "Bit of the Nez Perce Campaign," 21–24; Theodore W. Goldin, "The Seventh Cavalry at Canon Creek," in Cyrus Townsend Brady, *Northwestern Fights and Fighters* (Williamstown, Mass.: Corner House, 1974), 212–13.

14. S. D. Sturgis to G. C. Doane, September 5, 1877, Gustavus Doane Papers.

15. Interview with No Feather (Weptas Nut), February 15, 1915, WMC.

16. Goldin, "Bit of the Nez Perce Campaign," 26, 29; Greene, *Nez Perce Summer,* 212.

17. *NPJ,* 255.

18. On this strange notion of lesser cultures somehow melting away before the advance of superior ones, both in North America and elsewhere in the colonized world, see Patrick Brantlinger, *Dark Vanishings: Discourse on the Extinction of Primitive Races, 1800–1930* (Ithaca, N.Y.: Cornell University Press, 2003).

19. *Condition of the Indian Tribes. Report of the Joint Special Committee, Appointed Under Joint Resolution of March 3, 1865, With an Appendix,* Sen. Rpt. 156, 39th Cong., 2nd sess., Serial Set 1279, 1:4.

20. Richard Irving Dodge, *Our Wild Indians: Thirty-three Years' Personal Experience Among the Red Men of the Great West. A Popular Account of Their Social Life, Religion, Habits, Traits, Customs, Exploits, etc.* (Chicago: A. G. Nettleton, 1882), 56.

21. O. O. Howard, *My Life and Experiences among Our Hostile Indians* (Hartford, Conn.: A. D. Worthington, 1907), 551–52, 433.

22. Sherry L. Smith, *The View from Officers' Row: Army Perceptions of Western Indians* (Tucson: University of Arizona Press, 1990), 154–55.

23. *NPJ,* 60; General John Gibbon, "The Pursuit of 'Joseph,'" *American Catholic Quarterly Review* 4 (April 1879): 337; Dodge, *Our Wild Indians,* 440, 449, 451, 452.

24. Smith, *View from Officers' Row,* 28–29.

25. Anson Mills, *My Story* (Washington, D.C.: published by the author, 1918), 158–63.

26. Smith, *View from Officers' Row,* 135.

27. The standard work is Joseph C. Porter, *Paper Medicine Man: John Gregory Bourke and His American West* (Norman: University of Oklahoma Press, 1986).

28. For a gathering of Bradley's field notes and writings on plains Indians, see James H. Bradley Collection, SC 1616, MHS; Leutenant James

H. Bradley, *The March of the Montana Column: A Prelude to the Custer Disaster,* edited by Edgar I. Stewart (Norman: University of Oklahoma Press, 1961).

29. E[dward] Wynkoop to S. F. Tappan, January 2, 1869, Samuel F. Tappan Papers, Colorado State Historical Society, Denver.

30. Smith, *View from Officers' Row,* 29; Dodge, *Our Wild Indians,* 53.

31. Emily McCorkle FitzGerald, *An Army Doctor's Wife on the Frontier: The Letters of Emily McCorkle FitzGerald from Alaska and the Far West, 1874–1878* (Lincoln: University of Nebraska Press, 1962), 312; Smith, *View from Officers' Row,* 155.

32. Smith, *View from Officers' Row,* 122.

33. Richard Irving Dodge, *The Plains of the Great West and Their Inhabitants* (New York: Putnam, 1877), 395–97; Stanley R. Davison, "A Century Ago: The Nez Perce and the Tortuous Pursuit," *Montana* 27:4 (October 1977): 13.

34. George Crook, *His Autobiography,* edited by Martin F. Schmitt (Norman: University of Oklahoma Press, 1946), 16.

35. John G. Bourke diaries, copies, 25:12–13, Lansing Bloom Papers, Center for Southwest Research, Zimmerman Library, University of New Mexico, Albuquerque, New Mexico.

36. Michael McCarthy diary, June 27, 1877, Michael McCarthy Papers, Library of Congress.

## Chapter 15

1. *SW,* 510.

2. Ibid.; *NPJ;* Theodore W. Goldin to L. V. McWhorter, February 27, 1929, box 10, folder 69, item 104, McW.

3. As early as the pursuit of the Nez Perces across the Salmon River after the battle at White Bird Canyon, according to an officer, many thought that the bands might "escape and join the Sioux." Stephen Perry Jocelyn, *Mostly Alkali: A Biography* (Caldwell, Idaho: Caxton Printers, 1953), 229.

4. *Bozeman Times,* October 4, 1877; *St. Paul Pioneer-Press,* reprinted in *St. Louis Globe-Democrat,* December 7, 1877.

5. *SW,* 510.

6. Ibid., 527.

7. N. P. Langford, "The Wonders of Yellowstone," *Scribner's* 2:1 (May 1871): 3; *Letter from the Secretary of War, Communicating the Report of Lieutenant Gustavus C. Doane upon the So-called Yellowstone Expedition of 1870. March 3, 1871.* S.Exec.Doc. 51, 41st Cong., 3rd sess., Serial Set 1440, 1:3. Doane was effusive about the Yellowstone valley close by to what would soon the a national park: "Excepting the Judith Basin, I have seen no district in the western Territories so eligible for settlement."

8. J. W. Redington, "The Stolen Stage Coach," box 10, folder 69, item 70, McW; J. W. Redington, "Scouting in the Montana in the 1870s," *Frontier* 13:1 (November 1932): 60–61.

9. Fred H. Tobey diary, September 11, 1877, HL.

10. *NPJ*, 257.

11. Theodore W. Goldin, "The Seventh Cavalry at Canyon Creek," in Cyrus Townsend Brady, *Northwestern Fights and Fighters* (Williamstown, Mass.: Corner House, 1974), 219.

12. Theodore W. Goldin to L. V. McWhorter, February 27, 1929.

13. Ibid.

14. *YW;* S. G. Fisher, "Journal of S. G. Fisher," *Contributions of the Montana Historical Society* (Helena: State Publishing, 1896), September 13, 1877, 278.

15. "The Colonel Sturgis Fight," box 10, folder 69, McW.

16. Tobey diary, September 13, 1877.

17. *SW,* 511.

18. Fisher, "Journal of S. G. Fisher," September 13, 1877, 279.

19. In their versions of the fight, Howard and Sturgis both claimed that only one howitzer, that under Lt. Harrison Otis, made it into action. See *NPJ,* 259, and *SW,* 511. Others on the scene, however, make it clear that Guy Howard was there, too, albeit ineffectually and comically. "Howitzer at the Canyon Creek Fight," box 10, folder 69, item 59, McW, and Theodore W. Goldin, "A Bit of the Nez Perce Campaign," typescript reminiscence, NL. Probably Howard and Sturgis were dissembling to avoid embarrassing Howard's son.

20. Tobey diary, September 13, 1877.

21. Redington, "Scouting in Montana," 60.

22. *SW,* 512; *San Francisco Chronicle,* September 19, 1877. Fisher noted Sturgis's claim and wrote that it was "surely mistaken"; Fisher, "Journal of S. G. Fisher," September 13, 1877, 280 n.

23. *YW,* 189.

24. Fisher wrote that the Crows kept out of the fight and "staid in the rear and stole everything they could get their hands on," including his pack animals, clothing, and bedding. Fisher, "Journal of S. G. Fisher," September 13, 1877, 280.

25. *YW,* 189.

26. Edward S. Curtis, *The North American Indian; Being a Series of Volumes Picturing and Describing the Indians of the United States, and Alaska, Written, Illustrated and Published by Edward S. Curtis* (Seattle: E. S. Curtis, 1907–30), 7:167–68; Camille Williams to L. V. McWhorter, June 21, 1937, box 12, folder 84, McW. Crow tradition holds that their leaders assured the Nez Perces that they would only pretend to fight, but it is not clear whether the reference was only to the battle on Canyon Creek, in which they did not take part, and not to the next day or any other later time.

27. *YW,* 187.

28. G. W. Baird [for Miles] to G. C. Doane, August 12, 1877, Gustavus Doane Papers, Special Collections, Montana State University Library, Bozeman. For other correspondence on the army's strategy, see Gustavus Doane to Acting Assistant Adjutant General, Yellowstone Command, August 3, 1877, Nelson A. Miles to Governor B. L. Potts, copy of telegram,

August 5, 1877, Nelson A. Miles to S. D. Sturgis, August 12, 1877, G. C. Doane to Commanding Officer, Camp Baker, August 21, 1877, all in Gustavus Doane Papers.

29. Oliver Howe to Samuel Howe, November 11, 1877, Oliver R. Howe Papers, Special Collections, Montana State University Library.

30. Tobey diary, September 14, 1877.

31. *SW,* 512.

32. Redington, "Scouting in Montana in the 1870s," 61.

33. The absent supply train was the final effect of the political jockeying three weeks earlier, when Lt. Col. Gilbert had tried to catch and replace Howard. Back at Henry Lake, as Howard had prepared to enter Yellowstone Park, he had ordered three companies under Captain Henry Cushing to gather supplies at Fort Ellis for support of anticipated field operations. Cushing was to take the rations to the Crow agency and stand ready to help in blocking the Nez Perce escape. When it became clear that they would try to leave the park via the Clark's Fork area, Howard told Cushing to go there to supply Sturgis. Just then, however, word came from Gibbon countermanding Howard's order and telling Cushing to stay at Fort Ellis and be ready to help Gilbert, who presumably would be taking over the whole operation. But Gilbert was pushing his troops down all the wrong trails in Yellowstone Park, and when he finally gave up his botched errand, no one apparently told Cushing. He sat at Fort Ellis "awaiting definite information about what was going on," he wrote later, but "at last it seemed that no one knew anything as to what was going on." So he took the plunge and set off on his own. He arrived at Canyon Creek the day after the battle, hours after Sturgis and his hungry men had left on their tired pursuit. *SW,* 625–26.

34. Stanley R. Davison, "A Century Ago: The Nez Perce and the Tortuous Pursuit," *Montana* 27:4 (October 1977): 16.

35. *SW,* 628.

36. *YW,* 196–97.

37. William Moelchert to David Hilger, November 13, 1927, SC 491, MHS.

38. *YW,* 199; J. W. Redington to L. V. McWhorter, March 10, 1931, box 12, folder 84, McW.

39. Bruce Hampton, *Children of Grace: The Nez Perce War of 1877* (New York: Avon Books, 1994), 280.

40. *SW,* 558; John Samples reminiscence, SC715, MHS.

41. *HM,* 473–74.

42. Edwin James, *Account of an Expedition from Pittsburgh to the Rocky Mountains* (Philadelphia: H. C. Carey and I. Lea, 1823), 1:476, 480–81.

43. William R. Brown, Jr., "*Comancheria* Demography, 1805–1830," *Panhandle-Plains Historical Review* 59 (1986): 1–17.

44. David J. Wishart, *The Fur Trade of the American West, 1807–1940: A Geographical Synthesis* (Lincoln: University of Nebraska Press, 1979), 92–100.

45. Ibid., 81–83; Edward Thompson Denig, *Five Indian Tribes of the Upper Missouri: Sioux, Arikaras, Assiniboines, Crees, Crows* (Norman: University of Oklahoma Press, 1961), 95.

46. Merrill G. Burlingame, "The Buffalo in Trade and Commerce," *North Dakota Historical Quarterly* 3:4 (July 1929): 266, 268, 277–78; Isaac Lippincott, "A Century and a Half of Fur Trade at St. Louis," *Washington University Studies* 3, pt. 2, no. 2 (April 1916): 239–41; Hiram Martin Chittenden, *The American Fur Trade of the Far West* (New York: Press of the Pioneers, 1935), 2:807; Andrew C. Isenberg, *The Destruction of the Bison: An Environmental History, 1750–1920* (Cambridge: Cambridge University Press, 2000), 105–6.

47. An agent on the central plains in the mid-1850s estimated that the Cheyennes, Arapahoes, Kiowas, and Comanches on the upper Arkansas were killing about 112,000 bison a year—about ten per person. Among the more commercially involved Cheyennes and Arapahoes, the ratio was about thirteen per person. If these bands were using six bison annually to support each person, then trade accounted for roughly half the kills, perhaps more, since the agent wrote that hunters were also taking thousands of pronghorns, deer, elk and bear. J. W. Whitfield to Superintendant of Indian Affairs, January 5, 1856, Office of Indian Affairs, letters received, Upper Arkansas Agency, NA.

48. One authority estimated that hunters on the upper Missouri River alone had killed one and a third million bison in 1857. That was surely an exaggeration, but just as surely, the expanding hunt had taken a great bite out of the plains herds by the Civil War. J. A. Allen, *History of the American Bison, bison Americanus,* Department of the Interior, United States Geological Survey, *Ninth Annual Report* (Washington, D.C.: Government Printing Office, 1877), 563.

49. Gustavus C. Doane, "The Buffalo—Their Range and Numbers—Indian Hunting—The Wolfers," box 6, file 7, Gustavus Doane Papers.

50. This is not to say that bison could not be found. When the army's advance scouts came through, they found a large herd in the area of the Judith Basin and thought Crows had been hunting successfully there. Redington, "Scouting in Montana," 62. Nonetheless, the general trend is undeniable.

51. Contrary to popular impression, some meat was harvested and sold to nearby towns and military posts. The prodigious hunter J. Wright Mooar used hides to construct large vats for soaking bison hams in brine and temporary smokehouses of three thousand square feet. J. Wright Mooar interview, March 1939, Nita Stewart Haley Memorial Library, Midland, Texas.

52. David A. Dary, *The Bison Book: The Full Saga of the American Animal* (Chicago: Swallow Press, 1974), 103.

## Chapter 16

1. "The Last Battle. Prophetic Dreams of Wot-to-len," box 9, folder 56, McW.

2. Narrative of Ho-sus-pa-ow-yein (Shot-in-Head), box 6, folder 28, McW.

3. Robert H. Steinbach, *A Long March: The Lives of Frank and Alice Baldwin* (Austin: University of Texas Press, 1989), 128; S. Roy to W. M. Camp, July 10, 1911, WCP.

4. Jerome A. Greene, *Nez Perce Summer, 1877: the U.S.Army and the Nee-Me-Poo Crisis* (Helena: Montana Historical Society Press, 2000), 253–55. The news of Cow Creek was in a letter from George Clendenin, an agent for the company running steamboats to Fort Benton. It included his opinion that "I think the Nez Perces are keeping up cow [Creek] & will pass through the [Little] Rockies & Bears Paw & go north to the line," which is in fact what they would do.

5. L. S. Kelly, "Capture of Nez Perces," folder 59, Walter M. Camp Collection, White Swan Library, Little Big Horn Battlefield National Monument. Louis Shambow reminiscence, MHS; "Baird's Account of the Service of Captain Maus against Chief Joseph & Geronimo," George W. Baird Papers, BL.

6. "Bear Paw Notes," Edward S. Godfrey Papers, Manuscript Division, Library of Congress. Godfrey's longer account of the campaign quotes Hale as saying "this cold morning," a version found in some accounts of the battle. "Bear Paw Notes," however, seem to be corrections of that longer account.

7. Nelson A. Miles, *Personal Recollections and Observations of General Nelson A. Miles* (Chicago: Werner, 1896), 268.

8. John F. Finerty, *War-path and Bivouac, Or the Conquest of the Sioux* (Norman: University of Oklahoma Press, 1961), 232.

9. *YW,* 205. Probably the man delivering the warning had been one of a dozen or so hunters seen by Miles's scout, Louis Shambow, who thought, interestingly, that the hunters had binoculars and had seen him and the other scouts. Louis Shambow Reminiscence, MHS; *YW,* 205n.

10. Ibid., 205.

11. "Account of the Bear Paw Battle," 17, Edward S. Godfrey Papers.

12. Captain Godfrey called the three companies the "weakest troops" of the command. "Account of the Bear Paw Battle," 1.

13. Quoted in Greene, *Nez Perce Summer,* 274. See also S. Roy to Walter Camp, December 18, 1909, and [Jones] to Walter Camp, January 26, 1912, WCP. A participant estimated that the riders were only fifty or so feet from the bluff's edge and that some of the riderless horses went over it. James Clark interview, item 10, Robert S. Ellison Papers, Western History Collection, Denver Public Library.

14. Peter Allen, "Military Expedition and Campaign and Battle of Bear Paw Mountains, M.T., September 30, 1877," FF12, Walter M. Camp Papers, Western History Collection, Denver Public Library.

15. Myles Moylan to E. A. Garlington, August 16, 1878, copy, folder 25, National Archives Non-accessioned Files, White Swan Library, Little Big Horn Battlefield National Monument.

16. "Account of Bear Paw Battle," 19.

17. Henry Romeyn interview, October 14, 1912, WMC.

18. Henry Romeyn, "The Capture of Chief Joseph and the Nez Perce Indians," in *Contributions of the Historical Society of Montana* (Boston: J. S. Canner, 1966), 2:288–89; "'We Have Joseph and All His People': A Soldier Writes Home about the Final Battle," *Montana* 27:4 (October 1977): 32.

19. Henry R. Tilton, "After the Nez Perces," in Peter Cozzens, ed., *Eyewitnesses to the Indian Wars, 1865–1890: The Wars for the Pacific Northwest* (Mechanicsburg, Pa.: Stackpole Press, 2002), 554.

20. *YW,* 206.

21. Narrative of Peo Peo Tholkekt, box 6, folder 31, McW; "Black Eagle's Narrative of the Last Fight," box 10, folder 62, McW; *YW,* 206–7. For an account by Cheyenne scouts, see "Capture of Nez Perces. Young Two Moon's Account," White Swan Library, Little Big Horn Battlefield National Monument.

22. "Black Eagle's Narrative of the Last Fight"; Narrative of Peo Peo Tholkekt; YJIV, 428; *HM,* 483–84.

23. "Capture of the Nez Perces. Young Two Moon's Account."

24. YJIV, 428.

25. *YW,* 211.

26. "Yellow Bull's "Story," folder 59, Walter M. Camp Collection, White Swan Library, Little Big Horn National Monument; "Incidents of the last Battle and surrender," box 10, folder 62, McW.

27. "Items by Yellow Wolf," box 10, folder 62, McW.

28. Allen, "Military Expedition and Campaign and Battle of Bear Paw Mountains."

29. The Nez Perces in fact might have been able to hold on for a considerable time. A scout told later of seeing in the camp ham, bacon, "canned goods of all kinds," tobacco, and even candy and granulated sugar—ten sacks of it in one of the pits. Louis Shambow reminiscence, SC729, MHS.

30. By some accounts, Miles considered withdrawing and entrenching himself in some distant woods to wait for reinforcement. Edward S. Godfrey diary, October 1, 1876, Godfrey Family Papers, SC2000, MHS; "Brave Jerome: A Dashing Lieutenant's Experience in Chief Joseph's Trenches," in Cozzens, *Eyewitnesses to the Indian Wars,* 2:592.

31. George W. Baird, "Indian Campaigning with General Miles in Montana," BL. A variation by the company surgeon has it that the bison were approaching in precise single file, raising hopes that they might be cavalry reinforcements. Jerome A. Greene, ed., "An Army Surgeon's Account: Henry Remson Tilton's view of the Bear's Paw Mountains Expedition and the Conclusion of the Nez Perce War," *Montana* 56:2 (summer 2006): 21.

32. YJIV, 429.

33. *YW,* 214; *HM,* 495; Linwood Laughy, comp., *In Pursuit of the Nez Perces: The Nez Perce War of 1877* (Wrangell, Alaska: Mountain Meadow Press, 1993), 271. There is confusion over when he was killed. Yellow Wolf puts the death on the third day, although according to the way he places it in the events, it would have been on the second. McWhorter puts it near

the end of the siege on the eve of surrender. Another participant, Yellow Bull, later said that the action that brought Looking Glass out of the pit was a sally of mounted Nez Perces meant to deceive the troops. "Yellow Bull's Story," folder 59, Walter M. Camp Collection, White Swan Library, Little Big Horn Battlefield National Monument.

34. "Capture of Nez Perces. Young Two Moon's Account." This account tells of a poignant moment when the scouts were met by two men and a young girl, who spontaneously took off a bead necklace, placed it over the head of one of the scouts, Starving Elk, and shook hands with him. Other accounts say that Miles called for a truce. See, for instance, Greene, "Army Surgeon's Account," 21.

35. Romeyn, "Capture of Chief Joseph," 289.

36. Edward S. Curtis, *The North American Indian; Being a Series of Volumes Picturing and Describing the Indians of the United States, and Alaska, Written, Illustrated and Published by Edward S. Curtis* (Seattle: E. S. Curtis, 1907–30), 8:171.

37. Ibid.; "Capture of Nez Perces. Young Two Moon's Account."

38. At least one white, the army's surgeon Henry Tilton, got the gist of the matter: Joseph, he wrote later, "was inclined to surrender, but did not have control of the entire camp." Greene, "Army Surgeon's Account," 11.

39. *YW*, 215–16; "Brave Jerome," 591; interview with Yellow Bull, February 13, 1915, WMC.

40. On the one side, see *YW*, 217 and 217 n.; *HM*, 489–90; Interview with Yellow Bull, February 13, 1915, WMC. On the other, Charles Erskine Scott Wood to Harry Stinson Howard, February 20, 1942, box 234, folder 1, Charles Erskine Scott Wood Papers, HL. Joseph's words are in YJIV, 428. In his official report, Miles wrote that "While Joseph remained in our camp...[Jerome] went into the village and was detained (but not harmed)," implying that the Nez Perces were the ones improperly seizing someone under the truce flag. Surgeon Tilton's account similarly says only that "Joseph remained in our camp on the night of October 1." *SW*, 528.

41. It is unclear whether Jerome went into the camp on his own or was sent by Miles. He claimed that he was in the camp to reconnoiter on Miles's orders, or at least with his permission. "Brave Jerome," 591–92. Charles Erskine Scott Wood later claimed that when Miles heard of Jerome's being taken prisoner, he "was furious" and swore at Jerome because he would have to release Joseph and thus lose a bargaining chip.

42. Romeyn, "Capture of Chief Joseph," 290; *YW*, 220; "Incidents of the last Battle and Surrender," box 10, folder 62, McW.

43. Louis Shambow reminiscence, SC749, MHS.

44. *HM*, 513–14; "Mrs. Shot-in-Head's Sequel to Former Narrative," box 7, folder 38, Narrative of Peo Peo Tholekt, box 6, folder 31, McW.

45. *SW*, 628–30.

46. Ibid., 630.

47. Sturgis probably could have been on the scene, but nervousness over Sitting Bull once again intervened. At Carroll, he had gotten word of the fight late on October 2 and had immediately begun moving his men across

the Missouri. He would have moved ahead rapidly with his cavalry, but he reasoned that if the Sioux came south, they might attack his divided command piecemeal, and in any case he would need a united force to meet the threat. So he chose the slower option of waiting until his force was united at the Little Rocky Mountains and then advancing. He was close to Snake Creek when a courier appeared to tell him of the surrender. *SW,* 512–13.

48. *YW,* 222n; *HM,* 492, 625.

49. YJIV, 429.

50. The Cheyenne account, which has Miles telling Cheyenne scouts to tell the Nez Perces "if they surrender none will be harmed," is "Capture of Nez Perces. Young Two Moon's Account." The Nez Perce account has a white man in the army camp calling to the Nez Perces: "You will go back to your own country, Wallowa and the salmon. Babies will grow up, and you sill start anew. You will not be hung! Do not be scared!" "Personal Narrative of Wat-tes Kun-nin: Earth-Blanket," box 14, folder 104, McW.

51. *NPJ,* 66.

52. Yellow Wolf told how the army's two Nez Perce emissaries told the leaders that Miles was an "honest-looking man" who wanted the war to end. The deep mistrust of Howard was reinforced by his demeanor: "All Indians said, 'General Howard does not look good. He is mean acting!'" This set up what seems a crucial moment in a later meeting, when Howard spoke harshly and Miles pulled the leaders aside to assure them that he would return them home and that Howard "will forget all this." At that, Joseph appears to have decided that Miles was sympathetic and had the authority to protect them and to take them home: Miles was "a headman, and we will go with him." *YW,* 222–24.

53. Jerome A. Greene, ed., *Frontier Soldier: An Enlisted Man's Journal of the Sioux and Nez Perce Campaigns, 1877* (Helena: Montana Historical Society Press, 1998), 128.

54. *YW,* 224.

55. No Feather recalled that there were about forty persons with White Bird when he led them quietly away after dark, drawing no fire from soldiers. Interview with No Feather (Weptas Nut), February 15, 1915, WMC.

56. "Nez Perces Escaping from the Last Battle Computed by Black Eagle," box 10, folder 62, McW. In his official reports, Miles either made no mention of escapees or implied that most gave themselves up, saying that after he had sent word out that they would be allowed to return home, they "cheerfully complied" with his call to surrender. In congressional testimony the next year, he said that "a few escaped during the fight," those out hunting or "stealing." Howard wrote of "a few Indians, including White Bird," creeping through the lines and later of White Bird escaping with two wives and fourteen followers and of "other fugitives" and several "squads" who sought refuge among nearby tribes and ran to the mountains. *SW,* 76, 529, 631; *The Reorganization of the Army. A Report of the Sub-committee of the Committee on Military Affairs Relating to the Reorganization of the Army. March 21, 1878,* H.Misc.Doc. 56, 45th Cong., 2nd sess., Serial Set 1818, 4, 240.

57. This seems to be the meeting Joseph referred to when he later wrote that Miles "said to me in plain words, 'If you will come out and give up your arms, I will spare your lives and send you back to the reservation.'" YJIV, 429.

58. *YW*, 224–25.

59. Charles E. S. Wood, "The Surrender of Joseph," *Harper's Weekly,* November 17, 1877, 906; Charles Erskine Scott Wood to L. V. McWhorter, September 1, 1935, box 9, folder 56, McW.

## Chapter 17

1. Fred Bond, *Flatboating on the Yellowstone, 1877* (New York: New York Public Library, 1925), 21–22.

2. *SW,* 630.

3. The headline over the speech's first publication referred to Joseph as "the Great Chief" and the account as "a Remarkably Pathetic and Suggestive Communication." *Bismarck Tri-Weekly Tribune,* October 26, 1877. For examples of subsequent appearances, see *New York Times,* November 16, 1877, and *Harper's Weekly,* November 17, 1877, 690.

4. Those words are from Joseph's own account, dictated in 1878. Variations exist in the accounts of both Howard and Miles. None of these includes anything beyond these few words. Haruo Aoki, "Chief Joseph's Words," *Idaho Yesterdays,* 33 (fall 1989): 17–18.

5. During a trip to the nation's capital soon after the war, Wood wrote Howard that "Gen. Townsend," probably Edward Davis Townsend, had asked for a copy of "Joseph's reply" to file alongside the famous speech attributed to the Mingo chief Logan in 1774. Wood complied. C. E. S. Wood to Oliver Howard, November 16, 1877, ser. M91 OOH. Wood later said that he tried to retrieve the document but it had been lost.

6. Sherry L. Smith, *Reimagining Indians: Native Americans through Anglo Eyes, 1880–1940* (New York: Oxford University Press, 2000), 23.

7. C. E. S. Wood, "Diary on Nez Perce Campaign," June 28, July 17, 1877, box 26, folder 1, Charles Erskine Scott Wood Papers, HL.

8. C. E. S. Wood, "Diary," July 20, 1877; George Venn, *Soldier to Advocate: C. E. S. Wood's 1877 Legacy* (La Grande, Ore.: Wordcraft of Oregon, 2006), 49 n. Wood's last entry was on June 23.

9. C. E. S. Wood, "Famous Indians: Portraits of Some Indian Chiefs," *Century Illustrated Monthly* 46 (July 1893): 437.

10. Quoted in Venn, *Soldier to Advocate,* 60.

11. George Venn, "Chief Joseph's 'Surrender Speech' as a Literary Text," *Oregon English Journal* 20:1 (spring 1998): 69–73.

12. The comment is in an inscription, dated December 1936, from Wood to "My dear Son Erskine" in a copy of Chester Anders Fee, *Chief Joseph: The Biography of a Great Indian* (New York: Wilson-Erickson, 1936), in the restored library of Erskine Wood, School of Law at Lewis and Clark College, Portland, Oregon.

13. *Chicago Daily Inter-Ocean,* November 9, 1877.

14. *San Francisco Chronicle,* October 7, 1877.

15. Standard works on the evolving image of Indians during these years are Brian Dippie, *The Vanishing American: White Attitudes and U.S. Indian Policy* (Middletown, Conn.: Weslyan University Press, 1982), Philip Deloria, *Playing Indian* (New Haven, Conn.: Yale University Press, 1998), Smith, *Reimagining Indians,* Alan Trachtenberg, *Shades of Hiawatha: Staging Indians, Making Americans, 1880–1930* (New York: Hill and Wang, 2004).

16. Along the way, vague suggestions had been made to do just that. In the first known reference to the idea of a national park, the artist George Catlin in 1832, soon after painting Rabbit Skin Leggings and No Horns on His Head during their visit to St. Louis, had a "melancholy contemplation" on the passing of Indians and the great herds of bison. Then a thought: what if the government should create "a *nation's* park, containing man and beast," where "the world could see for ages to come, the native in his classic attire, galloping on his wild horse" after his fleeing prey? As late as 1871, the railroad kingpin William Jackson Palmer was able to envision something similar. He was about to found Colorado Springs as an elite resort, an "inner sanctum of Americanism" apart from the "foreign swarms" washing in from Europe. Around this refuge of the true republic he pictured a great preserve where threatened wildlife could be saved "with a…few Indians," so future generations might see in the flesh what would otherwise survive only in storybooks: "Can you imagine anything more delightful?" George Catlin, *Letters and Notes on the Manners, Customs, and Conditions of the North American Indians,* I (New York: Dover, 1973), 261–62; John S. Fisher, *A Builder of the West: The Life of General William Jackson Palmer* (Caldwell, Idaho: Caxton Printers, 1939), 164, 202.

17. *Frank Leslie's Illustrated Weekly,* October 27, 1877.

18. *Harper's Weekly,* September 1, 1877, 680, August 16, 1880, 644.

19. *New York Times,* August 14, 1877; Larry Cebula, "Filthy Savages and Red Napoleons: Newspapers and the Nez Perce War," *Pacific Northwest Forum* 6:2 (summer–fall 1993): 9. The *San Francisco Chronicle* (August 6, 1877) considered the hostiles "by far the pluckiest and most intelligent" fighters the army had ever faced.

20. F. L. M, "The Nez Perce War," *Galaxy* 24:6 (December 1877): 826. Miles interview in *Chicago Tribune,* reprinted in *Little Rock Daily Arkansas Gazette,* December 5, 1877; *Milwaukee Daily Sentinel,* July 13, 1877; *Prescott Weekly Arizona Miner,* August 31, 1877.

21. *Little Rock Daily Arkansas Gazette,* July 4, 1877; *Nation,* August 2, 1877, 69–70; *Harper's Weekly,* September 1, 1877, 680; *Frank Leslie's Illustrated Weekly,* September 1, 1877, October 27, 1877.

22. *New York Times,* October 15, 1877.

23. *St. Louis Globe-Democrat,* December 2, 1877. The dateline is from Bismarck on November 21, two days after Joseph's arrival.

24. Henry R. Tilton, "After the Nez Perces," in Peter Cozzens, ed., *Eyewitness to the Indian Wars, 1865–1890: The Wars for the Pacific Northwest* (Mechanicsburg, Pa.: Stackpole Books, 2002), 556–56.

25. Jerome A. Greene, *Nez Perce Summer, 1877: The U.S. Army and the Nee-Me-Poo Crisis* (Helena: Montana Historical Society Press, 2000), 325.

26. Nelson Miles, *Serving the Republic: Memoirs of the Civil and Military Life of Nelson A. Miles* (New York: Harper, 1911), 180–81.

27. Robert H. Steinbach, *A Long March: the Lives of Frank and Alice Baldwin* (Austin: University of Texas Press, 1989), 131–32.

28. YJIV, 429.

29. John A. Carpenter, "General Howard and the Nez Perce War of 1877," *Pacific Northwest Quarterly* 49:4 (October 1958): 144; *Bismarck Tri-Weekly Tribune,* November 21, 1877; Alfred A. Terry to Adjutant General, November 14, 1877, Special File of Letters Received, War Department, Division of the Missouri, NA; Nelson Miles to O. O. Howard, January 8, 1878, ser. M91, OOH.

30. Sherman to Sheridan, August 31, 1877, and October 10, 1877, Nez Perce War, Special File of Letters Received, War Department, Division of the Missouri, NA.

31. Sherman to Sheridan, October 10, 1877, Nez Perce War, Special File of Letters Received, War Department, Division of the Missouri, NA.

32. Commissioner of Indian Affairs, in *Report of the Secretary of the Interior, 1877,* H.Exec.Doc. 1, pt. 5, vol. 1, 45th Cong., 2nd sess. Serial Set 1800, 8:409. Charles E. S. Wood, in the capital working on Howard's behalf, ran into the Idahoan Frank Fenn, prominent in the early fighting against the bands, as Fenn was leaving interior secretary Carl Schurz's office. Fenn said that his neighbors feared that if the fugitives returned they would unearth caches of weapons and once again attack and harass the settlers—a view he presumably passed on to Schurz. Wood gave his opinion that the Nez Perces posed no threat. Charles E. S. Wood to Oliver O. Howard, November 16, 1877, ser. M91, OOH.

33. Charles E. S. Wood to Oliver O. Howard, November 16, 1877. Schurz went on to say that he thought all Plateau tribes should be "gradually and gently consolidated" on one large reservation.

34. William Sherman to Oliver Howard, December 12, 1877, ser. M91, OOH.

35. *Bismarck Tri-Weekly Tribune,* November 23, 1877

36. Pope also wrote Sheridan that if the bands were to stay with him, he at least might build some sheds of rough lumber. There is no record of a reply. Pope to R. C. Drum, Assistant Adjutant General, November 13, 1877, Pope to Sheridan, November 23, 1877, Sherman to Sheridan, November 25, 1877, Pope to Sheridan, November 25, 1877, Pope to Sheridan, November 27, 1877, Nez Perce War, Special File of Letters Received, War Department, Division of the Missouri, NA.

37. Commissioner of Indian Affairs, in *Report of the Secretary of the Interior, 1878,* H.Exec.Doc. 1, pt. 5, vol. 1, 45th Cong., 3rd sess. Serial Set 1850, 9:464; *HM,* 529–30.

38. "Testimony Taken by the Joint Committee on Transfer of the Indian Bureau," S.Misc.Doc. 53, 45th Cong., 3rd sess. Serial Set 1835, 3:79.

39. Commissioner of Indian Affairs, in *Report of the Secretary of the Interior, 1878,* 9:464; J. Stanley Clark, "The Nez Perces in Exile," *Pacific Northwest Quarterly* 36:3 (July 1945): 215.

40. The quotation is from the *San Francisco Daily Evening Bulletin,* May 16, 1878. For the debate, see *Congressional Record,* 45th Cong., 2nd sess., vol. 7, pt. 4, 3235–41, 3257–66.

41. Ibid., 3236.

42. Ibid., 3260.

43. Ibid., 3260. Senator John J. Ingalls of Kansas took up a more muted theme. The fertile, salubrious Indian Territory in time should be opened to white settlement. Keeping it only for Indians would be "un-American," and sending more tribes there only worsened the situation. Crowding in more Indians would also complicate opening the territory to railroads (3237).

44. Ibid., 3266.

45. "Mrs. Shot-in-Head's Sequel to Former Narrative," box 7, folder 38, McW.

46. *HM,* 511 n. "The Story of Pe-Na-We-Non-Me [Mrs. Shot-in-Head]," box 8, folder 43, McW; Jerome A. Greene, "The Nez Perces in Canada," manuscript in my possession, 78–82. Greene carefully compiled various reports of deaths, which total forty-two, although it is not clear whether some reports overlap. See also "Warriors Escaping from Last Battle Killed by Enemy Tribes," list compiled by Many Wounds and Black Eagle, box 11, folder 79, McW, and Otis Halfmoon, list of Nez Perces killed by Assiniboins in Canada, July 25, 2005, Nez Perce in Canada vertical file, NPHP. Hugh Scott told of hearing from a band of Assiniboins that they had followed protocol and given five escaping Nez Perces a fine dinner ("give them the best you have got, for it is the last one they will ever eat," they admonished each other) and that once they had left, several young warriors chased them down and killed and scalped them. Yellow Bull told much the same story. Hugh Scott to Walter Camp, September 2, 1913, Interview with Yellow Bull, February 13, 1915, both in WMC.

47. Hugh Lenox Scott, *Some Memories of a Soldier* (New York: Century, 1928), 771; Hugh Scott to Walter Camp, September 2, 1913, Marion Maus to Walter Camp, February 8, 1914, WMC.

48. At the end of August 1877, General George Crook sent word to invite the renowned Sioux warrior Crazy Horse to join the campaign Crook was assembling in case the Nez Perces escaped Yellowstone Park. Crazy Horse either accepted but had his words mistranslated or, more likely, refused outright. Whatever happened, the conversation helped bring about his arrest and killing on September 5, the day the Nez Perces made their move to leave the national park. The fullest discussion of this much-debated episode is in Jeffrey Ostler, *The Plains Sioux and U.S. Colonialism from Lewis and Clark to Wounded Knee* (Cambridge: Cambridge University Press, 2004), 85–105.

49. Unidentified author to Cora, May 21, 1890, transcript, archives, Glenbow Museum, Calgary, Alberta.

50. William A. Dobak, "Killing the Canadian Buffalo, 1821–1881," *Western Historical Quarterly* 27:1 (spring 1996): 47–49.

51. "Governor General's Office Numbered Files, File 2001–1," copy, "Nez Perce in Canada," vertical file, NPHP.

52. Hugh A. Dempsey, "The Tragedy of White Bird: An Indian's Death in Exile," *Beaver,* February–March 1993, 23–29.

53. "White Hawk Escapes to Sitting Bull," box 14, folder 104, McW.

54. *YW,* 278.

55. Ibid., 288, 288 n.

56. *HM,* 511.

57. *St. Louis Globe-Democrat,* July 25, 1878.

## Chapter 18

1. Commissioner of Indian Affairs, *Report of the Secretary of the Interior, 1877,* H.Exec.Doc. 1, pt. 5, vol. 1, 45th Cong., 2nd sess. Serial Set 1800, 8:409.

2. A recent book thoroughly covers the Nez Perce exile and return: J. Diane Pearson, *The Nez Perces in the Indian Territory: Nimiipuu Survival* (Norman: University of Oklahoma Press, 2008).

3. J. Stanley Clark, "The Nez Perces in Exile," *Pacific Northwest Quarterly* 36:3 (July 1945): 221–23.

4. *YW,* 289. Raven Spy recalled: "Babies and children dying; one hundred of them." "The Narrative of Kul-Kul Si-Yakth: 'Raven Spy,'" box 7, folder 38, McW.

5. Chief Joseph [translator James Reuben] to O. O. Howard, June 30, 1880, ser. M91, OOH; Thomas J. Jordan, in Commissioner of Indian Affairs, *Report of the Secretary of the Interior, 1881,* H.Exec.Doc. 1, pt. 5, vol. 2, 47th Cong., 1st sess. Serial Set 2018, 10:152.

6. Clark, "Nez Perces in Exile," 222.

7. William H. Whiteman, in Commissioner of Indian Affairs, *Report of the Secretary of the Interior, 1879,* H.Exec.Doc. 1, pt. 5, vol. 1, 46th Cong., 2nd sess. Serial Set 1910, 9:181; Thomas J. Jordan, in Commissioner of Indian Affairs, *Report of the Secretary of the Interior, 1882,* H.Exec.Doc. 1, pt. 5, vol. 2, 47th Cong., 2nd sess. Serial Set 2100, 11:137; *New York Times,* October 29, 1883.

8. William Whiting, in Commissioner of Indian Affairs, *Report of the Secretary of the Interior, 1880,* H.Exec.Doc 1, pt. 5, vol. 1, 46th Cong., 3rd sess. Serial Set 1959, 9:207.

9. Clark, "Nez Perces in Exile," 221–27; *Report of the Committee on Indian Affairs, United States Senate, On the Condition of the Indians in the Indian Territory, and Other Reservations, etc., 1886,* S.Rpt. 1278, pt. 1, 49th Cong., 1st sess. Serial Set 2362, 8:298–300.

10. Lewellen E. Woodin in Commissioner of Indian Affairs, *Report of the Secretary of the Interior, 1883,* H.Exec.Doc. 1, pt. 5. vol. 2, 48th Cong., 1st sess. Serial Set 2191, 2:137.

11. William Whiting, in Commissioner of Indian Affairs, *Report of the Secretary of the Interior, 1880,* 9, 208.

12. Tilden, a boy at the time of the war, later became a prominent source in recording its details. See for instance, "Statement by Samuel Tilden," box 10, folder 62, McW. On Gould: *New York Times,* October 29, 1883.

13. *San Francisco Daily Evening Bulletin,* April 25, 1878.

14. *St. Louis Globe-Democrat,* January 19, 1879, January 26, 1879.

15. *New York Times,* January 18, 1879; *St. Louis Globe-Democrat,* January 26, 1879; *Concord (NH) Independent Statesman,* January 30, 1879.

16. *Testimony Taken by the Joint Committee Appointed to Take into Consideration the Expediency of Transferring the Indian Bureau to the War Department,* 1879, S.Misc.Doc. 53, 45th Cong., 3rd sess. Serial Set 1835, 3:78.

17. YJIV, 432–33.

18. *Bismarck Tri-Weekly Tribune,* November 23, 1877.

19. *Chicago Daily Inter-Ocean,* December 31, 1881.

20. Chief Joseph [translator James Reuben] to O. O. Howard, June 30, 1880.

21. O. O. Howard to Chief Joseph, July 20, 1880, ser. M91, OOH.

22. *Boston Daily Advertiser,* January 3, 1882; *New York Times,* October 29, 1883.

23. *Boston Daily Advertiser,* January 3, 1882, February 11, 1882, July 27, 1882; *New York Times,* October 29, 1883.

24. *New York Times,* October 29, 1883.

25. Ibid.

26. Lewellen E. Woodin, in Commissioner of Indian Affairs, *Report of the Secretary of the Interior, 1883,* H.Exec.Doc. 1, pt. 5. vol. 2, 48th Cong., 1st sess. Serial Set 2191, 2:137, 330–31.

27. Eric Foner, *Reconstruction: America's Unfinished Revolution, 1863–1877* (New York: Harper and Row, 1988), 80–81; Leon F. Litwack, *Been in the Storm So Long: The Aftermath of Slavery* (New York: Random House, 1979), 296–97.

28. Thomas J. Jordan, in Commissioner of Indian Affairs, *Report of the Secretary of the Interior, 1881,* 10:152.

29. Ibid.; Lewellen E. Woodin, in Commissioner of Indian Affairs, *Report of the Secretary of the Interior, 1883,* 2:137; *HM,* 537.

30. For the Cleveland memorial see *Congressional Record,* 45th Cong., 2nd sess., vol. 7, pt. 4, 2916, and for Dawes's remarks, 4496. Other petitions noted: 3164, 3779, 3850, 3909, 4093, 4094, 4095, 4137, 4243.

31. Pearson, *Nez Perces in the Indian Territory,* 280–82.

32. *HM,* 540–42; *YW,* 289–90; Camille Williams to L. V. McWhorter, May 19, 1940, box 7, folder 34, McW; Mrs. Frances Monteith to L. V. McWhorter, December 11, 1934, box 8, folder 34, McW; G. L. Deffenbaugh, in Commissioner of Indian Affairs, *Report of the Secretary of the Interior, 1885,* H.Exec.Doc. 1, pt. 5, vol. 2, 49th Cong., 1st sess. Serial Set 2379, 12:299.

33. Hugh L. Scott to Walter Camp, September 2, 1913, WMC; "Narrative of Kul-kul Si-Yakth: Raven Spy," box 7, folder 38, McW.

34. Pearson, *Nez Perces in the Indian Territory,* 266–68.

35. Sidney D. Waters, in Commissioner of Indian Affairs, *Report of the Secretary of the Interior, 1886,* H.Exec.Doc. 1, pt. 5, vol. 2, 49th Cong., 1st sess. Serial Set 2379, 12:411–12.

36. *YW,* 290.

37. *New York Times,* April 24, 27, 28, 1897.

38. *New York Times,* April 24, 1897.

39. *Portland (OR) Morning Oregonian,* August 14, 1899.

40. James McLaughlin, *My Friend the Indian* (Lincoln: University of Nebraska Press, 1989), 366.

41. Albert M. Anderson in Commissioner of Indian Affairs, *Annual Reports of the Department of the Interior, 1900,* H.Doc.5, pt. 2–1, 56th Cong., 2nd sess. Serial Set 4101, 27:393; Albert M. Anderson, in Commissioner of Indian Affairs, *Annual Reports of the Department of the Interior, 1898,* H.Doc.5, pt. 2, 55th Cong., 3rd sess. Serial Set 3757, 15:298.

42. On Erskine's time at Nespelem in 1892 and 1893, see Erskine Wood, "A Boy's Visit to Chief Joseph," *St. Nicholas* 20:11 (September 1893): 815–19, Erskine Wood, "Partial Account in Erskine Wood's Hand of His First Visit with Chief Joseph," box B, folder 5, Wood Family Papers, Special Collections, Lewis and Clark College Library, Portland, Oregon, and "Diary of 2nd Visit to Chief Joseph," box B, folder 8, Special Collections, Lewis and Clark College Library, as well as correspondence between Erskine Wood and his parents in Wood Family Papers. For his poetic answer: Erskine Wood to mother, October 15, 1892, box 3, item 2, Wood Family Papers.

43. *Harper's Weekly,* October 20, 1900.

44. *New York Times,* February 13, 22, September 16, 18, 1903.

45. M. Gidley, *Kopet: A Documentary Narrative of Chief Joseph's Last Years* (Seattle: University of Washington Press, 1981), 38–39.

46. Ibid., 66–67.

47. *New York Times,* September 24, 25, 1904.

48. Gidley, *Kopet,* 82–83.

49. Ibid., 91–92.

## Epilogue

1. *Time,* April 5, 1971.

2. *Indian Country Today,* January 16, 2006.

3. Allen P. Slickpoo, Sr., and Deward E. Walker, Jr., *Noon Nee-Me-Poo (We, the Nez Perces): Culture and History of Nez Perces* (Lapwai, Idaho: Nez Perce Tribe of Idaho, 1973), 210.

4. Deward E. Walker, Jr., *Conflict and Schism in Nez Perce Acculturation: A Study of Religion and Politics* (Moscow: University of Idaho Press, 1985), 64.

5. A. F. Parker, "Idaho and the Nez Perce Reserve," *West Shore* (July 1889): 381–82.

6. "Comments and Opinions of Other Officers re: Campaign," Mss FD 869, Fort Dalles Collection, HL.

7. W. B. Audlip to Howard, October 29, 1877, ser. M91, OOH.

8. As the book's subtitle indicates, Howard also perpetuated the fiction that Joseph was responsible for the war's start and was in command throughout: *Nez Perce Joseph: An Account of His Ancestors, His Lands, His Confederates, His Enemies, His Murders, His War, His Pursuit and Capture* (Boston: Lee and Shepard, 1881). In a book written for young readers thirty years after the war, Howard called Joseph "the greatest Indian warrior I ever fought." O. O. Howard, *Famous Indian Chiefs I Have Known* (Lincoln: University of Nebraska Press, 1989), 198.

9. John Gibbon, "Adventures of American Army and Navy Officers," pt. 3, "The Battle of the Big Hole," *Harper's Weekly,* December 28, 1895, 1235.

10. Erskine Wood, "Reminiscence of Fishing at Chief Joseph's Camp," box B, folder 16, Wood Family Papers, Special Collections, Watzek Library, Lewis and Clark College Library, Portland, Oregon; *St. Paul and Minneapolis Pioneer Press,* August 1, 1881, clipping, box 5, folder 13, Jerome Greene Research Papers, NPHP.

11. "Dec. 4, 1919, Howowenew and David Scott at my house…," final page of "Diary of 2nd Visit to Chief Joseph," box B, folder 8, Wood Family Papers.

12. Alan Trachtenberg, *Shades of Hiawatha: Staging Indians, Making Americans, 1880–1930* (New York, 2004), 9.

13. Anthony F. C. Wallace makes this point in his excellent study of Thomas Jefferson's policies toward and treatment of native peoples. Under the hierarchical British Empire, there was little need for cultural common ground exactly because its subjects had so little say in public affairs. As power was opened to popular influence in the American republic, the need to speak out of some common tradition logically led to marginalizing those considered too far outside that tradition, notably Indian peoples. Anthony F. C. Wallace, *Jefferson and the Indians: The Tragic Fate of the First Americans* (Cambridge: Harvard University Press, 1999), 17–18.

14. *YW,* 13–19.

# INDEX

About Asleep (Eelahweemah),
    156, 189, 274
Absaroka Mountains, 227–232, 234–235
A Company (Gibbon), 187, 190
A Company (Miles), 272
Aguinaldo, Emilio, 313
Albert, Joe (Elaskolatat), 155
alcoholism, 150
Alexander, Charles, 201
Alpowai band, 105, 141–142, 152
Alvord, Benjamin, 87
American bison
    see bison
American Bison Society, 263
American Fur Company, 24, 35
American presence
    fur trade, 24–28
    Oregon country, 58–61
    pioneer immigration and settlement,
        31–32, 46–49
Amherst, Jeffrey, 57
annexation of Texas (1845), 59
antelopes, 9
Apaches, xviii
Appomattox, 292
Arapahoes, 17, 79, 96
Arkansas City, Kansas, 311
Army Medical Museum, 315
Asiatic cholera, 55, 149
assimilation policies, 43–46, 85, 102–105
Assiniboins, 257, 269, 297, 315, 371n46
Astoria, 24
Astor, John Jacob, 24
Atsinas, 21, 22

authority structure, 12–14, 31–33,
    109, 158–160

Bacon, George, 205–206, 210
Bad Boy/Rough Customer
    (Nez Perce), 236
Baird, George W., 298
Baker, James, 126–127
balsamroot, 11
Bancroft, Eugene, 155
Bancroft, Hubert Howe, 77
bands, 11–13, 17–18
Bannack City, Montana, 202, 204
Bannocks
    Battle of Canyon Creek, 249
    geographic barriers, 14
    and Howard, 209
    Howard's advance scouts, 202, 203,
        225–226
    military conflicts, xviii
    Yellowstone National Park, 215, 218
baptism, 51
Baptists, 103
Barstow, A. C., 113
battle casualties
    Battle of Bear's Paw, 272–273,
        275–277, 279
    Battle of Big Hole, 189–193, 196,
        201–202
    Battle of Clearwater, 157–158
    loss of pride, 317
    monetary costs, 316
Battle of Bear's Paw, 3–4, 268,
    269–279, 270

Battle of Big Hole, 184–196, *188*, 199–200, 317
Battle of Canyon Creek, 244, *246*, 247–248
Battle of Clearwater, 153–168, 198
Baxter Springs, Kansas, 300
B Company (Bradley), 187
bears, 8
Bear's Paw Mountains, 257, *268*, 268–269
beaver skins, 24–26, 28–29
Beecher, Henry Ward, 104
Benedict, Isabella, 126, 127, 133, 136
Benedict, Samuel, 124–125, 126
Benson, Henry, 209
Benteen, Frederick, 150, 245, 247
berries, 9
Biddle, Jonathan, 272
Big Hole, 182, 184–185, 226
Big Hole National Battlefield, 315
Big Snowy Mountains, 251
Big Thunder, 89, 92
Birch Creek, 204
Bird Alighting (Peopeo Tholekt), 141–142, 156, 274, 279
biscuitroot, 9–10, 11
Bismarck, North Dakota, 55, 177, 216, 283, 295
bison, 9, 258–263, *261*, 363nn47–51
*Bison antiquus*, 258
*Bison bison americanus*, 258
Bitterroot Mountains, 5, 7, 14, 169
Bitterroot River, 171
Bitterroot Valley, 171–177, 181–183
Black Eagle (Wep-tes-tse-mookh Tse-mookh), 36, 274, 281, 316
Black Feather (Whylimlex), 136
Blackfeet
    bison hunting, 259
    capture of Nez Perce girl, 21
    geographic barriers, 14
    impact of guns and horses, 18
    intertribal conflicts, 12
    Lewis and Clark Expedition, 22, 23
    origins, 4
    Yellowstone National Park, 215
Black Hair, 206
Black Hills, South Dakota, 79, 109
Blanchet, Augustine, 38
Blanchet, Francois, 38

blueback salmon, 8
Blue Mountains, 7, 14
Blue Mountains geological province, 5
Board of Indian Commissioners, 103, 304
Bonneville, B. L. E., 28, 38
Bourke, John Gregory, 240, 242
Bow and Arrow Case (Phillip Evans), 140
*Boy Scout Handbook*, 290
Boy Scouts of America, 290
Bozeman, Montana, 220, 221, 225, 231
Bradley, James, 183, 184–185, 187, 190, 240, 241
Brave Seventeen, 144–145
Brice, Patrick, 127, 136
Bridger, Jim, 182
British presence
    confrontations with the Wallawallas, 327n10
    fur trade, 24, 25–26
    Oregon country, 58
    religious influences, 37
The Broken Arm (Tunnachemoontoolt), 21
Brouillet, J. B. A., 50, 330n15
Buck, Henry, 173, 202
buffalo
    *see* bison
buffalo berries, 253
The Bull's Head (Kentuck), 27

Cain, Andrew J., 79
Calapooya River, 50
California, 49, 55, 76, 96
Calvalry cemetery, St. Louis, 316
Camas Creek, 206
camas lilies, 9–10
Camas Meadows, 206, 208, 209, 225
Camas Prairie, 128, 143
*Camassia quamash*, 9–10
Cameahwait (Shoshone Chief), 203
Camp Chopunnish, 23
Camp Norton, 143–144
Camp Rains, 144
Canadian exile, 296–299
Canyon Creek, 244–247
Captain John, 279–281, 284–285
Carleton, James, 238

Carlisle Indian School, 104, 290,
      303, 313
Carnahan, J. M., 177
Carpenter, Frank, 219, 220, 222, 226
Carpenter, Ida, 219, 220, 222, 226
Carson, Christopher "Kit", 96
Cascade Mountains, 7
Catholicism, 38
Catlin, George, 35, 369n16
Catlin, J. B., 183–184, 187, 191, 202
Cayuses
   confrontations with white settlers, 48
   disease epidemics, 49, 55, 57
   fur trade, 25
   kinship and social bonds, 13
   missionaries, 29
   origins, 4
   religious practices, 39
   social structure, 69
   treaty negotiations, 61–65, 67–68
   Whitman massacre, 49–50, 58
Centennial Mountains, 205
Chamberlain, John, 128, 129,
      140, 343n14
Chapman, Arthur "Ad"
   Battle of Clearwater, 153
   battle with the Nez Perces,
      134, 135
   civilian troops, 131
   as interpreter, 282, 284–285,
      299, 304
Charlot (Chief of the Flatheads), 182
Cherokees, 45, 296
Cheyennes
   Battle of Bear's Paw, 274
   disease epidemics, 55
   impact of guns and horses, 18
   and Miles, 251, 268
   military conflicts, 79, 96, 199
   trade networks, 17
*Chicago Tribune*, 285
chief, 12–13
Chief Joseph Dam, 314
*Chief Joseph: The Biography
      of a Great Indian* (Fee), 288
chinook salmon, 8
Chipmunk (Nez Perce), 124
Choctaws, 45, 296
chokecherries, 9, 11
cholera epidemic, 55, 149

*Christian Advocate and Journal and Zion's
      Herald*, 35–36
Christianity
   enforced conversions, 85, 99,
      102–104, 310
   federal government policies, 81
   and Howard, 112
   missionaries, 36–39, 41–51
   *see also* missionaries
Chuslum Hahlap Kanoot
      (Naked-footed Bull), 223
Civil War
   historical perspectives, xiii–xvi
   implications, 318–319
   and Miles, 251
   post-war policies, 100
   and Sturgis, 232
   technological impacts, 180–181
   and western expansion, 95–97
Clarke, John, 25
Clarke, Newman S., 71
Clark, Fanny, 245
Clark's Fork, Yellowstone River,
      228–232, 234–236, 244
Clark, William, xviii, 16, 20–23,
      33, 35, 168
   *see also* Lewis and Clark Expedition
Clearwater River, 6, 7–8, 75–76,
      152–153
Cleveland, Grover, 309
climate, 7
Clyman, James, 27
Cochise (Chiricahua
      Apache leader), 108
Cody, William F. "Buffalo Bill",
      224, 311
Cody, Wyoming, 227
Coeur d'Alenes, 4, 13, 71–72
collective/shared activities, 12–13
Colorado gold strikes, 76, 79
Columbia Plateau, 5
Columbia River, 6
Colville, Washington, 76, 310–311
Comanches
   impact of guns and horses, 18
   military conflicts, 199
   Red River War (1874-75), 251, 262
   trade networks, 17
combines, 11
Congressional Peace Policy, 101–105

Conner, Patrick, 96
contact diseases, 52–54
Cooke City, 228
Cooke, Jay, 216–217
Corinne, Utah, 171, 254
corporal punishment, 41
Corps of Discovery, xviii, 20–23, 58–59
    see also Lewis and Clark Expedition
Corvallis, Montana, 171, 183
Cottonwood Creek, 130, 140, 141,
    145, 152–153
Cottonwood House, 128, 143
Coulson, Montana, 244–245
cous, 9–10, 11
Cowan, Emma, 219–220, 221, 222,
    223–224, 226
Cowan, George, 219–221,
    222, 226, 228
Cowan party, 219–224, 222, 241
Cow Creek, 254–256
Cow Island, 254–256, 268, 279
Coyote, legend of, 4, 168
Crandall Creek, 234
Crazy Horse, 290, 297, 371n48
Creeks, 45
Crees, 297
Crook, George, 112, 151, 230, 241
Crow Agency, 231
Crows
    bargaining power with white
        population, 249–250
    Battle of Canyon Creek, 248–249
    Battle of Clearwater, 166
    bison hunting, 259–260
    confrontations with
        Nez Perces, 249
    confrontations with
        the Sioux, 250
    origins, 4
    relationships with the Nez Perces,
        171, 174, 182, 183, 204, 227
    trade networks, 17
    Yellowstone National Park, 215, 218
cults, 84
Curry, George, 92, 93, 97
Curtis, Edward S., 159, 162
Cushing, Henry, 231–232, 253, 362n33
Custer, George Armstrong
    Little Big Horn, 110, 147, 177,
        198, 232, 250

    social contact with Native Ameri-
        cans, 239
The Cut Lip, 20, 21
cutthroat trout, 8

Daily Graphic (Chicago), 285
Daily Inter-Ocean (Chicago), 284
Daily Union (Sacramento), 97
Darrow, Clarence, 287
Dawes Allotment Act (1887), 309, 316
Dawes, Henry L., 309
Day, Lew, 128, 129, 343n14
Daytime Smoke (Halahtookit),
        23, 27, 168, 302
D Company (Gibbon), 187
D Company (Moylan), 272
Dead Indian Hill, 234, 235
Dead Mule Trail, 140
Deer Lodge, 171, 202, 205
Deitrich, Richard, 223
Demers, Modeste, 38
Denig, Edward, 259
desertion, 149–150
Devil's Gate, 236
Devine, Richard, 124
disease epidemics, 48–50, 52–57,
        149, 295, 302
displacement policies, 44–46
Doane, Gustavus
    on bison hunting, 260
    and the Crows, 250, 253
    pursuit of Nez Perces, 223,
        227, 229, 232
Dodge, Granville, 311
Dodge, Richard, 238, 240
Doolittle Commission, 100
Doolittle, James R., 100, 102
Double Ditch archaeological site, 55
Dreamers, 81–85, 83, 114
Dull Knife (Cheyenne Chief), 199
Dunraven, Windham Thomas
        Wyndham-Quin, Earl of, 217,
        224
dysentery, 49, 55, 149

Eagle in the Light, 72–73, 89, 92
Eagle Robe (Tipyahlahnah Siskan), 124
Edmunds, George F., 296
Eeikish Pah (The Hot Place), 300–304,
        308–309

Eelahweemah (About Asleep), 156, 189, 274
Elaskolatat (Animal Entering a Hole), 155
elderberries, 9
Elice (Ellis), 33, 37–38, 41, 59
elk, 8
Elk City, Idaho, 7, 77, 78, 80
elk thistles, 9
Emerson, Ralph Waldo, 306
*eneynu ti-to-qam* (provincials), 17–18
English, Lieutenant, 194
*Equus caballus*, 197
Eskoomskee (No Feet), 133, 160, 298
European contact, 15
Evans, Phillip (Bow and Arrow Case), 140

farming settlements, 29, 260
*Far West* (steamboat), 177
F Company (Gibbon), 187
F Company (Ilges), 256
F Company (Perry), 134, 135
federal government policies
    exile of the Nez Perces, 294–296
    military troops, 146–150
    Nez Perces, 101–105, 107–109, 111–120
Fee, Chester Anders, 288
Fessenden, William, 88
Fifth Cavalry, 230–231
Fifth Infantry, 268–269, 272–273
Findley, A. B., 110–111
firearms, 15, 18–19, 22
fireberries, 11
Firehole River, 219, 221, 225–226, 227
First Cavalry, 254
First Red Feather of the Wing (H-wow-no Ilpilp), 158–159
fish, 8
Fisher, Stanton, 225–226, 228, 229, 236, 248, 254
fish headman, 12
Fitzgerald, Emily, 139, 167
Fitzgerald, John, 139, 201, 211, 221, 240, 317
Five Crows, 64, 68
Five Fogs (Pahka Pahtahank), 189
Five Wounds (Pahkatos Owyeen), 140, 162, 183, 195–196, 315
Flatheads
    Battle of Clearwater, 165

fur trade, 25
    impact of guns and horses, 18
    intertribal conflicts, 12
    kinship and social bonds, 13
    Nez Perce retreat, 182
    trip to St. Louis, 36
Florence, 77–78, 80
*Fontenelle* (steamboat), 268
food availability, 8–11
Forse, Albert G., 110, 145
Fort Abraham Lincoln, 293
Fort Belknap, 315
Fort Benton, 176, 254, 256
Fort Boise, 170
Fort Brave, 171
Fort Ellis, 176, 183, 220, 231, 245, 253, 362n33
Fort Fizzle, 173, 177, 182
Fort Hall, 203, 225
Fort Harker, Kansas, 149
Fort Lapwai, 87, 166
Fort Laramie, 239
Fort Laramie Treaty (1868), 100
Fort Larned, Kansas, 147
Fort Leavenworth, Kansas, 295, 299
Fort Nez Perces, 25
Fort Riley, Kansas, 295
Fort Run, 171
Fort Scott, 299–300
Fort Shaw, 176, 183, 209, 211–212
Fort Skidaddle, 171
Fort Vancouver, 108, 167
Fort Walla Walla, 50, 116
*Frank Leslie's Illustrated Weekly*, 291
frasera, 9
Freedmen's Bureau, 108, 112, 139
Frenchman Creek, 276, 279
fur trade, 23–29

Garrison, William Lloyd, 103
Gass, Patrick, 23
G Company (Gibbon), 187
G Company (Romeyn), 273
geological background, 4–5
geological surveys, 216
Geronimo, 318
Ghost Dance, 83
Gibbon, John, *192*
    Battle of Big Hole, 199, 317

Gibbon, John (*Continued*)
  and Howard, 201–202
  impressions and admiration of Native Americans, 238
  impressions and admiration of Nez Perces, 242
  post-war life, 317
  pursuit of Nez Perces, 176–177, 183–196
  supply problems, 362n33
  troop morale, 150

Gilbert, Charles C., 228–229, 232, 362n33
Godfrey, Edward, 272
Goldin, Theodore, 177
Goldman, Emma, 287
gold strikes, 59, 70, 75–81, 85–86, 96
gooseberries, 9, 11
Gould, Jay, 304, 310
Grande Ronde River, 6
Grangeville, Idaho, 7, 128, 131, 141
Grant, Ulysses S., 103, 107, 108, 214
Gray, William, 330n15
Greater Reconstruction, xvi–xix, 59, 151, 292, 318–319
Great Hunt, 258–263, 261
Great Plains, 17, 18, 96–97, 258
Great Small-pox Chief, 57
Greeley, Horace, 46
Grimes, James W., 337n53
Grizzly Bear Youth, 206, 351n16
Gros Ventres, 297, 315
Grover, LaFayette, 107–108
guns-for-horses diplomacy, 22, 26, 250
gun trade, 15, 18–19, 22

Hahtalekin, 105
Hair Combed Over Eyes (Wottolen), 156, 158, 207, 267, 298
Halahtookit (Daytime Smoke), 23, 27, 168, 302
Hale, Calvin H., 88–90, 92–95, 97
Hale, Owen, 269, 272
Halfmoon, Otis, Jr., 315
Hallalhotsoot (Lawyer), *91*
  conversion to Christianity, 51
  mining frontier impacts, 80
  treaty negotiations, 64–69, 72–73, 89–90, 92–93, 97

Hamilton, Montana, 171
Hand in Hand (Nez Perce), 133, 160
Hardin, Edward E., 186
*Harper's Weekly*, 284, 285, 291
Hasenahmahkikt, 298
Hawaiians, 25
Hayden, Ferdinand, 216–217
Hayes, Rutherford B., 163, 293, 304
Hayt, E. A., 301, 304
H Company (Trimble), 134
headman, 11–13
Heart Mountain, 232, 234–235
Heart of the Monster, 4, 41, 168
*Heavenly Discourses* (Wood), 287
Heh-yookts Toe-nihn (Rabbit Skin Leggings), 36
Heinmot Tooyalakekt (Young Joseph), 51, 59, 84, 106–107, *113*
  *see also* Joseph (Chief of the Nez Perces)
Helena, Montana, 221, 223
Hell's Canyon, 7
Hemene Moxmox
  *see* Yellow Wolf (Hemene Moxmox)
Henderson ranch raid, 223, 227, 357n31
Henry Lake, 205, 210–212, 221, 225, 231
herald, 12
Heyoooom Iklakit (Grizzly Bear Lying Down), 274
Hickok, James Butler "Wild Bill", 224
Hidatsas, 17, 19, 54
Hill, Tom, 277–278
historical perspective of nineteenth century America, xiii–xix
Hogan, Sgt., 192–193
Hohots Ilppilp (Red Grizzly Bear), 20, 21, 22, 31, 33–34
Holmes, Oliver Wendell, 181
homeland geography, 5–7
Homestead Act (1862), 95
Hoodoo Basin, 229
Hornaday, William, 263
Horse Prairie, 203
horses
  Battle of Bear's Paw, 270–271, 273–275
  Battle of Clearwater, 196, 198–199
  as food, 253

importance, 16–17, 18, 196–200, 203
as military strategy, 198–199
Nez Perce drawing, *198*
raids by the Crows, 248–249
theft of Howard's horses, 206–208
Howard, Guy, 248, 361n19
Howard, Oliver Otis, *138*
    arrival at Fort Vancouver, 108–109
    arrival at Snake Creek, 279–280
    Battle of Clearwater, 153–168,
        198–199
    battle preparations, 137, 139–140
    battle with the Nez Perces, 133,
        140–143, 152–153
    and civilian population, 145–146,
        204–205
    Civil War battles, 137
    confrontations with white
        settlers, 110
    exile of the Nez Perces, 293, 295
    Freedmen's Bureau, 108, 112, 139
    and Gibbon, 201–202
    impressions and admiration of
        Native Americans, 238
    and Joseph, 307, 311, 313–314
    and Miles, 279
    nontreaty Nez Perce bands,
        123–124, 130–131
    and Perry, 145
    post-war life, 317
    pursuit of Nez Perces, 169–174,
        201–213, *207*, 225, 228–232,
        235–237, 243, 250–251, 253–254
    and Sherman, 211–213, 228
    supply problems, 362n33
    surrender of Nez Perces, 280–285
    treaty negotiations, 111–120
    troop morale, 150
    use and care of horses, 198–199
    use of the telegraph, 177, 211–212
Howe, L. D., 88
Howowenew, 318
huckleberries, 11
Hudson's Bay Company, 58
Huggins, E. L., 82
Humble, John, 183, 351n20
hunting impact on bison, 258–263, *261*
Husishusis Kute (Naked Head),
    105, 119, 275
Hutchins, Charles, 88, 92, 93

H-wow-no Ilpilp (First Red Feather
    of the Wing), 158–159
*Hyracotherium*, 196

I Block Up (Tumokult), 189
ice trade, 28
I Company (Gibbon), 187
Idaho, 96, 98, 316
Idaho City, 135
Ilamnieenimhoosoos, 298
Ilges, Guido, 256–257
Illinois, population increases, 47
Imnaha River, 6, 8, 106
Indian Congress, 313
Indian Peace Commission, 100–101
Indian problem, 88, 100–101
Indian Removal Act (1830), 45
Indian removal policies, 44–46
Indian reservations
    and Calvin Hale, 88–90, 92–95
    Congressional Peace Policy, 101–105
    current status, 316
    federal government policies, 96
    and Isaac Stevens, 61
    Nez Perces, 94, 99
    treaty negotiations, 64–65, 94
Indian Territory, 45, 293, 295–296,
        300–304, 308–309
Indian Treaty Act (1850), 60
indigenous prophets, 55–56, 81–85
intermarriage, 11, 13, 69
In-who-lise, 351n16, 353n18
Iowa, population increases, 47
*ipetes*, 36
Irving, Washington, 27, 28
Irwin (captured soldier), 226
Iskumtselalik Pah, 182

Jackson, Andrew, 45
Jackson, Helen Hunt, 218
Jackson, William Henry, 216
Jefferson River, 352n34
Jerome, David H., 113–114
Jerome, Lovell, 278
John (Nez Perce), 39
*Johnson v. McIntosh*, 60, 94
Jokais (Worthless/Lazy/Captain John),
        279–281, 284–285
Joseph (Chief of the Nez Perces), *113*,
        *161*, *312*

Joseph (Chief of the Nez Perces) (*Cont.*)
    baptism, 51
    Battle of Bear's Paw, 270–271, 273,
        275, 278
    Battle of Big Hole, 196, 199–200
    Battle of Clearwater, 156, 160,
        162–163, 165
    battle with Perry, 133
    contact with white public, 304–309,
        311–314
    conversion to Christianity, 307
    death and funeral, 314
    exile, 299–300, 302
    and federal government policies,
        106–120
    gathering at Tepahlewam, 125
    and Howard, 307, 311, 313–314
    and Miles, 278, 311, 313
    move to White Bird Canyon, 130
    public perception, 290–292
    return from exile, 310–313
    and Roosevelt, 313
    and Sherman, 304
    surrender, xviii, 280–282, 290,
        291–292
    surrender speech, 283–285, 287–288
    trip to New York City, 311, 313
    trip to Washington D. C., 304–308
    and Wood, 285, 287
    Yellowstone tourist encounters, 220
    *see also* Heinmot Tooyalakekt
        (Young Joseph)
Judith Basin, 254, 260
Judith Gap, 231, 251, 253, 254
Jyeloo (Nez Perce), 129

Kamiah, Idaho, 4, 163, 167–168, 170, 298
Kamiakin (Yakima chief), 67,
    69–70, 71, 73
Kanakans, 25
Kane, Paul, 49
Kansas, population increases, 260
Ka-ow-poo (Of the Dawn), 36
Kapkap Ponmi (Noise of
    Running Feet), 274, 298–299
K Company (Gibbon), 187
K Company (Hale), 272
Keeler, A. D. C., 163
Kelley, James, 71
Kenck, Charles, 222, 223

Keogh, Miles, 147
Ketalkpoosmin (Stripes
    Turned Down), 204
Kill Devil Mountains, 5
King, Clarence, 216
kinship bonds, 11, 13–14, 69
Kiowas
    impact of guns and horses, 18
    military conflicts, 199
    Red River War (1874-75), 251, 262
    trade networks, 17
Kipkip Owyeen (Wounded
    Breast), 159
Koolkool Snehee, 89
Kul-Kul Si-Yakth (Raven Spy), 302
*k'usaynu ti-to-gan* (sophisticates), 17

ladder teaching device, 38
LaForge, Thomas, 166
Lake Yellowstone, 226, 227
Lakota Sioux
    *see* Sitting Bull (Sioux Chief)
Lamar River, 226, 229
Lamatama band, 105
Lang, William, 226
Lapwai (Place of the Butterflies)
    Fort Lapwai, 87, 166
    Lapwai Creek mission, 39, 50
    Lapwai Indian agency, 86–88, 101,
        115–120, 309–311
Lawyer, Archie, *303*, 303, 308–309
Lean Elk (Poker Joe)
    arrival at Nez Perce band, 174
    Battle of Bear's Paw, 275
    loss of leadership, 357
    retreat from Big Hole, 202–203
    retreat from Clearwater, 182
    supplies at Cow Island, 255
    wagon train attack, 256
    Yellowstone tourist encounters,
        219–220
Lee, Daniel, 38–39, 330n20
Lee, Jason, 38–39, 330n20
Lee, Robert E., 292
legal jurisdictions (Nez Perces), 98–99
legend of Coyote, 4, 168
Lemhi Shoshonis, 203
Lepeet Hessemdooks (Two Moons),
    134, 158–159
Lewis and Clark Expedition

contact with Nez Perces, 21, 22–23, 26, 31, 33
contact with Shoshonis, 203
disease epidemics, 55, 57
fur trade, 24–25
prophet movements, 56
Lewis, Meriwether, xviii, 16, 20–23
Lewiston, Idaho, 77
fur trade, 24
and Howard's troops, 169–170
mining frontier impacts, 76, 78, 80, 86
precipitation, 7
*Liberator* (Garrison), 103
*Life on the Plains*
(Wild West Show), 313
linguistic ties, 13
Linn, Lewis, 47, 59
Little Belt Mountains, 251
Little Rocky Mountains, 257, 269
Livingston, Montana, 226
Lochsa River, 8
Logan, William, 190
Lolo Pass/Trail, 20, 23, 163–174, 176
*Lomatium canbyi*, 10
*Lomatium cous*, 9–10, 11
Lone Bird (Peopeo Ipsewaht), 182, 275
Long, Stephen H., 258
Looking Glass (Alalimya Takanin)
Battle of Bear's Paw, 275, 277
Battle of Clearwater, 162, 166
battle with the scouting party, 152
battle with Whipple, 141–143
gathering at Tepahlewam, 123–124
meeting with Howard, 118–120
nontreaty Nez Perce bands, 105
and Rawn, 172, 176
resumption of leadership, 257–258, 267, 269
retreat from Clearwater, 182–183
Looking Glass (Apash Wyakaikt), 65–67, 89
looting, 157
lower Nez Perces, 17–18, 80, 89
Loynes, Charles, 189, 191–193, 194
Lyon, Caleb, 98

Mackenzie, Ranald, 199
Madison River, 225
malaria epidemic, 53, 54, 57, 295, 302

Mammoth Hot Springs, 220, 221, 222, 223, 225, 227
Mandans, 54, 55
Manifest Destiny, 179
Man of the Morning, 316
Manuel, Jack, 126–127, 129, 343n14
Manuel, Jennet, 126–127, 129, 343n14
Manuel, John, 127, 129, 343n14
Manuel, Maggie, 126, 127, 136, 343n14
Many Wounds, 257
Marias River, 21
Marshall, James, 79
Marshall, John, 60, 94
Martin, John (Giovanni Martini), 147
Mason, E. C., 169, 173, 212, 221, 240–241
Mason, Harry, 127
Massachusetts Bay, 54
*Masses*, 287
Maxey, Samuel B., 296
Mayer, Frank, 262–263
McCaffrey, Corporal, 192–193
McCarthy, Michael, 135–136, 145, 155, 158, 242
McDougall, Duncan, 57
McDowell, Irvin, 163, 171, 204, 211, 212
McKenney, Thomas, 102
McKenzie, Donald, 24–25
McKinley, William, 318
McLaughlin, James, 312–313
McNall, Wells, 110–111
McWhorter, Lucullus, 321
measles epidemic, 49–50, 52–53, 55
medicine line, xiii, 297
Medicine Lodge Creek Treaty (1867), 100
Medicine Tree, 182
Meopkowit (Baby/Know Nothing/ Captain George/Old George), 279–281, 284–285
Merritt, Wesley, 245, 247–248
Methodists, 38, 99, 103
Mexican War (1846-48), 59
Miamis, 300, 301
Miles City, Montana, 244
Miles, Evan, 154
Miles, Nelson, 252
Battle of Bear's Paw, 269–282
impressions and admiration of Nez Perces, 240

Miles, Nelson (*Continued*)
    and Joseph, 278, 311, 313
    and the Lakota Sioux, 297, 317–318
    post-war life, 317–318
    pursuit of Nez Perces, 212, 244,
        250–251, 267–269
    surrender of Nez Perces, 283–285,
        292–293, 367n50, 367n52
military conflicts, 70–72, 96,
        133–136, 140–144
military impressions and admiration
        of Native Americans, 237–242
military troops, 146–150, 160
Milk River, 257, 279
Mill Creek council grounds, 61–70, 63
Miller Creek, 229
Miller, Henry, 78
Miller, Marcus, 154, 156, 160, 165
Mills, Anson and Nannie, 239
mining frontier impacts, 78–79
Minnesota, 96
Misery Hill, 152–153
missionaries
    arrival in the Pacific Northwest, 29
    Christian conversions, 99, 330n20
    and the Indian population,
        38–41, 43–51
    Nez Perce refugees, 297
    as reservation agents, 103
    White's laws, 31
Missoula City, 169, 170, 183
Missouri Breaks, 253, 254
Missouri, population increases, 47
Missouri River, 214, 253–255, 268–269,
        279, 292–293, 295
Modoc Indians, 108, 300, 301
Moelchert, William, 255
Monida Pass, 204, 205
Monroe, James, 45
Montana, population increases, 96
Monteith, John B., *303*
    meeting with the Nez Perces,
        115–117, 119–120
    missionary activity, 99
    as reservation agent, 99, 104–105,
        107–108, 110, 175
Moore, Joe, 128, 129
Moran, Thomas, 216
Morrill Land Grant Act (1862), 95
Morse, Jedidiah, 179

Morse, Samuel Finley Breese, 178, 179
mountain goats, 8
mountain man ideal, 24, 28
mountain sheep, 8
Mount Idaho, 127–128, 130–131, 133,
        136, 139–140
Moylan, Myles, 272
Muir, John, 218
mule deer, 8
mules, 208
Mullan Road, 96, 169, 170
Musselshell River, 253, 268
mythic role of Indians, 288–290

*Nation*, 291
Navajos, 96
Nebraska, population
        increases, 96, 260
Neolin (Delaware prophet), 83
Nesmith, James W., 88,
        100–101, 337n53
Nespelem Creek, 311, 313, 314
Nespelems, 311
"new" American perspectives,
        288–290, 305–308
Newell, Robert, 80, 99
New Ulm, Minnesota, 96
*New York Times*, 284, 291, 308, 311
*New York Tribune*, 291
Nez Perce National
        Historical Park, 315
Nez Perce National
        Historical Trail, 315
Nez Perces
    assimilation policies, 43–46, 85,
        102–105
    Battle of Bear's Paw, 3–4, 269–279
    Battle of Big Hole, 184–196, *188*,
        199–200
    Battle of Canyon Creek, 244, *246*,
        247–248
    Battle of Clearwater, 153–168, 198
    battle with Perry, 133–136
    battle with the scouting party,
        152–153
    battle with Whipple, 143–144
    birthplace, 4
    Canadian exile, 296–299
    citizenship rights, 318
    confrontations with Crows, 249

confrontations with white settlers, 110–111, 124–130, 145–146, 254
contact with white population, 20–35, 78–81, 85–88, 107–109
conversion to Christianity, 310
cultural changes, 27
dissolution of nation, 93, 97
distrust of white population, 203
Dreamers, 81–85
and Elijah White, 29, 31–34
exile, 293–296, 299–300
federal government policies, 101–105, 107–109, 111–120
food availability, 8–10
gathering at Tepahlewam, 124–126, *125*
gold strike impact, 78–81, 85–86
homeland geography, 5–7
Indian Territory, 300–304, 308–309
legal jurisdictions, 98–99
Lewis and Clark Expedition, 21, 22–23, 26, 31, 33
loss of homeland, 92–95, 97
marksmanship skills, 157–158
and Miles, 244, 250–251
military conflicts, 72
military impressions and admiration of Nez Perces, 237–242
mortality rates, 301–302
negotiation strategies, 67–70
Nez Perce Territory, 6
Nez Perce War Outbreak, *132*
public perception, 290–292
and Rawn, 172, 175–176
relationships with the Crows, 171, 174, 182, 183, 204, 227
religious practices, 36–39, 41, 43–44, 50–51, 99–100, 316
remembrance observances, 315–316
reservation life, 94, 99, 119–120, 300–313
retreat along the Lolo Trail, 163–174, 176
retreat from Big Hole, xiii, 202–213, 218–219, 224–232, 234–237
retreat from Clearwater, 163–177, 181–185
retreat to Canada, 243–251, 253–257, 267–269
return from exile, 309–313

revenge attacks, 124–130, 203
and the Sioux, 243, 296–298
social structure, 10–14, 17–18, 31–33, 69, 109
supplies at Cow Island, 255
surrender, 280–285, 367n50, 367n52
theft of Howard's horses, 206–208
trade networks, 15–19
treaty negotiations, 61–74, *63*, 87–90, 92–94
trip to St. Louis, 35–37
understanding of American culture and technology, 174–177, 181
wagon train attack, 255–256
Yellowstone National Park, 215, 218–225
Yellowstone tourist encounters, 219–226, 357n31
Nez Perce Sam, 298
Nez Perce Territory, 6
Nez Perce War Outbreak, *132*
Nimiipuu (Real People), 4, 168, 318
*see also* Nez Perces
No Feather (Nez Perce), 236
No Feet (Eskoomskee), 133, 160, 298
No Flesh (Sioux), 239
No Heart (Teminisiki), 196, 199–200, 270–271
No Horns (Ta-weis-se-sim-ninh), 36
Noise of Running Feet (Kapkap Ponmi), 274, 298–299
nontreaty Nez Perce bands
band characteristics, 105–106
gold strike impact, 80
loss of homeland, 107–112, 114–120
reservations, 89, 97
treaty negotiations, 92
Norris, Philetus, 218
*North American Review*, 305, 306–307
Northern Pacific Railroad, 216–217
North West Company, 24, 25
Norton, Benjamin, 128, 343n14
Norton, Hill, 128, 343n14
Norton, Jennie, 128, 343n14
Norwood, Randolph, 206, 208–209
obsidian, 215

Odeneal, T. B., 107
Ogden, Peter Skene, 26, 50
Old George, 279–281, 284–285

Old Joseph
    see Tuekakas (Old Joseph)
Ollokut (Frog)
    Battle of Bear's Paw, 275
    Battle of Big Hole, 196
    Battle of Clearwater, 154,
        158, 160, 162
    battle with Perry, 133
    confrontations with Crows, 249
    gathering at Tepahlewam, 125
    and Joseph, 110
    meeting with Monteith, 115
    move to White Bird Canyon, 130
    religious practices, 84
Ollokut's widow, 299
Olympia (WA) Pioneer and Democrat, 81
Omohundro, John B. "Texas Jack", 224
Oregon
    and Elijah White, 328n26
    missionary activity, 330n20
    pioneer immigration and settlement,
        29, 39, 46–48, 58–61, 70
    population increases, 59–60, 98
    Wallowa County, 316
Oregon Donation Act (1850), 59
Oregon Territory, 58–59
Oregon Treaty (1846), 58
Oregon Weekly Times, 70
Orofino Creek, 75–76, 79
Orofino, Idaho, 8
Otskai, 207
Otstotpoo (Fire Body), 157
Ott, Larry, 124
Over the Point (Teeweeyownah),
    159–160
Owhi (Yakima chief), 64, 65, 71–72
Owyeen (Wounded), 191

Pacific Railroad Act (1862), 95, 180
Pacific Telegraph Act (1860), 180
pack mules, 208
Pahit Palikt, 190
Pahka Pahtahank (Five Fogs), 189
Pahkatos Owyeen (Five Wounds),
    140, 162, 195–196, 315
Palmer, Joel, 61, 62–65, 68–70
Palmer, William Jackson, 369n16
Palo Duro Canyon, Texas, 199
Palouses, 13, 69, 72, 119
Pambrum, Andrew, 69–70, 334n43

Parker, Samuel, 39, 329n6
Parnell, William, 135, 147, 157
Peace Policy, 101–105
Pelican Creek, 226
Pend Oreilles, 4
Peopeo Ipsewaht (Lone Bird), 182, 275
Peopeo Kiskiok Hihih (White Bird)
    gathering at Tepahlewam, 124
    nontreaty Nez Perce bands, 105
    revenge attacks, 126
    treaty negotiations, 89, 90
Peopeo Moxmox (Yellow Bird),
    49, 64, 65, 67–68, 70–71
Peopeo Tholekt (Bird Alighting),
    141–142, 156, 274, 279
Peorias, 300, 301
Perry, David, 131–136, 144–145, 156, 158
Pickering, John, 329n12
Pierce City, 76–77
Pierce, Elias D., 75–76, 79
pioneer immigration and settlement
    disease epidemics, 54–55
    and Elijah White, 328n26
    impact on bison, 260
    Oregon, 29, 58–61, 70
    population increases, 46–49
    White's laws, 31–32
Place of the Manure Fires
    (Tsanim Alikos Pah), 258
The Poet in the Desert (Wood), 287
Polk, James K., 58, 178
Pompey's Pillar, 253
Poncas, 301
Pope, John, 295
Popham, George, 127
Possossona (Water Passing), 152
Potts, Benjamin, 171, 172, 177
Powder River, Montana, 199
Powell, John Wesley, 216
Pratt, Richard Henry, 104
precipitation, 7–8
Presbyterians, 38, 39, 51, 99, 103, 316
prophet dances, 56, 82–84
prophet movements, 55–56, 81–85
prostitution, 150
Protestantism, 38, 41–44, 51
public perception of Indians, 288–290
Puget Sound region, 60–61

Qualchen, 71–72

rabbits, 9
Rabbit Skin Leggings (Heh-yookts Toe-nihn), 36
Radersburg, 221
rail construction, 61, 95, 179–181, 216–217
Rainbow (Wahchumyus), 140, 154, 162, 172, 195–196, 315
rainfall, 7–8
Rains, Gabriel, 70
Rains, Sevier, 143–144
Randall, Darius, 144–145
Raven Spy (Kul-Kul Si-Yakth), 302
Rawn, Charles, 171–173, 175–176, 182, 191
Raynolds Pass, 210
Ready, Pete, 128, 343n14
Real People
    see Nimiipuu (Real People)
Red Cloud (Sioux), 239
Red Grizzly Bear (Hohots Ilppilp), 20, 21, 22, 31, 33–34
Red Heart, 166–167, *167*
Redington, John Watermelon, 202, 248
Red Moccasin Tops (Sarpsis Ilppilp), 124–126, 134, 172, 195
Red River Anglican school, 37
Red River War (1874–75), 251, 262
Red Wolf, Josiah, 189, 315
religious practices
    Christian conversions, 99, 102–104
    cults, 84
    Dreamers, 81–85, 114
    Nez Perces, 36–39, 41, 43–44, 50–51, 99–100, 316
rendezvous, 25–27, 29, 39
reservations
    and Calvin Hale, 88–90, 92–95
    Congressional Peace Policy, 101–105
    current status, 316
    federal government policies, 96
    and Isaac Stevens, 61
    Nez Perces, 94, 99, 119–120, 300–313
    treaty negotiations, 64–65, 94
return from exile, 309–311
Reuben (Tip-ia-la-na-uy-lala-te-skin/ James), 80, 303, *303*, 307–310, 350n37
Richard (Nez Perce), 39
"right of discovery" concept, 60
"right of occupancy" concept, 60

river systems, 6–7
Rocky Mountain geological province, 5
Roman Catholics, 38, 51, 99, 103, 316
Romeyn, Henry, 273
Roosevelt, Theodore, 263, 313, 318
Ross Hole, 201

Sacagawea, 203
Sahaptin linguistic family, 13
Salish linguistic family, 13
salmon, 8, 11
Salmon City, Idaho, 204
Salmon River, 6, 77, 98, 105, 131, 140–141
Sal Poils, 311
Sand Creek massacre, 96
Sanford, George, 208, 254
*San Francisco Chronicle*, 186, 288
Santee Sioux, 96
Sarpsis Ilppilp (Red Moccasin Tops), 124–126, 134, 172, 195
Schurz, Charles, 295, 304, 370n32
Scott, David, 318
Scott, Hugh, 297, 358n32, 371n46
*Scouts of the Prairie*, 224
*Seattle Post-Intelligencer*, 314
Second Cavalry, 268–269, 271
sego lilies, 9
serviceberries, 9, 11
Seventh Cavalry, 231, 232, 243, 254, 267–269, 271–273
    see also Sturgis, Samuel
shaman, 12, 36–37
Shearer, George, 145
Sheepeater Shoshonis, 215
*Shepherdia argentea*, 253
Sheridan, Philip, 176, 177, 204
Sherman, William T., *294*
    on the Battle of Big Hole, 186
    Doolittle Commission, 100
    exile of the Nez Perces, 293, 295
    and Howard, 211–213, 228
    and Joseph, 304
    on the Lolo Trail, 169
    on military conditions, 147–148, 149–150
    Montana/Wyoming tour, 211–212
    Peace Policy, 105
    pursuit of Nez Perces, 230, 290
    use of the telegraph, 177
    on western expansion, 181

Shively, John, 218–219, 224–225, 227

Shore Crossing (Wahlitits), 124–126, 134, 182, 190, 195

Shoshone (Stinkingwater) River, 227, 230–232, 234–236

Shoshonis
    geographic barriers, 14
    and Howard, 203–204
    impact of guns and horses, 18
    Lewis and Clark Expedition, 203
    military conflicts, 96
    trade networks, 15
    Yellowstone National Park, 215, 218

Shot-in-Head, 274

Shoup, George L., 204

silver salmon, 8

Sioux
    confrontations with Crows, 250
    disease epidemics, 55
    impact of guns and horses, 18
    Little Big Horn, 110, 250
    and Miles, 251, 268
    military conflicts, 79, 96, 109–110
    and the Nez Perces, 243, 296–298
    origins, 4
    trade networks, 17

Sitting Bull (Sioux Chief), 231, 243, 250, 276, 290, 296–298

slavery, 53–54, 102–103

smallpox epidemic, 18, 54, 56–57

Smet, Pierre de, 38

Smith, Asa, 41, 43, 46

Smith, Gerrit, 102–103

Smith, Jedediah, 25, 28, 182

Smith, Rachael, 50

Smith, Sara, 41

Smohalla, 81–85, 100

Snake Creek, 257–258, 267, 269–271, 276, 279, 315

Snake River, 6, 7–8, 80, 105, 206

social contact with Native Americans, 239, 239–242, 285, 287

social structure
    authority structure, 12–14, 31–33, 109
    bands, 11–13, 17–18
    chief, 12–13
    combines, 11
    headman, 11–13
    kinship and social bonds, 11, 13–14, 69
    villages, 10–11

Soda Butte Creek, 228

South Pass, 28

Spalding, Eliza (daughter), 50

Spalding, Eliza (wife), 39–41, 48, 50

Spalding, Henry, 40
    confrontations with Indian population, 48–50
    as interpreter, 89
    missionary activity, 39–41, 43–46, 99
    Wallowa Valley, 106

Speaking Owl, 72

spirit dances, 36–37

spiritual relationships
    cults, 84
    Dreamers, 81–85, 83, 114
    Nez Perces, 36–39, 41, 43–44, 81–85, 99–100
    prophet movements, 55–56, 81–85

Spokan Garry, 37, 38, 45

Spokans, 13, 25, 71–72

Spotted Tail (Sioux), 239

Springtime (Joseph's wife), 156

Spurgin's Beaver Slide, 228

Spurgin, William, 228

Steffens, Lincoln, 287

Steptoe, Edward J., 71

Stevens, Isaac Ingalls, 60–73, 89

Stevensville, Montana, 171, 173, 175

Stickney, William, 113

St. Louis Globe-Democrat, 291

Stripes Turned Down (Ketalkpoosmin), 204

Strong Eagle (Tipyahlahnah), 134, 143

Sturgis, James G., 234

Sturgis, Samuel, 233
    Battle of Bear's Paw, 279
    Battle of Canyon Creek, 247–248
    pursuit of Nez Perces, 212, 231–237, 243, 245, 247–250, 253–254
    supply problems, 362n33

Sully, Alfred, 148

sunflowers, 9, 11

Sutter's Mill, California, 79

Swan Necklace (Wetyetmas Wahyakt), 124–125

sweat lodges, 11, 49

Tamootsin (Timothy), 51, 64, 72, 92

Targhee (Tacher) Pass, 210

Ta-weis-se-sim-ninh (No Horns), 36

Taylor, Nathaniel G., 100, 102

Teeweeyownah (Over the Point), 159–160

telegraph lines, 95, 176, 177–181,
178, 211–212

Teller, Henry, 296

*tel-lik-leen* (ceremony), 124, 125

Teminisiki (No Heart), 196,
199–200, 270–271

temperatures, 8

temporary leadership, 12–13

Tendoy (Lemhi Shoshoni Chief), 203

Tenskwatawa (Shawnee prophet), 83

Tepahlewam (Joseph's daughter), 156

Tepahlewam (Split Rocks/Deep Cuts),
124–126, 125

Te-pah-le-wam Wah-kus-pah
see Canyon Creek

Terry, Alfred, 177, 230, 297

*tewat*, 12, 36–37
see also Toohoolhoolzote

Texas annexation (1845), 59

The Cut Lip, 20, 21

The Dalles, 17, 76

Theller, Edward, 134, 135

Thompson, David, 25

Tilden, Samuel, 304

Timber Creek, 234

*Time*, 315

Tip-ia-la-na-uy-lala-te-skin
(James Reuben), 80, 303, 303,
307–310, 350n37

Tipyahlahnah Siskan (Eagle Robe), 124

Tipyahlahnah (Strong Eagle), 134, 143

Tolo Lake, 123

Tongue River cantonment, 212, 244,
267, 292–293

Tonkawa, Oklahoma, 301

Toohoolhoolzote
Battle of Bear's Paw, 275
Battle of Big Hole, 196
Battle of Clearwater, 153, 158, 162
meeting with Howard, 116–120
nontreaty Nez Perce bands, 105
treaty negotiations, 89

tourists, 219–226, 241, 357n31

Trachtenberg, Alan, 319

trade networks, 15–19, 254–255,
259–261

Trail of Tears, 45

transcontinental railroad, 61, 95, 179–181

transcontinental telegraph, 95, 176,
177–181, 211–212

trappers, 24–29

treaty negotiations, 60–74, 87–90, 92–94

treaty Nez Perce bands
gold strike impact, 80
treaty negotiations, 89

tribes (political units), 68–69

Trimble, Joel, 134, 135

*Tri-Weekly Tribune* (Bismarck), 283

troop morale and living conditions,
146–151

Tsanim Alikos Pah (Place of the
Manure Fires), 258

Tuekakas (Old Joseph), 73
conversion to Christianity, 51
kinship and social bonds, 69, 72
loss of homeland, 97
military protection, 87
nontreaty Nez Perce bands, 105–106
treaty negotiations, 67, 72, 89, 90

tuli-m cult, 84

Tumokult (I Block Up), 189

Tunnachemoontoolt (The Broken
Arm), 21

Twisted Hair, 20, 21, 22

Two Moons (Lepeet Hessemdooks), 134,
158–159

Umatillas
kinship and social bonds, 13
social structure, 69
treaty negotiations, 61, 64–65, 67–68

Union Pacific Railroad, 254

Unitarians, 103

upper Nez Perces, 17–18, 84–85, 89

U.S. Highway 12, 4

Utes, 17

Vail, Alfred, 178, 179

Vancouver, George, 55

vector diseases, 52–54

vegetation zones, 8

Vicious Weasel (Nez Perce), 134

villages, 10–11

Virginia City, Montana, 79, 211,
212, 222

Virginia City, Nevada, 76

"virgin soil" epidemics, 52–54

wagon train attack, 255–256
Wahchumyus (Rainbow), 140, 154, 162, 172, 195–196, 315
Wahlitits (Shore Crossing), 124–126, 134, 182, 190, 195
Waiilatpu mission, 39, 50
Walker, William, 35–36, 45
Wallawallas
    confrontations with the British, 327n10
    disease epidemics, 49, 55
    kinship and social bonds, 13
    military conflicts, 70–71
    treaty negotiations, 61–65, 67–68
Walla Walla, Washington, 76, 79
Wallowa Lake, 14, 106, 313
Wallowa Mountains, 5, 7, 106
Wallowa Valley, 105–112, 114–120, 311–313
Wallula, Idaho, 311
Wanapams, 81
Warner, Olin, 287
War Singer (Camille Williams), 220
Washani (Dancers), 81
Washington, 60–61, 316
Washington Territory
    gold strikes, 75, 79, 81
    Lapwai Indian agency, 87
    Mullan Road, 96
    population increases, 86, 96, 98
    see also Hale, Calvin H.
Water Passing (Possossona), 152
Wat-ku-weis (elderly woman), 20
Wawawai band, 105
Weeahweoktpoo (William Wheeler), 156
Weikert, Andrew, 223–224
Weippe Prairie, 20, 22, 80, 164, 165, 168, 226
Wep-tes-tse-mookh Tse-mookh (Black Eagle), 36, 274, 281, 316
western expansion
    assimilation policies, 85
    fur trade, 27–34
    historical perspectives, xiii–xix
    implications, 318–319
    telegraph lines, 177–181
    see also disease epidemics; gold strikes; missionaries; pioneer immigration and settlement
Westport, Missouri, 46

Wetistokaith, 187, 190
Wetyetmas Wahyakt (Swan Necklace), 124–125
wey-ya-kin, 36–37
Wheeler, George S., 216
Wheeler, William (Weeahweoktpoo), 156
whipman, 12
Whipple, Stephen, 108–109, 111, 115–116, 141–145, 166
whiskey, 80–81, 130, 150, 204, 343n14
White Bird battlefield, 134–136, 315–316
White Bird Canyon, 130, 131, 133, 158, 242
White Bird Creek, 98, 126, 127–128, 133, 140–141, 145
White Bird (Peopeo Kiskiok Hihih)
    Battle of Bear's Paw, 275
    Battle of Big Hole, 189, 190–191
    battle with Perry, 133
    Canadian exile, 298
    escape to Canada, 281–282, 367n56
    gathering at Tepahlewam, 124
    meeting with Howard, 117, 118–120
    nontreaty Nez Perce bands, 105
    revenge attacks, 126
    treaty negotiations, 89, 90
White, Elijah, 30
    arrival in the Pacific Northwest, 46
    proponent of Oregon settlement, 328n26
    as subagent, 29, 31–34, 49, 93
    White's laws, 31–33, 41, 42
whitefish, 8
Whiteman, William, 301–302
white population
    confrontations with Nez Perces, 110–111, 124–130, 145–146, 254
    contact with Nez Perces, 14
    disease epidemics, 48–50, 52–57
    gold strike impact, 75–81
    homesteading opportunities, 95–96, 107
    impact on bison, 260
    invasion of Nez Perce land, 78–81, 85–88, 107–109
    military conflicts, 70–72
    pioneer immigration and settlement, 29, 31–32, 46–49, 58–60, 70

population increases, 98
trade networks, 20–29
White, Richard, 87
White's laws, 48, 59
whitetail deer, 8
Whitman, Marcus, 39, 46–50, 56–57
Whitman massacre, 49–50, 58
Whitman, Narcissa, 39, 46, 50
Whitman, Perrin, 89
Whylimlex (Black Feather), 136
wild carrot, 9, 11
wilderness protection, 217, 289
wild game, 8–9
wild plants, 9–10
Wilhautyah (Wind Blowing), 110–111
Willamette River valley, 29, 39, 46
Williams, Camille (War Singer), 220
Williams, Mark, 303
Wilmot, Lew, 128, 145, 152–153, 343n14
Wind Blowing (Wilhautyah), 110–111
Wind River, 227, 230
Wood, Charles Erskine Scott, *286*
    Battle of Clearwater, 154, 160, 162, 163
    battle with the Nez Perces, 139–140
    and civilian population, 205
    exile of the Nez Perces, 294–295
    and Joseph, 285, 287
    Joseph's surrender speech, 285, 287–288
    pursuit of Nez Perces, 198–199, 206–207, 211
    social contact with Native Americans, 239, 285, 287
    surrender of Nez Perces, 282
Woodcraft Indians, 290
Wood, Erskine, 287, 313, 318
Wood, Henry Clay, 109–110, 111, 113–114, 145
Woodruff, Charles, 189, 194–195
Wool, John E., 71
Worcester, Samuel, 44
Wottolen (Hair Combed Over Eyes), 156, 158, 207, 267, 298
Wounded Breast (Kipkip Owyeen), 159
Wounded Head (Nez Perce), 135, 136
Wounded Knee massacre, xviii, 318
Wounded (Owyeen), 191
Wright, George, 71–72
Wyandots, 45

Wyeth, Nathaniel J., 28
Wynkoop, Edward, 240

Yakimas
    kinship and social bonds, 13
    military conflicts, 70
    treaty negotiations, 61, 64, 67–70
yampa, 9, 11
Year of the Belly Ache, 55
yellowbell, 11
Yellow Bird (Peopeo Moxmox), 49, 64, 65, 67–68, 70–71
Yellow Bull, 110, 182, 304, 310, 311
yellow fever, 53
Yellowstone Act (1872), 214, 216
Yellowstone National Park, 211, 213–225, 263
Yellowstone Plateau, 214–215
Yellowstone River, 226, 227–229, 244, 292–293
*Yellowstone* (steamboat), 35
Yellow Wolf (Hemene Moxmox), *320*
    Battle of Bear's Paw, 3–4, 273–274, 276
    Battle of Big Hole, 189–190, 193, 196
    Battle of Canyon Creek, 247
    Battle of Clearwater, 156, 157, 158
    battle with Perry, 135
    battle with the scouting party, 152
    confrontations with Crows, 249
    exile, 302
    meeting with Howard, 120
    post-war life, 319, 321
    on religious conversion, 310
    retreat from Clearwater, 182
    retreat to Canada, 254
    return from Canada, 298
    return from exile, 311
    supplies at Cow Island, 255
    surrender, 281–282, 367n52
    Yellowstone tourist encounters, 219–220, 223
*Yellow Wolf, His Own Story* (McWhorter), 321
Young Chief (Cayuse), 48, 68, 334n35
Young Joseph
    *see* Heinmot Tooyalakekt (Young Joseph)
Young White Bird, 187, 189